Families
and Communities

A New View of American History

David J. Russo

THE AMERICAN ASSOCIATION FOR STATE AND LOCAL HISTORY
Nashville, Tennessee

Library of Congress Cataloguing-in-Publication Data

Russo, David J.
  Families and communities.

  Bibliography: p. 301
  1. United States—Historiography.   2. Local history.   I. Title.
E175.R87   973'.07'2   74-11389
ISBN 0-910050-29-5

For
Page Smith
Daniel J. Boorstin

Contents

Contents

Preface

Sometimes it is important to pick the best brains—as I have unashamedly done here, especially when their collected writings suggest a grand new synthesis. Such is the case now in the field of American history.

For several years it has been my intention to write a full-length history of Deerfield, Massachusetts, an inquiry into the shifting role of the small town through American history. In the course of my research, as I examined certain general studies about towns and cities, it occurred to me that the best work being done in "local" history, if viewed in the widest possible framework, implies—but does not spell out—a new way of looking at the whole of our historical experience. Instead of maintaining a national perspective, we should assume moveable vantage points that take account of the levels of communities all Americans live in simultaneously: countryside or town or city, state, region, as well as nation. And if the study of important individuals, family life, and Americans in the aggregate is added to community studies, then a new organizing principle of far greater scope, complexity, and validity than our textbooks now offer comes into bold relief.

What follows relies upon writings that *generalize* in important ways about the American past. This is the only possible basis for the kind of proposal I make. Otherwise, there would always have been one more monograph to look at, one more article to peruse. The occasional inclusion of long quotations is deliberate. At times, I felt that certain historians summed up their far-reaching theses far better than I could, and the reader is asked not to look for further analysis or summation at the end of such quotations. The chapters should be read consecutively, as the thesis is gradually constructed and the writing is meant to be cumulative in its impact. For example, Chapter 9, "The New Scheme: A Brief Sketch," would seem sketchy indeed if the reader were not already familiar with the earlier chapters dealing with scholarship of a slightly broader character.

In general, I have sought to present the essence of important recent studies, to relate those studies to each other in the context of the new scheme I present, and to criticize them only when I felt there was some obvious or major shortcoming. My overriding concern was always to show how such scholarship leads us to a new way of looking at our past.

It is hoped that what follows will be of interest not only to teachers, scholars, and various kinds of students of American history, but also to members of historical and genealogical societies, to the sort of people who buy books offered by the History Book Club. I believe that general accounts focussed on the proposal I present can reunite the amateur and professional elements of history's audience, so that historical writing can once again have the broad appeal it had in the nineteenth century, before there was a historical profession or an academic field, when writers who tried to explain our past—such as Bancroft and Parkman—had immense popularity.

I should like to thank a number of colleagues and friends for giving me the benefit of their understanding of certain facets and fields of history: Donald Friary, Patrick Peterson, Charles Jago, and Thomas Willey. William Alderson, Director of the American Association for State and Local History, has had faith in the worth of this project from its inception. His loyalty and optimism are much appreciated. I am also grateful to Margaret Belec for her fine typing.

David J. Russo

Hamilton, Ontario
September 1973

Families and Communities

Introduction

I

Local history is now fully in the mainstream of American historical writing and, indeed, may well drastically change the course of that writing. Page Smith's thesis in *As a City upon a Hill: the Town in American History* has the potential of revolutionizing the way we—historians, students, and the general population alike—look upon our past. The over-all mental picture we all have of the shape of American history could eventually be changed beyond recognition.

Smith's thesis is shockingly simple: "[If] we except the family and the church, the basic form of social organization experienced by the vast majority of Americans up to the early decades of the twentieth century was the small town."[1] Smith also sketches out, but does not adequately develop, a conception of Americans living in various *levels* of community at the same time. Of these, the local community exerted the most profound and comprehensive influence on the lives of Americans until their society became urbanized. So, in order to understand the total pattern of American life in the United States from its colonial beginnings through the nineteenth century, one's focus should be, not on the *nation*, but on the town.

To elaborate on Smith's thesis is to draw from it even more far-reaching implications. Smith, with perfect consistency, could have gone on to argue that the whole outline of American history should be redrawn to highlight the level of community of most consequence in

---

1. Smith, *As a City Upon a Hill; The Town in American History* (New York: Alfred A. Knopf, Inc., 1966), vii.

1

each stage in the development of American society. In other words, American society has been in the most basic way a *federal* entity—not just politically, but socially, economically, and culturally, as well. And within this federation, the locus of power and influence has shifted——unevenly, to be sure, but unmistakably in the long term—from the town to city, state, and region, and finally to the nation.

The former primacy of the town is now being established in some of the best work being done in the whole field of American studies. The present primacy of the nation is obvious, but the *way* in which this largest of communities attained its pre-eminent position is not as obvious, simply because few studies presented from the national perspective bother to offer an explanation.[2] Regionalism in the United States has long been a matter of interest to historians, both with reference to the Civil War and to the continuous territorial expansion of the nation across the North American continent. But the "South" and a succession of "Wests" have not been viewed typically—by historians, at least—as the most obvious instances of a *general* phenomenon: the existence of "regional communities" which at particular times became more influential than any other kind.[3] There have been many studies of individual states, of course, but few attempt to define the state as a *type* of community that can be *generalized* about, in the same way that political scientists write about state government, or, indeed, as historians are now generalizing about towns. Urban history is further developed in that there are a number of influential studies that comment on various kinds of cities at different periods of time.[4]

Work is therefore under way—however unevenly—that *could* result in the creation of a general version of American history opening with the town as the center of attention, moving on to consider the growing importance of cities, states, and regions, and ending with the piecemeal "nationalization" of American life, a process still going on. Though the focus would shift, over time, from the town to the nation—since those

2. The first general study of a recognized period of American history to take the scheme now being proposed into account is Robert Wiebe, *The Search for Order, 1877-1920* (New York: Hill and Wang, 1967).

3. Howard Odum and Harry E. Moore, *American Regionalism: A Cultural Historical Approach to National Integration* (New York: Henry Holt & Co., Inc., 1938); Merrill Jensen, editor, *Regionalism in America* (Madison, Wisc.: University of Wisconsin Press, 1952).

4. For example, Carl Bridenbaugh, *Cities in the Wilderness* (New York: The Ronald Press Co., 1938) and *Cities in Revolt* (New York: Alfred A. Knopf, Inc., 1955); Richard Wade, *The Urban Frontier: The Rise of Western Cities* (Cambridge, Mass.; Harvard University Press, 1959).

levels of communities in between did not achieve the clear-cut pre-eminence of either extreme—cities, states, and regions will have to be dealt with concurrently in some fashion. But the basic *direction* of the focus of attention is clear: It will have to be steadily "upward," from the local to the national community.

The most obvious impact of such an organizing principle for the American past is that levels of community other than the nation will be *consistently* dealt with in general accounts. No longer will the town sud-denly emerge as part of a catch-all chapter on the colonial period, only to disappear from view thereafter. No longer will cities receive only sporadic, passing reference, as in allusions to the colonial cities along the Atlantic coast, to the urbanization that accompanied industrializa-tion after the Civil War, to bosses and political machines, and to the municipal reforms of the earliest, lowest level of Progressive improve-ment. No longer will states be given prominence only under the Arti-cles of Confederation, where their importance was obvious, and in such instances as the Jacksonians acting at the state level, or the states aiding and regulating development of the economy before the Civil War, or some states leading the way after the war in regulating busi-ness, or other states becoming "laboratories" of Progressive reform in the first decades of this century. And no longer will the focus be on re-gionalism only as it related to crisis or territorial expansion.

The piecemeal coverage of all these "lower" levels of community derives from the national perspective in general accounts of American history. Since the efforts of Charles Beard and Morrison and Com-mager in the 1920s and 1930s, textbooks have been written in the same old mold to the same old formula: the nation is the frame of reference; governmental activity is constantly in the foreground, creating the very periodization through which we view our past. That other *kinds* of in-stitutions and activities have not fitted into this periodization is awk-ward, but it is dealt with in occasional chapters existing in isolation be-cause no systematic attempt is made to *relate* these "other" aspects of life to each other or to politics and government. This concentration in our texts on the nation-state in its political and territorial aspects has only slowly broadened to include subjects recently dealt with in American historical writing. One of the wonders of our historical profession is the extent to which standard general accounts *fail* to incorporate what our better monographic and periodical writing suggest should be noticed.

The extremely uneven, sporadic reference to local, state, and reg-ional history is the product of generalizations based upon a national framework. Towns, cities, and states are included only when some national development found expression there. But in the new scheme of things, this characteristic will be reversed; the whole thing will be "flipped": what happens in the *national* community will be noticed only when it represents the nationalization of something in American life. Local and other subnational communities remain the frame of reference until it can be demonstrated that they have lost their primacy.

Of course, influence flowed in *both* directions. Some things—such as the national government's control over international relations, coinage, weights and measures, a communications or postal system, and interstate commerce; widespread commitment to ideals formed before and during the revolution; the influence of world- and continent-wide supply and demand on the cost of items produced outside but consumed within a given locality; even the pre-eminence of foreign and national news in the early journals—all are instances of village and rural life influenced by broader, outside patterns from the beginning of our life as a nation. Such examples only underscore the obviously awkward character of the progressive nationalization of American life, something that gained strength during wars and other crises and subsided somewhat afterwards, though never to the extent that the process was reversed or made stagnant.

Briefly put, clear pre-eminence for the national community, or for Americans in the aggregate, comes economically, socially, politically, and culturally: *economically*, when the corporation becomes characteristically a nationwide organization (from the 1870s to the 1920s approximately); *socially*, when the class-spread created by industrialization produces self-conscious interest groups—such as laborers, farmers, businessmen—with national dimensions and cohesiveness (roughly from the 1870s to the 1930s); *politically*, when the national government becomes the regulator of those interests and provides for the security and welfare of the whole population (beginning roughly with Theodore Roosevelt's Square Deal, cresting with Franklin Roosevelt's New Deal, and continuing sporadically since that time); *culturally*, when ideas, values, information, art, and entertainment are conveyed through national magazines, network radio, and network television. In addition, many institutions, associations, and activities have undergone nationalization at different rates and at different times since the mid-nineteenth century.

Of course, not *all* corporations have become nationwide; not *all* farmers, laborers, and businessmen have joined national associations; and not *all* the interests and activities of the American people have been subjected to government regulation. The point is that such development came, in this period, to characterize broad, significant areas of American life. But the process itself is incomplete and continuous. Whether limits can be imposed upon this process by a concerned population is a question to be dealt with later.

There is evident irony in the fact that Americans created, in their revolutionary act of independence, a new political entity, a nation, long before that nation became durable and powerful and cohesive. But what has not sufficiently been noted is that, for Americans, the "nation" was an abstraction whose significance to their lives was far less than that of their town or city or state. Much more often than not, the national community has become their primary frame of reference only in this century.

II

But what is a community? If the scheme now being suggested is to find wide acceptance, there should be a generally shared definition, one that covers villages, towns, cities, states or provinces, regions, nations—even empires and federations of nations.

The most recent attempt at definition has come, appropriately enough, from a sociologist. Rene König's *The Community* is a volume in the British-based International Library of Sociology and Social Reconstruction, sponsored, apparently, by the Institute of Community Studies. In *Community*, König discusses the enormous linguistic confusion that has marked the usage of the term in such countries as Germany, Great Britain, Italy, France, and Spain. He goes on to seek a definition broad enough to include the various levels of community just mentioned. His term is "a global society on a local basis," or, in more specific terms, human societies existing all over the world, restricted in size, and embracing families, neighborhoods, and groups of all kinds.[5] Though at times König seems to limit unduly the work of "community sociologists" by suggesting that they ought to leave political and economic aspects of community life to others, he properly deemphasizes the community as an administrative or political unit with territory and borders. What determines a community's actual size and shape is its existence as a social unit, a human creation with definite structures, functions, and values, as well as physical space; in short, not

5. Rene König, *The Community* (London: Routledge & Kegan Paul, Ltd., 1968), pp.22-30.

an abstraction, but a "social reality." Thus, there can be several communities in a township, for instance. A community must never be confused with families or kinship groups, classes, or other groups, all of which it *contains*, all of which are abstractions unless located in specific communities. So, too, with neighborhoods, which König defines as the universal practice on the part of those who live in communities to associate with a smaller, more intimate group, sometimes a contiguous one in a geographic or physical sense, but sometimes not. Once sociologists accept this definition of community, König urges them to go on and study the relationship between the population and its physical setting, or the "spacial layout of the community," what König calls the "social ecology," the "structural aspects" of community life—such things as leadership groups, power, status, and class—and, finally, the values the people live by.

There are problems with König's scheme. "A global society on a local basis" is general enough as a definition—indeed, *too* vague to satisfy everyone. Are empires or nations "local" even if they exist all over the world? If so, what is not local? We are pretty far away from common notions of "local" when discussing the Roman or the British Empires. Moreover, König does not take the next step and differentiate among an empire, a nation, a city, or a town. One is left with an incomplete system of classification for the various types of human societies in existence. Armed with König's definition of community, we still do not know what to *call* the community we happen to be observing or studying.

Perhaps the most influential recent attempt made by a social scientist to define community is that of an anthropologist, Robert Redfield.[6] Though dealing only with what he calls the "little community," Redfield is quick to call village or town "a human whole," something it shares with a person, a people, a nation-state, a civilization: that is an "integral entity . . . describable on its own characteristics as a whole." Therefore, Redfield insists, a community should be *studied* as a whole; specialized studies dealing with specific aspects of life do not grasp the essential integrity or wholeness or inter-relatedness of the subject: indeed, "such a way of thinking breaks up the whole."[7]

Redfield goes on to discuss the work of other anthropologists who have studied the relationship among various levels of community in particular societies. He even includes diagrams to show those

---

6. Robert Redfield, *The Little Community* (Chicago: University of Chicago Press, 1956).
7. *Ibid.*, p. 10.

relationships.[8] Though restricted to primitive communities and without apparent concern for definitions covering civilized societies as well, the work of anthropologists exploring the nature of community at all levels goes beyond that to be found in any other discipline.

Redfield hastens to add that "no words describe all that a community is." All that interests him are words and concepts "that cover much that goes on throughout all of human life for everybody in that community."[9] His categories for community study do not differ much from König's later list: ecological system, social structure, and so on. But on one vital matter König and Redfield are at great odds. Konig is quite firm in his assertion that Redfield's emphasis on integration and "wholeness" has led to a view of community that can blind one to division and conflict. Genuine community "does not exclude the existence of powerful inner tensions, definite power groupings, and even a lack of inner homogeneity, which can under certain circumstances break into open conflict."[10] This argument over integration is important because true consensus on the meaning of community will not exist among social scientists as long as they argue over a term so central to any full-blown conception of the subject.

In any case, the sociological perspective on community is incomplete. True, all major aspects of community life as traditionally defined by historians—political, economic, cultural, intellectual, as well as social—can be analyzed from the sociologist's vantage point. Investigations of groups, institutions, and activities cover a wide spectrum of human behavior—but not all of it. What about the role of the individual? What about the definition or perception that the inhabitants themselves have of their community, of their village or state or nation? How do *they* define community? What does it mean to them? And what about a spiritual, instead of just a "natural" definition of community? König places human society in the broader context of natural or animal community life. All species, he says, build communities. But what about the human community as a spiritual creation, as the by-product of man's relationship to God?

Such a definition is outside the realm of most recent historical and sociological inquiries into the nature of modern societies. But certain recent religious philosophers have continued to insist upon the essentially spiritual nature of a *genuine* human community. Of course, any

8. *Ibid.*, p. 117.
9. *Ibid.*, p. 11.
10. König, *The Community*, p. 130.

theologian has to deal with the impact of belief on the organization of human society. The character of a group's religious belief will obviously help to shape the kind of community it develops. Since religious belief is at the heart of all theological inquiry, it is natural for theologians to define as genuine only those communities whose inhabitants have faith at the center of their lives.

The problem with this definition for community is that it does not cover a good deal of the texture of life in recent Western civilization, where large segments of the population have lived out their lives without significant reference to religious faith, especially in our own century. So, even if the spiritual nature of community life in the West was evident, therefore, in the ancient and medieval worlds, and into the modern period as well, this has not been true of the recent past. This means that historians and social scientists, whose definition of human life generally precludes a spiritual dimension, could not point to the church as the central institution in the life of cities and nations of the modern West, even if they wanted to. What needs to be explained, however—*within the context of community*—is why and how the church, and religious belief, lost their significance. Even if historians discount the divine origins of faith, they have to provide explanations in naturalistic or humanistic terms.

Modern theologians can still argue—and none has done so with more pertinence than the recent Jewish theologian Martin Buber—that man has lost "true" community along with his faith, and that if he is to reconstruct a proper society in the future, he must have a sense of community based upon a common religious purpose. As Buber puts it: "The real essence of community is to be found in the fact—manifest or otherwise—that it has a center. The real beginning of a community is when its members have a common relation to the centre overriding all other relations."[11] Though this center reflects something divine in nature, the community itself must be solidly earthly and human, for

> it is here the truth of the centre is proved . . . . The primary aspiration of all history is a genuine community of human beings—genuine because it is *community all through*. A community that failed to base itself on the actual and communal life of big and little groups living and working together and on their mutual relationships, would be fictitious and counterfeit . . . . [Therefore, it] is community of tribulation and only because of that commun-

11. Martin Buber, *Paths to Utopia*, paperback edition, (Boston: Beacon Press, 1958).

ity of salvation . . . . A community of faith truly exists only when it is a community of work.[12]

Buber goes on to sketch a conception of a whole human society constructed of levels or layers of communities[13] whose relationships could shift and flow through time, depending on the circumstances, for "[community] should not be made into a principle; it too should always satisfy a situation rather than an abstraction. The realization of community, like the realization of any idea, cannot occur once and for all time; always it must be the moment's answer to the moment's question, and nothing more."[14]

A utopian socialist, Buber believed that human beings should direct their aim toward the creation of a society whose means of production, distribution, and consumption are commonly owned. But of even greater importance was the on-going problem of what he calls

> the right line of demarcation that has to be drawn ever anew . . . between the sphere which must of necessity be centralized and those which can operate in freedom; between the degree of govermment and the degree of autonomy; between the law of unity and the claims of community . . . [in short,] *the custody of the true boundaries*, ever changing in accordance with changing historical circumstances; such would be the task of humanity's spiritual conscience; a Supreme Court unexampled in kind, the right true representation of a living idea.[15]

Leaning on definitions made by Ferdinand Tonnies, the founder of German sociology, Buber makes the assertion that small-scale communities are natural, while large-scale ones are artificial to the inherent nature of human beings. The little human community developed in the distant past was a social world made up of persons "at once mutually dependent and independent [and] differed in kind from all similar undertakings on the part of animals, just as the technical work of man differed in kind from all the animals' works."[16] So much, argues Buber,

12. *Ibid.*, pp. 135, 133, 134, 135.
13. "An organic commonwealth . . . will never build itself up out of individuals but only out of small and ever smaller communities; a nation is a community to the degree that it is a community of communities." *Ibid.*, p. 136.
14. *Ibid.*, p. 134.
15. *Ibid.*.
16. *Ibid.*, p. 130.

for the false connections of the sort later made by sociologists like König between human and other animal societies.

During the long course of human history, clans formed communities in which divisions of labor or function occurred and in which customs and laws took root. In each, the individual human, having felt at home, "felt himself approved in his functional independence and responsibility." These little communities Buber calls the natural product of the "social principle"—that is, the result of human beings' coming together in free association and living in a manner that furthered their distinctively human nature. Opposed to this is the "political principle," the creation of great power centers, large, autonomous, "artificial," centralized communities. The chief product of the political principle—the State—can be likened to some great plague that has sapped genuine community of its vitality:

> The crucial thing here was not that the State . . . .weakened and gradually displaced free associations, but that the political principle with all its centralistic features percolated into the associations themselves, modifying their structure and their whole inner life, and thus politicized society to an ever-increasing extent . . . . In the monstrous confusion of modern life, only thinly disguised by the reliable functioning of the economic and State-apparatus, the individual clings desperately to the collectivity. The little society in which he was embedded cannot help him; only the great collectivities, so he thinks, can do that, and he is all too willing to let himself be deprived of personal responsibility; he only wants to obey. And the most valuable of all goods—the life between man and man—gets lost in the process; the autonomous relationships become meaningless, personal relationships wither; and the very spirit of man hires itself out as a functionary.[17]

Western civilization is therefore in crisis because genuine community has given way to an artificial one. The never-ending problem for humanity in the future is not to try to do away with the state, but to limit its principle of centralization to an absolute minimum. This is, from the modern liberal perspective, a profoundly conservative prescription. The liberal—in social-economic-political terms in the twentieth-century West—has been one who believes the state *should* exert power for the common good and, at least in the United States, is also one who

17. *Ibid.*, pp. 131-132.

looks upon the local community as a refuge for antiliberal ways of life.

Buber does not respond to this point, nor does he make detailed suggestions as to how the line of demarcation between the political principle that is the State and the social principle that is genuine community ought to be, or, indeed, can be adjusted. Instead, he refers his readers to the Jewish village communes in Palestine during the 1940s as an encouraging example—that is, communities communal in nature, yet spiritual in purpose, though, significantly, not without problems involving efforts at co-operation.

But is Palestine the world? What are the prospects for communal life in on-going societies like the Chinese, Russian, or American? Is not a scheme based upon "social" and "political" principles too schematic and historical? Does it really offer much insight into the ways human societies have actually evolved? Are communities above the local level necessarily political, centralist, artificial —the State? Is it not possible for genuine community to exist in cities, states, nations, and empires? And even in villages and towns, what can the "center" be in "nationalized" societies largely emptied of spiritual purpose? Even with such questions, Buber's brief *Paths in Utopia* remains the most incisive statement on community offered by any recent theologian or philosopher, and it has had increasing influence among intellectuals in the Western world, one of whom is Page Smith.

What makes all these efforts at definition by sociologists like König and theologian-philosophers like Buber ultimately unsatisfactory is the failure of these individuals to be good historians, as well. Their attempts to grasp the essential nature of community are excessively schematic. Just as the meaning of the term *community* has changed, over the centuries of Western history, so too have the actual shape and substance of the communities themselves changed. Sociologists, in their attempt to understand contemporary society, are not sufficiently aware of the long, varied life of humanity in villages, cities, and nations to make definitions that stand the test of time. Philosophers are too concerned with the ultimate meaning of community to be sufficiently aware of the complicated and variegated shape of their subject when it is examined in the matrix of actual human experience.

This means that historians are—theoretically, at least—in the best position to comment on the meaning of community through human history. As to definition, one is tempted to urge that students of community allow the people whom they study to say what a community is.

The people who live in them have always had some perception of what communities are. This suggestion is contrary to much of twentieth-century philosophy, as well as social and physical scientific theorizing, which has placed a great deal of emphasis on a search for linguistic precision. But it is by no means obvious whether the lack of consensus—and precision—that frequently follows such efforts leaves us in a better position than we were in when we relied upon the vague, imprecise terms evolved in common parlance.

In any case, what people meant by *community* has varied enormously over the centuries of organized human life, especially in recent times; and, since part of historical reality is the understanding of contemporaries and not merely the later wisdom of historians, the student of community must accept a certain amount of imprecision in the very definition of his subject. Historians are perhaps more accustomed to living with such ambiguity than those in the related but younger disciplines of social science.

The proposition to be examined here is that a state, a region, or a nation are as much a human community as a town or a city, although obviously different in character. All communities are social and ecological—that is, they involve relationships between human beings living in association with each other and within their physical environment. Sociologists, geographers, and theologians bring only partial perspectives to their inquiries into community life. The sociologist defines everything as social, ignoring individuals and distinctions between the purely social and other aspects of life. The geographer focusses on the physical setting and the relationship of human societies to that setting. The theologian is primarily concerned with spirituality or its absence. Only the historian—and the anthropologist—can view human life whole, if the task is to explain why and how human life through all generations has come to be what it is now. And the historian has the best categories for such a broad assignment: political, economic, social, cultural, and intellectual sum up humanity's life rather better than any other list yet devised. If these activities are examined as they apply to individuals, groups, and institutions in various levels of communities formed by human beings, the historian approaches the comprehensive perspective that modern scholars must reach for if we are not to succumb to lack of understanding of our contemporary world.

As a spatial entity, the neighborhood, village, town, and city all have limited size. All are "local," are places people live in and belong to. People do not live in a state, region, or nation in the same sense, although they can feel loyalty and a sense of belonging to these larger communities. Individual life has assuredly been influenced by involvement with them, even before the creation of what sociologists call our contemporary "mass society." True, the state and the nation have a political existence denied the region, at least in the American system. And the exercise of political power exerts an influence over the lives of all inhabitants of local communities. But these larger entities must be seen as having a nonpolitical character as well, just as towns are not properly investigated as communities if only their administration and territory are in view.

The fact is that human beings live simultaneously in a hierarchy of communities, from the neighborhood to the nation, and sometimes on up to empires and federations of nations. The pages that follow attempt to define the full nature of those communities, one by one. Only then can we begin to understand the passing of what Peter Laslett[18] has called "The World We Have Lost," the pre-industrial village society, and its replacement by the nationalized mass society of our time. Only then can we see the consequences of human life organized on ever shifting levels of community.

18. Peter Laslett, *The World We Have Lost* (London: Methuen & Co., Ltd., 1965).

2

The Little Community: Towns (and Rural Areas Too?)

I

It must be stressed that historical writing in the United States did not always have the national perspective we so naturally associate with it. In fact, there was local history in what is now the United States long before there was national history. Those who wrote about towns and colonies and states and regions during the seventeenth, eighteenth, and nineteenth centuries are guilty, in J. H. Plumb's apt phrase,[1] of "using the past," of creating histories to serve some purpose other than to understand, on its own terms, what happened. There can be little doubt that nonprofessional historical writing during all these years developed largely as a response to various practical considerations, usually the need to justify or praise the author's group or colony or state in some historical controversy. David van Tassel, in his *Recording America's Past: An Interpretation of the Development of Historical Studies in America, 1607–1884*, documents the long-term efforts of those who "used the past" in this way and thereby created a corpus of ahistorical literature and documentation that underlay the professional work that began to appear at the end of the nineteenth century.

In the colonial period—at least, in New England—the most influential historical writing was characterized by its religious focus, by what Peter Gay, in his *A loss of Mastery: Puritan Historians in Colonial America* calls "a modernized, Protestant, Anglicized theory of history developed more than a thousand years before by Orosius and St. Augustine. . . . [This theme] clarified the religious experience and or-

---

1. J. H. Plumb, *The Uses of the Past* (London: Macmillan & Co., Lt., 1970).

ganized the historical knowledge of Christian Englishmen. It gave God his glory, man his place, events their meaning—and England its due."[2] This Christian view of history was used by each religious group against the others: Anglican against Puritan; Puritan against Anglican; and both against Rome. The great histories of Puritan New England— William Bradford's *Of Plymouth Plantation*, Cotton Mather's *Magnalia Christi Americana*, Jonathan Edwards's *History of the Work of Redemption*—all fit the old mold, with a Puritan twist, even as the historical craft was elsewhere assuming its modern form. Whether dealing with a colony—such as Bradford's Plymouth or Mather's Massachusetts Bay—or with a village—the Reverend John Williams's *The Redeemed Captive Returning to Zion* is a good example[3]—Puritan historical writing attempted to explain God's will in the affairs of a group of like-minded people who attempted to sustain a religious community in the face of continuing hardship and travail. Theirs was a great drama, a rousing story with dimensions both human and divine.

Gay's thesis must not be allowed to stand alone, however, for there were many other colonial "histories" whose orientation was far more secular. Indeed, Van Tassel reveals another whole stream of historical writing from the pre-national period, something that could be called justificatory prose pieces presented as defenses for the colonial side in just-concluded controversies. As early as the 1680s, William Hubbard wrote an official history of New England commissioned by the Massachusetts legislature, and

> was inclined to accept the naturalistic interpretations of the more worldly ministers who were beginning to make inroads upon Puritan orthodoxy. In his history he did not emphasize the thesis that New England was a protectorate of God; he chose to ignore or to explain by natural causes instances attributed by his predecessors to Providential intervention on behalf of the Puritans.[4]

This subnational perspective continued to be natural long after the story of Americans was largely divorced from religious themes. Even after the Revolution, long after the creation of the political nation, as

2. Gay, *A Loss of Mastery* (Berkeley, Cal.: University of California Press, 1966), pp. 9–10.

3. *The Redeemed Captive* is an account of the massacre at Deerfield in 1704, during which French troops and Abenaki Indians killed and carried off to Canada as captives a large portion of the village's population.

4. David van Tassell, *Recording America's Past: An Interpretation of the Development of Historical Studies in America, 1607–1884* (Chicago: University of Chicago Press, 1960), p. 20.

Daniel J. Boorstin puts it, "The history of states and regions seemd primary; the history of the United States contrived and derivative. Many years would pass before Americans would see their history the other way around. . . . Not until after the Civil War would a national perspective on American history seem normal."[5]

As state historical societies set themselves to the task of collecting documents—Van Tassel calls it "Documania: A National Obsession Locally Inspired"[6]—fact-laden state and town histories were written in quantity in the decades after the revolution. Though Van Tassel does not discuss them at length, these writings appear to have been shorn of the religious meaning at the heart of their influential colonial predecessors and tended to be partisan to family, town, state, or section. It was in this setting that Van Tassel finds—and rescues from oblivion—a loose community of young writers who, during the 1850s and 1860s, brought a critical spirit to bear on their investigations into facets of state and local history that happened to interest them. Under the aegis of the New England Historical and Genealogical Society, *The Historical Magazine* was founded in 1857 as a journal for this group and became in the 1860s the embodiment of the new emphasis. Van Tassel's point is that the critical frame of mind we so naturally associate with modern, professional historical writing was already making headway among amateur local historians before the rise of the historical profession in the decades following the Civil War.[7]

A serious defect of Van Tassel's book is that it equates local history with statewide historical activities and writings. He presents only a few shreds of evidence about truly local historians, those who wrote of villages and towns. The fact is that during the course of the nineteenth century, local—or, more properly, town history—became the property of writers who sought to memorialize the lives of their own ancestors, the early settlers of their communities. This was history whose purpose was, as Harvard's Albert Bushnell Hart unabashedly put it, the "worship of ancestry."[8]

A good example of the shifting character of local historical writing in the United States during the nineteenth century is the career and writing of George Sheldon of Deerfield, Massachusetts.[9] Sheldon was

5. Boorstin, *The Americans*; 3 vols. (New York: Random House, 1958–1973). Quotation is from Vol. 2, *The National Experience*, pp. 363, 367.

6. Van Tassel, p. 103.

7. *Ibid.*, pp. 121–134.

8. Pocumtuck Valley Memorial Association, *Proceedings*, VI (1911), 619.

9. The following section dealing with Sheldon is based upon my "The Deerfield Massacre of 1704 and Local Historical Writing in the United States," Paul Fritz and David

one of the more notable of the antiquarian town historians who were keepers of the past during the late nineteenth century. Long-time president of the local historical society, curator of its museum, and author of a two-volume history of Deerfield, Sheldon dominated the historical activities of his fellow townsmen to an unusual extent. These were impressive achievements for a man who had no education beyond that of the local academy, who had no long-term occupation other than farming, and whose only public office beyond one term was that of justice of the peace. Though largely self-educated and initially without economic or social prominence, Sheldon recognized that his own family was every bit as prominent as any other, if viewed *historically*.[10] His dedication through half of his ninety-eight-year life to the task of preserving the past of family and town was what one associate called, simply, "a labor of love."[11] Sheldon's second wife, Jennie Arms, had a more elaborate explanation. Sheldon, she thought, had been driven by a vision:

> In one word it was a MEMORIAL. A memorial of the men, women, and children of early New England, especially of the valley of the Pocumtuck. The lives and deeds of these people should not perish from the earth, but should live on in their records of stone and iron, of wood and manuscript page. These records should be snatched from destruction, gathered together and reverently preserved. The babe unborn to remote generations should know of the brave beginnings of New England in this frontier of our old Commonwealth.[12]

How did he come to that vision?

> He had seen, as a child through the eyes of his grandmother, the early inhabitants whom we call Indians, peeking at eventide

Williams, editors, *The Triumph of Culture: 18th Century Perspectives* (Toronto, Ont.: A. M. Hakkert, 1972), 315–333.

10. The Reverend Mr. Williams may have been the massacre's most prominent survivor and captive, but a Sheldon led them out of captivity. In his *History*, Sheldon wrote of his ancestor: "In the efforts for the recovery and redemption of the captives from Canada, Ensign John Sheldon was a central figure. To his tenderness of heart, to his unflagging faith, is due in large measure the success that followed." Ensign Sheldon built the "Old Indian House," where the stiffest defense against the attackers was made during the massacre (George Sheldon, *History of Deerfield, Massachusetts*, 2 vols. [Deerfield, Mass.: Pocumtuck Valley Memorial Association, 1895–1896], pp. 324–325).

11. P.V.M.A., *Proceedings*, IV (1901), 241–242.

12. *Ibid.*, VII (1921), 60.

through the windows of the Old Indian House. He had felt through his grandmother's stories the frightfulness of Indian captivity. As a mature man he had lived, in thought, with the white pioneers until, in very truth, he had become one of them, not only in blood but in spirit. Loyalty had changed to love—then the vision was born. Pondering alone in the firelight, the love-passion and the vision developed into an all-controlling purpose.[13]

Sheldon's interest in the past was, from the beginning, an interest in both the written record and surviving artifact; the two meshed, became inseparable in his historical imagination. He was upset when the Old Indian House was torn down in 1847; he belonged to the Deerfield Society for Rural Improvements in the 1850s and helped "to improve the streets and public grounds of the village;"[14] he was on the committee that built a monument right after the Civil War and managed to dedicate it to both the dead of that war and to the early settlers as well; and, in 1870, Sheldon was founder of the Pocumtuck Valley Memorial Association, whose purpose was "the collecting and preserving of such memorials, books, papers and curiosities, as may tend to illustrate and perpetuate the history of the early settlers of this region, and of the race which vanished before them."[15]

The P.V.M.A. was a successful antiquarian society if judged solely in terms of its stated objectives. Over the half-century of Sheldon's leadership, it came into possession of the town's academy building and converted it into a "Memorial Hall"; it amassed a large collection of furnishings from the colonial period, including the battered door from the Old Indian House, as well as Indian artifacts; it opened its hall for public inspection; its president put together an impressive collection of family papers, tracts, pamphlets, brochures, and books dealing with local history; it had annual meetings indoors and field meetings outside at various places around the valley, with antiquarians of widely varying capacity and ability making addresses; it commemorated many events, persons, and families, and in doing so, left a trail of memorial tablets strewn throughout the village and surrounding country.[16]

13. *Ibid.*

14. Constitution of the Deerfield Society for Rural Improvement, Papers of the Deerfield Society for Rural Improvement, Pocumtuck Valley Memorial Association Library, Deerfield, Mass.

15. This statement appears in the association's Constitution.

16. P.V.M.A., *Proceedings*, I (1880), 434–442; VI (1920), 554–565. The field meetings had long programs including hymns, prayers, dedicatory addresses, chorales, dirges,

The people who were active with Sheldon in the P.V.M.A. were, typically, prominent in their own communities: the roster of the association's membership reads like a "Who's Who" of Franklin County. What Sheldon provided in his role as historical impressario- —cajoling, persuading, hinting, planning, scheduling, and generally keeping up enthusiasm for an undertaking beyond the unassisted talent of most of his associates—was a much needed focus for those whose families had lived in the area for a long time and who shared his view of the past. What is most remarkable, in a social sense, is that Sheldon- —largely by virtue of his fame as an antiquarian-local historian—became, by all accounts, one of the most prominent persons in his own community.

Sheldon's own historical writings tower above those of his associates in the P.V.M.A. His persistence, dedication, and seriousness of purpose were distinctive. All lauded his efforts, but no one could emulate him. Though largely self-trained, he had a brief but significant partnership with the Reverend J. H. Temple. Both the scope and scale of Sheldon's own *History* are clearly forshadowed in their collaborative history of the nearby town of Northfield, published in 1875, a decade before his own work on Deerfield was serialized in the local newspaper. Sheldon and Temple were certain they were expanding what had hitherto constituted "local history." "The field of these researches," they wrote, "is to a great extent new ground." Theirs was a work based consistently on "manuscript documents," which they listed: town and church records, county records, state archives, family papers, memories of aged persons, and tradition.[17]

How Sheldon appears to have revelled in the accumulation, preservation, and close reading of the materials he worked with for a decade in writing his history! In his preface, he "thanks the owners of the hundreds of garretts, closets, and trunks which I have ransacked at will.[18] He used the same kinds of sources he and Temple had listed earlier with one simple aim in mind: "[To] write as far as [possible] from original sources of information."[19]

---

audience marches, basket lunches, band music, open singing, historical addresses, poems, and "miscellaneous speaking interspersed with music." Though they had the atmosphere of an outing, these meetings gave members and guests an opportunity to reflect on their view of the past and on the meaning of the important events in their town's history.

17. George Sheldon and the Reverend J. H. Temple, *A History of the Town of Northfield, Mass.* (Albany, N.Y.: J. Munsell, 1875).

18. Sheldon, *History of Deerfield, Massachusetts,* I, iv.

19. *Ibid.*

Sheldon's massive, sprawling *History of Deerfield* goes on and on for 1,401 pages. Hailed as a "triumphant model of local historical writing" by an awed colleague, Sheldon's *History* was, in fact, a good example of late-nineteenth-century town history, a version that greatly expanded upon the earlier efforts of the pre-Civil War years. These earlier efforts usually reflected their author's particular interests—genealogical, biographical, military, or religious—or whatever records the writer happened to come upon. But Sheldon and others who shared his approach tried to utilize *in a systematic fashion* the whole array of town, court, church, and even family papers that no one had bothered to investigate before.

The result was *not* the comprehensive history we expect to find, given the means adopted. True, Sheldon expanded upon established areas within local historical writing, such as geneology and war history. He also added considerably to the scope of what had been included in earlier town histories. A great array of subjects receive at least brief attention. But there is no attempt at analysis and interpretation. Great chunks of information are lifted, in undigested form, from the mass of material he examined so closely. The result is more of a catalogue or chronicle than what we would call historical writing.

Thus, Sheldon, though he expanded what was already developed in local history, significantly failed to develop other areas of town life beyond the mere listing of information. Mesmerized by the sources he labored over for so long, he did not have the capacity to analyze them. Local historical writing, in his hands, thus expanded in length and scope, but did not significantly alter in character.

Sheldon's definition of *community* is implicit throughout his two-volume work. "Deerfield" is never the township; it is not an entity defined by its borders; it is not, in short, a political or an administrative unit. "Deerfield" is the original village and the families who lived in it during its formative years. In other words, to Sheldon and the members of the P.V.M.A., the town was simply an extension of family; together, they comprised one's community. From the perspective of the late twentieth century, Sheldon's view of history appears quite narrow. Indeed, how constricted a view of his own community he had, even though it was accurate for the period that he wrote about. But, in the very years when he and his associates were most active, great numbers of Irish, French-Canadians, and Poles moved into the Connecticut Valley and, in particular, into the southern part of the township of Deerfield. This influx of Catholic immigrants and the development of industry and technology would transform the rural, agricultural, cohesive, Yankee small town Sheldon so fondly remembered. And yet there is not the slightest hint of any of this in his *History*. His view of the past precluded his paying any attention to such things—at least as part of his town's *History*. Sheldon's interest all but ends with the Revolution. The short portion of his *History* dealing with the nineteenth century is highly fragmentary. The only genealogies he prepared on his own initiative were those for families living in the town *before* the Revolution. At times, in the last section, he almost seems bored with it all, as if fulfilling some obligation to bring the story into his own time. The account does not end—it just stops; the reader does not know where he has been left. For Sheldon, the drama and adventure of his heroic ancestors ended with that great triumph of liberty over tyranny, the Revolution. Thereafter, his view of historical time became vague and misty. The New England town had been established through great effort during the colonial period and had placed itself under a national government dedicated to human freedom as a result of a successful revolution. That was all one really needed to know; that is all George Sheldon cared to know.[20]

Appropriately enough, Sheldon's own most balanced statement on the meaning of Deerfield's past came in an address on the bicentennial of the massacre:

> We honor our ancestors for their bravery and their steadfastness; we sympathize with them in their sufferings, and are grateful to them for the results—which are ours. They filled that measure which the world of today demands as the pride of its homage——they were successful. . . . We meet today in vain if we are not stronger for their strength, and more faithful, preserving, industrious and economical for their example.[21]

Sheldon readily admitted that the Puritans were, by his standards, bigoted, self-centered, superstitious, and intolerant, "but speaking broadly in the perspective of the centuries, this other fact remains; we see in them a people sifted out from the deeper darkness and despotism which they left behind them in Old England: we see them as the pioneers and the vanguard of civil and religious freedom for the nations."[22] Here, then, was a new meaning for the story of Americans;

---

20. Nor did his successors in the P.V.M.A. want to know any more. In all the years after his death that the Association published addresses and articles, not one word was ever printed about the nineteenth century, industrialization, the Irish, the Poles, or the changing character of the community they lived in.
21. P.V.M.A., *Proceedings*, IV (1903), 385–386.
22. *Ibid.*

they were pioneers whose efforts to build durable communities furthered the cause of civil and religious liberty.

Sheldon's worship of ancestry, his emphasis on the pre-national period, especially his portrayal of early Americans as torchbearers of liberty, all echoed what George Bancroft said in his monumental history of the United States.[23] Bancroft's was the first sustained attempt to provide the reading public of mid-nineteenth-century America with an account of the past from a national, rather than from a regional or local perspective. One of a number of gentleman-amateur writers—we call them "men of letters"—who turned to history only after dabbling in poetry, fiction, or critical essays, Bancroft and the other New Englanders of this group regarded historical writing as a literary art, as great human drama, a story of compelling interest to anyone who read literature. The "romantic" historians, as later analysts have dubbed them, thus attempted to re-create the past, not to analyze or interpret it. Theirs was, according to Richard Hofstadter, a "moral drama . . . told in pictorial terms."[24] Like Sheldon, "what they found most generally and consistently was progress toward liberty, progress which they interpreted with a distinct Protestant bias."[25] Though most in this group—Parkman, Preşcott, Motley—ranged far from presumably prosaic American themes, Bancroft insisted that the American story itself provided the most noble theme of all. If history was about the movement in human affairs toward liberty under God, then surely the history of the United States, the freest of all nations, was worthy of the most attention. Indeed, Americans were properly pictured as being in the vanguard of the human race: "American history could be seen as a kind of consummation of all history."[26]

Sheldon and Bancroft shared much in common, and it is likely that Sheldon had read Bancroft's history before writing his own.[27] There was great similarity of theme, time period covered, even style. Both focussed on heroic individuals and dramatic situations; both fail to bring the story in to the nineteenth century. Bancroft's successors did, however. Hofstadter calls John B. McMaster, Herman von Holst,

23. George Bancroft, *The History of the United States of America from the Discovery of the Continent*, 10 vols. (Boston: Little, Brown & Co., 1834–1874).

24. Richard Hofstadter, *The Progressive Historians: Turner, Beard, Parrington* (New York: Alfred A. Knopf, Inc., 1968), p. 13.

25. *Ibid.*, p. 14.

26. *Ibid.*, p. 16.

27. Coincidentally, Richard Hildreth, Bancroft's chief rival in the rather competitive practice of offering multivolume histories, was from Deerfield, though he did not live there during his adult life.

James Schouler, and others "conservative nationalists," in the sense that they wrote from a national perspective but were conservative in outlook regarding their own society and its recent past. In multivolume narrative accounts that include the period through the then-recent Civil War, they—like Sheldon, once again—avoided discussion of corrupt politics, disruptive industrialization, rapid urbanization, massive immigration, sporadic agrarian and labor revolts—except to condemn earlier historical manifestations whenever they found them.[28] In short, what they avoided at the national level, Sheldon avoided at the local level. All shared a rather narrow conception of what was fit for historical narration. Even though much of what was happening in their country at the time they wrote must have disturbed them, however, such developments had no place in an essentially "WASPish" success story.

Therefore, Sheldon—and probably other local historians of his kind in the late nineteenth century—shared a lot in common with our earliest "national" historians—including a common audience. The same people who turned to Parkman, Bancroft, and Schouler for the national or international story, also read Sheldon, Temple, or Judd for their local stories. It made no difference: all wrote history as literature, as art, as human drama, whether about the people of a nation or of a town, or even of colonial empires.[29]

This rather comfortable nexus of gentlemen-amateur writers, of a largely old-stock, upper- and middle-class audience, and of historical works that told the heroic story of common ancestors all fell apart at the turn of the nineteenth century. It did so in part because the Progressive successors of the Conservative Nationalists became professionals who sought to make history a social science and change its purpose. They would have had it analyze, not recreate; amass statistical as well as literary evidence to establish a point, not simply appear as vivid detail. Their characteristic genre of writing was the monograph, analytical studies of small subjects that, taken together, might establish a new

---

28. Hofstadter, pp. 24–29, 41.

29. Bancroft's popularity was immense. Boorstin explains: "Royalties from his *History* made Bancroft a wealthy man. Within ten years, that first volume went through ten 'editions'; it had gone through twenty-six by 1878. And people bought and read later instalments in large numbers as they appeared. . . . Never before or since has an American national historian been so widely acclaimed abroad. At home, too, his fame increased with the years. Twenty-one years after he had served as the official congressional eulogist on Andrew Jackson's death in 1845, he delivered the Lincoln memorial speech before a joint session of Congress, on February 12, 1866 . . . When he died in 1891, President Harrison ordered the flags at half-mast as Bancroft's body returned to his native Worcester [,Mass.]" (Boorstin, *The Americans: The National Experience*, p. 372). Sheldon's popularity as a local historian was also notable, though on a much smaller scale

overview, but were not themselves to be mistaken for the full story.[30] Under the influence of scholars like Turner and Beard and others whom they trained, American historical writing became increasingly technical or scientific. History of this professional kind did not completely ignore subnational activity, but the most natural frame of reference continued to be the nation. Even when the sectional factor was emphasized, as in Turner's later writings, the focus remained on the impact of sectional controversy on *national* policy. Therefore, narrow lines of inquiry probed, not layers of community, but slices of national life. A world power by 1900, the United States was henceforth regarded by its historians as having been a truly national society from its very beginnings. The mountain of monographic literature amassed over two thirds of a century by scholars has had an audience, of course. In textbooks from the 1920s onward, generations of students have been exposed to detailed analyses that add up to a presumably rounded view of why and how the United States became powerful and influential. Thousands of high school teachers have further distilled this analysis for millions of school children.

But those old-stock Americans who grew up to have an interest in local history continued to view the town as did Sheldon's generation: as an extension of family. Forceful members of historical societies after 1900 continued to be from families active in the early life of the village or surrounding area. A standard type of local history evolved: a narrative of largely political and religious events, followed by brief "histories" of various clubs and organizations. This blended with historical artifact and monument to produce an involvement with the past that was personal, descriptive, still in story form, and understandable to anyone who was interested. The labors of professional historians seemed far away and unrelated. The professional wrote about the nation in an analytical or technical manner. Except in textbooks, where could one read the story of America, even if one wanted to?[31] Surely, the great popularity of historical novelists stems in part from the cravings of those untrained in academic history, but who have a layman's interest in a national history of dramatic events and heroic figures. The audience—outside of university-trained historians—had not changed; professional historical writing had.

30. Hofstadter, pp. 35–43.
31. Morison's and Commanger's textbook (New York: Oxford University Press, 1930) went through five editions over the three decades following its initial publication. Its great popularity was always directly linked to its "literary" qualities. Morison's own *History of the American People* (New York, Oxford University Press 1965) was actually a best seller for some weeks!

III

Viewed in this broad perspective, Daniel J. Boorstin's *The Americans* becomes more than the first significant attempt at broad synthesis since Beard's *The Rise of American Civilization* [32]: It is also the first effort of a general character to reintegrate local and national history. Writing before Smith's study on towns appeared, Boorstin entitles Part I of his second volume "Community," and Part II, "Nationality"; and he emphasizes community-building as having been more successful than nation-building, at least through the 1860s. Americans constructed tangible towns and cities as they lived and moved on the land, but their nation remained vague, unfinished, something whose reality was suggested in abstractions and symbols more than in a central government whose powers were fuzzily drawn and hesitatingly used, or in territorial boundaries whose dimensions were imprecise and shifting.[33]

But Boorstin is himself imprecise. He gives "community" several definitions and often confuses the reader as to the applicability of his observations. Do his views relate to towns and cities generally, or just to cities? Are his views as true of Eastern or Southern places as they are of mid-Western ones? Boorstin treats New Englanders and Southerners as having well-defined regional characteristics, which concern him far more than their community-building aspect. In his *The Americans: the Colonial Experience*, he devotes whole sections to the Virginians and the Puritans and concludes that they constructed widely-divergent communities that profoundly affected colonial life in their respective regions. But he still is not concerned about *local* community-building. Only the Midwest provoked that sort of an interest. And so, although Boorstin has made "community" an organizing principle now familiar to American historians (because of the wide circulation of *The Americans*), he has not been consistent or thorough in his investigations of life at the subnational level.

This is why Smith's study is such a seminal work. The thousands of towns in which most Americans lived until this century have to be studied *in the aggregate* if we are to make sound generalizations about the community that exerted the most influence on the pattern of American life before, say, World War I. In his pioneering attempt to do this, Smith offers a tentative division of American towns into two types: covenanted and cumulative. The covenanted town obviously fascinated and held his attention to the point of overemphasis and distor-

32. (New York: The Macmillan Co., 1930).

33. Boorstin, *The Americans: The National Experience*, pp. 113–118, 221–274, 325–430.

tion. Defined as any community whose founders were "bound in a special compact with God and with each other" to uphold their faith or some moral reform or a special kind of life,[34] the covenanted community maintained its unity and was durable basically because it had a purpose, a reason for existing recognized and adhered to by the homogenous group that settled in it. By contrast, the cumulative town was created without a plan and just grew, usually rapidly "by the accumulation of miscellaneous individuals whose common interest was wholly material."[35] The classic covenanted community was the Puritan town in colonial New England, a type of town that was easily colonized or reproduced along the Atlantic coast and in mid-Western areas by disgrunteld, conservative New Englanders who thought their original communities were not pure enough. Other examples of covenanted-colonized towns were religious communities that attracted people of a common faith from many areas of the country; communities of foreigners from particular places outside the country; towns settled by railroads;[36] communities that were experiments in communal living; and temperance towns.

One perhaps unintended result of Smith's focus on the covenanted community is the new perspective in which communitarian reform movements such as the Owenites, Brook Farm, the Shakers, and the Mormons are placed. These were not distinctive, isolated instances of Americans trying to form model communities organized on communal or communistic principles in sharp contradistinction to American society as a whole; we find, instead, that among the thousands of small communities of that society, one of the *two* major types was very much like those reform communes, except that other covenanted towns generally maintained the private ownership of property, the exception being the original proprietors of the New England towns. Indeed, throughout his study, Smith gives the impression that the covenanted community was the distinctive American small town, whereas the cumulative community typically became the American city.

As useful as his definitions of types of towns are, Smith's insights are seriously weakened by a number of questions left unresolved. For instance, how many covenanted and how many cumulative towns have there been? The statement that "It is impossible to say what proportion

34. Smith, *As a City Upon a Hill*, p. 6.
35. *Ibid.*, p. 31.
36. This seems misplaced. Such towns were colonized, but were they in any sense covenanted?

of new towns should be credited to colonized or cumulative settlement" is disingenuous. Surely, it is a matter of someone's taking the time to check and count! Are we to believe that *all* cumulative towns became cities? And what about covenanted towns, such as Boston and Salt Lake City, that became cities?[37] If most towns were in fact cumulative in their origins, which is probably the case, is not the *typical* American town the uncovenanted, unplanned community, after all? Indeed, how unplanned was the cumulative community, anyway? John Reps's study of town planning clearly shows that many towns, especially those that later became cities, were in fact initially *planned*, though these plans were often later revised or even scrapped as the community grew.[38]

And why are material aims any less cohesive and unifying in their impact than spiritual or moral ones? Communities that exist for a single economic activity, such as mill, mining, or "company" towns, generally have the homogenous character of Smith's formally covenanted ones. Why present colonization as a phenomenon relating only to the covenant, to a desire for the purification and replenishment of the original compact? Even covenanted communities must have had people who left for economic as well as religious reasons. Surely new towns in rural areas were sometimes formed because there were too many people trying to farm in the initial land grant or because it was felt that another trading center for farmers farther on would be economically more satisfactory than the present one.

Indeed, why define towns with reference to purpose, anyway? One possible alternative is to give primacy to the geographic aspect of town life—that is, to a community's physical layout. In this context, towns divide into "closed" and "open" categories. The New England town plan, whether in the shape of streets around a square or of one long street, did not indicate that the founders expected the village to expand indefinitely; it was to be, spatially, a closed community. The "grid" pattern which predominated in the mid-Atlantic Coast and mid-West, however, presupposed future growth and thus created a physical setting for an open community.[39] But the problem remains: this definition is

37. Darret B. Rutman's *Winthrop's Boston: A Portrait of a Puritan Town* (Chapel Hill: University of North Carolina Press, 1965) shows how the most famous of the covenanted towns began to act suspiciously like a cumulative town within twenty years of its founding.

38. John Reps, *Town Planning in Frontier America* (Princeton: Princeton University Press, 1969).

39. *Ibid.*, pp. 145–223.

no more comprehensive than is Smith's. The former deals with ecology, the latter with values; neither, by itself, is complete.

The fact is that Smith, a biographer of John Adams[40] and therefore well informed about colonial New England, adopted Buber's essentially spiritual definition of community when he found that the Puritan settlers regularly formed Buber's kind of community and even carried their form of settlement with them as they migrated across the northern half of the expanding nation during the eighteenth and nineteenth centuries. It was, therefore, relatively easy to devise a scheme in which the Puritan's spiritual, or covenanted, community could be regarded as one of the two basic types of American towns. Such a scheme gave the spiritual element of community life in America a significance it had never had before, certainly not in recent writings concerned about towns generally. The decline of the town is thus linked directly to a decline in its religious vitality and cohesiveness.

In presenting his scheme, Smith largely ignores what has probably been the most influential of all proposals for the study of towns, that of the anthropologist Robert Redfield, in his *Little Community*. Redfield begins with the proposition that "[the] small community has been the very predominant form of human living through the history of mankind." Even in our presumed "urban age," a decided majority of the world's population still live in villages. Redfield goes on to define the small community in terms of its attributes, thus avoiding any flat definition of what it "is." Generalizing on his own studies of primitive villages, he concludes that distinctiveness, smallness, homogeneity, and all-pervading self-sufficiency[41] are basic features, but features realized only in some degree in actual communities. They are, in other words, ideal attributes. The more they are present, the more one is observing a genuine little community.

Redfield points to the ecological system and the social structure as two main areas of investigation for community life, but adds a category that sociologists generally ignore: "a generalized biography" or "the community as if it were a single personality,"[42] by which he means taking typical kinds of individuals and tracing their whole pattern and cycle of life from birth to death, so that one writes from the perspective of the individual who lives in a village, and not just the view of the community itself.

40. Page Smith, *John Adams*, 2 vols. (Garden City, N.Y.: Doubleday & Co., Inc., 1962).
41. Robert Redfield, *The Little Community* (Chicago: University of Chicago Press, 1956), p. 4.
42. *Ibid.*, pp. 55, 68.

It can be argued, of course, that Redfield's schemes flow out of studies relating to primitive villages and therefore do not provide reliable guides for explorations into the nature of town life in modern America, especially since Redfield himself admitted his four characteristics are schematic in nature. Still, Redfield's suggestions for community study are more broad-gauged than Smith's covenanted-cumulative or spiritual-material division, restricted as it is to the goals of townspeople. The Redfield scheme has the additional advantage of offering itself as a guidepost against which American town life can be measured as it has evolved over the last three centuries.

Also pertinent here is Maurice Stein's *The Eclipse of Community: Toward a Theory of American Communities* an attempt to define local community studies in a way that goes beyond what Stein calls the incomplete focus of such sociological pioneers as Robert Park, Helen and Robert Lynd, and Lloyd Warner. Stein claims that all three concentrated on one of the processes of change that transformed the small community each chose for study. For Park, urbanization (in Chicago) was central; for the Lynds, it was industrialization (in Muncie, Indiana); for Warner, bureaucratization (in Newburyport, Massachusetts).[43] Stein concludes that future studies of town and cities must concentrate on the social structure of a community and on why and how it has changed, over a period of time. Central to any explanation for change are the incomplete emphases of Park, the Lynds, and Warner: urbanization, industrialization, and bureaucratization. The result of change has been a "trend toward increased interdependence and decreased local autonomy," something that has resulted in the creation of a "mass society."[44]

Stein's proposal is somewhat marred by its being excessively schematic, however. The fact is that Park, the Lynds, and Warner wrote about far more than urbanization, industrialization, and bureaucratization, and to subsume their study under such rubrics unnecessarily simplifies the complex texture of the evolutionary process whereby town life was transformed. Certainly, the impact of large-scale immigration and vast changes in communications and transportation are two further factors that deserve equal billing with Stein's list.

Smith largely, though not completely, ignores the work of Redfield, Stein, and Laslett.[45] What emerges in his *As a City upon a Hill* is a blur-

43. Stein (Princeton, N.J.: Princeton University Press, 1963), pp. 13–93, 94–113.
44. *Ibid.*, pp. 107, 275–303.
45. Ignored also is Arthur J. Vidich and Joseph Bensman, *Small Town in Mass Society:*

red, incomplete sketch of a generally homogenous community that stressed conformity, to be sure, but that also created the setting for full, open, personal relationships in what Smith views as the most durable, successful community that Americans have ever devised. Smith's sketch is based mainly on old town histories and memoirs. The histories include places from New England across New York state through the mid-West into the plains states; and from various memoirs, he illustrates his subject, in an investigation whose fundamental categories are those used for a long time by historians: political, economic, social, intellectual, and cultural.

The small town's religious life turns out to be just that of the Puritan covenanted communities of New England and the mid-West, with their emphasis on the community of saints and the public redemption of sinners. Beyond this, Smith refers to the revivals of the evangelically oriented sects that both revivified the original covenant and kept alive the religious experience as both covenanted and cumulative communities in the nineteenth century settled into a pattern of containing various Protestant denominations.[46]

Economically, the small town was originally made up of undifferentiated, versatile farmers whose added craft skills were sloughed off and taken over by specialists during the nineteenth century. But the town that Smith portrays was generally a failure in efforts at industrialization, something that fits in with his preoccupation with nonmaterially oriented covenanted communities. Still, Smith finds evidence of countless attempts to nurture industrial enterprise in both New England and in the mid-West, in both covenanted and cumulative communities. Though admitting that "cumulative towns, especially in the mid-West, were business ventures . . . [which]progressed to the specialized functions of rural 'trading centers'," Smith rightly goes on to stress the obvious point that those communities, of whatever origin, which *remained* small towns were those that did not succeed in becoming industrialized.[47]

The politics of the town, at least in New England, were not democratic by theory or design, but were based upon the social uniformity and homogeneity of the community itself. Thus, the town meeting simply gave its formal approval to what was already politically accepta-

Class, Power and Religion in a Rural Community (Princeton, N.J.: Princeton University Press, 1958, 1968).
    46. Smith, *As a City Upon a Hill*, (New York: Alfred A. Knopf, Inc., 1966), pp. 55–83.
    47. *Ibid.*, pp. 84–109.

ble. Later, in the mid-West, the small-town politician continued the tradition by ignoring specific issues, by not disrupting the harmony of community life, by embodying the diverse interests and aspirations of his constituents. All this led to "a fondness for unifying abstractions," "evasiveness on particulars," "dependence on inflated rhetoric"—in short, to "the orator, the compromiser, the pragmatic politician"—to Abraham Lincoln.[48]

The law in small towns also became personal, judicial officials and lawyers alike applying common sense with reference to the great principles of the common law. The courtroom thus became a type of "theatre in which morality plays of a kind were acted out," and those who broke the town's rules were examined and judged, but also redeemed, as punishment—at least, until the nineteenth century—was public, short, and humiliating. But there is also evidence that towns tolerated or ignored minor kinds of deviant behavior. Their law enforcement agencies and churches concentrated on serious crimes and sins that were thought to be in need of redemption.[49]

Socially, the classless unity of the small town was maintained by common ceremonies and festivals, such as church services, weddings, baptisms, funerals, town meetings, militia training, agricultural fairs, and the national independence day. Community life was "improved" or "elevated" by debating societies, lyceums, mechanics institutes, and workingman's societies. The universal improvement or reform, to be more precise, was temperance, as drinking came to be regarded in the nineteenth century as the greatest threat to a community's health; and, in covenanted communities, the temperance crusade became a means, like revivals, to replenish a town's commitment to its covenant by warring on sin.[50]

The choice of careers open to an exceptional, intelligent youth was quite limited in the small town, of course. Outside of farming and the trades or crafts, there were the professions: the ministry, teaching, law, and medicne. The extraordinary number of denominational colleges, academies, and seminaries founded in towns—typically covenanted ones—by local churches provided the means whereby bright youngsters were trained for these professions. By the mid-nineteenth century, "teacher's institutions" and the "normal" school

48. *Ibid.*, p. 125.
49. *Ibid.*, pp. 132, 127–144, 63–64.
50. *Ibid.*, pp. 157–182, 145–146.

appeared and standardized both the eudcation of teachers and the public school system generally.[51]

Finally, the small town's ideology was a definition of the Protestant ethic that stressed "industry, frugality, equality, neighborliness, and loyalty"—a cluster of ideals that gave a distinctiveness and direction to life, especialy in the case of the covenanted towns when their original utopian purpose no longer seemed vital. Each generation learned this ideology though Webster's and McGuffey's eclectic readers, which were filled with moral aphorisms.[52]

This survey of small-town life, while neatly balanced and quite broad, is not exhaustive, especially in the social and cultural spheres. Smith also conspicuously fails to take into account Southern, mid-Atlantic, and far Western towns, an understandable failure in one sense: there is no body of literature on which to draw. Therefore, we do not know whether there is anything distinctive about towns in these regions, as there is in New England and the mid-West. Of course, it would be ironic if each major *region* is found to have had distinctive towns, as if it were somehow the region and not the towns themselves that determined the character of town life. But influence works in all directions, and one of the manifestations of regionalism may well have been to impart to local communities the distinctive, rather than common, features that they had.

One thing is certain: in *all* sections, towns were founded as soon as settlement began in the colonial period, "whether as market centers, bases for exploration and exploitation of natural resources, military camps for subjugation of a region, ports for fishing and trade, or havens from the religious persecutions of Europe,"[53] and this was true of the *South* and the *mid-Atlantic*, as well as New England.[54] Colonial legis-

51. *Ibid.*, pp. 239–247.
52. *Ibid.*, pp. 183–212, 228–230.
53. Reps, *Town Planning in Frontier America*, p. 3.
54. Carl Bridenbaugh, in his study of colonial Southern society, wrote: "A highly significant . . . phenomenon of growth in the Back Part was the rise of more than twenty little inland villages and towns between 1683 and 1776 . . . These towns grew up in answer to certain deeply felt needs of the inhabitants, and . . . have continued to thrive, for the most part because they met the economic demands of today. They started at a crossroad, on the banks of a river at a ferry, near a gristmill, or at a county courthouse, and always in the midst of a well-populated district. Obviously, they served as stages along [main roads], supplying entertainment and shelter for travelers at their taverns. Soon too they became neighborhood centers, attracting artisans and serving as market towns as well as providing for the needs of government" (Bridenbaugh, *Myths and Realities: Societies of the Colonial South*, paperback edition [New York: Atheneum, 1963], pp. . 147–148).

latures passed acts establishing procedures whereby land for townsites could be bought (except in New England, where it was given away), though land companies were sometimes allowed to act on their own. Beginning in the 1780s, Congress determined by law the manner in which the public land could be bought for the establishment of towns. States also incorporated and granted charters to towns. In all these ways, the local community was the creation of state and national government.

In any case, the identification of community-building with the spread of settlement across the continent is something that Smith emphasizes, as does Boorstin and as Richard Wade does, in his *Urban Frontier*.[55] This identification has had the effect of altering the emphasis that Turner gave to the processes by which the American frontier moved from the Atlantic Coast to the Pacific Coast. It is clear that organized community life was *concommitant* with the movement of individuals. There was no universal progression from explorer to trapper to trader to miner to rancher to farmer to town to city. Towns were planned along with initial settlement or, in the case of forts and places founded by the Spanish or the French, actually preceded settlement. Indeed, Boorstin properly emphasizes that there was community before government in the caravan migrations across the plains and in the claims clubs of farmers in the Mississippi Valley and those of miners in the far West.[56]

Boorstin and Smith both suffer from Turner's habit of generalizing on the basis of particular regions or groups, however, For example, there definitely was "community before government," but only in the trans-Mississippi West, not in the trans-Appalachian West, where no "floating" migrants or claims clubs existed. And community-building, Midwestern style, should not be presented as if it were somehow typical nationally, at least not without direct evidence. Smith focusses similarly on New England and the Midwest, ignoring the South, the mid-Atlantic, and the far West: yet, he presents generalized analyses of town life. These portraits contain insights, but the reader is confused as to their universality in terms of time and place. Smith tries to present a progression from colonial times to the twentieth century in his probings into major aspects of community life, but what results is a series of uneven fragments dealing sometimes with New England in the eighteenth century, sometimes with the Midwest in the nineteenth. Also,

55. Richard Wade, *The Urban Frontier: The Rise of Western Cities*, 1790–1830 (Cambridge, Mass.: Harvard University Press, 1959).

56. Boorstin, *The Americans: The National Experience*, pp. 51–90.

his tendency to equate the small town with the covenanted community to some extent predetermines the features of life that receive his attention.

IV

There is little doubt that the town in colonial America, wherever found, was the most important community in the life of the average transplanted white European and his offspring. In this sense, colonial life was not different from what Laslett has found to have been the case in England.[57] The semi-isolated, semiautonomous, preindustrial village, while lacking the purity of Redfield's primitive communities, was far closer to them in the substance of its life than it is to towns in contemporary America. This simple fact calls for a good deal of historical empathy if one is to feel the enormous gap that has opened—rather suddenly, as historical times goes—between the eighteenth-century world and our own.

The only colonial town that Smith paid any attention to in *As a City Upon a Hill* is the "covenanted" New England town. Many aspects of life in the New England town have received the attention of good historians for a long time, but not until the studies of Zuckerman, Clark, and Lockridge[58] were published, in 1970, did anyone use modern sociological analysis to probe the essential nature of these towns.

Zuckerman's "New England Towns in the Eighteenth Century" turn out to be nothing more than the fifteen Massachusetts towns that happened to publish their records. "They are not," the author admits, "an altogether random sample, but, given the rampant localism of the era they will do." Founded at intervals through both the seventeenth and eighteenth centuries, "among them were port towns and island villages, agricultural communities and inland commercial ones, and proto-suburbs within the orbit of the provincial capital."[59]

Lockridge directs his inquiry into the life of one town—Dedham, Massachusetts—during its first one hundred years; but he is concerned about towns generally, for "only from such knowledge, geographically

57. Laslett, *The World We Have Lost*, pp. 23–83.

58. Michael Zuckerman, *Peaceable Kingdoms: New England Towns in the Eighteenth Century* (New York: Alfred A. Knopf, Inc., 1970); Kenneth Lockridge, *A New England Town—The First Hundred Years: Dedham, Massachusetts, 1636–1736* (New York: Wm. Norton & Co., Inc., 1970); Charles E. Clark, *The Eastern Frontier: The Settlement of Northern New England: 1610–1763* (New York: Alfred A. Knopf, Inc., 1970).

59. Zuckerman, p. 2.

confined but comprehensive in terms of human activity,[60] can there emerge truly sophisticated hypotheses about all such towns."[61]

Both Lockridge and Zuckerman effectively utilize town records, but ignore literary evidence—letters, diaries, reminiscences—which, if it exists for their towns, might well have added to or altered their findings. They also draw on a growing body of literature about various aspects of colonial New England life.

What emerges is a portrait of what Lockridge called the "Christian Utopian Closed Corporate Community," or, if that is too much of a tongue-twister, what Zuckerman calls "Consensual Communalism." With either definition, New England towns were Smith's covenanted community. They were also, according to Zuckerman, "Peaceable Kingdoms" whose very nature as small, isolated communities with a uniformity of purpose, meant that their continued existence depended upon *voluntary* consensus, compromise, and a basic unity of opinion and action. Zuckerman investigates religious and secular values, social make-up, certain political procedures and activities, and everywhere finds a stress on harmony, conformity, peace.

Lockridge's Dedham, for its first *fifty* years, looks a lot like Zuckerman's Dedham, or any of his other fourteen towns, for that matter. But Lockridge stresses *disunity* after 1686, for the very period in which Zuckerman stresses peace and unity. Lockridge points to "the relentless logic of growth"—specifically to the growth of population, its spread into outlying areas, the end of available or productive land around the original townsite, all of which led to divisions among the villagers. These divisions found expression in increasingly argumentative town meetings, in the development of economic-political-social distinctions, and, ultimately, to secession and the formation of *new* towns for those living in the periphery.

Zuckerman admits that sections of towns seceded, but gives quite a different meaning to the phenomenon. Secession was simply *another*

60. This is inaccurate if applied to the author's own work, as he deals only with political, economic, and religious aspects of life.

61. Lockridge, p. xiv. Edmund S. Morgan, as early as 1961, suggested the New England town as a proper focal point of study, but he was interested in enhancing our understanding of Puritanism and did not regard the study of local communities as meriting our attention on its own terms. In his words, "If we . . . study the history of early New England by localities, town by town and church by church, I believe we could discover a great deal not only about the diversity of Puritanism but also about its range and penetration within society. . . . Such a study would require a thorough examination of the records of a large number of town" (Edmund S. Morgan, "New England Puritanism: Another Approach," *William and Mary Quarterly*, XVIII, no. 3 [1961], 236–242, 237).

way towns kept their peace, harmony, and uniformity: "Where differences developed in religion, occupation, ethnic extraction, or anything else deemed relevant, separation was often seen as the only solution." True enough, but because he ignores demographic and economic factors in his concentration on values and behavior, Zuckerman missed the dynamics of *change* that surely existed, even while brilliantly perceiving the notable stability of the colonial New England town. Zuckerman thus fails in his task, which was "to comprehend the culture of provincial Massachusetts whole."[62]

How typical are Lockridge's and Zuckerman's portraits? This is a fair question, since both offer their studies as attempts to generalize about the New England town—"Indeed," Lockridge adds, "about the entire history of colonial America, a society dominated by rural settlements."[63] Lockridge makes a good case for the typicality of Dedham in his final chapter, "Dedham and the American Experience," in which he ironically points to Zuckerman's dissertation, as well as other studies about aspects of New England life relating to towns, as evidence of Dedham's typicality. But Dedham was not necessarily typical as to the *pace* and *timing* of change. For instance, many features of life in Kent, Connecticut, a frontier community of the mid-eighteenth century, recall to mind Lockridge's early Dedham, *before* "the relentless logic of growth" got hold of it.[64] Perhaps the over-all *stage* of development of any given town has to be determined before Zuckerman's "peace and harmony" label or Lockridge's "disunity and change" label can properly be affixed.

Indeed, Charles E. Clark, in his *The Eastern Frontier: The Settlement of Northern New England: 1610–1763*, questions the whole notion of a region—New England—based on a certain kind of village society. He found that

> [the] settlers of that corner of America which became New Hampshire and Maine differed from Southern New Englanders in place of origin, motives of settlement, religion, politics, temperament, and way of life. These differences, and those of geography, resulted in a regional distinction between northern and southern New England that was as marked as the time-honored separations that are usually observed between New England and

62. Zuckerman, p. vii.
63. Lockridge, p. xiv.
64. Charles Grant, *Democracy in the Connecticut Frontier Town of Kent* (New York: Columbia University Press, 1961).

the Middle Colonies, and between the Middle Colonies and those of the Cheasapeake. . . . One cannot hope for a total comprehension of "colonial New England" if he fails to understand that it was not in the beginning all of a piece.[65]

Clark also found what he calls "imperialism" on the part of Massachusetts Bay, a persistent effort by this Puritan-dominated colony to extend its pattern of life throughout the region north of the Merrimac River during the seventeenth and eighteenth centuries. He adds: "Given the power, the vigor, and the size of the province that lay to the South, [this attempted 'Puritan conquest'] was probably inevitable."[66]

If inevitable, it was also only partially successful, however. Though Maine was brought under Massachusetts's jurisdiction, New Hampshire retained its independence. More important—and relevant—was the different character of towns that developed in northern New England. The early fishing villages were overwhelmingly materialistic in orientation. And even

> [the] interior town of northern New England as it developed in this period differed in several important respects from the typical seventeenth-century community of eastern Massachusetts or the lower Connecticut Valley. The motives for settling this area were complex and in most cases entirely secular. They included defense, land hunger, the speculative urge, intercolonial politics, and plain restlessness.[67]

In many ways the pattern of settlement in northern New England was initially controlled by the Puritan-oriented Massachusetts colonial government. "[Townships] were granted either by the Bay province or under pressure from it, and then settlement was subject to conditions conceived originally by Massachusetts magistrates." Thus each township had to provide for a church and a school and its own defense. But the continued focus on the possession of land in the interior settlements led to the stretching and deformation of villages planned after the Massachusetts model. "By the 1750s, [in] their place . . . communities of dispersed, integrated family farms, located according to the suitability of the land and the desire of the individual

65. Clark (New York: Alfred A. Knopf, Inc., 1970), pp. vii–viii.
66. *Ibid.*, p. viii.
67. *Ibid.*, pp. 265–266.

settler rather than according to an imposed scheme—grew rapidly to maturity."[68]

Though Clark's study is about the whole development of an area, and not just about towns, he does succeed in demonstrating that the classic Puritan village of Massachusetts and Connecticut was not established in New Hampshire and Maine. What remains doubtful is his assertion that northern New England should be regarded as a distinctive region, on a par with the mid-Atlantic region, whose hallmark, after all, was its variety. What Clark, perhaps unwittingly, does, is to call into question the whole concept of region as defined on the basis of local communities. The Puritan village did not wholly define New England, because one was not coterminous with the other.

Colonial America in all probability was "a society dominated by rural settlements"—or, more accurately, those segments of the colonies with contiguous townships may well have exerted the most influence on the lives of British provincials in those areas. But how typical was the relationship between Massachusetts towns and their provincial government? In eighteenth-century Massachusetts, Zuckerman clearly shows, the towns were easily the most powerful unit of government. Representation in the colony's legislature was based on towns, not people, and the evidence seems overwhelming that people using power and making decisions did so in far more important ways in their local communities than on the provincial level. In vivid, concrete ways, the towns played the pre-eminent political role in the lives of those who lived in the colony. In Zuckerman's words: "Local history, which has heretofore resisted most efforts to make it more than local, can be endowed with a larger significance, for in the instance of eighteenth-century Massachusetts, it provides a prospect of actually accounting for developments instead of simply describing them."[69] The town was also the basis of provincial representation in the other New England colonies—Rhode Island, Connecticut, and New Hampshire; but New York, New Jersey, Virginia, and Maryland had mixed systems, while Pennsylvania, Delaware, the Carolinas, and Georgia used the county as their unit.[70] None of the colonies had an outright district system based directly upon population. Until further study is done, it is not possible

68. *Ibid.*, pp. 267, 219.

69. Zuckerman, p. 222.

70. Cortland F. Bishop, *History of Elections in the American Colonies*, reprint (New York: Ben Franklin, 1965), pp. 7–45.

to generalize about the relative importance of local and provincial governments. Zuckerman's study is the model.

* * * * *

In 1954, twelve years before Smith's study appeared, Lewis Atherton presented the first modern generalized account of any type of American town, *Main Street on the Middle Border*, a study of what he called "a cultural and economic history of midwestern country towns from 1865 to 1950," towns defined as "service centers" for farmers, with less than 5,000 population.[71] Writing before sociological concepts of community had penetrated very far into the historical profession, Atherton wrote as one who had grown up in such a small town and who thus had a feeling for his subject, the kind of rapport that naturally led him "to read all the reminiscences, autobiographies, and novels depicting the region and period of which I am writing," in addition to such more orthodox sources as magazine articles, scholarly studies, and country newspapers—but not town records. He adds:

> I have tried to avoid making this another "I remember" story by eliminating my own personal experiences in mid-western country towns and oral traditions of my family going back to the Civil War and before. . . . Nonetheless, my own interest in research has been determined by family background and I have also felt more competent to judge the records and experiences of others when my own family has participated in so many of the same things.[72]

Atherton's "cultural" emphasis, while broad-ranging, ignores such things as political activity and factors making for economic growth or decline—which are serious omissions. But what Atherton *does* concentrate on he deals with effectively. His *forte* is vivid description that enables the reader to "see" a typical country town and perceive much of its essential character—description that provides analysis, even though the language used is not particularly analytical. Atherton's introductory device is simple: the reader is taken on an imaginery tour of a generalized Main Street, it being Atherton's assumption that what lines that street should reflect what the town is all about.[73]

---

71. Paperback edition (Chicago: Quadrangle Books, 1966), p. xiv. The Middle Border consists of Ohio, Indiana, Illinois, Missouri, Michigan, Minnesota, Wisconsin, Iowa, and the "eastern farming fringe" of Kansas, Nebraska, and the Dakotas.

72. *Ibid.*, p. xvi.

73. *Ibid.*, pp. 33–64.

The Midwestern country town was clearly built for materialistic purposes. Those who founded them entered into a frenzy of speculative enterprise in real estate, competing for settlers. And those who settled competed with those in other towns to act as service men for farmers in the adjoining countryside.[74] In short, the mid-Western country town was Page Smith's cumulative community, but a community that remained small while *wanting* at the same time to become bigger fast —all of which makes it contrast neatly with the New England covenanted community, and presumably its colonized version in the Midwest, as well.

Transportation—the horse—determined both the spacing of these rural trading centers and their relative isolation and self-sufficiency.[75] In many ways, they were not unlike the earlier New England towns, which strengthens the view that Smith's equating the covenanted community with the "classic" small town distorts as much as it enlightens. Like their counterparts back east, the Midwestern villages stressed conformity and were, in fact, largely unstructured, homogenous communities whose values and virtues, suggested by the Protestant ethic, were quite similar—even if their primary purpose, economic enrichment, was different. Because of the Midwesterners' obvious materialistic preoccupations, all aspects of the practical and useful, noncultural and nonartistic, are given more attention by Atherton than they received in the studies on colonial New England towns.[76]

Even so, the evident similarity between colonial New England towns and nineteenth-century Midwestern ones suggests that, contrary to Smith's assertion, *purpose* is less important than such things as values, isolation, and self-sufficiency in determining what is distinctive and important about any group of towns. Those who sought to produce a model or pure religious community did not, in a broad sense, create towns essentially different from those who emphasized the material aspects of life. Small-town values and society could accommodate *both*.

In any case, Atherton believes that "the history of the middle border has been largely the history of its towns"; and within these towns, life centered on community-wide activities, local crafts, services, and professions, and such local institutions as the church and the school, with little reference to the outside world.[77] Relationships with the outside world did exist, of course, most obviously with the farmers in the

74. *Ibid.*, pp. 3–32.
75. *Ibid.*, pp. 33–43.
76. *Ibid.*, pp. 65–88, 109–119.
77. *Ibid.*, pp. 143–192.

surrounding countryside. This farmer-villager relationship was something quite different from the New England experience, where towns were coterminous with the whole territory. A less obvious outside influence was the presence of merchandise produced in bulk elsewhere and sold to the villagers in general stores. Material self-sufficiency was never complete, though very much in evidence. Ironically, the McGuffey readers, through which small town values were passed on from one generation to the next, were an "outside" product, from the East. But Atherton regards the aphorisms of these readers as the quintessence of country town "culture." The irony disappears, therefore, if the readers are regarded as nineteenth-century American town values "generalized" in print for all to use. Popular culture or entertainment was also a product of the outside world, whether in the form of circuses or theatrical productions at catch-all opera houses.[78] In all, there is assembled a not very impressive list of outside influences.

* * * * *

More recently, in 1968, Robert R. Dykstra's *The Cattle Towns* presented a fairly comprehensive analysis of a special type of Midwestern town. Though largely ignoring social-cultural aspects of life, Dykstra captures what was distinctive about the five towns that became trading centers for those who brought cattle north from the Texas ranges. These frontier communities constitute a good example of what Dykstra considers to be a *general impulse* of town-building: that is, "most American small towns would be cities if they could."[79] In this case, the dynamics of growth involved continued efforts to get, to hold, and to increase the volume of the cattle trade. This imperative occasionally created dissatisfaction among neighboring farmers who regarded the towns as rural service centers, like other Midwestern communities.[80] Dykstra focusses on the one major aspect of town life that Atherton ignored: politics. He found a "politics of factionalism" or of conflict, not the harmony that Zuckerman asserts was central to New England towns in the eighteenth century. Factionalism took the form of periodic divisions within the towns over all manner of issues, both serious and humorous—political antagonisms that existed between long-lived cliques.[81] Whether the political life of the cattle towns was that of Midwestern country towns generally is yet to be demonstrated.

78. *Ibid.*, pp. 65–88, 127–142.
79. Robert R. Dykstra, *The Cattle Towns* (New York: Alfred A. Knopf, Inc., 1968), p. 3.
80. *Ibid.*, pp. 178–206.
81. *Ibid.*, pp. 207–292.

While Dykstra's study does not fundamentally alter the view we now have of the local community in the Midwest, it may be hoped that it will inaugurate a new era in the writing of local history: the systematic study of special types of towns. Other obvious candidates for such study are the Western mining town, the Southern mill town, fall line or early factory towns, and various kinds of "company" towns. More generally, attention should be given to temporary communities, to towns that were short-lived or failed altogether—"ghost-towns."[82] It is as important to know why towns *failed* as it is to know why they *endured*—or became cities.

V

All those who have already generalized about towns agree—whether explicitly or implicitly—that their influence was profound. How profound is yet to be determined. For most areas of the country during most periods in our past, the primacy of the town will most likely be found to have varied, depending on its relationship to other levels of communities and on the extent of its isolation and self-sufficiency.[83] The essential nature of the small town in America through the nineteenth century already appears in the writings of Smith, Lockridge, Zuckerman, Clark, Atherton, and Dykstra. Lockridge describes it as "pre-industrial village society." It is "a world we have lost . . . in the tides of migration, mechanization, and urbanization which have since altered western civilization."[84] All but Dykstra and Clark underscore this point and emphasize the basic differences between village life and that of modern American society. Even features of life that were evident then and are still present now *meant* something profoundly different in the earlier setting. The essential unity and conformity of the town imparted to such fundamentals as

82. James B. Allen, *The Company Town in the American West* (Norman, Oklahoma: University of Oklahoma Press, 1966), has written about one special type of town in one region, at least. He found nearly two hundred company-owned towns in the manageable region he chose. Whether a lumber, copper, coal, or industrial settlement, the company town was varied: "In some towns serious abuses of power occurred, while in others sincere and commendable efforts at company-employee co-operation were made. In some cases employees hated the managers . . . In other instances the workers were highly satisfied and even disliked leaving at the termination of their employment. . . . Some [towns] evolved from tent towns, mining camps, and other rugged frontier communities. Others were well planned from the beginning. Most were fully paternalistic, although the degree of company control varied widely," (p. 145).

83. This supports the views of Redfield and Laslett.

84. Lockridge, p. xil. The source is Laslett.

democracy, capitalism, and the Protestant ethic definitions vastly different from those that prevail now. At the heart of the matter was the primacy of the community over the individual, something that Boorstin has also stressed in his general interpretation of the period between the Revolution and Civil War.

The "communalism" was democratic in the general sense: there existed wide participation in town affairs, no extremes of wealth and poverty, and no clearly defined social classes or large ethnic, religious, or racial minorities. But it was a democracy profoundly antiliberal and conservative. As Smith puts it:

> It provided no room for tolerance of other creeds, religious or political; it was not based on the assumption that government represented a consensus among disparate groups with different interests and different conceptions of the truth. For the town there was only one truth—its own. The town in its homogeneity, in its racial and cultural "purity," was for the most part able to avoid those conflicts between rival groups and interests out of which modern democratic practice and theory developed.[85]

Zuckerman underscores this view. So does Lockridge in a general, ambiguous way, but he is also anxious to show the colonial origins of the breakdown of cohesion in town life. And Dykstra clearly found conflict in the post-Civil War frontier cattle towns. The applicability of Smith's general assertion thus requires more study.

The towns were also capitalistic, but were generally preindustrial at the same time. Smith convincingly documents the failure of those communities that remained small towns to develop successful industrial enterprise, even though many—even covenanted towns—repeatedly tried to do so. Generally speaking, townspeople did not have the capital, managerial skill, labor supply, or access to faraway markets. "The relation of the town to a wider economy was so casual and uncoordinated that the town was defenseless against relatively minor shifts in the economic pattern," Smith adds.[86] But how long did this situation last? And what about the agricultural economy of the towns? To what extent did it become specialized and commercialized in the sense that local products were sold, as in the cattle towns, in distant markets? Did this process occur only in "one-crop" rural areas? What *was* the relationship of the town's preindustrial economy to outside markets?

85. Smith, *As a City Upon a Hill*, p. 111.
86. *Ibid.*, p. 87.

There is general agreement that the Protestant ethic, from which values were derived, was given an anti-individualistic, communalistic emphasis in the towns. This meant laboring for the common good and not primarily for individual material gain. But what about all those towns whose population was caught up in speculative manias? Was not this sort of frenzy a kind of *secular* revival? Did it not indicate a concern for individual, as well as, communal, enrichment?

There are a number of pertinent questions relating to the general nature of small-town life in America that remain unanswered, even though a broad outline of that life is coming into view. It may be hoped that the kind of overview Smith has outlined will become sounder and firmer when we have more studies of the caliber of Zuckerman's, Lockridge's, Clarke's, and Atherton's.

* * * * *

It is important to know more than the main feature of the world we have lost, however, We should also know how and when we lost it. As to when, those who have generalized about towns are not in complete agreement. Lockridge writes vaguely about a new society of "pluralism, individualism, and liberty" predominating about the time of Andrew Jackson's presidency. But Atherton and Smith both point to the turn of the nineteenth century as the time when the small town was clearly losing its primacy.

Atherton and Smith are also in agreement as to how and why. The villain of the piece is unquestionably the city, or more generally, an urbanized society. Smith offers an impressive catalogue of urban-oriented changes that, taken together, account for the decline and fall of the town. It was the city that defined the Protestant ethic in such a way that rampant individualism and self-enrichment (or the "Gospel of Wealth") triumphed over the communal orientation of the ethic in the town. It was the city that provided the appropriate setting for the accumulation of capital and the development of giant corporations that went on to direct the small town's economy through branch plants. It was the city, with its structured society, that imposed styles of living on the rural population, making it more class conscious, impersonal, and apt to join organizations binding portions of it to groups extending far beyond the local community.[87]

Atherton shows more graphically how outside influences increasingly broke down the substantial self-sufficiency and isolation of the midwestern country town. Public utilities were formed by outside

87. *Ibid.*, pp. 104–107, 177–180, 205–210.

corporations because towns did not have the resources for them. Goods produced elsewhere were increasingly given brand names by rival producers. Mail-order houses and then chain stores brought outside merchandizing. Railroads, electric interurbans, and the automobile revolutionized transportation and transformed not only the relationship of villagers to faraway places, but also the dependency of farmers in the surrounding rural areas. Organizations in the towns became formal and were nothing more than local chapters of something created in the outside world. The Protestant churches accepted the social gospel movement and got involved in the newly organized community life. High schools were consolidated and values were passed on through the new conduit of scientific, secular, humanistically oriented school books. Radio, movies, and television replaced live entertainment—over which there had been a measure of local control. Chambers of Commerce sought outside industry so that the towns could "progress" and grow and become like cities.[88]

Atherton thus shows in concrete ways how one type of American town shifted in the organization of its life from a largely local to an increasingly national basis. The problem with Smith's larger and broader analysis of the decline of the small town is its lack of proportion. By concentrating on the covenanted town at the expense of the cumulative, he shows more concern for the decline of spirituality than for the wide range of developments whose cumulative effect was to undermine the small town's relative self-sufficiency. And by turning the city into a villain, he oversimplifies the context for certain important developments. It is a distortion to argue, for example, that railroads, automobiles, radio, television, the national corporation, nationwide social and labor-farmer-industrial organizations are simply a product of the city, as if urbanites somehow plotted and carried into effect the changes that altered the face of a society. Smith also gives excessive attention to the substance of town life *in relation to* his explanations for the ways that life was altered almost beyond recognition. Smith's study ignores other factors that helped to break down small-town isolation, the impact of large-scale immigration being the most notable.

* * * * *

What we have lost has brought forth differing personal reactions from those whose writings have been examined. Smith clearly regrets the decline of the local community in America, as does Atherton. They both try to understand its decline, but regret it, since what has replaced

88. Atherton, pp. 217–330.

the small town has not been successful as a human community:

> If it is true as history suggests that the preservation of the sense of
> a viable and open future is dependent upon the preservation of
> such "publics," [that is] communities in which human encounters
> dominate the encounters of people with "things," or of people
> with fictionalized personalities, or with individuals abstracted
> into a single function in a large collective society, the destruction
> of the town has serious implications for the future of our
> country.[89]

What to Atherton is sad, to Smith is human tragedy of limitless dimensions. What is implied in Smith's statement just quoted is that modern, secular, industrial-technological, humanistic society has failed to create a "good" human community to replace the one it has wrecked. But to Zuckerman, what has been lost is not what we regard as "good," either. Individualism of whatever kind, tolerance, liberty, have all come out of the society that has replaced the village. Thus Smith and Zuckerman, each in his own way, invest local history with a broad human significance for both the United States and the whole Western world.

Nowhere in their writings do Smith, Zuckerman, and the others flatly define what an American town was. Like Redfield, they are far more concerned with the task of delineating its chief characteristics than in plunging into a quest for an ever receding linguistic consensus. By contrast, Peter Laslett defines the preindustrial English village as a community that "consisted of households in association. To the factors of geography, being together in the one place, were added all the bonds which are forged between human beings when they are permanently alongside each other; bonds of intermarriage and of kinship and co-operation in matters of common concern."[90] This is not at all a bad attempt at definition, but is one largely ignored by the American scholars whose works are being discussed.

In colonial southern New England, the steady practice of "outlivers"[91] petitioning the legislature and receiving approval for the right to establish new towns simplifies the question of what a true

---

89. Smith, *As a City Upon a Hill*, p. 303.

90. Laslett, *The World We Have Lost*, p. 81.

91. "Outlivers" were those who moved away from the original settlement in a New England township when, with the growth of the population, it made sense to move closer to land holdings quite distant from the town center.

community was. Continuous areas of settlement thus ordinarily continued to be distinct communities, both in terms of their relative social homogeneity and in their political or administrative independence. But, the situation became more complicated in the nineteenth century, when the splitting off of older townships stopped for reasons as yet unknown. At that point, the New England town assumed its modern form: sporadic clusters of settlement surrounded by open farm land, all within the political unit of a single township. The amateur local historians of that century—like George Sheldon of Deerfield—often thought of the original village in the township as their community, where family continuity and social cohesion made possible the felt connections between family and community that characterize these historians' writings. When modern historians get around to writing on New England towns in the nineteenth century, it is quite probable that they will continue to de-emphasize political and administrative boundaries and focus on village communities that have a social as well as a geographic or political reality.

This problem of the town as a real community does not exist to the same degree in the Midwest, the only other area of the country whose village life has thus far received the attention of modern scholars. If Atherton's account is accurate, there was a fairly clean line of demarcation between the trading center that was the Midwestern village and the surrounding countryside.

In any case, future students of the American town must continue to be aware of the difference in dealing with a genuine community and one that is not. The town as a political or territorial entity and the town as a social structure may well diverge, not coincide. If the "local" or "little" community is to have any cohesion as a unit of historical study, Redfield's characteristics—distinctiveness, smallness, homogeneity, and all-pervading self-sufficiency—must be borne in mind as ideal attributes. And it bears repeating that the definition contemporaries themselves gave to their community must be evaluated along with terms of a more analytical character. This is something Sheldon and other amateurs of the nineteenth century knew instinctively; we forget it to our detriment. Perhaps Laslett's "households in association" should be the *sine qua non* when all else seems uncertain.

* * * * *

The town needs to be studied in *all* the major aspects of its life. Its study must not be reduced to "social" history, as Zuckerman and others do. Local history is not a branch of any of the established categories of historical study, but must exist as a separate entity, something that only Smith has thus far fully understood.

Redfield's "wholistic" approach, taken over by Smith, is more satisfying as a way of studying the town than is the far more common, restricted method, employed by such writers as Dykstra, Atherton, Lockridge, and Zuckerman, of selecting certain facets of town life for intensive examination to illustrate an over-all thesis.[92] Smith's account has a certain stateliness that results from its pleasing sense of balance and proportion. His examination of the town gains strength from his systematic explorations into all the major facets of community life. One comes away from the more specific studies just referred to with the feeling that the thesis might have been altered somewhat if only the author had decided to extend his coverage to other areas.

Of course, lack of evidence often limits inquiry in a completely arbitrary way: no sources, no analysis. But it is also true that writers on towns have typically slighted either statistical or various kinds of literary evidence. For example, Smith himself ignores completely the great array of statistical source material to be found in census, town, and church records. Then too, the "wholistic" approach must not be permitted to obscure division and conflict within towns. Smith, in his effort to be balanced and comprehensive, does not explore such matters. The reader is therefore surprised and somewhat shocked when he moves from Smith's general account and Zuckerman's more specific one to Lockridge's far from peaceable Dedham or to Dykstra's study of mid-nineteenth-century cattle towns, marked as they were by political and social disunity. Future students of town history should therefore strive to be both comprehensive and alert to signs of unity as well as to evidence of division in the life of the communities studied.

Smith's general account points out another limitation in the more specialized writings of recent years. By dealing with town life from the colonial period to the present, Smith tries to show the shifting place of the small community through the entire course of American history. Those who have written on representative towns or types of towns, restricting their examination to specific periods of time, leave the reader wondering whether the subject may be distorted through ignorance of what happened before and after. Maybe the period chosen was poorly defined; perhaps certain developments would take on a new meaning if seen in a longer course of time. True, those dealing with the origins

92. Dykstra deals with only political and economic aspects; Lockridge, with political, economic, and religious; Zuckerman, with the social and, to some extent, political, while Atherton omits certain aspects of economic life and neglects politics altogether.

of towns run fewer risks than others; surely this is at least a partial explanation for the great emphasis in local historical writing on the colonial period, though, of course, the town's obvious importance in the prerevolutionary period is also a factor. And it can be argued to great effect that studies have to be strictly limited if an author is to give more than a cursory treatment to his subject. But there is something very satisfying about a single writer's viewing a town "whole" in a temporal, as well as a spatial and social sense. Questions of proportion and emphasis are handled with more confidence. And the changing nature of town life is more clearly drawn.

Only one writer on towns has followed the lead of Smith on this matter of time. John B. Armstrong, in his *Factory Under the Elms: A History of Harrisville, New Hampshire, 1774–1969*, has presented a history of a single town through the entire "national" period of American history. Armstrong has no flashy or audacious sociological concepts to link his research to; his writing is bereft of the structured analyses of a Zuckerman. Indeed, with its rich detail and close association with the sources on hand, Armstrong's study reads something like those done by amateurs of Sheldon's generation—and after. But what lifts *Factory Under the Elms* far away from these earlier accounts is the over-all conception of local history that lurks behind the book's organization and coverage. Armstrong openly accepts Smith's view of town history. In doing so, he pays close attention to the relationship between the town and the outside world, gives systematic treatment—as far as sources allow—to the whole range of community life, and goes beyond Smith in his use of statistical evidence and in the attention given to elements of disunity in the town, to the power elites, to the influx of immigrants, to reasons for the village's durability, as well as to factors making it Harrisville, New Hampshire, and no other place in the world. Altogether, Armstrong's study has the proper balance to stand as a model for full-length, single-town history in the post-Smith era.

VI

But what of the truly rural population of the United States, those living outside settled communities of any kind? Redfield accepts the assertion made earlier by Newell Sims in *The Rural Community, Ancient and Modern* that isolated homesteads probably did not appear on a large scale until the settlement of the Americas by transplanted white Europeans.[93]

93. Redfield, p. 3; Sims (New York: Scribner's & Co., 1921), pp. 120–121.

Ruth Sutter is more precise:

> Around the Atlantic fringes of Europe, from Finland to parts of
> the Iberian peninsula, the traditional settlement pattern was one
> of single family and more or less self-sufficient farms. Homes-
> teads were dispersed, and a sense of neighborhood was probably
> maintained through kindship, trading associations, crossroads
> fairs, religious gatherings, and rural courts. . . . These *open-
> country neighborhoods* were scattered elsewhere in Europe too, but
> through much of England and trans-alpine Europe the commun-
> ity took the form of a *compact village*, a cluster of households sepa-
> rate from fields.[94]

But in the colonies: "With a great deal of land apparently available,
it is not surprising that the dispersed settlement pattern took hold and
spread, spread in fact across the continent, until in some areas it is hard
to find any community center or focus at all. There had been settled
homesteads in parts of Europe, but in North America they came to
characterize agricultural areas."[95]

If this be true, then a significant pattern of settlement in the British
North American colonies was unlike anything many colonists left behind. Unfortunately, the United States census figures on this subject
are misleading, so we do not have an accurate count of the rural population after 1790. The Census Bureau has defined places as rural if
they have fewer than 2,500 people. But such small towns are
communities and should not be confused with the element of the population that lives wholly outside communities. Rural sociologists typically
include what they call rural villages in their field of study,[96] but such an
inclusion would not make any sense in the scheme now being proposed. One thing is clear: the rural population, however defined, has
always been agricultural in its way of life.

Atherton points out that in large areas of the Midwest there were
farmers living outside the village trading centers. In the South, isolated
plantations and farms stretched over much of the inland areas, with
only occasional towns, cross-roads villages, or county seats as commun-

---

94. Ruth E. Sutter, *The Next Place You Come to: A Historical Introduction to Communities in
North America* (Englewood Cliffs, N.J.: Prentice-Hall, Inc., 1973), p. 33.

95. *Ibid.*, p. 83.

96. Lowry Nelson, *Rural Sociology: Its Origin and Growth in the United States* (Min-
neapolis, Minn.: University of Minnesota Press, 1969).

ity centers. Even in New England, in New Hampshire and Maine, Clarke tells us, the pattern of settlement came to be the isolated farm house. In purely political terms, outside of New England, only New York, Pennsylvania, Ohio, Illinois, Wisconsin, Minnesota, Missouri, and Arkansas developed the "township" system in which incorporated towns are coterminous with the entire territory of the state. In all other states, varying amounts of territory are directly under the jurisdiction of county government.[97] Such facts as these call into question Smith's assumption that most Americans live in towns, but do not necessarily undermine his assertion that most Americans were more influenced by the town than by any other form of community. Though the rural farming population lived outside the framework of community life, it was obviously affected in important ways by what happened in towns and cities. There are hints here and there in Smith's and in other general studies that the town served, economically, as a trading center for their hinterland, and, politically, provided politicians who acted as spokesmen for the farmers in state and national legislatures.[98] But even with such evidence, the rural element has yet to receive the attention of a historian who can generalize significantly about it. These were the people who most interested Turner, at least in their guise as pioneers on the frontiers. What is needed is a study of them in more settled, but still rural areas, where it already seems evident that they were, by turns, both conservative and (at least in the case of the Populist movement) radical.

97. *1970 Commercial Atlas and Marketing Guide* (Chicago, New York, and San Francisco: Rand McNally Co., 1970).

98. Smith, *As a City Upon a Hill*, p. 121; Atherton, *Main Street on the Middle Border*, p. xiv. Merle Curti's *The Making of an American Community: A Case Study of Democracy in a Frontier County* (Stanford, Calif.: Stanford University Press, 1959), is not an investigation of only the rural element in the population as defined here: Curti is also concerned with those who lived in towns. He concluded that (a) county history can be profitably studied through both literary and statistical evidence (he was one of the first to use the manuscripts from the 1850–1880 censuses later popularized by Thernstrom and others) and that (b) Turner's association of the frontier with democracy can be substantiated up to a point.

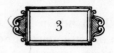

The Intermediary Communities: Cities, States, and Regions

I

The city, Lewis Mumford reminds us, has always been with us; indeed, "at the dawn of history, the city is already a mature form." The first urban centers of the ancient world were the result of what Mumford calls an "implosion," a coming together, under pressure, of "many diverse elements of the community hitherto scattered [about]," an "integration of shrine, citadel, village, work-shop, and market."[1] What followed was a succession of cities—ancient, medieval, baroque, commercial, the metropolis—all of which played a vital role in their respective civilizations.

These larger concentrations of people and the heightened efficiency, energy, and organization of their activities had what the thoroughly humanistic Mumford calls both positive and negative consequences:

> Through its concentration of physical and cultural power, the city heightened the tempo of human intercourse and translated its products into forms that could be stored and reproduced. Through its monuments, written records, and orderly habits of association, the city enlarged the scope of all human activities, extending them backwards and forwards in time. By means of its storage facilities (buildings, vaults, monuments, tablets,

1. Lewis Mumford, *The City in History: Its Origins, Its Transformations, and Its Prospects* (New York: Harcourt, Brace & World, 1961). pp. 4, 34, 569.

books), the city became capable of transmitting a complex culture from generation to generation, for it marshalled together not only the physical means but the human agents needed to pass on and enlarge this heritage. That remains the greatest of the city's gifts.[2]

Through their concentration of effort over many centuries, city dwellers have also unleashed the awesome and *explosive* power of the machine. Massive technological achievements have produced an overmechanized civilization in an increasingly urbanized world in which the human personality has been scattered by "vocational separation, by social segregation, by the overcultivation of a favored function, by tribalisms and nationalisms, by the absence of organic partnerships and ideal purposes"; an urbanized world in which "[quantitative] production has become . . . the only imperative goal in physical energy, in industrial productivity, in invention, in knowledge, in population. . . . "; in which there are even more alarming and malign explosions of energy that might disrupt the entire ecological system on which man's own life and welfare depends."[3]

In short, urbanized humanity has been overwhelmed by its excessive use of power. Like prehistoric civlizations, "we still regard power as the chief manifestation of divinity, or, if not that, the main agent of human development. [But absolute] power destroys the symbiotic cooperation of man with all other aspects of nature, and of men with other men."[4]

Mumford's thesis is that of the concerned humanist; it is, in sum, entirely his own. But, though unique, it rests on a foundation provided in 1921 in an article entitled "The Nature of the City," by Max Weber, the great German sociologist, who was the first social scientist in Europe to formulate a comprehensive definition for the city as a type of human community—a definition with as much influence as Redfield's later, similar attempt for the village or town.[5]

Whether Mumford's view is accepted or not, there can be no question that the American city plays a part in an urban drama of enormous consequence for all human life. And though entering the stage rather

2. *Ibid.*, p. 569.
3. *Ibid.*, pp. 573, 570.
4. *Ibid.*, p. 571.
5. Max Weber, *The City*, edited by Don Martindale and Gertrud Neuwirth (Glencoe, Ill.: Free Press, 1958), pp. 50–56.

late, places like Boston, New York, Philadelphia, and Baltimore played the vital role of cities elsewhere from the eighteenth century onward. Cities have been of great importance in American life from the early stages of white European settlement in the North American continent, even in the period of the preindustrial village society. Indeed, a considerable weakness in Peter Laslett's thesis in *The World We Have Lost* is the lack of attention given to the influence of seventeenth- and eighteenth-century London, even if it were the only urban center and contained only a small proportion of the country's population.

In 1963, Oscar Handlin, in an introductory essay to *The Historian and the City*,[6] tried to isolate the essential features of the *modern* city, of which most American cities are examples. To Handlin, the modern city is not simply a slow, evolutionary product,

> but a drastic break from the past. The continuity of history was ruptured by the emergence of something singularly new. . . . Handlin sees the catalyst of this remarkable phenomenon as the rise of the centralized nation-state, technological innovations, the novel developments in production and capital constituting the rise of modern industry, and the subsequent explosion of the urban population. . . . The American city, then, was born and grew into adolescence during the transitional stage between the preindustrial and modern industrial city.[7]

But what is a city? Like Redfield, Mumford avoids a precise definition: "No definition will apply to all its manifestations and no single description will cover all its transformations."[8] The U.S. Census Bureau is no help at all. For some time, it has defined as "urban" any place with 2,500 or more inhabitants. Such a definition makes "cities" out of many of Atherton's Midwestern "country towns." The city can, of course, be given a narrow legal and political definition—a corporate entity—just as the town can. But if one is to consider cities through history and around the world—"from the earliest urban islands that rose above the seas of agricultural villages, through city states, through preindustrial and postindustrial cities, to the megopolis of today"—then, as one

6. Oscar Handlin and John Burchard, editors, *The Historian and the City* (Cambridge, Mass.: M.I.T. Press, 1963).

7. Alexander B. Callow, editor, *American Urban History: An Interpretive Reader with Commentaries* (New York: Oxford University Press, 1969), p. 4.

8. Mumford, p. 3.

sociologist puts it, "it is well to keep a certain looseness in our conceptions of the city, for the city is many things—political, economic, and social, historical and geographic, physical, and even psychological."[9]

The astounding fact about professional historical writing on the American city is that it, like that on towns, is of recent origin, even though the historical profession matured as the nation became industrialized. So beholden have most professional historians been to the nationalistic approach to their academic field that, as recently as 1965, Charles Glaab could still ask that general surveys of American urban history be written without "a tendency to treat individual cities as locals in which events of national history can be examined. . . .The stages of an individual city's history do not really reflect the received divisions of national history. Periods in community history derive from critical turning points within the community itself."[10]

The great attraction of Turner's frontier thesis and Beard's economic thesis up to the time of World War II diverted attention from the obvious fact of urban growth. Historians focussed on conflict—between groups or sections—to the extent that, when they referred to urban phenomenon at all, "[cities] were treated almost exclusively as political and social 'problems.' A genuine disgust with 'urban' conditions combined with an ingrained rural romanticism . . . to spread the conviction that cities were costly deviants from some natural, more verdant, order of community life."[11] This contrasts rather sharply with the historical emphasis long evident in European scholarship on urban life. The contrast is, in a way, understandable: "While European students had materials from cities that had being going concerns for a thousand years, American cities were often not more than a few decades old."[12] In any case, not until the 1930s did historical scholars begin to pay attention to the city, something that was largely an outgrowth of interest in "an essentially descriptive social history concerned with the 'life of the people'."[13] The first scholarly investigations of urban life in the United States had been carried on by urban

9. Leo F. Schnore, "The City as a Social Organism," as quoted in Callow, p. 53.

10. Charles N. Glaab, "The Historian and the American City: A Bibliographic Survey," as quoted in Callow, pp. 662, 661.

11. Eric E. Lampard, "American Historians and the Study of Urbanization," as quoted in Callow, p. 633.

12. Weber, The City, p. 42.

13. Charles N. Glaab, "The Historian and the American City: A Bibliographic Survey," as quoted in Callow, p. 655.

sociologists, particularly at the University of Chicago in the 1920s[14] by Robert Park and his associates.

Park and his group developed the "concentric zone" theory of urban development, an essentially ecological theory of the city, seriously defective in its orientation toward the geo-physical rather than the social aspects of city life, by its primitive and excessively schematic concepts, and by its lack of attention to such sociological emphases as groups, institutions, and social structure. By 1930, Louis Wirth, an offshoot of the Chicago school, in an influential essay entitled "Urbanism as a Way of Life," sketched a more comprehensive and balanced definition for the urban community. He regarded it "as a physical structure with a population base, technology, and ecological order; as a system of social organization with a structure and series of institutions; as a set of attitudes, ideas, and constellation of personalities."[15]

Not until 1940 did a historian attempt to generalize about the role of the city in American history: Arthur Schlesinger, Sr., in the "History of American Life" Series of the 1930s, wrote *The Rise of the City*,[16] which forcibly brought urban growth, at least for the period from 1878 to 1898, into the mainstream of American history. In a paper before the American Historical Association Convention of 1940—in a manner begging comparison with Turner's action in 1893—Schlesinger announced that "[the] city marched westward with the outposts of settlement, always injecting exotic elements into pioneer existence, while in the older sections it steadily extended its domination over politics, economics and all the other interests of life. . . . A true understanding of America's past demands this balanced view—an appreciation of the significance of both frontier and city."[17]

Schlesinger's plea for an urban as well as a rural focus in American historical writing was immediately appreciated by other historians, but at least one expressed concern over the enormous ambiguity in the meaning and use of such terms as *city, urban,* and *urbanization*—an ambiguity that, not surprisingly, marred Schlesinger's own pioneering work.[18] By the 1960s, several historians had sufficient understanding

14. William Diamond, "The Dangers of an Urban Interpretation of History," in Callow, pp. 613–615.

15. Weber, pp. 22–24, 29–30, 38–40.

16. Arthur Schlesinger, Sr., *The Rise of the City*, (New York: Macmillan, 1933).

17. Arthur Schlesinger, Sr., "The City in American Civilization," as quoted in Callow, pp. 25–26.

18. William Diamond, "On the Dangers of an Urban Interpretation of History," in Callow, pp. 609–631.

of what urban social scientists (sociologists, geographers, and economists)—especially Louis Wirth—were doing to urge those who wished to study the history of American cities to give some much-needed structure and cohesion to their field. The pioneers had neglected the process of urbanization, had failed to define "urban" as a type of community, and had largely ignored all but the problems of city life.

In 1961, Eric Lampard argued:

> If the urban historian is to be more than a historian who happens to do his research and writing on the subject of cities, it will be necessary to show that the term *urban* explains something in history that cannot be better explained by recourse to other frames of reference. In short, *urban* must signify not subject matter alone but a scheme of conceptualization, in much the same way as *economic* or *culture* history. . . . [Urban] history is no longer regarded as a mere chronicle of local color and description, but as a potentially important perspective on many aspects of regional and national development. The study of particular communities and of general "urban problems" may illuminate subjects previously neglected or treated only within the "overaggregated" framework of the nation as a whole. . . . [But] we do not know enough about urbanization or "urban" characteristics in general to determine what is unique or otherwise in the experience of particular communities. The variant "facts of history" cannot be defined nor their significance appraised until they are treated in relation to larger conceptual frameworks, yet the conventional type of local history, though monumental in detail, seldom furnishes data in forms that are readily adaptable to macroscopic treatment. We lack, therefore, not only generalized frameworks of analysis but consistent and comparable data relevant to them.[19]

Not that the social scientists had all the answers. Lampard rightly accused sociologists of giving *city* and *urban* "circular or tautologous meanings." To Lampard, urbanization can most clearly be defined as a process "of population concentration . . . resulting in the formation of cities"[20]—that's all.

19. Eric E. Lampard, "American Historians and the Study of Urbanization," as quoted in Callow, pp. 639, 634–635.
  20. *Ibid.*, pp. 636, 635.

In 1967, Roy Lubove, again surveying the field, preferred "the process of city-building over time" as a definition for urban history.[21] More precisely, both agree that "human ecology," that is "community structure as the outcome of a changing balance between population and environment (including habitat and other populations) mediated by technology and organization," is of central importance,[22] though they disagree somewhat as to the exact range of urban life such inquiry should cover. Together, Lampard and Lubove bring to urban study the dual focus—social and geographic or physical—that the best writers on community have called for, a focus that the writers on towns, except for Atherton, have largely ignored. Urban historians thus have at least a conceptual framework generally lacking so far in recent scholarly town history.

And yet, when Charles Glaab offered "The Historian and the American City: A Bibliographic Survey," in 1965, he had to admit that urban historians had for the most part ignored Lampard's plea for a social scientific analysis of urbanization as a process.[23] Instead, Glaab commented on a growing literature of various kinds: "urban biography," or histories of individual cities; "period studies," or investigations of groups of cities at particular times, and studies he calls "special themes in urban history." Predicting that urban history, with or without a sociological orientation, would become important in an urban nation, he pointed to the planned establishment of programs in urban history at various universities, as well as to the preparation of textbooks on the subject.[24] Textbooks have indeed begun to appear, not the least of which is Glaab's own.[25] But the fact remains that until 1972 the only analytical or interpretive general study of American cities that might be classified in any sense with Smith's study of towns was Constance M. Green's *American Cities in the Growth of the Nation*,[26] a series of essays or

21. Roy Lubove, "The Urbanization Process: An Approach to Historical Research," as quoted in Callow, p. 643.

22. Eric Lampard, "American Historians and the Study of Urbanization," as quoted in Callow, p. 638.

23. Charles N. Glaab, "The Historian and the American City: A Bibliographic Survey," in Callow, p. 659.

24. *Ibid.*, pp. 669–670.

25. Charles N. Glaab and A. Theodore Brown, *A History of Urban America* (New York: The Macmillan Co., 1967).

26. Constance M. Greene, *American Cities in the Growth of the Nation* (Tackahoe, N.Y.: John De Graff, Inc., 1957).

lectures dealing with "aspects of the United States national history through case studies of sixteen individual cities in various periods."[27]

* * * * *

As for *period studies*, Carl Bridenbaugh is the pioneering synthesizer who, in his study of colonial American Atlantic seacoast cities—among the chief population centers of the British Empire by the eighteenth century—presented the thesis that "the first hundred years of town history on the American continent witnessed the foundation and gradual development of a truly urban society,"[28] alongside the rural and frontier ones. These nascent cities, located on sites geographically favorable for commerce, became trading centers, for people and ideas as well as goods, between their rural hinterlands and Great Britain. Richard Wade, in his study of "Urban Life in Western America, 1790–1830" asserted that "the towns were the spearheads of the American frontier. Planted as forts or trading posts far in advance of the line of settlement, they held the West for the approaching population [and] . . . many settlers moved across the mountains in search of promising towns rather than good land, their inducements being urban opportunities rather than fertile soil."[29] For the 1830–1860 period, Boorstin focussed on the "booster" towns in the Midwest and Rocky Mountain area,[30] towns that attracted our first businessmen, who, by "boosting" their towns in all-out competition with others, blurred what was private and what was public in community-building, making competition itself the most distinctive characteristic of the American city, at least in mid-America in the mid-nineteenth century. But even with the work of Wade and Boorstin, there are no general period studies for the whole of the nation between the Revolution and the Civil War. Blake McKelvey has written two general studies of cities from 1865 to 1966, but they are flat, descriptive, and textbookish, without sustained analysis of the essential *character* of American cities since the Civil War. McKelvey's failure is an important one, in that we do not know what we should know about cities during the very period that Smith and Atherton indicate as the time when the town went into decline because of the increasing influence of urban centers. Therefore period studies, in principle

27. Charles N. Glaab, "The Historian and the American City: A Bibliographic Survey," as quoted in Callow, p. 663.
28. Carl Bridenbaugh, *Cities in the Wilderness*, p. 467.
29. *American Historical Review*, LXIV (October 1958), 14–30.
30. Boorstin concentrates on Chicago, Cincinnati, and Denver.

of vital importance to our understanding of the city in American history, are still fragmentary in coverage and not always sufficiently analytical in nature.

As for *studies on urbanization*, it is something of an embarrassment that the only general work remains Adna F. Weber's *The Growth of the City in the Nineteenth Century: A Study in Statistics*.[31] An early attempt at quantification, this still influential study—"the first really sound comprehensive and complete contribution to urban studies by an American"[32]—confronts head-on the question of growth. According to Robert Dykstra, "most American small towns would be cities if they could."[33] Some of Smith's "cumulative" towns became cities, as did occasional covenanted towns such as Boston and Salt Lake City. As Kenneth Jackson and Stanley Schultz summarize: "The nation seemed to be alive with city boosters, each of whom could point to sharp increases in population and deliver excited speeches about the limitless possibilities of his particular town."[34] A word of caution, however: The "boosterism" made popular in Boorstin's writing should not, without further study, be applied indiscriminately to all periods of American history. Competition was in evidence in the growing urban centers of the seventeenth and eighteenth centuries that Bridenbaugh studied. But were there earlier, colonial forms of boosterism as well? Or was it a phenomenon that, for some reason that we do not yet understand, first flourished as Boorstin found it, in the 1830s in the Midwest?

In any event, the question here is, why did so many towns *fail* to become cities even with the best will at their command? What was different and distinctive about the few towns that kept right on growing into the urban centers of particular areas? With few exceptions, neither town nor city historians provide an adequate answer to this question, because neither group is sufficiently concerned about the other's community. Their respective frames of reference are such that they view largely in isolation what should be seen as closely related.

Not so, Adna Weber. With simplicity and clarity, Weber writes:

> The factor of chief importance in the location of cities is a *break in transportation*. A mere transfer of goods will require consid-

31. (New York: The Macmillan Co., 1899; reprint edition, Ithaca, N.Y.: Cornell University Press, 1963).

32. Adna Weber, p. ix.

33. Dykstra, *The Cattle Towns*, p. 3.

34. Kenneth T. Jackson and Stanley K. Schultz, editors, *Cities in American History* (New York: Alfred A. Knopf, 1972), p. 1.

erable machinery; and so we find commercial centres at the confluence of rivers, head of navigation, fords, meeting-point of hill and plain, and other places where the physical configuration requires a change of vehicle. But the greatest centres will be those where the physical transfer of goods is accompanied with a change in ownership; there is then added to the mechanical apparatus of temporary storage and transfer, the complex mechanism of commercial exchange. Importers and exporters, merchants and money-changers accumulate vast wealth and require the presence of other classes to satisfy their wants, and the population will grow rapidly. It is therefore easy to understand why so many of the large cities of the world are commercial centres, if not actual seaports. Every *great* city owes its emminence to commerce.[35]

Jackson and Schultz accept Weber's explanation: "Most large American cities received their initial impetus from commerce and were therefore placed at a natural 'transportation break'." But they quickly add that "a geographic site favorable to trade rarely sufficed to guarantee success." Another factor must be taken into account: "The difference between prosperity and stagnation for a city frequently lay in the quality of its leaders and the degree to which they were willing to risk their resources in the struggle for economic empire." In other words, "[Whether] a given city grew and prospered or stagnated and perhaps died depended on its locational advantages *and* the aggressiveness and foresight of its civic and business leaders."[36]

This is a generalization coming out of other work, but contains real insight into the nature of urban growth, nonetheless. What Jackson and Schultz are saying is that cities have grown, not only as a result of "accidents"—that is, the presence of favorable configurations of the landscape—but also because of the existence of energetic community leaders competing lustily with others for the domination of adjacent territory or urban hinterlands. In other words, people have not been passive agents in the urbanization process, herded together, as if by nature itself, around a bay, lake, river falls, or mountain pass; they have played an active role in determining whether a community turned into a Chicago or a Cairo, Illinois—into a city of mushrooming growth or a town of broken dreams, frustrated ambitions, and natural disorders.

35. Adna Weber, pp. 172–173.
36. Jackson and Schultz, pp. 3, 4, 2.

The most successful recent study to bridge the gap between town and city history—at least for the nineteenth century—is Michael Frisch's *Town into City: Springfield, Massachusetts, and the Meaning of Community, 1840–1880,*[37] a study of how and why one town turned into a city. Frisch is far more interested in the changing concept of community that emerged in the minds of Springfield's residents than he is in why this village blossomed, rather suddenly, into the leading city of its area. It was not commerce or transportation that made Springfield—and perhaps many other small nineteenth century cities—grow, but the presence of what Douglas North would call a special "carrier" industry that generated growth in related industries. In Springfield's case, the "carrier" industry was a large federal armory.[38] Frisch argues that, as Springfield grew, the population's response was based upon its changing perception of what their community was. Between 1840 and 1880, "[community] . . . was changing from an informal, direct sensation to a formal, perceived abstraction."[39] Before the Civil War, Springfielders

> tended to think, act, and view their community in direct, personal, informal, and nonabstract terms. . . . The public interest could appear to be the sum of the community's many private concerns because there was not the degree of highly formalized, segmented, and fragmented contacts between individuals that characterizes modern life, and similarly the life of the community, and individuals within it, did not resolve down into various public and private roles."[40]

As it grew into a city, under the stimulus of a Civil War boom, Springfield's inhabitants reversed their concept:

> By 1880, with relationships becoming more formal and people seeing themselves more fundamentally in terms of interest groups, the community was in the process of disintegrating as a real feeling of association. But, at the same time, the growing public functions of government and the accumulating results of

37. (Cambridge, Mass.: Harvard University Press, 1972.)
38. Douglas North, *The Economic Growth of the United States, 1790–1860*, paperback edition (New York: W. W. Norton & Co., 1966); Frisch, pp. 72–79.
39. *Ibid.*, p. 24.
40. *Ibid.*, p. 48.

rapid social and physical change were giving to the community a new meaning: it was becoming more important and comprehensive as a symbolic expression of interdependence. Community, in other words, was changing from an informal, direct sensation to a formal, perceived abstraction.[41]

Frisch probes the shift in community activity from a "private" to a "public" character and, though such a focus restricts his study unnecessarily to politics and government, he is able to show the relationship between such change and the way people viewed their community, as well as their own relationship to it. Paradoxically, as the wholeness of the town—people sharing a tactile, felt sense of association in a small, cohesive setting—gave way to the divisions of the city, with institutions and functions becoming structured and formalized, the Springfielder's fractured personality found a new sense of unity when related to the abstraction that was the city of Springfield. In other words, the city, at the same time it destroyed the personal associations of town life, replaced them with a developing sense of loyalty to an impersonal abstraction. Citizens still related to their community of Springfield, but in a vastly different way.[42]

Frisch also shows that at least one nineteenth-century town evolved into a city without important clashes among classes, interests, or ethnic elements. Springfield made the shift with an absence of deep divisions between businessmen and labor groups, or between immigrants and natives. Political parties thrived, but did not represent economic or social groupings nearly so much as traditionalists and innovators—those who wanted a government to act in the old way versus those who wanted the public sector reshaped to fit the changing nature of the community.[43]

Frisch is also concerned with the actual physical shape of Springfield and how the city's spatial layout reflected its people's perception of their community.[44] As Springfield grew to be the largest city of its area, such facilities as churches, libraries, courthouses, transportation terminals, and commercial buildings were built on a large scale in a central area, where they could symbolize, not just a neighborhood, but a whole community grown too large to be grasped visually all at once by

41. *Ibid.*, p. 247.
42. *Ibid.*, pp. 93–94, 107, 173–174, 212, 213.
43. *Ibid.*, pp. 241–250.
44. *Ibid.*, pp. 133–156.

its inhabitants. This new image of the city was abstract, but it allowed people to retain a sense of "their collective physical growth in terms comprehensive enough to permit such an environmental view to stand as living abstraction."[45]

The actual process by which the eighteenth- and early nineteenth-century commercial city was transformed into the modern metropolis is probed with great effect by Sam Bass Warner in *Streetcar Suburbs: The Process of Growth in Bostin, 1870–1900*. Emphasizing "individualistic capitalism" as basic to city life, Warner analyzes the way in which electrified streetcars, the revival of a rural ideal for community life, and the extension of municipal sanitation services and privately-owned utilities—gas, electricity, and telephones—combined to allow a growing middle class in an increasingly industrialized and commercialized urban area to leave the poor and the immigrants in the central city and to create, through thousands of individual decisions that took the form of a pattern, something new in human habitation: suburbs, settlements that were not self-contained communities in the traditional sense, but places based on income, not ethnicity, where middle-class people who worked in the central city lived. The result was a vast, new community whose social and economic and cultural boundaries extended far beyond the political territory of the old central city. Annexation of outlying areas stopped as middle-class suburbanites revived the rural ideal of a small community in the only way they knew how: politically. Just as the "outlivers" of New England townships in the colonial period wanted their own political identity, so, increasingly, did those who flooded into what were once largely rural towns outside Boston during the late nineteenth century. There was a crucial difference between the two kinds of migrants, however. The suburbanites were tied to the life of a central city; outlivers went on to create communities as cohesive and whole as those on the original village sites.

Warner finds that there were positive consequences of metropolitan urban growth:

45. *Ibid.*, p. 155. Or, as Sam B. Warner puts it: "The continual confrontation of large objects prevents the visual comprehension of the city and forces the ordinary citizen to think of his environment in terms of his street and his friends, or to think of the city in the terms of the newspaper abstraction, the political unit. This explains why city dwellers cherish a river view, a hilltop, or skyscraper panorama which allows the occasional opportunity to grasp at one time the totality of the city" (*Streetcar Suburbs: The Process of Growth in Boston, 1870–1900* [Cambridge, Mass.: Harvard University Press, 1962], p. vii. Frisch applies the view developed by Kevin Lynch, *The Image of the City* (Cambridge, Mass.: M.I.T. Press, 1960).

[Almost] all new suburban building from 1870 to 1900 included safe construction, indoor plumbing, and orderly land
arrangement. From the prosperity of the middle class and its
enthusiastic acceptance of the new sanitation and transportation technology came the popular achievement of the late-
nineteenth-century suburbs: a safe environment for half the
metropolitan population. . . . The apparent openness of the
new residential quarters, their ethnic variety, their extensive
growth, and their wide range of prices from fairly inexpensive
rental suites to expensive single-family houses—these visible
characteristics of the new suburbs gave aspiring low-income
families the certainty that should they earn enough money they
too could possess the comforts and symbols of success. Even for
those excluded from them, the suburbs offered a physical de-
monstration that the rewards of competitive capitalism might
be within the reach of all.[46]

Warner stresses even more the negative consequences, however:

Compared to transient conditions in older parts of the city, the
suburbs were more conducive to integration of the individual
into some sort of community activity. Their physical arrangement, however—the endless street grids and the dependence
upon the downtown for work and shopping—failed to provide
local centers where all the residents of a given area might,
through frequent contact, come to know each other and
thereby be encouraged to share in community wide
activites. . . . Aside from class segregation, there was nothing in
the process of late-nineteenth-century suburban construction
that built communities or neighborhoods: it built streets. The
grid plan of the suburbs did not concern itself with public life.
It was an economically efficient geometry which divided large
parcels of land as they came on the market. The arrangement
of the blocks of the grid depended largely upon what farm or
estate came on the market at what time. The result was, not integrated communities arranged around common centers, but a
historical and accidental traffic pattern.[47]

46. Warner, *Streetcar Suburbs*, pp. 155, 157.
47. *Ibid.*, p. 158.

The grid or geometrical pattern of settlement in late-nineteenth-century suburbs was, in fact, simply a continuation of the gridiron scheme associated with colonial Philadelphia and widely copied elsewhere as settlement spread westward in the eighteenth and nineteenth centuries.[48] Indeed, Congress encased this method of land division in federal legislation that imposed a sub-division something like a waffle-iron in rectilinear patterns over the public lands in vast areas of the continental United States.[49] Whether at the level of town or city, territory or state, such a policy ignored not only the social aspects of community life, but also the geographic or physical aspects, and thus, to some extent, economic aspects as well. Both suburban or municipal developers and congressmen "devised a cheap way of preparing land for market,"[50] as Boorstin puts it, and in doing so, did not take into account the natural geographic contours that provide the kind of social and economic cohesiveness upon which a viable community is based.

The impact on suburban community life was, in Warner's view, quite clear: "As a result of the centerless character of most suburbs, community life fell into fragments. Groups formed about particular churches, clubs, schools, and ward club rooms; rarely did any large fraction of the population of a suburban area participate in any joint endeavor."[51]

Other negative consequences of suburban growth were linked directly to the physical layout of the metropolis:

> Each decade brought an increase in the scale and complexity of
> economic and social life; each decade's problems demanded
> more wide-scale attention, more complex solutions. Because of
> the physical arrangement of the new metropolis, each decade
> also brought an ever greater fragmentation of community life
> into town and ward politics, church groups, clubs, and
> specialized societies of all kinds. The growing parochialism and
> fragmentation resulted in a steady relative weakening of social
> agencies. Weaknesses, in turn, convinced more and more indi-
> viduals that local community action was hopeless or irrelevant.
> The self-defeating cycle, begun by the streetcar metropolis, has
> continued with increasing severity to this day. . . . The essence

48. Reps, *Town Planning in Frontier America*, p. 221.
49. Boorstin, *The Americans: The National Experience*, pp. 244–247.
50. *Ibid.*, p. 247.
51. Warner, *Streetcar Suburbs*, p. 159.

of the new metropolitan plan was the separation of the vast areas of new construction from the old central city. . . . For the middle class the inner area of low-income housing became an unknown and uncontrolled land. . . . In part the rural ideal bore responsibility for the arrangement of the metropolis, for it had encouraged middle-class families to seek escape from the conditions of modern industrial life into an isolated family environment. More important, the dominant ideal of individualistic capitalism with its accompanying unwillingness to bring private profit to account had caused the economic division of the society. The slums and suburbs were the physical expression of this division. The conditions of the central city which so dismayed the middle class were the product of its failure to control the distribution of income, its failure to regulate housing and working conditions, its failure to develop an adequate welfare program for the sick and unfortunate, and its failure to devise a community program for integrating the thousands of new citizens who every year moved to the metropolis. These things, neglected, bore a harvest of middle-class fear. From fear came the late-nineteenth-century paradox of the growth of an economically integrated regional city . . . accompanied by an increase in the parochialism of its political and social units.[52]

The work of Frisch and Warner on the process of urban growth is imaginative and suggestive, but contains generalizations badly in need of further testing, something that can occur only with the study of other medium-sized cities and metropolises in other areas of the country. Also, studies on urbanization in the seventeenth and eighteenth centuries are needed to supplement those of Weber, Frisch, and Warner for the nineteenth. We do not know what the *general* determinants of urban growth in the preindustrial, or commercial, cities of colonial America were, even with Bridenbaugh's examination of the internal life of the leading coastal centers.

As for *special themes* studies, such subjects as immigration, the slums, municipal services, and politics have long received the attention of urban historians.[53] Probably the most influential study of recent years has been Stephan Thernstrom's *Poverty and Progress: Social Mobility in a*

---

52. *Ibid.*, p. 162–165.
53. Charles N. Glaab, "The Historian and the American City: A Bibliographic Survey," as quoted in Callow, pp. 667–669.

Nineteenth Century City,[54] in which the author shows that the stationary poor in at least one small nineteenth-century city slowly gained wealth and property, but not to the extent that the popular "rags to riches" ideal suggested. Thernstrom has not only focussed recent research on statistical evidence—the original manuscript schedules of the U.S. censuses from 1840–1880, as well as various kinds of town, city, and state records—involving masses of people in cities, but has also staked out topics new scholars are now assiduously pursuing: mobility, poverty, class, social elites, political power, residential patterns.[55] As of this writing, Oxford, Harvard, Yale, and perhaps other major scholarly publishers have series on urban history, something that will provide impetus for further specialized historical studies.

Tentative conclusions about geographic mobility are already emerging from this work. It seems likely that population movements in and out of the larger cities, as Peter Knights shows in his *Plain People of Boston: A Study in City Growth*,[56] were so pervasive that scholars should focus more than they have recently on the institutions that gave what cohesion there was to urban life. In the 1950s, Richard Wade argued, in his *Urban Frontier*, that, along with the shifting composition of city populations, common social and cultural institutions emerged to provide the cement of community of the kind that certain families gave to small towns simply by virtue of their longevity of residence. Therefore, though it is probably revealing and important to concentrate on the composition of small town inhabitants, a similar emphasis for urban groups may obfuscate much of what gave definition to community life in such places.

A difficulty with the lines of inquiry suggested by Thernstrom's study is that the distinctively *urban* character of these subjects is elusive and, at least in the essays included in *Nineteenth-Century Cities*, not adequately defined. To what extent does the city, as a type of community, give a particular shape to class, poverty, mobility, power, and the like?

A further problem with this kind of inquiry is not that it uses the city as a basis for the elaboration of national themes, as Glaab thought in the

54. (Cambridge, Mass.: Harvard University Press, 1964).

55. Stephan Thernstrom and Richard Sennett, editors, *Nineteenth-Century Cities: Essays in the New Urban History* (New Haven, Conn.: Yale University Press, 1969). Thernstrom has continued his study of the themes of mobility and migration in the setting of the modern metropolis in *The Other Bostonians: Poverty and Progress in the American Metropolis, 1880–1970* (Cambrdige, Mass.: Harvard University Press, 1973).

56. (New York: Oxford University Press, 1971).

mid-1960s, but that it does not present the city, as Redfield would put it, "whole." It still reduces the study of urban communities to fragmentary topics or "problems" and, in so doing, runs the risk of losing the over-all character of a human whole. The argument that the city is too complicated for a single scholar to treat is a strong one. It would be a lot stronger than it is if there were no significant studies of a wholistic kind to point to.

Urban biography or the history of individual cities is the oldest form of historical writing. Oscar Handlin thinks it is also the best form: "We need fewer studies of the city in history than of the history of cities. . . . [*How* general] developments unfolded, what was the causal nexus among them, we shall only learn when we make out the interplay among them by focusing upon *a* city specially in all its uniqueness."[57] But Charles Glaab, as recently as 1965, felt the need to emphasize

> the fact that urban history, at least in its ordinary forms, is as much related to the long-standing tradition of local history written by amateurs with an interest in their own communities as it is to the tradition of scholarly academic history. . . . It is impossible to establish any satisfactory criteria that would distinguish the "scholarly" urban biography from the best works produced by the amateur local historian. The urban biographer does not always escape altogether tones of "sentimentality, antiquarianism, and chamber of commerce advertising." It seldom does much to illuminate the general process of urbanization. There is little concern with what the city is and little indication that the problem has been more than casually considered.[58]

Eric Lampard adds: "As it is, the multiplication of case studies may only add to confusion, unless their findings can be related to larger and more comprehensive frames of reference."[59]

And, indeed, this is a real problem. But good histories of individual cities have been compiled and will continue to be written with as much understanding of the general process of urbanization as the alert scho-

57. Oscar Handlin, "The Modern City as a Field of Historical Study," as quoted in Callow, p. 23.
58. Charles N. Glaab, "The Historian and the City: A Bibliographic Approach," as quoted in Callow, p. 660.
59. Eric Lampard, "American Historians and the Study of Urbanization," as quoted in Callow, p. 635.

lar can muster. The corpus of urban historical writing will evolve and grow as it has already, as a result of an interaction between the particular and the general, between studies of individual urban communities and studies on urbanization generally.

Sam Bass Warner's *The Private City: Philadelphia in Three Periods of Its Growth* is probably the most successful attempt yet made to relate the study of a single city to a firmly held view of the nature of American cities generally. Elaborating on the thesis that underlay his earlier studies of Boston, Warner asserts that a pervasive "privatism," born of our emphasis on "individualistic" capitalism, is the most distinctive long-term feature of the American city. As he explains:

> The tradition of privatism is . . . the most important element of our culture for understanding the development of cities. . . . Its essence lay in its concentration upon the individual and the individual's search for wealth. Psychologically, privatism meant that the individual should seek happiness in personal independence and in the search for wealth; socially, privatism meant that the individual should see his first loyalty as his immediate family, and that a community should be a union of such money-making, accumulating families; politically, privatism meant that the community should keep the peace among individual money-makers, and, if possible, help to create an open and thriving setting where each citizen would have some substantial opportunity to prosper. . . . The tradition of privatism has always meant that the cities of the United States depended for their wages, employment, and general prosperity upon the aggregate successes and failures of thousands of individual interprises, not upon community action. It has also meant that the physical forms of American cities, their lots, houses, factories, and streets have been the outcome of a real estate market of profit-seeking builders, land speculators, and large investors. Finally, the tradition of privatism has meant that the local politics of American cities have depended for their actors, and for a good deal of their subject matter, on the changing focus of men's private economic activities.[60]

There have been many Philadelphias through the years since its founding, in both a physical and a demographic sense, but the

60. Warner, *The Private City: Philadelphia in Three Periods of Its Growth* (Philadelphia: University of Pennsylvania Press, 1968), pp. 3–4.

privatism just described remained and gave rise to a remarkably stable tradition. Justifying his concentration on one city with the statement that "It is my belief that Philadelphia's history has been repeated, with minor variations, again and again across the nation," Warner probes three periods of Philadelphia's past: the town of 1770–1780, the bit city of 1830–1860, and the industrial metropolis of 1920–1930. Most attention is given to the middle period,

> because this was the era when the big city and the American tradition of privatism first confronted each other. In these years the basic American municipal relationships between public and private functions were set, and the communitarian limits of a city of private money-makers were reached, and passed. This was the turning point in American urban history when tradition failed to adapt itself to modern urban and industrial life.[61]

Warner's study is thus rather episodic and certainly fragmentary in what it deals with. In all three periods, however, he finds plenty of evidence for the priority of privatism. Whether it took place in a colonial town where classes, residences, and work areas were all together; whether in a growing city enduring rapid, disruptive industrialization and, sometimes riotously, large numbers of immigrants; or whether in a relatively peaceful modern metropolis with home and work clearly separated—it did not matter. For example, Philadelphia's pre-Civil War efforts to create an effective waterworks and a public school system parallel the inability of the metropolis's early twentieth-century government to deal with maldistribution of income or inadequacy of building procedures, and illustrate the ineffectuality of a political system turned outward toward state and national politics. In short, through its history as a city, Philadelphia's governmental and public institutions did not deal with the urban community as a whole, did not treat it "as a public environment of a democratic society," so that "[in] 1930 Philadelphia, like all large American cities, stood as a monument to the tradition of the private city."[62]

Warner's studies—of both Boston and Philadelphia—lack balance. They ignore the respectable body of literature stressing the blurred lines between what was private and what was public in American cities

61. *Ibid.*, p. xi.
62. *Ibid.*, p. 223.

since the colonial period. They give "privatism" so much primacy that there is little sense of the *shifting* relationship between private and public through the several periods of American history. They stress the *physical* manifestations of urban growth more than other aspects. And they view city dwellers as atomistic money-earners, reduce people to their economic component, and ignore the crucial cultural aspect of city life that writers such as Lewis Mumford make so much of. Even with these shortcomings, however, no one has written more cogently than Warner about the processes by which the American city grew.

* * * * *

With efforts such as Warner's, urban historical writing has moved a long way from the "urban biography" of the amateur city historian. Since Schlesinger's paper of 1940, there has been a steady, though uneven, shift away from history focussed on the famous men and incidents of a city's past, on descriptions, based largely on various literary remains, of the development of associations and institutions—in short, the urban counterpart of the kind of town history that Sheldon and others offered. The shift has been toward a type of study thoroughly imbued with social science techniques, arising out of evidence—city records, census schedules—statistical in nature, resulting in a quantifiable analysis of the behavior of masses of urbanites. This shift constitutes a kind of revolution in the way people study the history of our cities.

Unfortunately, a piling up of period studies, inquiries into the nature of urbanization, monographs on special themes in city history, and urban biographies that treat one city as a microcosm of all has not yet led to the kind of synthesis that Page Smith attempted for the town in the mid-1960s. The literature on the American city is still rather diffuse and fragmentary.

Warner's *The Urban Wilderness: A History of the American City* only partially fills the need for a general account with the sweep and proportions of Smith's study on towns. Limited, by his own admission, to the "structural" approach to urban history, Warner continues in this latest effort to focus his inquiry on the physical growth of urban communities—much as town historians such as Sheldon exhibited great concern over who lived where and in what along village streets. But Warner also emphasizes more than before the economic sources of urban growth and the ways in which such development shaped certain institutions and groups, though his investigation is confined, without adequate explanation, to the post-1820 portion of our history.

Warner frankly offers *The Urban Wilderness* as something of use to all who would seek to alter the course of urban life, such efforts having heretofore lacked historical awareness:

> I have made the discovery that Americans have no urban history. They live in one of the world's most urbanized countries as if it were a wilderness in both time and space. Beyond some civic and ethnic myths and a few family and neighborhood memories, Americans are not conscious that they have a past and that by their actions they participate in making their future. As they tackle today's problems, whether with good will or anger, they have no sense of where cities come from, how they grew, or even what direction the large forces of history are taking them. . . . Without a sense of history, they hammer against today's crises without any means to choose their targets to fit the trends which they must confront, work with, or avoid.[63]

This sort of thing is Warner's forte: Perhaps no one writing on American history today can move back and forth between contemporary problems and their historical sources with such effectiveness.

Building on themes first presented in his earlier books on Boston and Philadelphia, Warner asserts that competitive, individualistic capitalism led to a kind of privatism in burgeoning urban centers that grew in response to the materialistic side of the American people. Such centers resulted in the emergence of communities in which the middle and upper classes attain at least material success, while the lower classes suffer deprivations of many kinds:

> Class and racial segregation and class, racial, and sexual discrimination lie at the root of almost all the pathologies of the current city. As manifestations of our nation's deepest feelings, of our long racist, capitalist, and sexist traditions, such behavior is both the most grievous, and the most difficult of all the burdens which the past has fastened upon the present. The essence of our urban history has been rapid growth and pervasive change working within the confines of ceaseless exploita-

63. Warner, *The Urban Wilderness: A History of the American City* (New York: Harper & Row, Publishers, 1972), p. 4.

tion of white over black, rich over poor, and men over women.[64]

If open competition, community, and innovation be regarded as three traditional goals of urban dwellers (though Warner offers no evidence that these three "goals" have in fact stood out throughout our history), then American urbanites

> have favored innovation and competition at the expense of community. New products and methods of production, new transportation, new ways of doing business have been introduced without regard for the dislocation and suffering they create. Skills have been wiped out, whole industries rendered obsolete, millions driven off the land or harried from one city to another. Competition for jobs, wealth, and power has been severe and even lethal, never completely open and fair. Blacks, women, immigrants, children, and old people have always been at a disadvantage. The inherent nature of our capitalistic system has bestowed differential and cumulative rewards so that the successful exercise a disproportionate control over the city and the lives of its residents. Consequently the strong prey on the weak, and to him that has shall be given. Today's state, serving the white middle class, is only the most recent manifestation of social and economic competition.[65]

The consequences of capitalism and privatism, Warner insists, are everywhere apparent and profoundly affect the shape of American urban life. Thus, the early definition of the possession of land, the private ownership of property, as a civil liberty, rather than as a social resource—as the Puritans, in effect, wanted it to be when they formed their covenanted towns—has meant that later efforts to control urban growth have foundered because the land involved is not under public ownership. Cities grew quickly in response to the desire of middle- and upper-income people to move away from the poor, but the resulting suburban communities lacked real centers because they were strung out along transporation lines. Later efforts at zoning and planning have typically been used by groups with economic and social power to keep out "undesirable" elements in the population. As a consequence,

64. *Ibid.*, p. 268.
65. *Ibid.*, p. 5.

such facets of urban life as housing and medical care have had a middle-class definition, featuring the privatism inherent in basing the construction of dwellings and the provision of medical services on the ability to pay. The most recent form of urban transportation, the motor vehicle, has been fitted to routes that keep alive middle-class commercial centers, but disrupt the lower-class slums, even though such routes allow for a natural decentralization of commercial life to other parts of the metropolis.

Warner is at his best when dealing with the modern, post-1870 city, which is fortunate in that, in terms of interpretation and analysis, this is precisely the time urban historians have dealt with least effectively. With great compression, but with real insight, Warner shows, in *specific ways*, how developments in technology and transportation created our "national network of cities," unevenly distributed through the Northeast, the Midwest, and California. At the same time, he shows how certain developments influenced urban growth *in particular*. Using New York, Chicago, and Los Angeles as his examples,[66] Warner deals with the "Big City: 1820–1870," the "Industrial Metropolis: 1870–1920," and the "Megopolis: 1920 —." His conclusions about the shaping of our modern city have a significance that stands out from the whole corpus of writing on this subject.

As for transportation: The wide spacing of rail terminals because of cost favored a few centers over others; the widespread ownership of cars for commuting and trucks for freighting has created a much greater residential and commercial mix in the physical form of the contemporary metropolis.[67]

As for economic growth:

> The ubiquity of power and machines in the late nineteenth and early twentieth centuries had profound effects on the American urban system. First, the new techniques encouraged urbanization in general by drawing more and more Americans into those economic roles which peculiarly favored the growth of cities. Mechanization of agriculture, mining, and lumbering freed a multitude of workers for alternative tasks in manufacturing, transport, finance, and the servicing of business. So successful were the new modes of factory production in saving manpower that in the fifty years after 1870 the ratio of Ameri-

66. *Ibid.*, pp. 60–64.
67. *Ibid.*, pp. 89–90, 117–118.

cans employed in marketing, transportation, and services, the very specialties of cities, grew more rapidly than the ratio of those in manufacturing itself.[68]

Accompanying this growth was a shift from partnership and proprietorship, with its concommitant mixture of public and private structures, and upper-, middle-, and lower-class residences to the corporation and the contemporaneous appearance of the carefully segregated city, with its commercial, industrial, and gradated residential zones; and most recently, a further shift has been to increasingly impersonalized and bureaucratized institutions of all kinds in our contemporary megalopolis, which displays contrasting eddies of centralization and decentralization.[69]

As for the distinctive social composition of the modern city:

> The reason that class is an inadequate key to the modern city is that, superimposed on the class-graded cultural variations of Americans, lie the broad bands of their racial and religious identifications: white Protestant, white Catholic, white Jewish, and black Protestant. These religious loyalties derive from our population history. We are a nation of immigrants, and these four socioreligious allegiances have matured out of the process of adaptation of immigrants to the circumstances of American urban life. Over time, these loyalties absorbed the immigrant's previous ties to the village, the region, the ethnic group, the religious denomination, or the nation, so that now all but a small fraction of our citizens identify themselves to a greater or lesser degree with the four broad socioreligious orientations.... All American families share a remarkably uniform urban experience, an experience compounded of class, ethnicity, and religion. The pattern is migration, followed by the ghetto or the slum or just hard times in the city, and this is succeeded by the eventual emergence into a stable income position, be it good or bad (and for many it is good), then the church and the suburb. Behind the migrations lay tribes, villages, or family farms, depending on whether the family memory went back to Africa, Europe, or the rural United States. But as each family lives through its experiences in this country, each one passes

68. *Ibid.*, p. 86.
69. *Ibid.*, pp. 60–64, 128–132.

through the acid of the city which burns off the special qualities of the past. . . . The sequence was, and still is, the sequence of urbanization of our rural migrants. Put most crudely, one brings to the city an extremely localized culture. After some years in the city, the culture becomes broader than the former village or town; it becomes ethnic.[70]

But, though divided, urban populations have a common culture, or at least shared concerns and hopes:

> The behavior of local government and the studies of social science show that a broad consensus on what constitutes a decent American life runs throughout the city. A decent job, a good education for one's children, a comfortable home, and adequate health care are on everyone's list of priorities, and the cultural variations by class, race, and religion which give wide specific meaning to these priorities are not very wide. . . . Working against this common culture, both its openness and its near-universal private family expectation, are two deeply ingrained attitudes which are endlessly reinforced throughout the metropolis: the tradition of white racism and the differential rewards of capitalism. The former poisons every neighborhood and institution, the latter segregates the city into clusters of families of similar class attainment and delivers the power and destiny of the modes of urban growth into the hands of the well-to-do. By their overwhelming purchasing power and control of most of the political, economic, and social institutions of the city, the upper income groups always have controlled and still do control the allocation of the city's resources and the determination of its patterns of development. . . . Our situation deserves to be called a disease, since most of its symptoms —poverty, slums, self-serving public institutions, violence, epidemics of drugs and diseases, misappropriation of land, and despoiling of the environment—grow upon a healthy body of everyday behavior and aspirations. . . . But because our political, economic, and social institutions have remained in the hands of the white and the well-to-do, who have chosen to interpret our common culture in terms of rewards for those who succeed and punishments for those who fall behind, the major

70. *Ibid.*, p. 156.

causes of our urban maladies have gone unattended. By stressing the value of private competition in the cluster of American aspirations, the well-to-do have legitimized their behavior.[71]

Warner's *The Urban Wilderness* thus in some ways reveals insight and broad analysis, but it is still rather restricted in its coverage of city life. Perhaps the most satisfying *over-all* brief account of the role of the city in the development of American society is still Richard Wade's essay, "Urbanization."[72] Drawing primarily on the work of Bridenbaugh and Warner, as well as on his own, Wade makes the claim that, for the urban historian, the shift of the American population from rural areas and towns to cities is "the single most important fact about our historical development."[73] Always, he asserts, there has been an urban frontier and an urban society, along with a rural one. Furthermore, this urban society provided

> each region with enclaves of a similar environment. For nineteenth-century cities had much in common. They all stemmed from commercial necessity; they all developed similar political and social institutions; they all created local governments which found the same range of urban problems. Moreover, their mercantile communities dealt with each other, and their local officials consciously borrowed ordinances and techniques for dealing with city affairs from other urban places. Thus American cities tended to look alike, to foster common characteristics, and to breed a texture of life that differed sharply from farm and plantation.[74]

And, even though until recently a minority of the population, urbanites have had from the beginning an influence over American life all out of proportion to thier number. It is clear that the economic character of cities from the beginning has been that of trading centers, places for the financing, storing, and distribution of goods, and only incidentally or in addition have they been industrial centers, or places for the

---

71. *Ibid.*, pp. 275, 154.
72. Richard C. Wade, "Urbanization," *The Comparative Approach to American History*, edited by C. Vann Woodward (New York: Basic Books, 1968), pp. 187–205. The author has added here and there to Wade's sketch.
73. *Ibid.*, p. 187.
74. *Ibid.*, p. 190.

actual production of goods. Rapid expansion of commercial activity generally explains the growth of cities, whether colonial towns, Midwestern frontier towns, or booster towns; and even after the Civil War, when industry was a major factor in the growth of cities, it seldom wholly determined their size or importance.

Intense urban rivalry—a pervasive competitiveness—in each area and period of our history led to the development of urban centers that overwhelmed their rivals and embarked upon a course of both economic and cultural imperialism. This process can be likened to nineteenth-century European empire-building or to the development of a kind of city-state.[75] In either case, urban dominance has been both regional in extent and plural in number. As these centers grew, they increased the orb of their influence. The result of this development is the modern metropolis.

Size at each stage was determined by available modes of transportation. Walking, the horse-drawn omnibus, the railway, the motor bus, the automobile—all allowed the city to increase its outer dimensions. As Wade has put it: "The extent of the city was determined by commuting time." This mass-transit revolution changed the compact city, with its mixture of rich, middling, and poor, its mixed residential and commercial uses of land, its conglomeration of industrial facilities, shops, and homes. All this gave way to a sorting-out process of commercial and residential areas, the latter organized largely according to income, with the wealthiest the farthest out and the poorest the closest to the center. Occupational and residential mobility has thus been a constant and pervasive feature of American urban life, at least since the industrialization of the nineteenth century.[76]

In a sense, urban economic imperialism looks like Atherton's Midwestern country town grown up. Cultural imperialism was also evident from the colonial period onward, however, and this was an almost wholly urban phenomenon. Boorstin writes of the colonial period: "No one of the five largest cities established an undisputed cultural dominance over cultural life as a whole. . . . [There] were influential local differences important for the future of American culture."[77] *Culture* in

75. For Canadian history, J. M. S. Careless has explored the possibilities of a "metropolitan" thesis in "Frontierism, Mettropolitanism, and Canadian History," *Canadian Historical Review*, XXXV (March 1954), 1–21.

76. Richard Wade, "Urbanization," in *The Comparative Approach to American History*, pp. 191–193.

77. Daniel J. Boorstin, *The Americans: The Colonial Experience* (New York: Random House, 1958), p. 295.

this definition includes the arts, science, philosophical inquiry, and entertainment diffused through books, periodicals, lecture tours, and touring shows, and preserved or displayed through museums, theaters, and halls of various kinds, as well as through schools. The cultural pluralism that resulted was a distinctive product of American urbanism. Only in the area of politics did the city not exert a significant influence from its beginnings. This was because American politics has always been based upon numbers, and, until recently, the urban population has been a minority. Indeed, like the towns, cities were, in political terms, creations of state government, and owed their very existence, both in corporations and charters, to the states.

As rural and foreign migrations into towns that became cities increased throughout the nineteenth century, the social structure became heterogeneous. At the same time, commercialization created an ever greater specialization of function. All of this resulted in the development of a community vastly different from the town—a community whose impersonal relations, varied composition, and new focus on individualism in its interpretation of the Protestant ethic led directly, according to Smith, to modern American, libertarian society.[78] In such densely populated communities, public agencies were formed—inadequately, to be sure, and in the face of a persistent tradition of privatism. Their purpose was to prevent natural and human destruction, to maintain order, and, gradually, to provide what came to be commonly recognized as public services. As communities became populous enough to be incorporated as cities, they dropped the direct democracy of the town meeting in favor of various forms of representative government, like those on the state and national levels. The expansion of public services and regulations led to the development of city government directly involved in important ways in its citizens' daily lives. Probably the towns followed the cities in this respect, retaining a voluntary character in their community functions sometimes well into the nineteenth century. Even with the development of mass society, city-derived forms of local government retain their primacy as the chief instrument through which daily public services are performed.

78. Thernstrom calls the ethic "the ideology of mobility" and focusses on industry, economy, occupational mobility, and the acquisition of property as its central features (Thernstrom, *Poverty and Progress*, pp. 57–79). For Warner, success in a capitalist society was associated with the ideals of hard work, thrift, and education (Warner, *Streetcar Suburbs*, p. 7). In reality, both writers attempt to define what Smith calls the Protestant ethic in an urban setting.

Cities—or "urban regions"—thus constituted a kind of way-station between the old village society and modern American society, and, indeed, were a most important catalyst in the making of our contemporary national community. Though urban society was local in its origins, rapid growth and economic-cultural dominance over wide adjoining areas combined to transform the world we have lost to the world we now have.

Although the dominant economic-social-cultural influence shifted steadily from the small town to the city during the eighteenth and nineteenth centuries, towns did not willingly give up their primacy. As long as most Americans lived in rural areas, the urban centers could not gain political hegemony. And in other spheres of activity as well, villagers resisted encroachments. Convinced of the superiority of virtuous town life over wicked city life, they damned city dwellers *at the same time* that many of them hoped their communities would grow into cities—an ambivalence not yet adequately probed or explained. In any case, historians have long pointed to the 1920s as the time when city-town enmity was at its most strident, probably because this was the last decade in which the town population was large enough to argue with effect against the complete destruction of a way of life that had already been much undermined.

As it turned out, the cities never did attain political pre-eminence within the nation. Power—outside the village—was granted by a rural population in 1788 to state governments. By the twentieth century, when the population had become urbanized, power shifted on to the national government. At the very time when cities acted as agents of modernity, their population was a minority. But now that most Americans live in urban areas, the society urbanization helped to produce is national in scope.

This brief sketch, while it errs in its tendency to equate the nineteenth-century city with *the* city in all American history, at least focuses on the basic factors making for urban development and highlights major characteristics of the urban community in America. There is, quite properly, a shift in emphasis from government to other facets of life. To restrict one's attention primarily to politics is to miss much about how and why the American city has become what it is.

* * * * *

To what extent are the developments that transformed American society from a rural, village-dominated society into an urban, city-dominated one simply a product of city life? As long ago as 1941—shortly after Schlesinger's paper appeared—William Diamond issued a warning "On the Dangers of an Urban Interpretation of History": "Since American cities grew during a period of rapid technical advance, when city and country were drawing more tightly together, many of the characteristics of urban life may have been but manifestations of cultural changes that were affecting the countryside too, but more slowly."[79]

Let's examine the assumption, held by Smith and other scholars who have generalized about towns, that the urbanization of American society produced the democracy and liberty we now have. Questions arise over the *political* element of that development. Simply put, the broadening of liberty in America does not generally appear to have been the work of urban politicians responding to a heterogeneous population. The separation of church and state, the placement of civil liberties in the frame of government itself, the establishment of the principle of nonelitism or rotation in office, the progressive broadening of suffrage (to include all adult males, both white and black, adult women, and people aged eighteen to twenty-one), the ending of the slave trade, the abolition of slavery, and the establishment of legal equality twice for the black population and once for the Indians—all have been the work of various politicians at various levels with various motives and purposes. Examined closely, none of these developments can be regarded simplistically as the product of urban politics. It is true that whenever a major party—usually the Democartic party—thought it could beneift from the support of cohesive immigrant groups that coalesced in the cities, it favored an open immigration policy and easy, quick citizenship procedures, or, in the case of black migrants to the North and West, legislation that established legal equality and social-economic opportunity. Such city-centered political action has not, by itself, usually broadened the *area* of liberty, however.

Furthermore, industry found a home in towns long before it moved to the cities. The efforts of the early industrialists to build factories at locations where water-power could be harnessed and where women and children of a still-rural society could live in a healthy environment are well-known. Only when known power sources expanded to in-

---

79. William Diamond, "The Dangers of an Urban Interpretation of History," as quoted in Callow, p. 625. Like Louis Wirth, Diamond warned against confusing urbanism with capitalism, industrialism, or liberalism. For Wirth's warning, see Louis Wirth, "Urbanism as a Way of Life," *American Journal of Sociology*, XLIV (1938), 7.

clude, first steam, and then electricity, was it feasible to locate industry in urban centers where, by the mid-nineteenth century, recent immigrants provided a large pool of unskilled labor.

Then too, at the same time that mass transit revolutionized transportation in the cities, railroads, and later automobiles, transformed distances in the countryside and towns as well. The railroads, by providing the first *nationwide* means of transportation, affected the growth patterns, even the location, of many villages.

Therefore, capitalism in American society constituted an economic system whose movers and shakers, innovators and entrepreneurs, developed corporate enterprise of, first, regional and then national dimensions, with a reach and linkages that went far beyond the urban centers where capitalists were generally located.

Even the development of economic and social organizations—of great variety from labor unions to the Elks and the professional baseball leagues—involved, in the nineteenth century, particularly, segments of a population still largely living in small towns and out in the countryside.

The point is that these were all *general* phenomena in which, it is true, the city often played an important role, sometimes a decisive one. But it is misleading to *equate* urban growth with these broader developments. Such a temptation leads urban historians to make flat assertions such as this:

> It was in the cities that road, canal, and railroad projects were instigated and fought for, and in city after city it was local as well as class interest that seemed to determine the direction and scope of transportation innovations. Because cities act somewhat like nations and seek to gain economic control of competing ceneers, transportation became a weapon in urban warfare. . . . Technology was itself largely a product of the city, both in its relation to ease of communication and in its dependence upon an intellectual creativity that found its most congenial environment in areas of dense settlement. . . . [The] cities produced new patents at a much higher rate than the nation as a whole. And the innovations in agriculture and industry made possible larger cities and reduced further the proportion of farms to the total population.[80]

80. Jackson and Schultz, editors, *Cities in American History*, pp. 5, 7.

Then comes the backtracking: As to transportation: "Smaller communities fought one another for survival too."[81] As for technology:

> But because urbanization encourages greater inventiveness, it produced a *feedback effect* on growth by promoting more rapid technological progress. In this way urbanization was a cause as well as a consequence of economic growth, and the circle of a self-sustaining process was closed. Though the existence of this feedback mechanism be granted, however, the magnitude of its influence remains open to conjecture.[82]

The actual range of urban contributions in the area of culture, health, and safety are great enough without such inflation: "These included the first struggle for innoculation, the first public schools, the first public health services, the first public libraries, the first victory for freedom of the press, the first fire protection systems and building codes, the best hospitals, and the finest cultural achievements."[83]

In explaining how and why we have developed an increasingly metropolitan society, it is utterly unnecessary to exaggerate the influence of the city, as if to compensate for an earlier overemphasis on the frontier.

II

The American states, it would seem, are simply political subdivisions of a political nation, the United States. As such, they are administrative and political units and appear to lack the other attributes that mark off towns and cities as full-bodied communities. And yet, the oldest of the states are considerably older than the political nation. The colonies were distinctive communities, each with its own origins and with special circumstances shaping its development. As Boorstin has shown, the Puritans of Massachusetts Bay, the Quakers of Pennsylvania, and the Virginians all founded colonies that were widely divergent in character—within a British context, to be sure, but clearly

81. *Ibid.*, p. 6.
82. Robert Higgs, "Cities and Yankee Ingenuity, 1870–1920," as quoted in Jackson and Schultz, pp. 20–21.
83. *Ibid.*, p. 7.

illustrating the variety and independence of the mainland British provinces.[84] The revolution and the Constitution that followed a few years later were the work of those who wanted national independence and then adequate national authority. Both took extraordinary determination, will, and faith in the future, but, of course, also deeply divided those who had been British colonists.

For years after the political nation had been created, it seems, the primary loyalty and identification for Americans was with one's state, though direct evidence for this is hard to find. "The United States are" was a common expression until the 1840s and 1850s.[85] We need to know about symbols, festivities, or other concrete manifestations of patriotism in the older states, as well as when and how and why such identification declined in fervor. And what of the new states, creatures as they were of the national government? Was their inhabitants' primary allegiance to territories and states that had no past, only a future? Did "boosterism" extend to the thirty-five states later admitted to the union, most of them during the nineteenth century? Did those who lived in states in the Mississippi Valley, the Plains, or the West Coast have the same relationship with their state as did those in the original states?[86]

We do not know for certain, but it seems clear that the amateur local historians, especially state historians, of the eighteenth and nineteenth centuries that David van Tassel writes about helped to keep alive a sense of identification with one's state.[87] And the fact that new states

84. Boorstin, *The Americans: The Colonial Experience*, pp. 3–32, 97–143.

85. Boorstin, *The Americans: The National Experience*, pp. 402–405; Daniel J. Elazar, *The American Partnership: Intergovernmental Co-Operation in the Nineteenth-Century United States* (Chicago: University of Chicago Press, 1962), pp. 319–321.

86. To one writer on the subject—Daniel J. Elazar—"Citizens of some states seem to have much more of a sense of attachment to their states than do the citizens of others . . . Evidently, certain factors in the history of individual states, perhaps including early patterns of settlement, unique contributions or experiences, and place in the total scheme of American history, combine with certain geographic factors, perhaps including degree of isolation and uniqueness of topography, to cause the development of state loyalties of different strengths. Evidence . . . indicates that the level of people's attachment to their states today is often misunderstood. This is at least partly because there is a tendency to evaluate loyalties on the basis of dualism, whereby the two loyalties are measured as to their mutual exclusiveness. In fact, the 'man in the street' tends to consider these loyalties as concurrent. He does not choose between state and national loyalties but embraces them both. Indeed, one is usually considered to be a function of the other" (Elazar, p. 320, fn.).

87. Van Tassel, *Recording America's Past*, pp. 45–66, 95–102, 121, 134.

quickly set up historical societies is a forceful indication of a rather pathetic insistence upon conjuring up a practically nonexistent past.[88]

It seems apparent that, with the possible exception of the 1780s, state communities did not constitute economic units, in either the British Empire or the American Union. Neither did any of them define "culture" in the broad sense, or create a social structure different from that of the other states. States probably lost their capacity to be full-fledged communities, gradually becoming little more than political units, when those who lived in the original states lost their collective memory of a common experience in a past that preceded the nation's existence. And yet, Americans *still* identify with their states. What does this identification mean with reference to the continuation of a real community? Probably not very much; but it does not die out, either, which suggests that communities can exist in the mind to help give identity to people, even though such communities have few tangible, concrete manifestations beyond territory and government. And so, at this point in the historical study of the American states, primary emphasis remains where it has always been: on the state as a political or administrative-territorial unit.

It seems certain that, until this century, the most important center of political power beyond the town was the state. During the 1770s and 1780s, the state's primacy under the Articles of Confederation was obvious. Economic life in a group of colonies that had gained political independence and then opted out of a largely self-contained economic trading unit was closely regulated during the disruptive aftermath. And under the Constitution as well, state governments continued to be involved in significant ways with economic development, though there was more emphasis on aid in the form of investment of public funds in the stock of private corporations for the development of risky economic and financial activities, such as banking and transportation, that would aid the *over-all* growth of the economy. When industrial and financial corporations grew to the point of producing antagonisms from farming, laboring, and smaller corporate elements, state governments reacted. After the Civil War, these governments began re-emphasizing regulation and became, after 1900, laboratories of progressive reform. Since the 1930s, the states have been generally eclipsed by the national government, galvanized into action by the cataclysm of the great depression, and have relinquished their primary role

88. Boorstin, *The Americans: The National Experience*, pp. 364–365.

as the government that both regulated and assisted the development of the world's mightiest economy.

All this is by now a familiar story, though only told here and there in general accounts. But although it is true that, until the twentieth century, no aspect of American life was affected by state governments as much as economic activity, we know surprisingly little about other areas of political action. For example, what about education, the care of deviants and dependents, licensing, or even the way law and order was maintained?[89] Given the primacy of state government in the domestic or internal aspects of our political system at least until World War I, it is important that we understand, in its historical dimension, the full range of significant legislative activity. But we must understand also the way in which laws are administered and enforced, the way judicial and penal institutions functioned at the state level, the way states established and financed asylums, penitentiaries, reformatories, almshouses, and hospitals, and the way things came to be regarded as fit subjects for state political action at all.

There have been many scholarly studies of various facets of the political history of individual states, especially since World War II. For a few states—Massachusetts, Pennsylvania, perhaps a few others —there are such studies for many consecutive years of the state's past.[90] Then, too, certain political developments—such as the Jacksonian and Progressive reform movements, or the reconstruction period of the 1860s and 1870s—have long attracted study organized at the state

89. Important studies on the schools and on institutions for deviants and dependents are Michael Katz, *The Irony of Early School Reform: Educational Innovation in Mid-Nineteenth Century Massachusetts* (Cambridge, Mass.: Harvard University Press, 1968), and David Rothman, *The Discovery of the Asylum: Social Order and Disorder in the New Republic* (Boston, Little, Brown & Co., 1971). Both are discussed in Chapter 6.

90. To take just one state, Pennsylvania: Robert L. Brunouse, *The Counterrevolution in Pennsylvania*, 1776–1790 (Harrisburg, Pa.: Pennsylvania Historical Commission, 1942); Harry M. Tinkcom, *The Republicans and the Federalists in Pennslvania, 1790–1801: A Study in National Stimulus and Local Response* (Harrisburg, Pa.: Pennsylvania Historical and Museum Commission, 1950); Sanford Higginbotham, *The Keystone in the Democratic Arch: Pennsylvania Politics, 1800–1816* (Harrisburg, Pa.: Pennsylvania Historical and Museum Commission, 1952); Philip S. Klein, *Pennsylvania Politics, 1817–1832: A Game Without Rules* (Philadelphia: Historical Society of Pennsylvania, 1940); Charles M. Snyder, *The Jacksonian Heritage: Pennsylvania Politics, 1833–1848* (Harrisburg, Pa.: Pennsylvania Historical and Museum Commission, 1958); Erwin Bradley, *The Triumph of Militant Republicanism: A Study of Pennsylvania Presidential Politics, 1860–1872* (Philadelphia: University of Pennsylvania Press, 1964); Frank B. Evans, *Pennsylvania Politics 1872–1877: A Study in Political Leadership* (Harrisburg, Pa.: Pennsylvania Historical and Museum Commission, 1966).

level. But historical studies that deal with the states *as a whole*—even if confined to the political sphere—are rare. The great variety inherent in a group that grew rather quickly—in about 120 years—from 13 to 48 is an obvious inhibitor to such an undertaking, though political scientists and scholars of government seem undaunted, if one judges by the continuous flow of textbooks and scholarly writings on state government since at least the early part of this century. It is far more demanding to generalize about state political life over periods of time than it is to probe the structure and function of such governments in the present, as political scientists ordinarily do.

Still, the fact remains that few historians have tried to generalize at all about the political life of what was in many ways the most important level of government through much of the nineteenth century. Allan Nevins was the pioneer. His *The American States During and After the American Revolution*[91] is an attempt to generalize about political life in the former colonies during a period in which the supremacy of the states over the nation cannot be questioned. But to what extent did the states *maintain* their central position under the Constitution? In the 1940s, the Committee on Research in Economic History sponsored a series of studies on particular states from various areas of the country from 1790 to 1860, approximately, to determine the role of government in the economy. The states selected were Massachusetts, Pennsylvania, and Georgia; the scholars who made the investigations were Oscar Handlin, Louis Hartz, and Milton Heath, respectively.[92] Out of these studies came the now-orthodox view of the continued primacy of the state governments in the development of a modern, integrated economy during the nineteenth century.

In another area, the rise of political parties on a federal basis meant that one common and important aspect of the states' political life was the organization and functioning of the institution Boorstin and others think made the political system of the United States workable and durable.[93] When "party" became—quite recently—a subject of investigation for historians, it was difficult to ignore its operations at the

91. (New York: The Macmillan Co., 1924.)

92. Oscar and Mary Handlin, *Commonwealth: A Study of the Role of Government in the American Economy: Massachusetts, 1774–1861* (Cambridge, Mass.: Harvard University Press, 1947; revised edition, 1969); Louis Hartz, *Economic Policy and Democratic Thought: Pennsylvania, 1776–1860* (Cambridge, Mass.: Harvard University Press, 1948); Milton Heath, *Constructive Liberalism: The Role of the State in the Economic Development in Georgia to 1860* (Cambridge, Mass.: Harvard University Press, 1954).

93. Boorstin, *The Americans: The National Experience*, pp. 427–430.

state level, especially with the work of political scientists as a guide. And yet, old habits died hard. In 1957, when Noble Cunningham, Jr., offered the first systematic investigation of the origins of party organization in the 1790s, he admitted that "[the] scope of the central theme has compelled a close adherence to national politics, and party politics of a state or local nature have been referred to only when they have a specific bearing on the development of national parties."[94] And yet, in 1963, when he presented a second volume on the same subject embracing the years of Jefferson's presidency, Cunningham confessed a change in focus:

> This is a study of the Jeffersonian Republican Party as a national organization, but I have aimed at presenting the national party structure with its components in the various states. Since American parties then, as now, operated both on the state and national level, a full view of the party nationally is impossible without including state organizations. A state-by-state survey of party machinery has thus been presented as an essential part of this book. Since there has been very little written relating to the operation of parties in many states in the Jeffersonian era, this section is aimed at making available a summary of party machinery throughout the nation.[95]

Even more recently, Richard McCormick, in *The Second American Party System: Party Formation in the Jacksonian Era*,[96] investigated the way in which the Jacksonian Democrats and the National Republicans—who became the Whigs—were organized in the late 1820s and the 1830s in every state in the Union. Though he found a great variety of circumstances, McCormick was able to generalize about the distinctive character of the second-party system. He contrasted its origins—state groups forming around the candidacies of Andrew Jackson and his opponents, as opposed to congressional divisions over certain issues in the 1790s—and its essential features—uniformity, national dimensions, and democratic organization as opposed to the variety and elitism of

94. Noble Cunningham, Jr., *The Jeffersonian Republicans: The Formation of Party Organization, 1789–1801* (Chapel Hill, N.C.: University of North Carolina Press, 1957), p. viii.

95. Noble Cunningham, Jr., *The Jeffersonian Republicans in Power: Party Operations, 1801–1809* (Chapel Hill, N.C.: University of North Carolina Press, 1963), p. viii.

96. (Chapel Hill, N.C.: University of North Carolina Press, 1966).

the first system—with those of the organizations that Cunningham had studied.

A recent effort by another author in the same vein is Lee Benson's *The Concept of Jacksonian Democracy: New York as a Test Case*.[97] Benson cites New York's political-social-economic heterogeneity as the reason for focusing on it. Concentrating on one election (1844) in one state, he develops the argument that both the Democratic and Whig parties appealed to essentially the same major, native, economic-social groupings, in slightly different percentages, at election time; they developed similar programs favoring the growth of a liberal, capitalist state, though the Whigs favored positive government action, while the Democrats negated this aspect; and they produced a leadership drawn from the same essentially middle-class social background. Therefore, the Jacksonian political movement is wrongly singled out in explanations for the growth of democracy and egalitarian sentiment during the 1830s and 1840s. Other developments, particularly in the field of transportation, should be examined as major causal factors. Benson closes with a tentative theory of voting behavior for U.S. political history.

All these conclusions are a great burden for research based primarily on one election in one state to bear, and Benson's argument favoring New York's typicality has been rightly criticized. Still, his study remains the single most influential attempt yet undertaken to generalize about the major parties primarily *at the level of the state*, even with the narrow "data base" so glaringly evident.

By 1970, even significant political issues—at least the most important one for the 1830s—were beginning to be treated in the dimension of state politics. James P. Sharp, in *The Jacksonians versus the Banks: Politics in the States after the Panic of 1837*, argues that research on the banking issue in the years following 1837

> is centered almost entirely on the national level, primarily the destruction of the Second Bank of the United States, with only scant attention paid to state politics, and then only to issues in the northeastern states of New York, Pennsylvania, and Massachusetts. And while there are a number of excellent works on individual states, there has as yet been no attempt to bridge the gap between a state focus and a predominantly national one.[98]

97. (Princeton, N.J.: Princeton University Press, 1961).
98. Sharp, *The Jacksonians versus the Banks: Politics in the States after the Panic of 1837* (New York: Columbia University Press, 1970), pp. viii-ix.

Sharp's study is presented as "a nationwide survey of banking and politics on the state level after the Panic of 1837," but a survey based upon "representative states," nonetheless.[99] The reason?

> Since it would have been virtually impossible, and needlessly repetitious, to have undertaken a close study of the political movement in all twenty-six states [as McCormick did], representative states from each of [four] geographic sections . . . the Southwest, Northwest, Southeast, and Northwest—each of which shared common characteristics and a certain cohesion . . . were singled out for intensive analysis. In each of these states—Mississippi, Ohio, Virginia, and to a lesser degree, New York and Pennsylvania—Democratic rhetoric and action on the state level were studied [,] a careful analysis made of the positions taken by the party on the bank issue in the state legislatures [, and] the basis of the party's grass-roots support . . . [was] examined [in certain constituencies]. . . . Other states . . . were dealt with in a more summary fashion with the aim of indicating similarities to and deviations from the experience in the representative states.[100]

His conclusion is that Democrats everywhere, politicians and voters alike, were united by a desire to establish "democratic control over banking and currency."[101]

Other scholars have begun to explore, again, in its *historical* aspects, "intergovernmental relations," that is, the over-all political relationship between the state and federal governments. In 1962, Daniel J. Elazar, under the auspices of the Workshop in American Federalism at the University of Chicago, which examined the hypothesis that "government in the United States is shared government on all levels," presented *The American Partnership: Intergovernmental Co-operation in the Nineteenth-Century United States*. Elazar concluded that the old emphasis on "duality," on hostility and conflict between the two levels, was misplaced. He found that there was "no exclusiveness of activity, no stand-offish separation. Aside from the Civil War, there is a continuous involvement of both the federal and state governments in all the great

99. *Ibid.*, p. ix.
100. *Ibid.*
101. *Ibid.*, p. 329.

domestic tasks of building and maintaining a continent-wide nation."[102] Elazar chose the "hard-case" method of investigation:

> Rather than attempt an over-all history of American government in the nineteenth century, specific, well-screened programs in selected states were chosen for investigation with a view to demonstrating that co-operation occurred where it was least likely to be found. . . . [The] greater part of the research for this study was done at the state level. . . . The states . . . could be assumed to have a greater stake in asserting their independence or their domination of a given program if such existed. Thus . . . if a pattern of intergovernmental co-operation similar to that with which we are familiar today should emerge from an examination of the states' records, it would lend additional support to the evidence in question. Furthermore, since the center of the political process generally lies in the party system, and since parties are state-based, a study of the operation of the federal system as a whole can justifiably be undertaken from the vantage point of the state, which lies at the center of the process.[103]

The four states extensively explored are Virginia, New Hampshire, Minnesota, and Colorado, chosen for their regional spread and for their typicality of different kinds of relationships between the states and the federal government. Linking intergovernmental relations continuously with the geographic and economic growth of the nation, Elazar found four major categories to probe, all arising out of major problems requiring governmental action: internal improvements, education, disposition of the public lands, and slavery. Whether co-operation was informal or systematized, it was pervasive, and it far outstripped conflict and duality of effort—again, with the notable exception of slavery. Early forms of grants-in-aid and services-in-aid involving federal assistance in the form of land, money, and services were thus features of American government from its inception; and, even though the slavery issue represented what Elazar calls "separatist tendencies," an emphasis in studies of the nineteenth century on duality rather than co-operation, and in studies of the twentieth century on the New Deal program as a revolutionary innovation in our federal system

102. Elazar *The American Partnership*, pp. xi, viii.
103. *Ibid.*, p. 2.

is misplaced, in both instances. Elazar's thesis finds support in Boorstin's view of "government as a service institution";[104] indeed, the Elazar view preceded Boorstin's by a few years.

In 1969, James T. Patterson, in *The New Deal and the States: Federalism in Transition* focussed on the shifting character of state-federal political relations during the depression of the 1930s. Patterson's generalizations about the states lack the systematic and comprehensive quality of, say, McCormick's, and, indeed are frankly selective and impressionistic:

> Generalizations on federal-state relations can be misleading. It may be that the most faithful way of describing them in the 1930s—or any period—is to begin with the assumption that only a state-by-state analysis would give proper emphasis to the great dissimilarities among the states. This is a tenable view, and distinctive state traditions and institutions indeed posed formidable and at times insurmountable barriers in the way of New Deal planning. But a state-by-state approach risks losing the forest for the trees, and it surrenders the chance of finding the generalizations which give meaning to history. Accordingly, I have tried to compromise, describing some to the countless variations in state responses, but searching always for whatever broad trends or patterns may have existed.[105]

Patterson succeeds in conveying a sense of the impact of the New Deal on the political operations of what had until that time been the most important government in the internal aspects of our federal system.

Under the spur of crisis, the states moved to take over some expenses of local communities: "The centralization of American life was forcing the states to assume local functions. Nothing since that time has reversed this invincible trend."[106] But the growth of state activity in the 1930s was not substantial. The federal government did goad states into more administrative efficiency and a wider merit system, hastened the spread of social legislation, awakened underprivileged voters to activity in state political life, and vastly increased grants-in-aid programs, fitting spending and tax policies at the state level to federal stipulations. But the results were fragmentary and incomplete:

104. Boorstin, *The Americans: The National Experience*, pp. 249–256.
105. (Princeton, N.J.: Princeton University Press, 1969), pp. vii–viii.
106. *Ibid.*, p. 202.

The New Deal produced neither federal dictation, a completely co-operative federalism, nor a state progressivism. Instead, it helped create a rather flat mixture of achievement, mediocrity, and confusion. For all the supposed power of the New Deal, it was unable to impose all its guidelines on the autonomous 48 states. . . . The causes of this mixed record defy simple explanation, but perhaps the most obvious was the limited nature of positive state action prior to the depression. Scholars have shown that the states contributed materially to nineteenth-century economic development, that they preceded the national government in regulating corporations, and that they often served as laboratories of social reform. But neither the states nor the federal government prior to 1929 had been forced to provide costly welfare programs, countercyclical spending, or legislation beneficial to organized labor. Since these were the staples of the new progression of the 1930s, it was not surprising that state leaders, like many New Dealers, were slow to implement them. And given the inexorable centralization of modern life, it is clear that the national government was better equipped to handle economic problems by 1933.[107]

Other factors were the lack of state revenues, largely based upon real estate and personal property taxes; delays in gaining constitutional sanction for New Deal programs directly involving the states; and a state political system with courts sometimes as hostile to reform legislation at the state level as the Supreme Court was at the national level. There were state constitutions that "obstructed the financing of new services"; legislatures that, through inequable districting, favored rural interests opposed to urban-focussed reform; and there were politicians who bickered constantly among themselves.[108]

Patterson concludes:

[The] most striking feature of federal-state relation during the 1930s was not the failure of the New Dealers, but the limits in which they had to operate. Time was short, courts hostile, state institutions obstructive, and political parties too often concerned with patronage instead of policy. Above all, state refor-

107. *Ibid.*, pp. 202–203.
108. *Ibid.*, pp. 203–205.

mers faced the same potent forces which eventually brought the New Deal to its knees: the durable appeal of materialistic, pro-business ideology and the stubborn resistance to a strong central government. . . . For all the apparent nationalism of the 1930s, states rights and strict constructionism remained remarkably healthy. Indeed, the system of federalism itself, far from serving as a flexible medium for change, revealed itself——in Canada as well as the United States—to be better suited to preserving dignity than to encouraging strong and coordinated national action.[109]

* * * * *

Those who have thus far attempted to generalize about American state political history have consequently done so in a variety of ways. Cunningham and McCormick made state-by-state surveys in their studies of party organization during the 1800s and the 1830s, also grouping the states into regions. But Sharp, in his investigation of the banking issue in the states in the late 1830s chose "representative" states, arguing that in-depth research is more valuable than the more superficial, total survey. Elazar and Patterson took similar stands in their probings into state-federal relationships. Another approach is that adapted by the Committee on Research in Economic History in the 1940s: the practice of assigning scholars to single states in various regions to focus on a particular aspect of state politics.

All approaches have merit, but the question nags: How, unless you survey *all* the states, do you *know* what is representative and what is not? Synthesizers such as Sharp point to work already done on single states, work on which it is possible to define the range of political practice. This is satisfactory as long as such scholarship exists. But what if it does not—for some other period or subject? What then? The question is especially germane as the total number of states spurted upwards during the course of the nineteenth century.

In any case, generalizations about the historical experience of the American states have not yet resulted in a work with the sweep and synthesis of Page Smith's *As a City upon a Hill*. Scholarship in this area is still too fragmentary.

* * * * *

109. *Ibid.*, pp. 206–207.

What should be stressed about states in their political capacity is their innovative role in the development of our society, something they clearly lost to the national government only in the crisis of the 1930s. The linkage of state government with the conservative aspects of American life is thus relatively recent in origin. Long-term primacy in the economic sphere, with respect to both aid and regulation, has already been alluded to. The states as innovators can also be seen in the process by which the United States was turned into a modern, liberal society, something Smith vaguely attributes to the city. State governments initially separated church and state, ended primogeniture and entail, abolished slavery (in the North), composed "Bills of Rights" and insisted (in the guise of the "Anti-Federalists") on a bill of rights being added to the federal constitution; they drew up new constitutions in the 1820s and thereafter that removed property qualifications to the suffrage, and initiated the suffrage for women. Much of the political apparatus of the modern liberal state thus originated at state level.

Though states from the beginning passed legislation respecting the founding, settling, and legal chartering of towns and cities, their role in this instance was of a vastly different character; they constituted a *conservative* influence, especially with reference to fast-growing cities. State governments did not generally lead the way in the development of more effective new political forms for such communities, probably because of the numerical supriority in state legislatures of those who represented the interests and concerns of the more numerous and stable towns.

In any case, the role of the state in both its innovative and conservative aspects with reference to local and national communities has not received the attention it deserves.

III

Regionalism exists in all societies, to some extent. And the larger and more varied in composition a society is, the more significant and obvious regional manifestations become. Like the term *community* itself, regionalism defies any simple or widely acceptable definition. But that sectional division and, on one occasion, open conflict, has played a major role in American history has not been in any doubt, at least since the time of the Civil War.

Frederick Jackson Turner in his later work stressed the historical centrality of a pervasive sectionalism. Paradoxically, while Turner and his followers were the first professionals to write about American history from a national perspective, in the very act of doing so, they highlighted sectional antagonism to such an extent that the nation was largely viewed *through its regions*.[110] In short, they effectively meshed nationalism and regionalism into one synthesis.

But their use of the term *sectionalism* was loose, its meaning vague. Desirous of more precision, two sociologists—Howard W. Odum and Harry E. Moore—published in 1938 the results of a thorough inquiry into the nature of regionalism of all kinds in American life. They found as many as seven attributes, overlapping to some extent: (1) a spatial unit, (2) characterized by flexible limits, with a center and fringe areas; (3) homogeneity in selected characteristics (closely related surface or geographic features); (4) uniform structural or functional aspects (common resources, transportation, power); (5) the "relative, composite homogeneity of the largest number of factors for the largest number of purposes in view"; (6) "a constituent unit in an aggregate whole"; and (7) organic unity "in land and the people, culturally conditioned through time and space relationships." They defined five types of regions: the natural region: soil, climate, topography, valleys, mountains, etc.; the metropolitan region; a loose section "from which loyalties, patriotism, and folkways radiate"; a region for administrative purposes; and a "group-of-states" region.[111]

Accusing historians of giving a negative meaning to sectionalism——focussing on antagonism and conflict—Odum and Moore distinguish regionalism from the more historical term and stress positive connotations, arguing that regionalism is desirable, indeed *necessary*, in a country as large and varied as the United States. Paradoxically, the existence of regions is vital to the continued growth of an integrated American society, for it is only through the free interplay of varied regional patterns of life that whatever is *genuinely* national in scope will emerge.[112]

Having criticized the Turnerian view of America's past, Odum and Moore go on to retain what historians had defined, however fuzzily, as "sections" as being the only acceptable basis for a definition of major regions in the United States. These large, composite, "group-of-state, major societal regions"—the Northeast, Southeast, Southwest, Northwest, and Far West—"comprehend both the natural factors and the

---

110. Frederick Jackson Turner, *The Significance of Sections in American History* (New York: Henry Holt & Co., 1932); Hofstadter, *The Progressive Historians*, pp. 93–103.
111. Odum and Moore, *American Regionalism*, pp. 14–16, 29.
112. *Ibid*., pp. 35-51.

societal factors which must, of course, include the American states and prevailing historic, economic, and culture traits."[113] The use of state boundaries to define the outer limits of composite regions whose definition depends on overlapping cultural, economic, social, and political patterns is somewhat less than satisfactory, but the authors could not find a better alternative.

Odum's and Moore's book quickly became the most influential study of American regionalism. By 1951, Louis Wirth was able to catalogue an impressive array of regional studies from "[geographers], historians, anthropologists, linguists, artists, economists, sociologists, political scientists, administrators, architects, engineers, and planners."[114] Whether defined by physical characteristics or cultural ones, whether set off sharply by barriers or defined by a focal point with a vague periphery, regionalism was being studied by a great number of scholars from a variety of academic disciplines. Wirth, while excited by this development, was also dismayed by a certain ineptness that he thought characterized regional studies:

> The failure to discriminate the many distinct factors that underlie the emergence and persistence of regions is a serious fault of present-day scholarship and research. It has led to the failure to distinguish between genuine and spurious regions. Areas of homogeneity have been mistakenly represented as areas of integration. It has been mistakenly assumed that physical regions also inevitably constitute economic, cultural, and political regions. . . . If the mark of a community is interdependence and the mark of society is consensus, it follows that many areas which have been conceived as regions are neither communities nor societies, for they show no convincing evidence of a common basis of existence or of a collective consciousness.[115]

Neither the efforts of Odum and Moore to define and spur on the study of regionalism or the later Symposium on American Regionalism held at the University of Wisconsin in 1949 has had much success in deflecting the focus of historical scholarship away from sectional conflict and antagonism, nor have such efforts enticed historians to study less obvious or distinctive forms of regionalism. Indeed, historians

113. *Ibid.*, pp. 32, 30.
114. Jenson, editor, *Regionalism in America*, p. 382.
115. *Ibid.*, p. 392.

have not accepted as workable a number of Odum's and Moore's definitions of regions. The reason, in part, is that those definitions are a product of the 1930s and do not always reflect historical reality in all periods; also, some of Odum's and Moore's regions—the Northwest, Southwest, Far West—appeared relatively late in American history. Most historians continue to treat New England, not the Northeast, as a section, refuse to break the South into the Southeast and the Southwest, and, similarly, deal with the Plains states, not the Northwest, as a unit. Series such as the "History of the South" continue to define that section as the states that formed the Confederacy. Other series, such as the New American Nation Series, continue the practice of focussing on a succession of Wests in the national period, either trans-Appalachian or trans-Mississippi.[116]

In any case, thorough, comprehensive studies of regionalism of the kind that Odum and Moore called for have not yet been written. The main reason that regionalism has received the attention it has thus far in American historical study is an old one: several *national* developments are inexplicable without reference to it: namely, the South and the Confederacy, the Civil War, and a succession of frontier "Wests" as settlement expanded from ocean to ocean.

Regionalism, in *all* its forms, as a regular phenomenon in American history, *should* be examined on its own terms, however. Even though lacking the political definition of states, or even towns and cities, regions viewed as a *level of community* are of considerable significance and, if studied as levels of community, can help to explain the over-all character of the American historical experience. Odum and Moore, before settling on the "group-of-states major societal regions" as the proper unit for study, delineate a number of other, more limited, but still useful definitions. Metropolitan regionalism has rightfully been staked out by urban historians and constitutes a kind of transitional zone between the city and regional studies.[117] Natural regions based upon climate and geography, however, along with "cultural" regions in which a given style in architecture, art, literature, etc., predominates, and religious regions, where certain kinds of ecclesiastical organizations or forms of Christianity prevail are three other kinds of regionalism that could profitably be studied with reference to economic, cultural, and religious developments.

116. Francis S. Philbrick, *The Rise of the West, 1754–1830* (New York: Harper & Row, 1965); Ray A. Billington, *The Far Western Frontier, 1830–1860* (New York: Harper & Row, 1956).

117. Careless, "Frontierism, Metropolitanism, and Canadian History."

A look at fine arts is one example. Benjamin Spencer has convincingly shown that localism and regionalism—from the regional variations of the colonial and antebelleum periods through the local-color schools of the post-Civil War years to the localism of the 1920s and 1930s—has marked American literature from its beginning, in spite of continuous pleas for distinctively national, expatriate, proletarian, and other antiregional styles. Architecture is always the product of the intermingling of "the social and religious customs of its builders," with the "geographic, geologic, and climactic conditions of the land of its inception," as Rexford Newcomb puts it. American architecture is no exception. Like others, it is a product of the commingling of people and geography in regional variations. Though largely derived from European styles until the twentieth century, buildings and homes in the United States also varied according to the landscape and the climate, as well as the exigencies of economic and social patterns. Only in this century, with the coming together of "new materials, new systems of construction, and new inventions"[118] did construction allow for the gradual development of a distinctively national or "American" style, in the form of the skyscraper and mass-produced house-styles.

But painting as an art form has not shared in these developments. As E. P. Richardson explains:

> Painting is . . . an art without the practical elements of architecture. Its materials are the same in all climates. A picture needs no adaptation to a Wisconsin winter or a Texas summer, as does the form of a house. The regional influences of climate and geography do not affect its practice as they affect architecture. Nor has it been used, like literary skill, to give expression to the strong practical currents of thought in which the life and conflicts of political sections have been expressed. . . . There is not even a theory of regionalism in painting. . . . The theoretical debate in the field . . . has been a simple one, between American nationalism, on the one hand, and loyalty to various cosmopolitan styles and points of view on the other. . . . There are no deep-rooted local schools. There are only individual artists who may for a time seem to give an individual flavor to the work of their community; or loosely connected groups of artists, which dissolve as easily as they are formed. National unity, and the unity of the climate of the mind that prevails through-

118. Jenson, editor, *Regionalism in America*, pp. 219–220, 273, 292.

out Western life, are stronger than any of these vague local associations. . . . Regionalism may be said, therefore, to be a relatively superficial phenomenon in the field of American painting, compared with its strong, objective existence in other fields. It does not exist as a theory. It seems to have no existence in the shape of firmly rooted regional trends or styles.[119]

Major regions of the "group-of-states" kind have continued to be an important element in American historical writing since Turner's time. Though lacking the precision and evenness and coverage that Odum and Moore call for, such writing has, nevertheless, focussed increasingly on the great variety that existed even in the historically defensible regions.[120]

Boorstin's *The Americans: The National Experience*, while it deals with community-building at the level of the town and city, is *organized* on the basis of sections—New England, the South, the Midwest—at least before the author goes on to deal with general or national developments, that is. In Boorstin's view, geography and resulting economic patterns have helped to produce regions. The long growing seasons and initially fertile soil in large areas of the South predisposed its population to grow staple crops on a large scale. The semiarid soil of the Plains states led to the extensive cultivation of single crops. And the mineral-rich Rocky Mountains naturally produced a preoccupation with mining in that area. The rocky soil of New England forced people to look to the sea or to develop industrial instead of agricultural enterprise. All these general geographic variations are properly associated with significant economic differences.

But the character of those who settled in certain areas also fostered regional distinctiveness. Boorstin's Puritans and Virginians profoundly influenced the whole colonial pattern of life and settlement in New England and the South (the former wanting to purify English society, the latter to copy it). These two groups had such an effect both because they had objectives in which they believed and because they had the practicality to be successful community-builders. But such groups as the Quakers in Pennsylvania, by contrast, though dominant at first, did not have long-term influence, because of their rigidity and

119. *Ibid.*, pp. 262, 272. For an account of regional economic development from 1790 to 1860, see Douglas North, *The Economic Growth of the United States*, pp. 101–176. This study is discussed in Chapter 9.

120. For a good account of the variety apparent in the South, see Clement Eaton, *The Growth of Southern Civilization* (New York: Harper & Row, Publishers, 1961).

impracticality and because of the built-in heterogeneity of the Mid-Atlantic colonists. Penn's colony stressed religious toleration and welcomed variety, not uniformity. From its inception, the Mid-Atlantic area lacked the uniformity that permitted groups with the distinctiveness of purpose and the pragmatic cast of mind of the Puritans and the Virginians to dominate a whole region.[121]

The continuance of regionalism into the national period of our history displays quite clearly the interplay of the factors just mentioned. In New England, when religious uniformity in the towns gave way, geographic and economic conditions asserted themselves, and Puritans became quite naturally what Boorstin calls the "Versatiles," or practical activists. Driven outward by a barren soul, shorn of a unifying religious purpose, New Englanders became the chief transplanters of European and especially British practices and processes, taking over the role that the Virginians played in the colonial period. Furthermore, emigration into New England gave to its population a heterogeneous character, something noticeably lacking in the colonial period. This variety stimulated reformers to work for all manner of changes in a *national* society whose nature New England more nearly approximated. In other words, the reform impulse in New England shifted from utopians of the homgeneous colonial New England town to nineteenth-century reformers in a society marked by its increasing variety.[122]

In the South, after independence, the maintenance of the Virginian ideal—that of the planter-gentleman—combined with the pre-eminence of staple crop agriculture and a large number of Negro slaves to produce a region whose people became self-conscious, especially when their interests were attacked by reformers in other parts of the country. Boorstin's great insight into the antebellum South is that the region became largely unified, *even though* it had as much variety as any other area, because Southerners asserted it was homogeneous and "belief in uniformity tended to create uniformity. . . . 'The South' became the most unreal, most powerful, and most disastrous oversimplification in American history." Why did this happen? The answer is ironic: "While these Southern Americans believed their region unified by its homogeneity, what actually drew it together and made it conscious of itself was its deep and (according to white Southern belief) ineradicable division—into white and black. . . . Leading Southerners persuaded themselves that only by dividing their communities into two

121. Boorstin, *The Americans: The Colonial Experience*, pp. 3–143.
122. Boorstin, *The Americans: The National Experience*, pp. 3–48.

could they make themselves one."[123] Thus, Negro slaves became "indelible immigrants" outside the Southern community and with none of their own. And so the planter leadership, embodying the way of life white Southerners aspired to, were able to convince the mass in a patriarchal society that there was no conflict and no division. They therefore were able to speak for the whole regional community—and indeed some of them led it into Civil War.

Southern regionalism has remained the most conspicuous since that conflict as well. In fact, the common experience of rebellion, a separate government, defeat, and military occupation gave to Southern regionalism a clarity and precision that it lacked *before* the war. Even so, the homogenizing influences of an increasingly "national" society have led to significant reductions in those postwar features of life that gave substance to that regionalism: poverty, racial segregation, an agricultural economy. As the South becomes increasingly similar to the rest of the country, one thing alone keeps alive its people's sense of distinctiveness, and that is what C. Van Woodward calls their common historical experience of defeat, failure, poverty, and pessimism—so contrary to the national experience of abundance, success, and optimism.[124] In this, Southerners are like those who lived in the Eastern states whose existence preceded the Union of 1776. Both responded to "communities" that had existed apart from the nation.

Like Turner, Boorstin is also concerned with the West. But in his treatment of "The Transients: the Joiners," those who moved west, and of "The Upstarts: the Boosters," those who built the towns and cities there, Boorstin ranges all over the trans-Appalachian and trans-Mississippi west to the extent that regionalism becomes so attenuated as to be almost emptied of meaning. We are left to wonder whether the distinctive patterns of migration and settlement he discusses for the Mississippi Valley, the Plains, the Rockies, and the Pacific Coast were in some way determined by the land, or whether the "western" way is to be somehow regarded as the "American" way as well. Why treat New England as a distinctive region, and not the Plains, or the Rockies, or the Pacific Coast, as well? What was there about migration featuring the "community before government" of the caravan and the "claims clubs" of the farmers and the miners or about settlement that took the form of highly competitive "booster" towns in which the private and public spheres of life became enmeshed—what was there

123. *Ibid.*, p. 170.
124. C. Vann Woodward, *The Burden of Southern History*, revised edition (Baton Rouge, La.: Louisiana State University Press, 1968), pp. 3–25.

about such migration and settlement that warrants its being associated with a region so vague in its boundaries and time period as to be almost without definition? And Boorstin clearly *presents* such activity as having been "western." By contrast, available evidence seems to suggest, first, that migratory patterns varied with their length, the terrain, and whether or not the U.S. government had already secured the territory; second, that boosterism and competitiveness were general nineteenth-century phenomena.

* * * * *

With the Boorstin synthesis, the historical study of regions has come a long way from the precision that Odum and Moore called for in 1938. The question of what constitutes a region in the *historical* development of American life is still a vexing one, even with the Odum-Moore efforts at definition. "Area" studies of architecture, literature, religion, geography, and the like, can have a certain amount of precision because of the built-in focus on one activity or one kind of setting. As such, they constitute a fruitful line of inquiry for the future and would force historians away from the regionalism-is-just-sectional-antagonism approach that Odum and Moore deplored. But what of the "group-of-state" regions? The fact is that historians have rarely found a convincing nexus of cultural-social-economic-geographic elements that add up to the regional unity that Odum and Moore thought they found all over the United States in the 1930s. Recent historians have rightly insisted upon the presence of either a widespread, common pattern of life (as in colonial New England and Virginia) or a well-developed sense of awareness, consciousness, and loyalty (as in the South of the national period) before investing broad and *varied* areas of the United States with the title of *region*. Frankly, it is doubtful that historians would get very far in a frenzied effort to project back into American history Odum's and Moore's five neatly packaged "group-of-states" regions. Regionalism, it would appear, is an important but devilishly uneven force in our historical experience.

Something else now needs more emphasis, however, and that is the role that this phenomenon played in the development of local communities. We all know how sections contributed to national crisis and territorial expansion. But the fact that New England and Midwestern towns were typically different from each other, to some extent, must have something to do with such features of regionalism as the influence of founding groups, geography, and economic activity. The influence of regions thus extends *downwards* as well as upwards as a contributor to the process whereby the American community received an ever wider definition.

4

The Big Community:
The Rise of the Nation

Writers on modern nationalism—Carlton Hayes, Hans Kohn, Boyd Shafer, David Potter—have largely defined, without knowing it, the nation as a "community," with attributes in common with other levels of community. Appropriating their definitions and terminology, one can construct a description of a nation that contains the same social and geographic or administrative-territorial dimensions that those who have written about towns, cities, and regions have featured. Of course, people do not "live" in nations the way they live in specific towns or cities, but they "belong" to a nation as much as they belong to a particular local community.

Just as one is an inhabitant of a town or a city by virtue of living within its boundaries, so, too, is one a citizen of a nation if residing in its territory. Just as one feels a part of a neighborhood or a village or a metropolis, so also does one have loyalty to a larger group, the people of a nation. Furthermore, both local and national communities can be studied in their psychological aspects—identification with and loyalty to a group—as well as in their institutional or sociological aspects—political-economic-social-cultural structures such as governments, law-enforcement agencies, churches, schools, armies, etc.[1]

Students of nationalism, such as Hayes, tell us that patriotism and nationality groups have existed through much of human history. Not

1. David M. Potter, *The South and the Sectional Conflict* (Baton Rouge, La.: Louisiana State University Press, 1968), pp. 36–41.

until they coalesced with political nation-states in Western Europe in the late eighteenth century, however, was there genuine, clearly recognizable nationalism of the kind characterizing a nation-state system that has, with the end of Western colonialism in our own time, encircled the globe and become almost universal. Americans have thus been directly, personally, and simultaneously involved with a hierarchy of community life. And though all historians of nationalism agree that the nation has become the pre-eminent level of community in our time, Potter rightfully stresses the concurrent nature of each American's involvement. Like Odum and Moore in the 1930s, Potter sees membership in subnational groupings as something not at all antithetical to the growth of nationalism:

> Historians frequently write about national loyalty as if it were exclusive, and inconsistent with other loyalties, which are described as "competing" or "divided" and which are viewed as detracting from the primary loyalty to the nation. Yet it is self-evident that national loyalty flourished not by challenging and overpowering all other loyalties, but by subsuming them all in a mutually supportive relation to one another. The strength of the whole is not enhanced by destroying the parts, but is made up of the sum of the parts. The only citizens who are capable of strong national loyalty are those who are capable of strong group loyalty, and such persons are likely to express this capacity in their devotion to their religion, their community, and their families, as well as in their love of country. The nationalism which will utilize this capacity most effectively, therefore, is not one which overrides and destroys all other objects of loyalty, but the one which draws them all into one transcendant force. A well-known phrase runs, "For God, for Country, and for Yale"—not "For God, or Country, or for Yale."[2]

And, like Hayes and Shafer, Potter stresses the existence of a national group apart from its political manifestation, the nation-state——something quite unusual among American historians of any kind. True,

---

2. *Ibid.*, pp. 48–49; Daniel J. Elazar, in *The American Partnership*, p. 320, makes essentially the same point.

institutionally, the nation assumes all the concreteness which a census of population, an inventory of resources, an army and navy, and all the apparatus of public authority can give to it. In psychological terms, a nation exists only subjectively as a convergence of men's loyalties; without this convergence there would be no nation. But once the nation has become institutionalized, men tend to regard the institution itself as transcendent—a thing on which the loyalties of men ought to converge simply because it does exist. Again, in theory, the nation survives as a unit because people continue to feel a psychological unity. But in operative terms, its survival may depend upon the power of the state to override divisive impulses and to control an aggregation of people as if they were one, even despite a significant degree of reluctance on the part of some of those who are being thus united. . . . The political state as we know it today possesses tremendous powerful devices for making the institutional aspects of nationality seem more real than the psychological aspects. With the paraphernalia of symbols (the flag, the crown, the national anthem, the constitution) it evokes the emotional responses of patriotism. By such means as citizenship, territorial boundaries, and sovereignty *vis-a-vis* other political states, it sets up demarcation which separate and even differentiate human beings on one side of an imaginery geographical line from human beings on the other side of this line. Even though it should be situated upon a terrain which lacks any natural geographical unity, it can employ the concept of a "common territory" so persuasively as to create the illusion of commonality for geographically diverse areas, whereas, in the absence of common political jurisdiction, real features of geographical unity will not be recognized as the basis for a commonality. . . . [The] operative importance of formalistic features, such as citizenship, jurisdiction, territoriality, and so on, tends to convey an image of nationality which is far more institutional than psychological. And this concept is, of course, far more categorical, more absolute, more unitary in its implications: the individual either is or is not a citizen; the public authority either does or does not have jurisdiction; the disputed area lies either inside or outside of the national boundary. None of these matters is partial, any more than sovereignty itself is partial—and sovereignty, it used to be said, is like virginity in that it cannot be surrendered in part.[3]

Potter thus reveals the inadequacy of historical inquiry that defines the nation in exclusively institutionalized—and primarily political-—terms. In this, he underscores the efforts of Hayes and Shafer to give a broad definition to nationality-groupings and patriotism, both of which flourished for centuries before the rise of the nation-state. He adds, however, the argument that the nation as an abstraction existing in the minds of the group is *still* as important as the nation-state in its institutional manifestations. Potter goes on to develop the view that nationalism "rests on two psychological bases: feeling of common culture on the one hand and feeling of common interests on the other." In other words, national group loyalty arises not only out of a distinctive cultural identity, but also out of a sense that the group has shared economic and social interests that the nation-state can further and protect.[4]

Boyd Shafer, writing in 1955 and 1972, when nationalism and the nation-state had made their way into Asia and Africa, expanded upon Haye's earlier efforts and produced a serviceable, broad, many-faceted definition for nationalism:

> The ten statements that follow do not define nationalism but, *taken together*, they describe its basic attributes, both real and mythical
>
> 1. A certain defined, even if vaguely, territory or land, whether this be large or small, inhabited by a people or desired by them.
> 2. A people, called a nation, who share or hope to share, in different and shifting ways, a common culture, and who are able to communicate with each other with some facility. The common culture generally includes language . . . or commonly understood languages . . . common literature, common symbols, common customs, and common manners.
> 3. Some dominant social (Muslim or Christian churches, for example) and economic (capitalist or communist) institutions. . . . Accompanying or behind these institutions there are common social and economic interests. If there are

3. Potter, *The South and Sectional Conflict*, pp. 40–43.
4. *Ibid.*, pp. 51–59.

deep conflicts over these institutions or interests, then the nation is likely to be divided.

4. A common independent or sovereign state (type does not matter), or, with rare exceptions, the desire for one.

5. A shared belief in a common history and often in a common ethnic origin, sometimes thought to be religious or racial. . . . The common past and ethnic origin may be real or imagined.

6. Preference and esteem for fellow nationals. . . . or at least greater preference or esteem for them than for members of other similar groups who do not share . . . the common culture, institutions, interests, and heritage.

7. A shared, a common pride . . . in past and present achievements, more often the military and economic than the cultural and social, of the group, and a shared, a common sorrow in its tragedies, particularly its military failures.

8. A shared indifference or hostility to other (not all) people similarly organized in nations . . . especially if the other nations seem to threaten the national security and hopes, the nation's survival in the present and the future.

9. A devotion to the entity (even if little comprehended) called the nation . . . that embodies or symbolizes the territory, the culture, the institutions, the interests, the heritage, and whatever else the people think they have in common.

10. A shared hope that the nation, the nation as a group, and the individuals belonging to it, will have a secure and happy future.

These ten attributes are . . . generally present. They do not all have to be present at the same time and in the same way or to the same degree. The varieties of combination and emphases are manifold. Before nationalism can be said to exist, however, most of them must be present, and when all are present at the same time, then nationalism will be strong.[5]

* * * * *

If the mountain of scholarship written from a national perspective since the turn of the last century is seen in the context of the preceding

---

5. Boyd Shater, *Faces of Nationalism*, (New York: Harcourt, Brace, Jovanovich, Inc., 1972), pp. 16–20.

general discussion of nationalism, much of it is not inaccurate, but misplaced in its emphasis. The great outpouring of monographic literature on various aspects of the institutional life of the nation—usually the activities of the national government—stemmed from an incomplete conception of what the nation was. Of even greater consequence was the wrongly placed focus on national institutions at a time when they were of less importance than the nation as a mental abstraction; for it can be strongly argued that Americans believed in and gave their loyalty to an abstraction embodying certain ideals long before the institutionalized apparatus of the nation-state they created directed the course of their lives with anything like the impact of the town, the city, or the state. This is what most writers on the American nation have not understood. And this is why so much of our monographic scholarship dealing with the United States before the twentieth century is misdirected. We have labored hard and long on something that was of *relative* insignificance, ignoring what mattered most in the shaping of American lives.

Even Shafer and other writers on nationalism have not adequately explained the distinctive character of the "national community" in what is now the United States. In 1957, Hans Kohn commented with great effect on the peculiar origins of American nationalism. According to Shafer's scheme, the rebelling British colonists had only a small chance of developing a national consciousness. They were not of a common stock, did not have a common church, had no historically defined territory, no distinctively "American" language or literature,[6] and no common pride in their own land or hostility toward others——certainly not during a revolution that was a civil war as well. All that the "Americans" had were certain dominant social and economic patterns or institutions, such as Christian churches and capitalism, which were hardly distinctive to that area of the British Empire.

But what they gained from their revolution was of immense importance: they set up their own nation-state and embodied certain general, eighteenth-century revolutionary ideals in their declaration of independence and in their frame of government: namely, a libertarian state whose government must protect and further the human rights of liberty, the pursuit of happiness and property, and equality under God. Thus, what made Americans members of a nation was the ideal to which that nation was dedicated from its inception—this, long before

6. Hans Kohn, *American Nationalism: An Interpretive Essay* (New York: The Macmillan Co., 1957), pp. 15–19.

the institutional apparatus of the nation-state became central to the lives of its citizens.[7] In Potter's terms, the psychological component was more important than the sociological.

I

The pioneer scholar in the study of the centrality of the nation in the American mind is Paul Nagel, in *One Nation Indivisible: The Place of the Union in American Thought, 1776–1861* and *This Sacred Trust: American Nationality, 1798–1898*. Drawing on an array of "orations, sermons, hymns, newspapers, books, magazines, letters, and diaries," Nagel concludes that these sources "contain the seminal elements of an ideology, dominated as they are by the voice of reflective persons:

> A persisting pattern of national consciousness throughout the century indicates the public's willingness to heed its articulate brethren. . . . Because there is not much material available that was written by the ordinary person, the historian must learn much from what was offered to the silent community. The public advocates of nationality provided the lore needed in a self-conscious republic. Furthermore, the intellectual historian makes no guarantees about the viewpoint of the so-called average American. Such a concern need not trouble those seeking only the dynamics of a nation's intellect.[8]

Nagel separates strands of thought, covering certain periods over and over again, and, while the approach is a bit dizzying in its effect, the cumulative impact is considerable: there is little doubt that the mental abstraction, the image of the Union, was of enormous consequence in the shaping of an American consciousness and, more than *anything* else, made people into Americans. Above all, Americans were Stewards of a Sacred Trust in the Vineyard of the New World; through triumph and adversity, plagued with doubt and anxiety as well as blessed with a sunny optimism, they nourished their trust. America's public leaders lashed out like modern jeremiahs against "the hazards of mammon, passion, and partisanship."[9] Leading the reader through alternating

7. *Ibid.*, pp. 20–25.
8. Paul Nagel, *This Sacred Trust* (New York: Oxford University Press, 1971), pp. xv–xvi.
9. *Ibid.*, pp. xiii.

sections of "Affirmations" or "Doctrines" and "Anxieties," Nagel demonstrates that Americans believed the Union to be, by turns, unique, special, everlasting, absolute, a great experiment with a mission, a destiny, a spirit all its own, something with a glorious past (the Founding Fathers), security, and progress. In the course of the nineteenth century, Americans come to love their Union deeply and to place great faith in it as an abstraction of transcendent importance. Symbols—such as the popular chain image, the ship of state, and the heavenly solar system—emphasized the "intactness" of what they stood for.[10]

But what of the sectional antagonism that culminated in Civil War? Even this conflict, viewed from the perspective of a developing national consciousness, takes on a fresh aspect. Potter argues quite effectively that both Northerners and Southerners had *multiple* loyalties in the early and mid-nineteenth century

> and what distinguished them was that one, being in the majority, was able to keep all its loyalties co-ordinated, and therefore undivided, while the other, being in a minority, was not able to keep them co-ordinated, with the result that they did become divided. Multiple loyalties do not inherently produce conflict, and the question whether conflict will develop is entirely separate from the question whether loyalties are multiple. . . . The North's so-called "nationalism" consisted . . . partly in its control over federal policy, and in the ability to keep it in alignment with sectional interests, while the South's "sectionalism" was, at least initially, an expression of the lack of such a capacity. . . . If North and South fought; if one was a "nation" and one was not; if the people of one were "loyal" and those of the other were "disloyal"; or, on the other hand, if they constituted two diverse civilizations, then the investigator is under strong compulsion to reduce the complex forces of the 1850s to simplicity and to come up with antitheses which will fit those dualisms. Hence, we have had a series of sweeping and dramatic contrasts which present North and South in polar terms. . . These antitheses are in a sense caricature, perhaps accurate in singling out some distinctive feature, but grossly distorted in the emphasis which they give it.[11]

10. Nagel, *One Nation Indivisible* (New York: Oxford University Press, 1964), pp. 211–221.

11. Potter, *The South and Sectional Conflict*, pp. 68, 75–76, 72, 73.

Potter's own explanation of the conflict is a factor that caused

> bitter disagreement even among a people who have much basic
> homogeneity. No factor, I would suggest, will meet this need
> better than the feeling, widespread in the 1850s in the South,
> that the South's vital interests were being jeopardized, and that
> the region was being exposed to the dangers of a slave insur-
> rection, as a result of the hostility of antislavery men in the
> North. Applied to the sectional crisis, such a view of the sources
> of friction would make possible the explanation of the Civil
> War, without making impossible the explanation of the rapid
> return to union after the war. No cultural explanation will do
> this. . . . [The] American Civil War must be interpreted less in
> terms of antitheses and dissimilarities between North and
> South, and more in terms of the prolonged sequence of in-
> terest conflict which crystallized along sectional lines. . . . By fo-
> cussing upon conflict of interest as a basic factor it is possible to
> explain the otherwise stubborn anomaly that the sectional crisis
> grew in intensity even as the republic grew in homogeneity.[12]

The Civil War itself also displayed the paradoxical nature of a growing nationalism. At the very time when a conflict of interest forced
Southerners to divide their normally concurrent loyalties and give
pre-eminence to sectional identification, Northerners, under Lincoln's
leadership, fought to retain the Union that, under the crisis of secession and rebellion, became in their minds an Absolute, something that
had to be preserved at all costs. In the very act of dividing with their
Southern brethren, Northern Americans greatly strengthened their
identification with their most potent mental abstraction: the Union.[13]

The view put forth by Potter and Nagel runs the risk of resting on
overgeneralizations, however. Their insights must be tempered with
the reminder that nationalism and sectionalism did not affect *all*
Northerners and Southerners to the same extent and in the same way.
Even more important, nineteenth-century nationalism was, at least in
its symbolic manifestations, rather tenuous and groping. Nagel's few
symbols aside, Boorstin shows that neither a national flag nor an anthem were matters of common agreement until after the Civil War, the
flag becoming official in 1911 and the anthem in 1931. Until the Un-

12. *Ibid.*, pp. 78–79, 80, 81.
13. Nagel, *This Sacred Trust*, pp. 129–193.

iform National Holidays Act was passed in 1968, there were few official national holidays, each state generally compiling its own list. Even Independence Day was not regularly celebrated on July 4 until around 1830, though it became, in Boorstin's phrase, "a festival of national purpose" at which times Americans were reminded of the existence and purpose of their nation. Then, too, in their search for national heroes, Americans found George Washington, whose name, life, writing, and remains became the subject of mythology, liturgy, and iconography.[14]

But other notable individuals, such as Jefferson, Franklin, and Patrick Henry, became subjects of local patriotism long before they were objects of national adoration. In the realm of folk heroes, Davy Crockett was the first to be known outside of a region, but even he was primarily a *frontier* figure, though Boorstin plays down this identification. Not until the twentieth century, when such heroes became planned, artificial creations or fabrications of profit-seeking promoters utilizing the mass media, did a Paul Bunyan become known everywhere as a symbol of giantism and physical strength. By this time, what had been the natural product of the tall tale was the deliberate symbol of the national corporation or the syndicated cartoon. In short, in their search for symbols, to use another Boorstin phrase, Americans in the eighteenth and nineteenth centuries "were long confused and troubled by undertainty and by competition among local and partisan loyalties." Only Washington immediately became, as "Father of his Country," an accepted national symbol, and even he was the subject of sectional controversy in the 1830s.

Furthermore, even the important mental abstractions suggested by the term *Union*, even those symbols and images on which there *was* a large measure of agreement, found *expression* in the still largely village society of the nineteenth century. Orations and celebrations in *particular* communities allowed an essentially rural population to mark their membership in a national community whose existence took the form of ideals expressed at the birth of the nation.[15]

This belief in the superiority of the American Union was unquestionably widespread, as Nagel demonstrates, and ran deep into community life during the late eighteenth and nineteenth centuries. Ear-

14. Boorstin, *The Americans: The National Experience*, pp. 337–358.

15. Smith, *As a City Upon a Hill*, pp. 160–161; Atherton, *Main Street on the Middle Border*, pp. 193–196, 202–206, 214–216; Ralph Gabriel, *The Course of American Democratic Thought*, 2nd edition (New York: The Ronald Press Co., 1956) pp. 91–104.

lier, the Puritans founded towns and colonies dedicated to the proposition that, on an "errand into the wilderness," they would construct model religious communities for the English to emulate. In a sense, the Americans nationalized the Puritan concept of a model community, though how conscious spokesman for the Union were of the Puritan example is difficult to assess.

Page Smith goes one step further with this Puritan-American analogy and argues that the federal Constitution can be viewed as the covenant of the secondary or national community, the way the covenants of New England towns and their offspring were the covenants of the primary community and, as such, "took on the character of a holy writ."[16] Again, there is not much evidence to show whether the Founding Fathers, *as a group*, related what they were doing to what the town fathers of colonial New England had done. Still, Smith, by this simple stroke, turns the whole nation into a covenanted society. When one explains, as Nagel did, the ways in which the Union was conceptualized in the years after 1787, there is much to be said for this analogy.

There is also a problem: the Puritan covenant was an all-embracing agreement between a religiously oriented group of people and God, whereas there is good evidence to indicate that the Constitution was a strictly limited political agreement that left large areas of human conduct out of account. This is what Yehoshua Arieli argues in *Individualism and Nationalism in American Ideology*.[17] Arieli found that those who drew up the Constitution, those who thought about, wrote about, talked about the nature of politics or who acted as politicians agreed that the nation-state, after 1776, should have a government whose writ was explicitly defined, so that there could continue to be a "free society", wholly outside the realm of governmental activity. As if somehow anticipating modern writers on nationalism and the rise of sociology, American state-builders thus clearly separated government from "society," or, in other terms, the existence of a national group from its political apparatus. This separation was enunciated most effectively by the Jeffersonians, but it remained the basic assumption in the political-social thought of nineteenth-century Americans. Therefore, if the Constitution was a covenant, its main emphasis was to delineate particular areas in which government had a right to operate, leaving a much wider range free from governmental interference, so that the individual could flourish in a "free society." In this way, the erstwhile

16. Smith, *As a City Upon a Hill*, pp. 14–15.
17. (Cambridge, Mass.: Harvard University Press, 1964).

British colonists made their government a lot less than they themselves were: a new nationality-group in the late-eighteenth-century world.

What is most striking about the flurry of state-building of the 1770s and 1780s in what became the United States of America is the continuity manifested everywhere. The states generally maintained the function of government they exercised under the Articles of Confederation, and before that, as provinces within the British Empire. So too did the new national government carry on the same over-all powers granted to the original Congressional form of government in the 1780s, which in turn related to those areas in which the British government acted before independence. In other words, the constitution, as it related to the *operational* aspects of government, codified and froze the *types* of power exercised by government in the eighteenth-century context, altering the *levels* at which power was exercised in such a way that the national government replaced the old imperial British government, just as state governments replaced the old provincial governments. The only important changes were in the form of structure and not the substance of power. The new central government was situated in the territory over which it had jurisdiction, and not overseas; it was republican, not monarchical; and it was directly representative, not virtually. Even these shifts in structure did not hide the many marks of the British models. Since the King was "responsible" for the revolution, royalty was out; but both the elected president and the monarch were given responsibility for administering the laws, suggesting policy, carrying on foreign affairs, and commanding the armies. Both the House of Commons and the House of Representatives were directly representational. In both countries, the judiciary was independent and appointive. The common law of one was the common law of the other. The powers of the central government—whether British, before 1776, or American, thereafter—involved international relations, the maintenance of law and order within the nation's borders, and the protection, aid, and regulation of the national economy. This was what government was all about in the eighteenth-century world. And the Constitution, by maintaining the status quo, assured that state and local government would continue to play the same primary roles that they had assumed during the colonial period. Therefore, throughout the nineteenth century, what state governments did about economic and social problems was of more significance than what the national government did. This state of affairs did not change until the federative character of American society changed.

National powers respecting currency, import duties, funds for public improvements, the public lands, the territories, and interstate commerce led to countless debates and proposals between nationalist-minded Congressmen, presidents—even jurists—and their state-rights counterparts. The uneven, jerky character of national policy on banking, tariff, internal improvements, public lands, slavery in the territories, education, and the regulation of transportation and industry was no match in influence for the broader, deeper, steadier flow of activity invovling state governments. And certainly the legislation that Congress did enact during the nineteenth century did not amount to the national government's becoming the catalytic agent that transformed the weakly integrated republic into a cohesive nation economically, politically, and socially—which is what articulate nationalists such as Hamilton, the later Jefferson, Clay, and Marshall envisioned. The point that needs stressing is: Given the *nature* of American society in the nineteenth century, it would have been astounding if the fledgling national government *had* played that role.

The United States's position in the world also contributed to a relatively weak central authority. As C. Vann Woodward has shown, no other fast-growing nation-state of the modern world had to devote so little of its resources to its defense.[18] Protected by two oceans from old world powers; blessed with the "trade, not further empire" policy of Britain, the world's mightiest sea-power; fortunate in being able to remain apart from European rivalries and in having able diplomats at hand when European involvement was unavoidable, the United States, during its century of maturation, often had something approaching free security.

The character of our armed services reflected this diplomatic isolation. During the colonial period, a village society relied upon amateur citizen soldiers, or militia, for defense when communities were threatened by an outside foe. Since British tyranny was associated with the quartering of a professional army in peacetime, the founding fathers maintained the militia system in the Constitution, charging Congress with the responsibility for establishing rules and leaving with the states the task of organizing and supervising the units. Free security, a genuine fear of large standing armies as a threat to liberty, and localized Indian wars resulted in a regular army and navy that were skeleton forces in comparison to population and resources. Even

18. C. Vann Woodward, "The Age of Reinterpretation," *American Historical Review*, LXVI (1960), 1–19.

though both Union and Confederate governments resorted to the draft during the Civil War, the huge, still largely volunteer armies disbanded shortly after the war. When the state militia system was reconstituted as the national guard in the 1870s, the concern was over domestic strife accompanying industrialization, not over foreign wars.[19]

The decentralized, federated character of American society in the eighteenth and nineteenth centuries was also evident in the lack of strong central or national institutions outside of government. Both Boorstin, in his *The Americans: The Colonial Experience*, and Stanely Elkins, in *Slavery: A Problem in American Intellectual and Institutional Life* stress this point with appropriate comparisons to such "centralized" European countries as Britain and Spain. In colonial times, American seaports became regional cultural centers. Colleges were founded in many different places and established close relationships with their community. Those entering the professions were trained in the apprenticeship system, rather than in advanced educational centers, and became loosely organized amateurs. Army personnel were village-based nonprofessionals who cared only about defending home and hearth—and community.[20] These were colonies whose political power was dispersed through many towns and counties and assemblies, whose religious authority was severed from an overseas hierarchy and placed without plan in vestries or in the congregation itself. All this contrasted with a more structured and centrally organized British society.

Even after independence and the creation of a nation-state, the lack of unifying national institutions with power and authority ranging through the whole society—as was the case in Spain, for example—remained, in the opinion of historians such as Stanley Elkins, the most conspicuous feature of a young society. With the territory of the nation expanding sporadically by leaps and bounds, with the outer rim of the United States clouded by meandering Indian tribes, and with pervasive geographic ignorance, Americans viewed the physical shape of their domain as hazy, unfinished, and growing. This sense that theirs was an uncompleted society influenced even their language: "tall talk," the blurring of fact and fiction, was the verbal manifestation of a people unsure of the physical reality of their own land. Americans forged their

---

19. Hugh D. Graham and Ted R. Gurr, editors, *The History of Violence in America: Historical and Comparative Perspectives*, paperback edition (New York: Bantam Books, Inc., 1969), pp. 56–57.

20. Boorstin, *The Americans: The Colonial Experience*, pp. 169–265, 291–316, 345–372.

own brand of English as a common language, mixing words from the languages of the non-English-speaking immigrants with verbal creations based up on new kinds of experiences. It was not, however, until the efforts of Walt Whitman in the 1850s and thereafter that a sustained attempt was made to convey in fictive terms what it meant to be an American; and even Whitman's faith in the future of the Union faltered in the years after the Civil War. There were no comparable efforts in the other arts—painting, sculpture, music, architecture, and so on—involving other ways of communicating. In short, Americans spoke and wrote a single language, which they on certain occasions put to nationalistic uses in orations and writings, but they conspicuously lacked a truly unifying culture, something ignored by Elkins and Potter and others in their concentration on institutions and interests.[21]

The nationwide presence of Christianity, capitalism, and representative-republican government in postrevolutionary America must not be allowed to obscure the fact that these religious, economic, and political forms were anything but uniform and centralized. As Elkins has noted, the absence of a state church, a strong central government, a large professional army, and organized or centralized professions[22] revealed a young society characterized by looseness, variety, and, above all, decentralization.

Protestant sects were so numerous that none could come anywhere near the favored position of the Catholic and certain Protestant sects in European countries. *And yet*, the importance of Christianity as a religious faith was everywhere apparent. Political power was divided into hundreds and thousands of units scattered through countless miles of territory. And those who became national politicians typically had short careers in the village that was the nation's capital, spending far greater amounts of time in state and local politics because that was where the more important exercise of political power occurred. *And yet*, representative-republican government as a form was supported everywhere as the only political system fit for American citizens. Capitalistic enterprise was divided into hundreds of plantations, dozens of mercantile houses, countless farms, mills, craft-shops, and even a few factories for the production of basic commodities such as cloth—all competitive, all local—or regional—in their scope of operation

21. Boorstin, *The Americans: The National Experience*, pp. 221–241, 264–274, 277–324, 307–324.

22. Stanley Elkins, *Slavery: A Problem in American Intellectual and Institutional Life* (Chicago: University of Chicago Press, 1959), pp. 28–32.

within the United States. *And yet*, capitalism, private enterprise, was defended everywhere as the proper mode of production.[23]

In such a decentralized society, it is hardly surprising that there is little evidence of the growth of nationwide social classes that would satisfy any rigorous, modern definition of that term.[24] Only the "seaboard aristocracy" of the late colonial and early national periods and, later, the Southern planters of the antebellum period come close.[25] It is precisely because of the ease with which men of wealth and talent could attain prominence in the style of Boorstin's "amateur gentleman" that these groups emerged in a setting where the avenues to wealth were restricted to commerce in a few Atlantic ports or on plantations, confined either to the tidewater or, later, to the "black belts." As the population grew and spread after the revolution, the avenues to wealth became more numerous and the places where the prominent could live too scattered for a cohesive aristocracy or governing class to form.[26] Outside of the plantation South, prominence in one activity did not typically spill over into others as it did in the time of Washington and Jefferson.

It would, of course, be ludicrous to present farmers as a class, comprising as they did the great majority of the population.[27] But it is also

23. Eugene Genovese argues effectively in *The Political Economy of Slavery: Studies in the Economy and Society of the Slave South*, paperback edition, (New York: Pantheon Books, 1967), that, in spite of many capitalist features, the plantation was not, if defined in terms of the planters' goals and pattern of life, a truly capitalist entity.

24. For a discussion of the definitions social scientists have given to the concept of class, see David L. Sills, editor, *International Encyclopedia of the Social Sciences*, 17 vols. (New York: The Macmillan Co. & The Free Press, 1968), XV, 296–325.

25. On the planters as a class, see Eugene Genovese, "Marxian Interpretations of the Slave South," in Barton J. Bernstein, editor, *Towards a New Past: Dissenting Essays in American History* (New York: Pantheon Books 1968), pp. 90–125.

26. Douglas T. Miller, *Jacksonian Aristocracy: Class and Democracy in New York, 1830–1860* (New York: Oxford University Press, 1967), p. 61: "New York's upper classes did not form a unified estate. There were various coteries of aristocratic persons. In the cities the best society was commercially centered, but also included professional persons such as eminent doctors, lawyers, literary figures, ministers, and professors. Even the fronter communities of western New York had their own local aristocracies composed of large landholders, merchants and industrialists, and lawyer-politicians." For a discussion of the common attributes of the antebellum *urban* upper class—at least in New York, Brooklyn, Boston, & Philadelphia—see Edward Pessen's *Riches, Class, and Power Before the Civil War* (Lexington, Mass.: D. C. Heath & Co., 1973).

27. Clarence H. Damhoff, *Change in Agriculture: The Northern United States, 1820–1870* (Cambridge, Mass.: Harvard University Press, 1969), discusses how technological changes forced farmers to become commercial in their orientation, to ask to an increas-

ridiculous to argue that laborers, whether craftsmen or factory operatives, had the cohesiveness, organization, self-consciousness, and identity of outlook required of a class. The feeble efforts of workingmen to
form unions and even parties were short-lived and never included very
many groups of craftsmen or, in the case of political movements, never
involved more than a few states.[28] The evidence that some laborers in
some places sought to act together to further their interests should not
be ignored; neither should the Workingman's Party's broad reforms,
which were of benefit to many groups other than strictly laborers, nor
the geographic and occupational limitations of the labor movement before the late nineteenth century.

Even the Negroes, the one group in the society set off in a separate
racial caste, did not behave as a class, oppressed as they were. The
slaves, of course, were quite restricted in their movements and were
largely ignorant of the geography and society that lay beyond a rather
small radius of thier owner's home or shop. Free Negroes in the Northern states were a small, scattered percentage of the population, and
their efforts to adopt common positions and goals at Negro conven-
tions held in various places were only partially successful.[29]

The only truly cohesive groups, outside the aristocrats already referred to, were the poor or Catholic and largely Irish immigrants of the
1840s and 1850s who congregated in the Eastern coastal cities. Not
surprisingly, they tended to vote as a group and were wooed by politicians as a group.[30] But the immigrants are the exception that points up
the rule: in nineteenth-century America, groups were located in par-

ing extent, "Does it pay?" Damhoff divides farmers, not into classes, but into "innovators," "imitators," "gradualists," and "traditionalists," to indicate their varied responses to the commercial orientation that mechanized production made possible. Earl
W. Hayter, *The Troubled Farmer, 1850–1900: Rural Adjustment to Industrialism* (De Kalb,
Ill., Northern Illinois University Press, 1968), discusses the difficulties farmers had ad-
justing their values and beliefs to the new patterns of agricultural life produced by technological innovations.

28. Walter Hugins, *Jacksonian Democracy and the Working Class: A Study of the New York
Workingman's Movement, 1829–1837* (Stanford, Calif.: Stanford University Press, 1960);
Edward Pessen, *Most Uncommon Jacksonians: The Radical Leaders of the Early Labor
Movement* (Albany, N.Y.: State University of New York Press, 1967). Pessen admits (p.
200) that many workers were not active in the labor movement of the 1830s. Local chapters of the trade unions of this period were quite numerous and far more durable than
the sporadic efforts to create national organizations (pp. 34–51).

29. Leon F. Litwak, *North of Slavery: The Negro in the Free States, 1790–1860* (Chicago:
University of Chicago Press, 1961), pp. 214–246.

30. Benson, *The Concept of Jacksonian Democracy*, pp. 165–207.

ticular communities and areas, conspicuously lacking a national identity. Only "Americans" had that.

In short, even though the young American nation—before the late nineteenth century—had religious-economic-political forms that were everywhere present, these forms were noticeably without cohesion and centralization. They were not organized on a national basis, even though they appeared, repetitively, in communities all over the nation.

II

The emergence of the mass "nationalized" society we know is the result of the complex interplay of many factors, but none are of greater significance than the revolutionary developments in communications and transportation that occurred, particularly from the mid-nineteenth century onwards.

The role of communications highlights the growing centralization of American life at the same time that communications made significant contributions to that centralization. The earlier form of communication over distance for Americans was the postal service, which, ironically, was under the supervision of, first, the British government and then the new national government, which was empowered to establish post offices and post roads. This power was used to good effect. Government-built post offices became public "communications" centers and government-built post roads became the first public transportation system. Indeed, communication by letter long retained its communal character: people were discouraged from having their mail delivered at home because they had to pay for such a service until the Civil War, after which there was free delivery in places of more than 10,000 population. Not until the turn of the century did rural free delivery become firmly established. Only in the twentieth century, then, has written communication been largely stripped of its public setting. Postmasters were often "publick printers" (printers of government documents) as well and, under the Jacksonians, became local party chieftains as political appointees.

Letter-writing became the means by which people in hundreds of villages new about what was happening elsewhere and led directly to the formation of journals or "newspapers" whose news was letters from paid or unpaid correspondents. Daily newspapers developed in various towns and cities. The wholly partisan party or political press that followed the lead of Washington journals and the commercial press featuring news of economic activity were the two most important kinds of newspapers that evolved after Independence. By the 1840s, the earliest mass or "penny" press appeared in major cities and relied on an association of regular reporters who concentrated upon important news items. As this kind of city newspaper grew during the remainder of the century, the country press flourished, as well, featuring news of the daily lives of those who lived in and around small towns, the kind of news that the mass press of the city largely ignored.[31]

In the meantime, the telegraph, in the 1840s, and the telephone, after the turn of the century, greatly increased the speed with which people could communicate on a personal basis. On the public level, magazines first nationalized communications; then came radio, in the 1920s, television, in the 1950s, bursting the regional limitations of the mass-circulation newspapers. In all—the telegraph, the telephone, magazines, newspapers, radio, and television—large corporations quickly dominated the field, organized in the manner of corporations in other sectors of American life. Only radio, and later, television were subjected to direct public regulation, by a Federal Communications Commission, though all could be prosecuted under the antitrust acts.

In terms of communications, what resulted was not a "global" but a "national village." All Americans can see and hear the news together each day. The very definition of news in newspaper and television journalism has broadened in this century to include the full range of social and cultural as well as political and economic development of both a long- and short-term character. The daily lives of people still receive the attention of the country press and radio-television stations in smaller communities. But the proportion of the population living in such areas has dramatically declined over the last century.

The enormously significant role that home-delivered mail, radio, and television have played in the nationalization of communications is obvious; but what is not so evident is the shifting character of the individual's relationship to these new means of communicating. The American was no longer a member of a "live" group with whom he could register his opinions or his response. He was now in a passive position, at the receiving end of a one-way process of communication, and ordinarily only those who shared his home were aware of his views. In

31. Bernard A. Weisberger, *The American Newspaperman* (Chicago: University of Chicago Press, 1962); Daniel J. Boorstin, *The Americans: The Democratic Experience*, pp. 130–132.

the very act of becoming instantaneous and universal, communication had created a "new segregation."[32]

Historians have long agreed that the railroad provided what its predecessors—wagons by land, boats over canals and natural waterways—lacked: the first all-weather, truly national transportation system. As the railroads spread across the nation from the 1830s to the end of the century, they displayed phases of all-out competition followed by consolidation that were to mark all major industrial activity of the post-Civil War decades. The first nationwide industry, railroads were, not surprisingly, the first sector of the economy to be regulated by the national government, with the passage, in 1887, of the Interstate Commerce Act, which was sporadically but progressively strengthened in the next three decades or so. The railroads conquered space as nothing had before, but they did more than that: in what Boorstin calls a "democracy of haste," they did away with social distinctions in travel and placed their emphasis on speed.[33] Given large land grants to thrust across the unsettled plains and mountains beyond the Mississippi, they actually hastened settlement through colonization schemes that resulted in the creation of trackside communities. In more settled areas, towns and would-be cities openly competed for track, the location of which often determined a community's over-all pattern of growth or decline, and, in any case, made possible fast and easy travel between neighboring places.[34] The railroad, in short, provided the means whereby people and goods could travel anywhere in the United States at any time.

After World War I, the motor vehicle continued the trend, shifting the mode of travel from public to private conveyances, further integrating the flow between city and town, and both with country, and greatly expanding trading centers. Ford, General Motors, Chrysler, and other large corporations consolidated production as had their railroad predecessors. National governmental aid took the form that state governments had granted turnpike corporations in the late eighteenth and nineteenth centuries: the expenditure of public funds for the construction of highways. The private motor vehicle became a popular means of transportation in the United States in the 1920s, considerably

32. On radio and television, see Eric Barnouw, *The Image Empire: A History of Broadcasting in the United States*, 3 vols. (New York: Oxford University Press, 1966–1970); Boorstin, *The Americans: The Democratic Experience*, pp. 390–395, 154–155, 132–133, 472.

33. Boorstin, *The Americans: The National Experience*, pp. 107–112.

34. John Stover, *American Railroads* (Chicago: University of Chicago Press, 1961).

earlier than it did in Europe. An already mobile U.S. population thereby gained a means of movement that was both private and unrestricted by public schedules or fixed routes, as streetcars had been and as subways are. And yet, even though the automobile provided a convenient means of moving freely about for vast numbers of people, the effect was to isolate all those who spent increasing amounts of time along highways insulated from the landscape, pedestrians, and communities. The more Americans traveled in these new private vehicles, the more they travelled alone.[35] Since World War II, bus corporations have made the highways "public," and trucking firms compete with trains as freight-carriers of the nation.

With the development of commercial airlines—again, since World War II—time and space have shrunk dramatically for an ever-increasing element of the population. Airline corporations are big and consolidated. National governmental aid has taken the form of airport construction—the plane's "highway"—while flight corridors criss-crossing over the continent-nation are, in a sense, the latest version of travel routes that began with postroads and continued in the form of canals, tracks, and highways.

From the beginning, then, Americans sought to overcome the handicaps of space through an ever faster, more convenient and flexible mode of transportation. In this search they have always been aided by their governments, as politicians invested whatever means were available with a *public* definition, and thus financial assistance, even though private corporations actually built the roads and canals and tracks, the wagons and boats, trains, cars, and planes. Thus have public and private remained blurred in a basic area of *national* life, just as the businessman in his booster city, or state governments in their aid to the economy, ran together what was public and what was private in the nineteenth century.

* * * * *

Economic change was also crucial. The nationalization of the American economy, so that a given commodity could be produced, distributed, and consumed all over the nation by one corporation was the work of many individuals, groups, and institutions. Of particular significance are state governments and their aid to transportation and

35. John Rae, *The American Automobile* (Chicago: University of Chicago Press, 1965); Boorstin, *The Americans: The Democratic Experience*, p. 270.

banking, as well as the great entrepreneurs like Rockefeller, Carnegie, and Morgan, who managed corporations in such a way as to make them sound and efficient. The financial and distributive activities of these economic empires were usually located in cities, but they involved areas beyond and between cities, as well. It is somewhat simplistic, therefore, to argue, as Smith does, that the nationwide corporation is a product of the city.

The process of consolidation and centralization that transformed, first, railroads, then "basic" industries such as oil and steel, spread rapidly after the turn of the nineteenth century. By the 1920s, increasing numbers of both raw material and consumer industries were affected, to the point that modern American industries generally assumed the form that they have retained ever since: each is dominated by an oligarchy of big corporations, though many still have a lot of small businesses, as well. After World War II, the corporate farm and the food-processing industry became the corresponding signs of bigness in agriculture. And corporate enterprise generally became more complicated, with the appearance of the multiproduct financial conglomerate.

This hierarchical structure has remained remarkably stable, even with the "trust-busting" efforts of Theodore Roosevelt, Taft, and Wilson, and Franklin Roosevelt's abolition of holding companies in the utilities industry. The only legislative source that the national government has ever had for its actions is the Anti-Trust Act of 1890, strengthened by the Wilson Administration in 1916, its aim being to prevent monopoly and promote competition but *not* to dismantle oligarchies or undo bigness.

The fact is that bigness came to corporate industry because the nationalization of transportation and communications and the mechanization of industrial processes created economic conditions favorable to the creation of nationwide organizations, in terms of both production and distribution. Those industrialists who became famous, rich, and the most successful entrepreneurs realized this and knew how to act accordingly.[36]

After the turn of the century, as Boorstin points out, the scientific management movement was an attempt at "packaging the unit of work," at making assembly-line production efficient and regular. By the 1920s, "flow technology" led to the introduction of the annual

---

36. Boorstin, *The Americans: The Democratic Experience*, pp. 49–52. John D. Rockefeller is a good example.

model in industry after industry—that is, to the creation of continuous demand through the displacement of objects that were still usable. After World War II, quality control, or "making things no better than they need to be" increasingly influenced the production plans of American industries. And throughout the century, "invention factories," beginning with Edison's and continuing with research and development units, devoted technological research to what would be marketable.[37] In all these ways, production came to be fitted to a national mass market.

In the meantime, corresponding ways of "nationalizing" distribution and consumption occurred. The department store ("the Consumer's Palace"), the five-and-ten-cent store ("the Consumer's Bazaar"), and mail-order firms all replaced or challenged older general or other local stores and displayed items at fixed prices. Chainstores standardized distribution everywhere, and, through the introduction of self-service, even did away with the need for salesmen. The franchised local outlet linked up a person with little capital and experience to large-scale capital, productive facilities, experimentation, advertizing, and reputation.[38]

The result of such activity was the creation of a vast consumer-public, comprised of individuals whose decision to buy or not to buy in service-less supermarkets was, paradoxically, far more private than it had ever been in the old general store—much like the apartness of individuals in the new world of electronic communications.[39]

The growth of corporate enterprise in consumer industries has, in turn, led to the development of an institution that David Potter portrayed as having vast and increasing social, ethical, and economic importance: advertising, itself a national industry, appealing, Boorstin adds, to groups of buyers, in a public, general way, in contrast to salesmen, who related to individuals in a private and personal manner.[40] Not only do advertising firms try to persuade the American consumer to buy one brand or another of essentially the *same* product, but, more significantly, advertising in newspapers, magazines, radio, and television actually creates *values* for the consuming American by telling him or her what is desirable or even necessary if one is to live the good life. And yet, as persuasive as this agency of our capitalistic, corporate

37. *Ibid.*, pp. 361–370, 546–555, 193–200, 527–546.
38. *Ibid.*, pp. 101–129, 429.
39. *Ibid.*, pp. 119, 444.
40. *Ibid.*, p. 145.

economy is, it operates under regulations so vague and loosely enforced that it is largely unaccountable, even though it performs some
of the same functions that the churches and schools used to perform.[41]
But Potter ignores another aspect of advertising that Boorstin rightly
emphasizes: the development of market research, scientific efforts to
determine what consumers themselves want.[42]

The rapid development in the size and scope of corporate enterprise after the Civil War, along with the increasing occupational
specialization concommitant with industrialization, created a social
order with much greater extremes of wealth and poverty than ever before, and spurred the growth of increasingly self-conscious socio-
economic groupings in the population on a scale that had never existed
before.

* * * * *

The new industrialists formed an upper class with a cohesiveness
that stands comparison with the antebellum planters and the colonial
merchants and planters. With wealth conspicuously displayed the new
aristocrats became social models for millions who viewed them as the
most successful Americans. Clustered in mansions grouped in various
cities, where they formed exclusive associations such as New York's
"400," the new rich lacked the physical cohesion of a true European
aristocracy, as did their planter and merchant predecessors; but,
through the vehicle of the national corporation, their actions had a far
greater impact than those of the smaller-scaled, regional mercantile
and agricultural enterprises of the eighteenth and earlier nineteenth
centuries. In this sense, our most recent, easily identifiable upper class
has been, appropriately enough, the most nationalistic.

E. Digby Baltzell, in *Philadelphia Gentlemen: The Making of a National
Upper Class*, broadens the definition of "upper class," calling it an
"American business aristocracy" and providing an analysis of the very
rich late-nineteenth-century families in the eastern seaboard cities
(Boston, New York, and Philadelphia) who "supported various exclusive institutions which produced, in the course of the twentieth century, a national, upper class way of life." He concludes:

41. David M. Potter, *People of Plenty: Economic Abundance and the American Character*
(Chicago, University of Chicago Press, 1954), pp. 166–188.
42. Boorstin, *The Americans: The Democratic Experience*, pp. 148–155.

[While] there are many middle and lower classes in America, there exists one metropolitan upper class with a common cultural tradition, consciousness of kind, and "we" feeling of solidarity which tends to be national in scope. The origin and development of this inter-city moneyed aristocracy in America quite naturally paralleled the rise of rapid communitications and the national corporate enterprise.[43]

In the decades following the Civil War, farmers and laborers organized broad social organizations whose purpose was, in part, that of any club: to provide a communal setting for people with common interests. In this, they were acting out the impulse to "associate" that foreign observers such as Tocqueville noticed as early as the 1830s. Even the trappings of secrecy and ritual that characterized so many of these associations marked the farmer and labor societies of the postwar period. The farmers' Granges, Farmers' Alliances, and the laborers' Knights of Labor[44] were—significantly—organized on a *local* level, with innumerable chapters founded in villages and cities all over the country and on regional and national levels, as well. Though "federal" in their structure, their local chapters were the most important units.

But the Granges, Farmers' Alliances, and Knights of Labor became something more than clubs. In a period of social and economic strain and dislocation, when industrialization and the mechanization and commercialization of agriculture brought about important changes in the way goods were produced and traded, insecure farmers and craftsmen used these organizations as a means to advocate reforms, such as equal pay for both sexes, the eight-hour day, the abolition of child and prison labor, the abolition of national banks, a substantial increase in the money supply, free coinage of silver, the reduction of tariff rates, public regulation of railroad and telegraph companies. In this way, organized farmers and laborers hoped to exert pressure on governments to provide a measure of regulation over the new large-scale industrial enterprise that seemed to undercut competition, con-

43. E. Digby Baltzell, in *Philadelphia Gentlemen: The Making of a National Upper Class* (Glencoe, Ill.: Free Press, 1958), pp. v, 389.

44. The shift from broad "reform unionism" to narrow "trade unionism" is analyzed by Gerald N. Grob in *Workers and Utopia: A Study of Ideological Conflict in the American Labor Movement, 1865–1900* (Evanston, Ill., Northwestern University Press, 1961). Corresponding shifts within the farmers' movements are traced, at least in the South, in Theodore Saloutous, *Farmer Movements in the South, 1865–1933* (Berkeley and Los Angeles: University of California Press, 1960).

trol wages, hours, prices, and the cost of moving goods for large numbers of small producers like themselves.

But the Grangers and the Knights went even beyond reforming the burgeoning capitalist system: they also harked back to the principles of co-operation and harmony that underlay the efforts of the communitarian reformers—the Owenites, the Brooks Farm transcendentalists, the Mormons, the Shakers, and the original proprietors of the New England towns—by advocating "co-operatives" for the buying and selling of goods. Of course, theirs were not to be in any sense spiritual communities, but communities frankly materialistic in aim, with the creation of produce "co-ops" located here and there around the country. At the very time, therefore, that farmers and laborers organized and groped their way toward *national* proposals for reform of the capitalist system that surrounded them, they also tried to set up *local* co-operatives not at all capitalistic in form. This duality of effort marked the path toward nationalization that farmers and laborers followed in the late nineteenth century and points out the remarkably tenacious appeal of co-operative, purposeful community life in the aspirations of Americans, even though the efforts to form durable co-operatives were generally no more successful than those of the secular utopian communities of the early nineteenth century.

The failure of the co-operatives accompanied stronger efforts at reform that led farmers in the more commercialized staple-crop areas of the Plains and the South to turn to politics and to a third party with proposals for reform of an economic order and a political system thought to be increasingly under the control of industrial plutocrats. When the Populists were absorbed by Bryan's Democratic Party and their general reforms were taken over by the broader Progressive reform movement after 1900, farmers again turned to nonpolitical associations, but ones more centrally organized—the National Farmer's Union (1902) and the American Farm Bureau Federation (1919)—and their concerns became much narrower. A "farm bloc" tried to devise acceptable schemes that would provide, for farmers, the same kind of aid that industrial corporations had secured for long periods ever since the 1790s. When the New Deal provided such aid in the form of government-regulated acreage and marketing procedures, the farmers lapsed back into conservatism of the pre-1870s period, having at last established the "parity" with industry that had so long eluded them—along with industry's hierarchical, oligarchical structure, it should be added.

Laborers, by contrast, took quite another course. During the 1880s, the difficulty of holding together craftsmen and drifting, ever-changing groups of unskilled workers, ever replenished through large-scale immigration, became apparent. In that decade, the American Federation of Labor (1881) gathered together under one centralized national organization many of the craft unions that had developed over the last fifty years. Its effective president, Samuel Gompers, concentrated on limited goals—shorter hours, higher wages, better working conditions—that quickly became the "holy trinity" of the organized labor movement. Deliberately avoiding the unskilled segment of the work force, the AFL thus—like farmers after 1900—narrowed the concerns of labor. Instead of reforming either the political or the economic system, the AFL chose to work within it, obtaining a better place for the skilled worker within the new industrial order. Nevertheless, corporations were hostile toward the organized labor movement and formed company unions, supported the issuance of court injunctions during strikes and boycotts, hired replacements and their own detectives, and pressed for "yellow dog" (prior agreement not to join a union) contracts with individual workers. Not until the New Deal of the 1930s was collective bargaining between organized unions and management guaranteed by government.

In the meantime, the efforts of the International Workers of the World to organize unskilled workers in the "One Big Union" movement during the World I years failed. William Haywood's attempt to unite all workers in a revolution to wrest power from existing governments and place it all in the hands of a labor council had little impact on a labor force either already organized or still too shifting, replaceable, and lacking in cohesion to be the foundation of a revolutionary movement. Not until the 1930s was the Congress of Industrial Organizations successful in organizing unskilled factory operatives. By that time, immigration and population growth had declined enormously; the lack of economic opportunity riveted factory workers in place; and a friendly Roosevelt Administration guaranteed collective bargaining. By 1955, the AFL and the CIO joined. For the first time in American history, unskilled and skilled laborers were in national unions under the leadership of one national council.

* * * * *

One measure of the nationalization of various groups in American society is the point at which a national organization was formed. The apogee of such activity is clearly from the Civil War to the Great Depression, but it has continued since that time and was somewhat in evidence before the 1860s. As for business, the American Banker's Association was formed in 1875, the National Association of Manufacturers in 1895, the national Chamber of Commerce in 1912, the American Association of Advertising Agencies in 1917, and the United States Junior Chamber of Commerce in 1920. Among professional groups, lawyers formed the American Bar Association in 1878; doctors, the National Medical Association in 1895; teachers or school administrators, the National Education Association in 1909, and the American Federation of Teachers in 1916; professors or university administrators, the National Association of Universities and Land Grant colleges in 1887, the Association of American Universities in 1900—and hardly a year went by from the 1880s to World War I without some academic discipline forming its own national organization. Clergymen formed the National Conference of Christians and Jews in 1928; scientists, the American Association for the Advancement of Science in 1848 and the National Academy of Sciences in 1863; artists, the American Academy of Arts and Letters in 1904, the American Federation of the Arts in 1909, the American Federation of Musicians in 1896, the American Association of Museums in 1906, Allied Artists of America in 1914, the Society of American Graphic Artists in 1914, the Actors Equity Association in 1914, the American Academy of Motion Picture Arts and Sciences in 1927, and the National Academy of Television Arts and Sciences in 1946.

This was also the spawning period of middle-class social and "service" clubs: the Elks (1868), the Eagles (1898), the Rotary (1905), and the Kiwanis (1915). Those from "old" families banded together in the Sons of the American Revolution in 1889, the Daughters of the American Revolution in 1890, the General Society of Mayflower Descendants in 1897, and the National Genealogical Society in 1903. Nativists founded the American Protective Association in 1887. Reformers were active from the 1830s onward: the American Anti-Slavery Society was formed in 1833, the American Temperance Union about the same year, and the American Peace Society, even earlier, in 1828, with the League of Universal Brotherhood, another peace organization, coming later, in 1846. After the Civil War, the Universal Peace Union (1866) kept alive the pacifist movement, while the interests of women were defended by the American as well as the National Woman Suffrage Association (both in 1869), the General Federation of Woman's Clubs (1890), and the League of Women Voters (1920), just as the Woman's Christian Temperance Union (1874) and the Anti-Saloon

League (1896) worked for prohibition.

For minorities, reform-minded whites formed the Indian Rights Association in 1882, the National Association for the Advancement of Colored People in 1909, the National Urban League in 1910, and for the poor, the National Conference on Social Welfare in 1874.[45]

The creation of such national organizations meant that groups located in communities all over the United States felt that they had common interests that ought to be protected or advanced everywhere and altogether, something made possible by developments in transportation and communication. It would be too strong to equate this activity with the rise of "social classes": the fact that farmers and laborers and businessmen and more specific groups in the middle classes founded nationwide associations does not mean that they suddenly transformed themselves into full-blown classes, with the requisite sharing of outlook, ease of identification by others, and common patterns of life. There was simply too much fuzziness around the edges, too much mobility from one group to another, and too little evidence that farmers and laborers consistently acted and thought *simply* as farmers and laborers. Only the colonial seaboard aristocracy, the antebellum Southern planters, the late-nineteenth-century industrial entrepreneurs, the poor Catholic and Jewish immigrants who bunched together in urban ghettos from the 1840s to the 1920s, and the poor blacks who have followed them into the ghettos since 1900—in other words, only the highest and lowest groups in our social order have had the cohesion necessary for a true "social class." In short, it has mattered a great deal in social terms if you are either rich and prominent or poor and ethnic.

The broad middle class with which most modern Americans generally identify is in a sense a refutation of class. But even within this framework, the sorting-out process that Warner found as cities became metropolises with suburbs has led to the *physical* separation of people in urban America, largely on the basis of income. As more and more Americans live in bigger and bigger urban areas, groups based on income gradations and physically separated into distinct neighborhoods or suburbs have become a prominent feature of the social structure. This would seem to indicate a movement toward a class-conscious society, especially as blacks, with the badge of color, replace older, poor, white, ethnic groups in the cities. Although blacks retain the cohesion of the poor white immigrants who preceded them, however, the mid-

45. *The 1973 World Almanac and Book of Facts*, paperback edition (New York: Newspaper Enterprise Association, 1972), pp. 254–269.

dle classes who surround them still do not *act* like a class: they are still "loose," vaguely defined, and mobile. Skilled laborers do not differ in fundamental ways from the clerical, managerial, and professional people who live near them.

This over-all lack of class-consciousness in most Americans, their continued faith in a liberal-capitalist society since the late nineteenth century, has meant what historians have long claimed: that those who have wanted to change the economic system—the Socialists and the Communists—or those who have wanted to change both the political and economic systems—the Communists—have not generally been very popular.

* * * * *

Around 1900, the so-called Progressive reformers, representing the unorganized middle class, arose to formulate, through their first leader, Theodore Roosevelt, a fundamentally new conception of the role of the existing national government in American society. Theodore Roosevelt is a pivotal figure in our history because he was the first president to argue that the *national* government must act as the regulator in a society that was rapidly becoming nationalized for the first time. Organized labor, agriculture, and business had become huge, nationwide interest groups. Government had to use power in the way that Hamilton and Clay envisioned: no longer to foster the nationalization of American life, for that had already occurred under different auspices, but to protect and to regulate those national interests and to correct the imbalances that had accrued from the rush toward monopoly during the late nineteenth century when the business sector had become too powerful for the other sectors. All groups must organize and protect their interests, while government acted as impartial mediator amongst them.[46] Whether Progressive reform be interpreted as having been basically and significantly split between those whose emphasis was on the restoration of competition (like the early Wilson) and those who favored bigness and sought the power to control it (like Roosevelt)—whether regarded as a movement to restore the economic imbalance created by industrialization, as an effort at making business more democratic, or just more efficient—however the Progressives are viewed, what is unquestionable is their having constituted the first

46. John M. Blum, *The Republican Roosevelt* (Cambridge, Mass.: Harvard University Press, 1954).

like-minded group of political reformers to *recognize* the essentially changed character of American society after the turn of the nineteenth century.[47]

And though they did not use governmental power broadly to deal with that change, they set the precedents that were developed in the 1930s by the New Dealers, who were able to act in ways appropriate to the new setting because of the economic crisis of that decade. Whatever else the New Deal amounted to—whether it be regarded as the savior of American capitalism through the introduction of the welfare state or as a conservative movement that missed a unique opportunity to undertake thoroughgoing reform[48]—it unquestionably represented the first sustained effort on the part of our national government to govern the *national* community in ways comparable to those that state and local governments had developed in connection with *their* communities. Welfare, health, job security, housing, and, through later extensions in the 1960s, education, culture, the environment—all became matters with which the national government has become directly involved through aid and regulation. As a result, political activity expanded into more and more of that area Arieli calls "free society," that is, the range of human activity that the framers of the Constitution left outside the competence of government in 1787.

* * * * *

This change was reflected in foreign affairs, as well. Theodore Roosevelt was also the first of our leaders to recognize that the United States was a world power and that its government had to *act* as if it were. This meant having strong armed forces, territories abroad, security in our "sphere of influence," maintenance of the balance of power in the Eurasian land mass (though of course no one "balanced" the Ameri-

47. Arthur S. Link, *Woodrow Wilson and the Progressive Movement, 1910–1917* (New York: Harper Brothers, Publishers, 1954); Samuel P. Hays, *Conservatism and the Gospel of Efficiency: The Progressive Conservation Movement, 1890–1920* (Cambridge, Mass.: Harvard University Press, 1959); Robert H. Wiebe, *Businessmen and Reform: A Study of the Progressive Movement* (Cambridge, Mass.: Harvard University Press, 1962); Gabriel Kolko, *The Triumph of Conservatism: A Reinterpretation of American History, 1900–1916* (Glencoe, Ill.: Free Press, 1963).

48. Arthur Schlesinger, Jr., *The Age of Roosevelt*, 3 vols. (Boston: Houghton, Mifflin Co., 1957–1960); Barton J. Bernstein, "The New Deal: The Conservative Achievements of Liberal Reform" in *Towards a New Past: Dissenting Essays in American History*, edited by Barton J. Bernstein (New York: Pantheon Books, 1968), pp. 263–288.

cans in the western hemisphere), the protection of American economic, religious, and cultural interests abroad, and the maintenance of peace and order in the world. The popularity of the older position of isolation and neutrality died out only slowly, as a cursory glance at the events from 1914 to 1945 shows: American sentiment shifted from disarmament, pacifism, and isolation to war again. Indeed, the struggle between the "old" and the "new" views was evident through the first four decades of this century, and only with World War II did isolation and neutrality cease to be an alternative, something underscored by the bipartisan posture of our major parties since that time. Only in the case of the war in Southeast Asia from 1965 to 1973 was there any serious questioning of the internationalist position, or any serious threat to bipartisanship.

During this period, the movement toward internationalism in foreign affairs found sporadic expression in the collective security apparatus of the League of Nations and the United Nations. Another manifestation of this impulse was financial and technical aid to less-developed nations, whether through the United Nations or directly by the United States government. Boorstin calls the foreign aid programs devised after World War II a secular, geographically broader version of earlier American Christian missionary efforts in various parts of the world. Both were stimulated by a faith in the universal applicability of the American "way of life"—that is, that recipient peoples would and should become increasingly like Americans. This was, in short, "do-goodism" on an international scale: "missionary diplomacy."[49]

This basic shift in our international position was, once again, reflected in the changing character of our armed forces. The development of a substantial regular army and navy dates from the early years of the century, and its growth was determined by the relative strength of the internationalist and isolationist positions. But though the government resorted to a draft in both world wars and has retained the draft since that time, the essential character of the American army has not changed: the average soldier is still the amateur, citizen, short-term soldier, though he has in this century been in units *not* organized according to locality or state. But he still needs something to fight *for*. Our government has therefore turned our wars into moral crusades to attract popular support and to fill army quotas.[50] In World War I, World

49. Boorstin, *The Americans: The Democratic Experience*, pp. 568–579.

50. George Kennan, *American Diplomacy, 1900–1950*, paperback edition, (New York: New American Library of World Literature, Inc., 1952), pp. 59–79. Veterans' groups

War II, and in the Asian wars, the United States was fighting totalitarian regimes that sought to subvert the independence and freedom, either directly or indirectly, of the world's "democracies." Tyranny threatened freedom, not in the context of the British Empire, but around the world. American security, once threatened by Indians or their white colonial allies, was later placed in jeopardy by the aggressive designs of the more distant Germans, Japanese, Russians, and Chinese.

The national government's "war boards" in both world wars greatly increased public regulation of the economy and created precedents for further government activity in times of domestic crisis, such as the depression of the 1930s or the recession of the 1970s. And, as was the case during the Civil War, people in rural areas, towns, and cities, were constantly focussed on national events during both world wars and the two recent Asian wars, something that contributed to growth of nationalist identification.

* * * * *

The national community that has emerged in this century has retained its cohesiveness throughout its development. Even during the period of large-scale industrialization from the 1870s to the 1930s, with its accompanying rise of group consciousness, social divisions, farmer or labor strikes, riots and marches which were sometimes violent, no significant groups within the emergent community felt hopelessly alienated or estranged. Hope for improvement and the desire to possess the material goods being produced in ever-increasing quantity were powerful, unifying sentiments. Serious alternatives to the emergent American system did not receive widespread popular support, even during the depression.

Another element in the cohesiveness of the national community was the restrictive definition given to it by those who proclaimed themselves to be in it. Americans retained their small-town proclivity toward defining as outsiders all who did not easily and comfortably fit into their "community." Indians constituted an "inferior" race, so they were regarded as wandering, "floating," tribal nations, whose land—as a matter of official policy, at least—should be bought and whose people

also founded national organizations after each war: the Grand Army of the Republic (after the Civil War), the Veterans of Foreign Wars (1899), the American Legion (1919), and so on.

should be civilized apart from the white society. Negroes also were an "inferior" race that was first enslaved, then segregated physically within white society, and, still later, socially placed in a separate caste. Immigrants—especially poor ones in the ghettos of larger towns and cities—were often regarded as alien and undesirable, the cause of society's problems. Nativists urged long apprenticeship periods before citizenship was granted and quotas on those from the more "unAmerican" European nations. And with industrialization, those who were poor were regarded as having a bad character and were accused of avoiding the virtues of the Protestant ethic. The nativist impulse and the desire of the "insiders" to define their community in such a way that it remained pure and homogeneous represents in a way the "nationalization" of an earlier impulse that found expression in the small towns: to keep out undesirables and aliens in order to maintain the peace, order, and harmony of the community.

Of course, there were always reformers who denied that the community should be so restricted. But it is a fact that only when a majority of ordinary politicians worked with these minorities did the very definition of the community broaden to include them as members. Radical Republicans tried but failed to include the Negroes after Lincoln ended their slavery during the Civil War. Progressives tried to include those who were not "making it" in a largely unregulated, increasingly oligarchical capitalistic system. The New Deal recognized the poor, Indians, Negroes, and women as regular parts of the national community it governed. Liberal Democrats and Republicans since 1960 have worked with blacks for legal and social equality, ended discrimination against immigrants, and are still trying to include the poor. These efforts at broadening the American community have been abrasive, and they have been resisted. Indeed, the community now seems less cohesive than it ever was when whites only were in it, even when they divided under the impact of industrialization. And so, ironically, just as the national community matures to the point that the great "interest groups" that industrialization gave rise to are becoming less cohesive, more vaguely defined, this same community has been jarred apart by the increasingly strident demands of racial minorities that they be recognized as fully equal parts of it.

* * * * *

As American society was becoming nationalized, nationalism became stronger and fuller. Americans gained an official flag (1911), anthem (1931), and uniform national holidays (1968). Symbols such as "Uncle Sam" stood for the nation with a totality that would have been impossible before the late nineteenth century. Lincoln has at least equalled Washington as the supreme embodiment of the nation among our mythologized hero presidents.[51] Paul Bunyan, with his image of giantism and power, contrived though he was as a folk hero, nonetheless eclipsed Davy Crockett as a symbol of the common American writ large, and was even less tied to a specific region.[52] The "Union" as a "Sacred Trust" that Americans labored as its "Stewards" to perfect in the "Vineyard" of the new world, became, at the turn of the nineteenth century, the union with a mission for the world. With the sudden addition of the remnant of the Spanish Empire in the Caribbean and the Pacific at the successful completion of the brief Spanish-American War in 1898, many Americans felt that they had to join their white European cousins, take up the white man's burden, and be tutors of the backward races of the world. In World War I, many Americans believed that they had to assure the survival of democracy in Europe and lay the foundation for a lasting peace through the collective security of a League of Nations. In World War II, most Americans rallied around a government that believed it had to stop the aggression of the totalitarian governments of Japan and Germany and establish lasting peace through the United Nations. In the Cold War, many felt that the United States must lead the free world against the aggressive designs of Communist Russia and Communist China. As a world power, the "Union," in the minds of its citizens, was invested with a transcendant significance. The United States was a nation-state with a special mission: to assure the survival and growth of liberty everywhere.

It is obvious that nationalism has been the strongest force in international relations in this century. By the time the United States became a world power, the nation-state system and the nationalist impulse had spread far and wide from its late-eighteenth-century western European roots. As Western colonialism ends, former Asian and African colonies reach for the nationhood of their colonial masters, just as Americans, in the late eighteenth century, and Latin Americans, in the early nineteenth century, had done.

---

51. David Donald, *Lincoln Reconsidered: Essays on the Civil War Era*, paperback edition (New York: Random House, Inc., 1961) pp. 144–166.

52. Richard Dorson, *American Folklore* (Chicago: University of Chicago Press, 1959), pp. 216–226.

Nationalism was so omnipresent that Carlton Hayes was prompted to study it as the pre-eminent political phenomenon of the post-World War I era. Summing up a lifetime of study in 1960, he concluded that nationalism was a "religion":

> The ritual of modern nationalism is simpler than that of certain other religions, but . . . it is already fairly well developed. Its chief symbol and central object of worship is the national flag. . . . There are universal liturgical forms for "saluting" the flag, for "dipping" the flag, for "lowering" the flag, and for "hoisting" the flag. Men bare their heads when the flag passes by; and in praise of the flag poets write odes, and to it children sing hymns and pledge allegiance. In all solemn feasts and fasts of nationalism, the flag is in evidence, and with it that other sacred thing, the national anthem . . . the *Te Deum* of the new dispensation; worshippers stand when it is intoned, the military at "attention" and the male civilians with uncovered heads, all with external respect and veneration. . . . Nationalism has its processions and pilgrimages. . . . its holy days, and just as the Christian Church adapted some festivals from Paganism, so the national state has borrowed from Christianity. In the United States, for example, the Fourth of July is a nationalist Christmas, Flag Day an adaptation of Corpus Christi, and Decoration Day or Veterans Day a patriotic version of All Souls Day, while in imitation of the saints' days of the Christian calendar are observed the birthdays of national saints and heroes, such as Washington and Lincoln. . . . Nationalism likewise has its temples, and he who would find the places and structures that are held most sacred by the mass of Americans should seek not Christian cathedrals but Independence Hall in Philadelphia . . . and, above all, the multidomed and columned national capital, a veritable mecca of popular pilgrimage, with its Temples of Congress and Supreme Court, its White House, its majestic monuments to Lincoln, Jefferson, and Washington, and its adjacent shrines of Arlington and Mount Vernon. . . . Moderns may regard their medieval ancestors' veneration of images, icons, and relics as savoring of "superstition," but let them replace, say, a statue of St. Joseph with a graven image of Lincoln, an icon of the blessed Virgin with a lithograph of Martha Washington . . . and a relic of the Holy

Cross with a tattered battle flag, and they display a fitting reverence.[53]

Other writers, such as Sidney Meade,[54] support Hayes's equation of nationalism with religion. Simply because Christianity was divided into innumerable sects—because, in other words, there was no state church—the Christian denominations increasingly linked themselves to the "Union," especially as it became more united and cohesive. Americans became strongly patriotic, and the mental abstraction itself evoked a faith with a religiosity of its own. The Christian cross and the American flag joined together in a place of worship is the symbolic union of two complimentary faiths.

But the equation of nationalism with religion, and especially Christianity, distorts as much as it illuminates. Though it is undoubtedly true that some Americans have had a faith in America as something that stands for all they believe in, their nationalistic faith rarely has totally replaced their Christianity, or Judaism, or Humanism, or atheism—or indifference. The nation or "Union" may have had divine origins or a providential mission in the minds of many Americans in the nineteenth and twentieth centuries, but these believers never *equated* the nation with God. There has always been something that transcends the nation—whether it be the growth of human liberty everywhere in the world, the viability of a league of nations, or God Himself.

III

If specific facets of life are examined for evidence of the nationalizing process, one is struck by the complicated and varied pattern of change. As a general rule, the stronger and more vibrant something was in the countryside and town, the longer it resisted nationalization, the more tenaciously it remained a local phenomenon.

The churches and the schools are good examples of this. There were all kinds of schools in colonial America, and the public school movement of the eighteenth and nineteenth centuries, was, to be sure, a drive toward uniformity and universality. But school systems, while

53. Carlton Hayes, *Nationalism: A Religion* (New York: the MacMillan Co., 1960), pp. 167–168.
54. Sidney Meade, "The 'Nation with the Soul of a Church'," *Church History*, XXXVI (September 1967), 262–283.

legally created by state governments, were left to the towns and cities for financing and management, something only very slowly altered. Colleges and universities were state creations or were founded by a church, and, in either case, as Boorstin has shown, were oriented toward the life of the community they were located in. There were occasional debates in Congress on the desirability of a national university in the early nineteenth century. When Congress finally acted and passed the Land Grant Act of 1862, however, it only provided financial aid for the further establishment of *state*-run colleges and universities. Not until the 1960s did the national government provide substantial, direct aid to primary and secondary schools, as well as to universities, and even then it was careful not to dictate in the area of curriculum and educational standards.

Several factors have worked against this rampant localism. Our public schools, in addition to teaching the languages of words, numbers, art, and music, plus a rudimentary knowledge of man and his world, have been an important vehicle for the transmission of our values through school books that have been as remarkable for their uniformity as our school system has been for its localism. Whether through the Bible, Webster's or McGuffey's readers, mail-order catalogues,[55] or modern elementary school books, our children have always been inculcated with the religious and material values and goals we have emphasized. The other development militating against localism has been the progressive enlargement of our high schools into district schools that do not relate to any real community at all.

The church, certainly the dominant institution in the New England covenanted community and its offshoots, was also of central importance in all the small towns. No matter how many churches there were, the services held for villagers and people in the country were the occasions when ministers interpreted the events in *this* world—both inside and outside the town—in relation to the word of God in the Bible. In this way, the clergy acted as a kind of medium, investing secular life with cosmic dimensions, holding out the Christian version of the good life, and exhorting the congregation to stop sinning and be virtuous.

In contrast to Europe, the presence from the beginning of so many Christian sects, along with the resulting absence of a state church, meant that religious influences at the national level have been insignificant in comparison to the role played by individual parishes in

55. Boorstin, *The Americans: The Democratic Experience*, p. 129.

towns and cities throughout the land, even though all denominations have had some kind of hierarchical structure to fit in some mesure the federative structure of American society. Though the National Conference of Christians and Jews founded in 1928 represents yet another instance of the nationalization of American life, it came at a time when the influence of religion was in decline.

* * * * *

The slow shift in power and influence from the local community to the state, and, finally, to the nation can be seen quite clearly in a number of activities. In health, education, and welfare, the primacy of city health departments, local school boards, and "Overseers of the Poor" gave way awkwardly and unevenly to state departments during the nineteenth century. They, in turn, gradually shared authority with a patchwork of federal agencies, usually formed in the decades after the Civil War and given cabinet status with the creation of the Department of Health, Education, and Welfare in 1953,[56] after the emergency programs of the 1930s served as a kind of prelude. So too with law enforcement agencies: the constables and sheriffs of towns and counties and small cities shared their tasks with police departments first created as a response to ethnic and religious rioting in the fast-growing cities of the 1830s and 1840s. Then state-controlled "national guard" units formed in response to the rapid industrialization and depression of the 1870s; and finally, the Federal Bureau of Investigation evolved a national police force dating from the 1920s—a time when the activities of crime syndicates clearly extended beyond state lines.[57] Similarly, leisure activities, or recreation, lost the natural or communal character they had in the country and town, where log-rollings, barn-raisings, corn huskings, stump-clearing bees, harvesting

56. On poverty, see Robert H. Bremmer, *From the Depths: The Discovery of Poverty in the United States* (New York: New York University Press, 1956) and *American Philanthropy* (Chicago: University of Chicago Press, 1960); Samuel Mencher, *Poor Law to Poverty Program* (Pittsburgh: University of Pittsburgh Press, 1967); Walter I. Trattner, *From Poor Law to Welfare State: A History of Social Welfare in America* (Riverside, N.J.: The Free Press, 1974). On health: Wilson G. Smillie, *Public Health, Its Promise for the Future: A Chronicle of the Development of Public Health in the United States, 1607-1914* (New York: the Macmillan Co., 1955). On education: Lawrence Cremin, *American Education: The Colonial Experience* (New York: Harper & Row, Publishers, 1970).

57. Graham and Gurr, editors, *The History of Violence in America*, paperback edition, (New York: Bantaam Books, Inc., 1969), pp. 56–57, 445–459; Harry A. Overstreet, *The FBI in Our Open Society* (New York: W. W. Norton & Co., Inc.), pp. 76-78.

celebrations, quilting parties, spinning bees, and so on,[58] all represented a fusion of community social gatherings and work, and became, first in the city and then in the nation, structured and "artificial" sports and games with formal rules and nationwide associations, vacations planned by a nationwide "travel industry," and parks and recreation areas built by cities, then states, and finally the nation, on its public lands.

* * * * *

Other activities are more difficult to categorize in this fashion. For example, cultural life at the level of the fine arts has become somewhat nationalized in the institutional sense, with nationwide artists' associations, with a number of state art councils, and, since 1963, a National Endowment for the Arts to ensure public financial support. But high culture has rarely developed a distinctively *national* or "American" style or substance; and when it has, especially since World War II, as in the case of recent schools of painting (such as abstract expressionism, minimal art, and pop art), the style and substance have become international in scope, whether created here or imported from abroad. The best in American fine arts has, by and large, been regional and local in source and inspiration: one usually looks in vain for something that defines what is American in artistic terms, finding much that is "Midwestern," "Southern," "New England," or of "New York," "Chicago," "San Francisco," "New Orleans," or "Indiana." Study of American writers, painters, sculptors, composers, playwrights, and so on, typically concentrates on artists who, whatever else they do, are unable to embrace the quintessential "Americanness" of life as they interpret it. Twentieth-century writers have stressed the American abroad, the American in the town, the American moving to and living in the city, the American in the East, West, North, and South, but *not* the American as a type of person or the American way of life as a distinctive way of life. The result has been that the most famous American literary artists have contributed to a broad mosaic, reflecting nothing so much as the persistence of local and regional variations in our culture, rather than the emergence of common or national literary tradition thought to be one hallmark of a vibrant nationalism.[59] Only in the more abstract

58. Russell Nye, *The Cultural Life of the New Nation, 1776–1830* (New York: 1960), pp. 143–144.
59. It can be argued that literary and other artists have more important things to do than to discover what it means to be a member of their national society, such as what it

arts of architecture and music have there been successful attempts to surpass regional and local definitions and to give a distinctively American or national character to artistic creation. Charles Ives infused European-derived classical musical forms with the rhythms and sounds of American folk, popular, religious, and patriotic music. Louis Sullivan and Frank Lloyd Wright created public and domestic architecture whose "form followed function," organically related to the natural world around it. Capable of being constructed anywhere, freed from the necessity of regional variations by the universal availability of their materials and utilities, Sullivan's and Wright's buildings and homes were truly national—and American. The dizzying heights of a Sullivan-inspired skyscraper reflects the reach of our commercial spirit. The organic interaction with its natural setting of a Wright-inspired house gives apt form to our centuries-long belief that we play out our lives in an endlessly raw and open landscape.

In general, however, it is at the level of the popular arts that Americans have attained the common culture that writers such as Shafer on nationalism claim a people should have. In all areas of creative endeavor—whether in the subliterature of the eighteenth- and nineteenth-century almanac and the late-nineteenth-centucy dime novel; in entertainment provided by minstrel shows, circuses, medicine shows, vaudeville, and Broadway musicals; in folk songs, jazz, or popular songs; in the art of sign painters, primitive portraitists, nature painters, carpenter-builders, and craftsmen who made furnishings of all kinds—Americans from the colonial period on created popular cultural forms that were a far sounder reflection of their over-all character as a people than were the efforts of self-appointed artistic spokesmen to find a distinctively American style in the fine arts culture that was largely a creation of the aristocratic element in European societies, anyway.

Some of these popular forms—such as Vaudeville and musicals—have been centered in New York, or have been regional in their range, as was jazz. But others were almost everywhere long before motion pictures, followed by radio, television, and the paperback book, provided means whereby these kinds of popular entertainment gained a truly nationwide audience in the twentieth century. It is essentially a mystery why people flung over a continent-nation, with few means of

means to be human. Shafer probably does not mean that a "common literature" is one that deals *only* with a literary abstraction: the "American," "German," "Englishman," and so on.

large-scale communication would everywhere respond to the same forms of entertainment and creativity. But wandering cultural organizations responded to that need and perhaps helped to mold it. The widespread sale of almanacs and dime novels, the large number of traveling minstrel shows, circuses, theatrical troupes, and vaudeville performers, along with many peripatetic singers and painters and craftsmen—all helped to form something approaching a national style long before technological changes created the mass culture so prominent in our time.

* * * * *

The most difficult aspect of life to fit into a scheme involving the nationalization of American society is thought. It is not an exaggeration to say that Americans had a common *frame of mind* long before they organized their *activities* into common patterns. Why was this so? Why did a population living in semi-isolated villages and in open countryside share a mental framework to an extent that has allowed historians to make plausible-sounding generalizations about the American mind before, say, 1865?

Unfortunately, there are no answers for these questions, thus far; but we do know that the essentially local character of church and school has meant that, until recently, religious and secular thought in American society has been filtered by these institutions to take account of the interests of people in many different towns, cities, and regions. Thought, as a determinant of political, cultural, social, and economic institutions and activities, has generally been influenced more by the mass of people and less by intellectual elites than has been the case elsewhere in the West. Formal philosophy and theology taught in our schools have been highly derivative. Dominant philosophical notions have generally come from Europe. Not surprisingly, then, the most distinctive American contribution to philosophy—pragmatism—has as one of its central tenets the assertion that truth is what "works." Ideas and beliefs that work or are practical have found favor with a people whose very spirit is pragmatic. This is not to suggest that professors and clergymen and other theorists have been without influence in American life. Until at least the Civil War, the college-educated members of any community finished their careers with a course in moral philosophy. Only with the rise of the secular university in this century have philosophy and religion ceased to hold a central place in the education of our intellectual elite.[60] But the ideas, values, beliefs, and attitudes that were most important in the shaping of American institutions had to be *interpreted* by preachers and teachers and writers to the mass of people in such a way that the people could understand them and try to mold their lives with reference to them. In this sense, intellectual elites, from the beginning figures of prominence in *local* communities, did not possess the cohesiveness and power to shape American institutions "from above" to the extent that European intellectuals tried to do in more hierarchical or centralized societies.

Boorstin believes that

> Americans formed the habit of accepting only those ideas which seemed already to have proved themselves in experience. They used things as they were as a measure of how things ought to be; in America the "is" became the yardstick of the "ought". . . . No American invention has influenced the world so powerfully as the concept of knowledge which sprang from the American experience.[61]

What was it?—the belief that there should not be a special class of "knowers" as in Europe. "Men here were more interested in the elaboration of experience than in the elaboration of 'truth'." Common notions about philosophy were thus rooted in the Americans' collective relationship to their environment.[62]

But Perry Miller indicates[63] that certain groups in American society—such as clergymen, lawyers, and jurists—interpreted religious and legal ideas for their community. Of particular interest here is that they drew on the very subtleties of theology and law that Boorstin attempts to remove from consideration in his accounts of the American historical experience. Miller thus shows the movement of intellectual currents downward, and not just upward.

Richard Hofstadter[64] attempts to show how, in religion (with its evangelical spirit), in politics (with its democratic emphasis), in "cul-

---

60. Frederic Rudolph, *The American College and University: A History* (New York: Random House, 1962).

61. Boorstin, *The Americans: The Colonial Experience*, p. 158.

62. *Ibid.*, p. 160.

63. In his *New England Mind*, 2 vols. (Cambridge, Mass.: Harvard University Press, 1953–1954), and *The Life of the Mind from the Revolution to the Civil War* (New York, Harcourt, Brace, & World, Inc., 1965).

64. In his *Anti-Intellectualism in American Life* (New York: Alfred A. Knopf, Inc., 1962).

ture," (with its heavy concentration on the practical), and in education (with its commitment to "life adjustment"), American life displays a pervasive distrust of the intellect.

All of these major historians thus view the American intellect differently. Their divergent interpretations underscore the lack of concensus within the field of American intellectual history.

This stands in sharp contrast to the broad, synthetic interpretation of American religious history offered by Sidney Ahlstrom,[65] with its wide definition of what constitutes a religious group and its insistence that religious life be examined in the same critical manner as any other and be viewed in relationship to the social and cultural life of a people.

In any event, it is clear that the Protestant ethic was defined for school children and congregations alike and became the major religious source of values for the civil, secular, material life of the population. So, too, did the clergy make sense out of God's world, strongly resisting the deistic interpretation with its mechanistic universe, accommodating to the Darwinian interpretation with its biological world, and reinterpreting until the "scientific" view of existence has been accepted as real or true, with God being everywhere or nowhere. This retreat before the advance of an increasingly scientific definition of the world was orderly, by and large, and was led by clergymen whose sense of God's world, however much it changed, was made intelligible to the congregation. Likewise, a theology developed which continuously shifted away from the omnipotence of God and depravity of man to the innate goodness, indeed the perfectibility, of man, a shift that occurred within a context of increasing secularization and materialism. This led, in turn, to churches that emphasized a Godly life evolving into organizations that favored "doing good" in this world.

As the British colonies matured in the eighteenth century, the philosophic views embodied in the European Enlightenment influenced in various ways the outlook of the provincial population. But since the main sources of the Enlightenment were British—the views of Newton and Locke—the colonists retained an outlook that was largely British. Indeed, the whole pattern of colonial society reflected views derived from the mother country: governments divided in structure and limited in power with a body of civil liberties to uphold; a mercantilistic, capitalistic economy; and a hierarchical social order with a governing class, a broad middling class, and black slaves—a colonial inno-

65. In his *A Religious History of the American People* (New Haven, Conn.: Yale University Press, 1972).

vation—as a separate caste. The Lockean synthesis that was the philosophical counterpart of these systems was widely recognized among the colonists. Even the earlier Puritan variant related in many ways to Locke's new synthesis: the Puritan covenant and Locke's social contract were the religious and secular versions of the same thing. Both believed magistrates were instruments of God and must be obeyed unless they became tyrannical. Both believed in human rights or civil liberties that it was the duty of government to uphold. Both believed in the sanctity of private property. And both believed in a hierarchical social order.

The need to fashion their own government forced the colonists to articulate their political views. What emerged in the Declaration of Independence was a more nearly perfect *British* political system: representative government on a grand scale. The central question that divided the erstwhile colonists in both 1776 and 1787 was how to establish a government based upon the principle of equality that would both effectively govern for the "common defense and general welfare," uphold civil liberties defined by Enlightenment thought, and hold power so organized and balanced that it would not become tyrannical (as the British government had). Debate over this question led to the framing of the Constitution with the addition of a bill of human rights.

In the process, the erstwhile colonists, with radical British theories as their major source, added two new elements to modern Western thought and practice: republican government over a large territory and the indivisible sovereignty of the people. Both of these innovations, characterized by what Gordon Wood calls their piecemeal formulation—diverse and scattered authorship—were created in response to the pressures of democratic politics. Even so, they were original, theoretically consistent, and complete in their constitutional aspects. This was political theory that was "diffuse and open-ended," but still "worthy of a prominent place in the history of western thought."[66]

The major unresolved question was: Who was *in* the political community? Periodic debates led to the progressive implementation of the principle of equality and the obliteration of the "stake-in-society" theory, so that the suffrage was extended from property-holders to adult white males, to adult black males, to women, to adult blacks, to young people. These extensions came about as the result of competitive, popularly oriented political groups looking for potential voters if

---

66. Gordon Wood, *The Creation of the American Republic, 1776–1787* (Chapel Hill: University of North Carolina Press, 1969), p. 615.

public sentiment would allow such an expansion of the suffrage. They were, however, accompanied by an insistence that the principle of equality, if properly applied, meant that these groups should be regarded as members of the political community.

Beyond expressed concern that government be broadly representative, libertarian, and not capable of becoming tyrannical, Americans have not concerned themselves about political theory. The Southern planters were the only minority with power and influence who felt that the government was *not* protecting their rights and *was* becoming tryannical, and—in the proposals of Calhoun—they came up with alternative forms of government that were unworkable in a political system based upon numbers. As a group, they tried to leave the political system altogether. Generally, Americans, as Potter and Boorstin have indicated, have had a pragmatic approach toward government. When people have not had the sense of adventure or the capital to construct something that would be of benefit to all, the government aided corporations; it became then, in Boorstin's phrase, a "public service" institution. When any significant portion of the population seemed to have artificial or natural barriers to equality of economic opportunity, then government acted, says Potter, to remove those obstacles.[67] This approach to government related to the experience villagers had with local politics, whose form, as Zuckerman shows, was basically determined by the practical needs of a small, homogenous community.

The liberal state was therefore largely formed *before* Americans had developed an integrated, national community. Though the ordeal of industrialization and urbanization strained the society contained within the liberal state, its form has remained remarkably stable. Since the New Deal first articulated the principle of welfare and security for all, the main debate over the theoretical aspects of politics is whether human rights includes such social-economic facts of life as income and job security for all, health care, education, housing, and food. And, even more recently, the problem of pollution has raised the question of whether a libertarian government has the right to plan the way man uses his environment, instead of allowing private corporations to do so. And so, human rights, civil liberties, and the general welfare have all been tossed together by the national American community since the 1930s. The debate over meaning now takes place in a largely secular, humanistic framework. Thus have the civil liberties defined in the

67. Boorstin, *The Americans: The National Experience*, pp. 249–256; Potter, *People of Plenty*, pp. 111–127.

eighteenth century's Enlightenment been greatly blurred and broadened in the context of twentieth-century humanism. These newer rights are not in our eighteenth-century Constitution. Are they, then, outside what Smith calls the "national covenant"—or do we now operate with reference to an unwritten covenant, as covenanted towns did when they were in decline or on their way to becoming something else?

The blurring of private and public, which has been a feature of American economic and political life, makes economic theorizing something more than a simple affirmation of faith it capitalism. In contrast to Europeans, Americans have regarded wealth, not as something fixed or scarce, but as ever expanding.[68] This attitude, plus the country's abundance of material resources, has made capitalism the natural economic form for Americans,[69] but our history shows throughout its course that the private ownership of property has always existed in a community context. The small town often exhibited a delicately balanced mixture of private gain and community service. And though fast-growing cities often developed with a minimum of public regulation and planning, the same cities went on to outright ownership of utilities and services, still the most notable instance of "socialism" in our entire system. True, there were regular debates over whether the United States ought to be an "open" or a "closed" economic unit—that is, whether there should be free trade or protection *vis a vis* foreign economies; but there has been wide agreement that the economy ought to be competitive, and not monopolistic, something written into law by Congress in its first major instance of regulation after the onset of industrialization. With the cataclysmic depression of the 1930s came the welfare capitalism of the New Deal and its successive aftermaths. This is a story of a mixed economy: public and private are blurred; government and corporation are in alliance, but the former regulates as well as aids the latter.

In the meantime, our *attitude* toward material things and economic activity remained stable until the depression of the 1930s. The Protestant Ethic stressed the virtue of honest labor. Its corollary was that if someone was poor, it was basically because of defects in his character. Only with mass poverty did Americans alter that view to include a proviso that government should provide welfare and security for the un-

68. *Ibid.*, pp. 78–90.
69. Carl Degler, *Out of Our Past: The Forces that Shaped Modern America* (New York: Harper & Row, Publishers, 1959), pp. 1–8.

employed because their undesirable state was not simply their own fault. Work is still regarded as the only virtuous source of income, however.

The hierarchical conception of colonial American society was increasingly challenged after 1790 by a view that emphasized equality of opportunity, especially as the patriarchal character of American families, groups, and institutions gave way to organization and form that was more loosely framed and inclusive, rather than exclusive and elitist. Americans theorizing about their society increasingly stressed its "open," mobile features, with family, character, occupation, and intelligence giving way gradually to wealth as the chief determinant of status. The argument was that no one *in* the community—whether it be town, city, region, or nation—should have his advanced blocked by artificial barriers. He should become all that his ability allows him to become. This view was held in a society with a distinctive tendency toward mobility, to be sure, but it was also a society whose upper classes have continued to hold real power and influence, who indeed have acted as social models.

Much of the strain and lack of consistency between American thought and practice has come from a noticeable difference in the *rate* of change between their political ideals and social reality. As early as 1776, on becoming an independent nation, Americans affirmed their belief in human equality. This principle has been easier to apply to the political community than to the social community. The granting of political rights to "outsiders" has always come before social acceptance and eventual cohesion. An answer to the question, "Why has this been so?" would resolve the most glaring contradiction between American thought and action in our historical experience from the seventeenth century to the present. This much can be said: The proclamation of equality in a period when the white race believed other races to be inferior in various ways is probably at the heart of the matter. Since racial equality has become an acceptable alternative view (in the United States only since the 1930s), the divergence between reality and this new, extraordinary view (extraordinary, in the broader perspective of the Western world) has created the tension that exists among Americans at the present time.

As in the political community, so in the social community: the principle of equality combined with pressure from those who felt blocked—minorities and their self-proclaimed spokesmen—to broaden the definition of what is American from native white, to immigrant, to Indian, to black. The outsiders, those who had constituted a kind of caste system beneath the world's most mobile society, have gyrated between a desire to maintain their non-American heritage and an insistence that they be treated just like anybody else *in* the community.

American social thought therefore supported *both* an open, mobile, essentially classless society at the same time that it took account of gradations and hierarchies and even caste based upon wealth and ability and race. The narrow definition of who was *in* the American community—namely, native whites—also helped to keep theory and practice together for "insiders," at least until this century.

* * * * *

One aspect of life in the "national community" that writers on nationalism ignore altogether is environmental history. This is unfortunate, because it unnecessarily restricts the range of study that focusses on the nation. It is as if writers on cities or regions were to ignore geography or the ecological setting of the communities they study. Environmental history, in Roderick Nash's definition, is "the total contact of man with his habitat and includes everything from urban design to wilderness preservation." He adds: "It assumes that one can learn about American character and culture by examining what Americans have done to their lands." Nash goes on to restrict this definition unnecessarily by adding, "I regard [environmental history] as a variety of intellectual history, an approach to understanding the history of thought." Actually, rightly conceived, environmental history is the *total* interaction between the American people and their geographic setting, or "what men have done to and thought about the physical world."[70] Central to it, at the national level, is the question of how both government and people dealt with the common or public lands within the nation's territorial boundaries from 1776 onward, with particular emphasis on federal land policy and patterns of settlement in their geographic manifestations. In short, the national community must have at least as broad a definition as towns, cities, states, and regions.

---

70. Roderick Nash, "The State of Environmental History" in Herbert J. Bass, editor, *The State of American History* (Chicago: Quadrangle Books, 1970), p. 250.

The Result . . . and the Decline
of Everything Else?

It should now be possible to try to define *community*, whether in the form of a town, a city, a state, a region, or a nation. All show certain attributes, and our understanding of any one of them should be enhanced by our recognition that a nation is, in many ways, like a town. It should be quickly added, however, that states and regions are incomplete communities. States have not been much more than political-territorial entities, certainly since the Civil War. Granted that the original states had existed as separate colonies before the Revolution; granted that, for a long time after the establishment of nationhood, a citizen's primary loyalty remained with his state, a circumstance especially long-lived in the South, where national loyalty was overriden by more localized forms of identification—granted these certainties, one is still left with the fact that states, as communities, never extended much beyond a territory, its government, and a vague feeling of belonging to that territory on the part of its inhabitants. Even though their political role in American history is an extremely important one, states never come to have social cohesion, cultural distinctiveness, or after the adoption of the U.S. Constitution in 1787, economic independence.

Similarly, regions or "areas" have not had any political or formal territorial existence, quite the obverse of states. And yet, who can deny the immense importance of geographic and economic, cultural, religious, even social manifestations that have appeared in "areas" subnational in extent but clearly beyond the scope of towns, cities, and states. There is much in American history that could not be grasped if such regional or area phenomena were left out of account. And the reference here extends far beyond an ever-receding frontier and a South that seceded and set up its own national government.

Still, Page Smith's definition of the town as the primary community and the nation as the secondary community[1] contains real insight in the sense that towns—cities, as well—and the nation are the only "total" communities: that is, communities containing both a political-territorial and a social-cultural definition. Those who write about the nation, especially historians, would benefit considerably by viewing their subject in the same light as those who write about towns and cities, and, to a considerable extent, on regions, as well. The nation is to society what a township or a county is to the settlements within them: the two *may* coincide, be coterminous; but, in reality, they rarely are. What formed the United States in territorial terms at any given time did not necessarily define a society that included "outsiders" like Indians, Negroes, Asians, and Catholic-Jewish immigrants, any more than town or city boundaries defined the outer limits of viable local communities. Just as "outlivers" wanted to secede from a township and establish one of their own, so, too, on occasion, did New Englanders and Southerners feel sufficiently estranged from American society to countenance the creation of an independent state. Just as groups of dissatisfied townspeople left and established "colonized" towns elsewhere, so, too, did settlers from many areas emigrate across territory not yet possessed by the national government and settle far from where they had lived before. Just as growing cities opposed further annexation on the grounds that communities should be small and familiar, with limits, as towns had always been, so, too, did some Americans oppose continued expansion with the argument that a nation cannot remain viable if it continuously grows territorially, taking in a variety of strange and alien people. Just as there was a blurring of "public" and "private" by "booster" businessmen in nineteenth-century towns and cities, so, too, have the "technocrats" of the large national corporations of our century blurred the distinction between the corporate and the "public" interest. And, if towns, cities, and regions must be viewed as social or human communities that interact ecologically with their geographic setting, so, too, should the nation be viewed as a people who build and move on the land of a great continent.

The thesis here is that Americans have always lived simultaneously in various levels of communities and that the level of most consequence

1. Smith, *As a City Upon a Hill*, p. 14.

has shifted by stages from the little community—the town—to the big community—the nation. The ineptness of this development should not be allowed to obscure its persistence.

A question intrudes at this point: How important was community life to the individual American at various periods of American history? There has been a definite shift away from the emphasis on individualism in American life associated with Turner's thesis. Writers such as Smith, Boorstin, Wade, Zuckerman, and many others are insistent that Americans lived out their lives in the context of community and communal effort. In their view, to see the American as a rural individualist before he was herded into big cities is to misread the American historical experience in a very fundamental way.

And yet, *how* basic was community to the development of distinctive features of American life? This is a fair question, because the natural inclination to live in communities is hardly uniquely American. In fact, the pattern of settlement that took the form of isolated farm houses spread over vast rural areas is, if anything is, the distinctive North American contribution to the way people settle on land. Those who stress community generally do not take sufficiently into account the truly rural segment of the population, with the notable exception of Lewis Atherton, and to some extent, Robert Dykstra, in their studies of midwestern country towns. The emphasis up to this point given to colonial New England, where townships were coterminous with the entire territory of the state, has doubtless been a factor in this neglect. But until we know as much about rural people as we do about townspeople, there is a danger that we will stress to excess the role of community in American history.

Beyond this, there is the question of how central were public, communal, or even institutional forms to the material or economic life of the individual American. Both Stanley Elkins and Sam Bass Warner argue that what stood out about American capitalistic enterprise was its unbridled individualism. For example, the Southern planter, lord of his own community in the rural south, was the individual capitalist *par excellence*.[2] Also, Warner stresses that urban centers grew as the result of thousands of individual capitalistic decisions on the part of middle-class Americans to buy a better home, the cumulative impact of which was the fast growth of large cities with a persistent tradition of

2. Eugene Genovese rejects the assertion that the planter was a capitalist in *The Political Economy of Slavery* and "Marxian Interpretations of the Slave South" in *Towards a New Past*, edited by Barton J. Bernstein, pp. 90–125.

privatism.[3] Even in the towns, Smith adds, the steady scramble for industrial enterprise, even with the high rate of failure because of a lack of talent, nonetheless weakened the fabric of community life. And those towns with a wholly materialistic purpose—the cumulative communities—tended to grow, Smith argues in line with Warner, because individuals wanted to get rich and worked hard at it. So: whether in rural areas, towns, or cities, some writers find that the individual American's continuous desire for the attainment of wealth has checked the growth of the "public" sector of society—that is, the development of strong, vital government, whether at the local, state, or national level. Indeed, this desire has checked the growth of institutions of any kind that would seriously limit the free play of the individual capitalist.

If this is true, then what is one to make of the emphasis in the work of Zuckerman, Boorstin, Wade, and others on the centrality of community in American history? What are we to make of all that community-building across the continent, all those "booster" businessmen and, more recently, all those corporate "technocrats" who have made private enrichment synonymous with the public weal? At this point, it is not possible completely to reconcile these divergent emphases. But this much seems clear: the individual pursuit of wealth in America has indeed worked to undermine community. On the national level, government in the Constitution was strictly limited, or as Arieli puts it, there was to be a large area of human activity beyond the power of government to interfere with. The nation itself became an unplanned community, with sporadic territorial acquisitions that were more the result of the quick deal or the short war than the product of government policy persistently applied. Efforts by such nationalists as Alexander Hamilton and Henry Clay to forge programs or "American systems" were adopted, if at all, only in piecemeal fashion. Even town- and city-planning was reduced to a minimum during periods of fast growth in the nineteenth century.

And yet, efforts to develop planned communities persisted, as well. The Puritan New England town and its offshoot, the covenanted town everywhere, were living monuments to such efforts. But beyond this, the public services of town, city, and state government expanded enormously in the course of the nineteenth century, often to the enrichment of special groups who equated their own material gain with the public interest. But gradually, the public sector went beyond the

---

3. Warner, *Streetcar Suburbs*, pp. 153–166; Warner, *The Private City*, pp. x–xii, 3–4.

purview of the more prominent elements and through either organized pressure or peaceable expansion, came to include laboring
and immigrant groups, as well. By the twentieth century, the "public
interest" had a broad definition, made broader still by the trauma of
the great depression. It was in the 1930s that federal administrators
talked about the need for national planning and priorities and government regulation of all the significant interests of the people. In the
meantime, towns and cities began to plan through zoning ordinances
and often established planning boards of their own. More recently, environmental problems involving pollution and energy-resource scarcity has spurred the growth of resource, regional, and urban planning
councils, which, with tighter zoning regulations, have moved us even
closer to the planned community.[4]

American society is now poised between a tradition of individual
wealth-seeking, with concommitant privatism in its community life,
and a tradition of communal life that comes out of the Puritan town
and later utopian settlements. The recent effort to plan community life
is no longer linked to spiritual purpose, of course. How far planning
and economic regulation will go without provoking a serious reaction
from those who argue for limited government and connect freedom
with private enterprise is not now known. Even if the planned community, under the spur of ecological crisis, becomes a fact, it cannot be
said how viable such communities would be without any ostensible
spiritual purpose.

Another question involves the extent to which the nationalization
of American life has changed the ways in which people live. It can be
argued that village life was always subject to outside influences, even in
the seventeenth and eighteenth centuries, and that the historian who
deals with any period is forced, to some extent, to go outside the town
to explain its pattern of life, especially changes in that pattern. Therefore, outside influences—such as the development of trade patterns,
the exercise of higher governmental and ecclesiastical authority, the
appearance of travelling cultural groups and itinerant persons of all
kinds, the desire for news of other people and places—served to break
down the isolation of small communities long before transportation

---

4. The emphasis given here to the "planned" versus the "unplanned" community is a
shift in focus away from Smith's covenanted-cumulative scheme. Planning and its opposite should have broad definitions, which take account of goals as well as physical layout.
Missing is any reference to the spiritual-materialistic distinctions that Smith found so
central, though goals can certainly include a religious dimension.

and communication made possible the nationwide organization of various activities.

Is "mass society" really more uniform than the earlier village society? Villagers and rural people may have lived out their lives in small areas, knowing and caring relatively little about what went on elsewhere, but they all shared common forms of government, economic activity, religious beliefs, and even popular forms of culture and entertainment. The *uniformity* of life in the eighteenth- and nineteenth-century towns and countryside is remarkable, given the relative lack of involvement on the part of each with the outside world. Such uniformity makes studies like Smith's, Zuckerman's, and Atherton's possible. The only plausible explanation for this uniformity is that the earliest settlers brought common ideas and practices to the task of community-building and that the forms of town life they established were repeated endlessly, though with regional variations, as a continent was settled. The conservative nature of the small community is nowhere better displayed than in the tenacity with which villagers adhered to tested ways of constructing and maintaining a town. Seen in this perspective, fast-growing towns and cities stand out as innovators, being far more varied in composition and, under the pressure of growth, more open to new ways. And yet, even nineteenth-century cities had much in common, even in the midst of changing their ways.

It is difficult to argue that the nationalization of life that has occurred largely in the last century has brought noticeably *more* uniformity. In fact, it seems more likely that life in the village-dominated society before, say, the time of the Civil War, was far *less* varied in outward appearances and in the range of opinion and beliefs and even what we now call "life styles" than is our own presumably homogenized contemporary society. Great waves of immigrants from Europe and migrants from the countryside, along with the occupational explosion produced by industrialization, created a heterogenous urban society. Americans may now be organized on a national basis, but they have *far more* to organize than they had a century or more ago. The transcience, novelty, and diversity that Alvin Toffler found abundant evidence of for his *Future Shock* supports the assertion that mass society—at least in its middle and upper classes—contains, not bleak uniformity, but a swirl of fast-changing, varied patterns. And so, if there has been a uniform direction of any kind, the movement toward nationalization has been accompanied by a corresponding movement toward greater social-cultural variety and tolerance, both of which have developed, however, within the strict, rather narrow framework of a largely secular liberal capitalist state—a point that Toffler, a former editor of *Fortune* magazine, ignores.

I

In sum, it is important to understand what the nationalization of American life has changed and what it has not. There can be no doubt about the declining role of towns, states, and regions, however. As more and more people move into urban areas, cities have become the typical local community for people living in mass society; but the cities' classic role of economic and cultural metropolitan imperialism has diminished at the same time.

Regionalism in the group-of-states sense has become increasingly artificial and administrative. National organizations and corporations have typically divided the country into regions for purposes of administration, management, production, or distribution, with offices centered in the largest metropolitan center in the area, whether it be New England, Mid-Atlantic, South Atlantic, Midwest, Plains, Rocky Mountains, or Pacific Coast. So, too, with government: the Census Bureau has divided the nation statistically into similar regions. Such divisions are not established out of deference to widely divergent regional populations, but rather constitute an admission that the United States, territorially, is still too vast to be dealt with whole.[5] In a sense, these "administrative" regions—usually following the lines of actual, historical ones—are the culmination of a centralizing process that began with the Midwestern country trading town and continued with the city.

Since the 1930s, the states, in V. O. Key's felicitous phrase, have been converted "into governments that spend money they do not raise and raise money they do not spend."[6] He continues:

[As] the prophets of doom proclaimed the passing of the states during the ferment of the New Deal, state governments were expanding their staffs, enlarging the scope of their activities, spending more and more money. . . . Along with the growth in

5. Odum and Moore argued in the 1930s that a legitimate form of regionalism was that for administrative purposes.

6. V. O. Key, Jr., *American State Politics: An Introduction* (New York: Alfred A. Knopf, Inc., 1956), p. 8.

the scale of its operations, the state has come to occupy a new and pivotal administrative and fiscal position in the governmental structure. One development contributing to its altered position has been the extension of the system of federal grants to states to cover more and more governmental activities. Under the grant system the states become, in effect, the agents of Congress to receive federal funds to aid in the support of governmental activities of national concern. In turn, the states often dispense federal funds—depending on the program and the particular state—to their local governments which actually administer the aided program. . . . In a parallel development, state governments in greater and greater degree have come to the financial support of their local governments by collecting taxes and distributing the proceeds, either as subventions for particular purposes or as shared taxes, among the localities. The states tapped new sources of revenue, such as the income tax and the sales tax, to supplement the resources of local governments, which had exploited to the maximum the general property tax—historically their fiscal foundation.[7]

With the shift of power and innovation to the national government in the 1930s, the states also became defenders of the conservative position on public issues, supporting rural interests against ever larger urban ones because their legislatures were typically based on geographic or political units (like counties) and not on people. Regional and metropolitan planning and direct aid to cities has pushed state governments even closer to the rural population. The Supreme Court's 1966 ruling that state governments must have representation in both houses based upon people may result in legislation that more accurately reflects the interest of the whole population in the states, but the question now is: Can government of *any* kind act effectively on this level? With the nationalization of American life and the urbanization of the population, it is doubtful, in administrative terms, at least, whether the states as political units now have *any* justification, except for the unwillingness of their governments to end their own existence.

But, what of the city, the characteristic "local" community of modern Americans? It continues to exhibit contrasting patterns of economic, technological, and cultural unity, all made possible by inno-

7. *Ibid.*, p. 7.

vations in communication and transportation—the elevator, the telephone, the automobile, bus, train, subway, radio, television, newspapers—with striking evidence of social and political disarray.[8] The city is a place with problems—pollution, slums, racial tension, violent crime, widespread middle-class fear—so vast that its future as a durable human community is uncertain. It is, in Mumford's humanistic terminology, the great monument of a civilization whose people went power-mad and subdued the natural world through the creation of a technology and an economy that has pulled apart the human personality and fragmented social groups living in close proximity. It is also where more and more Americans live.

But, even though the process of urbanization has created grave problems concerning the nature of community in modern, mass society, Mumford is convinced that its reformation and rejuvenation, not abandonment, is the only hope for humanity's future. His proposal for a revitalized urban community involves a reordering of human priorities of a kind so basic that one wonders how his prescriptions for change will ever occur:

> The recovery of the essential activities and values that first were incorporated in the ancient cities, above all those of Greece, is accordingly a primary condition for the further development of the city in our time. Our elaborate rituals of mechanization cannot take the place of human dialogue, the drama, the living circle of mates and associates, the society of friends. These sustain the growth and reproduction of human culture, and without them the whole elaborate structure becomes meaningless—indeed actively hostile to the purposes of life. . . . We must now conceive the city, accordingly, not primarily as a place of business or government, but as an essential organ for expressing and actualizing the new human personality—that of "One World Man." The old separation of man and nature, of townsman and countryman, of Greek and barbarian, of citizen and foreigner, can no longer be maintained: for communication, the entire planet is becoming a village; and as a result, the smallest neighborhood or precinct must be planned as a working model of the larger world. Now it is . . . the individual and corporate will of its citizens, aiming at

8. Hans Blumenfeld, "The Modern Metropolis" in Callow, pp. 166–177.

self-knowledge, self-government, and self-actualization, that must be embodied in the city. Not industry but education will be at the center of their activities; and every process and function will be evaluated and approved just to the extent that it furthers human development, whilst the city itself provides a vivid theater for the spontaneous encounters and challenges and embraces of daily life. . . . [The] innovations that beckon urgently are not in the extension and perfection of physical equipment: still less in multiplying automatic electronic devices for dispersing into formless sub-urban dust the remaining organs of culture. Just the contrary: significant improvements will come only through applying art and thought to the city's central human concerns, with a fresh dedication to the cosmic and ecological processes that enfold all being. We must restore to the city the maternal, life-nurturing functions, the autonomous activities, the symbiotic associations that have long been neglected or suppressed. For the city should be an organ of love; and the best economy of cities is the care and culture of men. . . . In order to defeat the insensate forces that now threaten civilization from within, we must transcend the original frustration and negations that have dogged the city throughout its history. Otherwise the sterile gods of power, unrestrained by organic limits or human goals, will remake man in their own faceless image and bring human history to an end.[9]

Equally concerned over the future of the city, particularly the American city, is Sam Bass Warner. Warner's proposals are in some ways as far-reaching as Mumford's, but they are also far more concrete. A radical who asks Americans to alter significantly the dividing line between what is public and what is private, Warner avoides advocating an outright socialist program. Instead, he argues that relatively unrestrained, individualistic capitalism has led to a tradition of privatism so strong that the very future of urban life itself is threatened. What must be done to assure that future? First, government must control urban land, build mixed public housing on a large scale, and provide direct transportation for the poor as well as for other groups. Then, more broadly, Americans must seriously consider making their national,

9. Mumford, *The City in History*, pp. 569–570, 573, 575–576.

private corporations into public institutions, since these corporations exert such enormous power over community life in America. We must somehow devise "methods for the democratic control of production and services by consumers or democratic control of the mode of work by the employees," must somehow end the bureaucratized metropolis.[10]

As for the town, it still contains its old form but has lost much of its substance. Church and school, which in the nineteenth century became the main institutions for the transmission of secular and religious values in the small-town setting, have been unable to maintain their centrality. Smith and Atherton point to the establishment of district high schools as solid evidence of the disassociation of the school with particular communities. And Smith sees the development of fundamental Protestantism in rural areas and towns since the turn of the nineteenth century as a sound indication that Protestantism has become the preserve of a minority desperately trying to cling to a faith that no longer dominates in a secular community:

> As secular society developed alternatives to the narrow social life of the churches, the churches fought stubbornly to preserve their control over the towns. Many of them stuck to a rigid fundamentalism which made the literal interpretation of the Bible the principle test of faith. . . . The contemporary Holiness sects are made up of socially marginal groups whose sense of rejection has turned their churches into fortresses the primary function of which is to reassure their members that as individuals they stand outside the judgments of society. . . . Members belong to these churches primarily because they have failed in terms of the most insistently publicized values of our society. Obsessed by a feeling of social helplessness, they have turned toward religious groups that place their emphasis on salvation and the life hereafter.[11]

How different from the churches in covenanted communities or during community-wide revivals! There is a great distance between the Puritans, who dominated their communities, and the Holiness sects, who are almost literally "out of" theirs. These are the extreme examples in the changing role of religion in the life of the small town.

10. Warner, *The Urban Wilderness*, pp. 268–272, 131–132, 274.
11. Smith, *As a City Upon a Hill*, pp. 73, 81.

What, then, does remain of the small town? Smith's answer is, "Not much!" Small towns continue to lose population. Some have become suburbs; others are dominated by exurbanites; still others are the location of branch plants whose decisions are made elsewhere and in a regional or national, not local, frame of reference. Occasionally, towns have also become adjuncts to some cultural institution, such as a private school or a college. Towns generally are increasingly places for retired and old people: indeed, a few are quite literally "living" museums, with restored homes and buildings open for public inspection, sometimes accompanied by a revival of older crafts and trades. Those with the most vitality remain country trading centers for an agricultural hinterland. The local covenant is dead.

Smith argues persuasively that in its period of decline, the greatest contribution of the town to the nation as a whole has been the migration of its ablest young people into cities where they have formed a disproportionately large number of notable persons in the various elite groups of contemporary mass society. The bright youngster from the town received his community's attention and concern. He was educated on a personal basis, was highly motivated to excel at his calling, and because of the town's distinctive interpretation of the Protestant Ethic, was trained to use his excellence in the public service. Thus Smith finds that most lists of prominent persons now available bear out his contention. There are two exceptions: businessmen and cultural leaders. Industry and culture, having flourished in the cities, are largely the product of an urban environment.[12]

Smith links—somewhat too simplistically—the creation of able young people with the covenanted town, which leads him naturally to a further generalization:

> The cumulative town, the essentially inchoate community, dispatched the great majority of its youth to other towns and to the cities to constitute again a lower-middle- and middle-class element, if they did not indeed sink to an even lower occupational and social status in the city.[13]

Smith also views the town as an intermediary staging area in the long-term movement of population from rural areas to the cities: "The town, with its essentially rural tradition and its relatively sophisticated

12. *Ibid.*, pp. 235–237.
13. *Ibid.*, pp. 256–257.

and complex social and cultural life, prevented the development of a rural peasantry in America and bridged what in most cultures has been a wide gap between farm and city."[14]

Social scientists who have studied the American town in this century[15]—especially Arthur Vidich and Joseph Bensman, in their *Small Town in Mass Society*—have stressed the great impact that agencies of a nationalized, mass society have had on the life of small communities. As Vidich and Bensman put it: "[This] study is an attempt to explore the foundations of social life in a community which lacks power to control the institutions that regulate and determine its existence."[16] They continue:

> The central problem which evolved in our study of Springdale was the discovery of the relationship between Springdale and the larger society. In our initial contacts with the community, we had found that even those local accomplishments of which the people were so proud were the result of operations of the large-scale, impersonal machinery of outside organizations whose policies in most cases were not even addressed to Springdale as a particular place but to Springdale as one of hundreds of similar towns which fell in a given category. . . . Despite our attempt to find original and indigenous sources of the community's culture and values, we were unable to find any. Instead we found external sources and origins for everything that the community cherished as being most genuinely representative of its own spirit. Moreover, we found that the community harbored genuine resentments against the urban centers and institutions by which the process of invidious comparison devalued by their very pervasiveness all that the community was, stood for, and believed in.[17]

What are the small town's values?:

> The dominant culture and life styles so remarkably preserved in Springdale were representative of almost all of the American

14. *Ibid.*

15. Maurice Stein, *The Eclipse of Community*, provides the best analysis of these social scientists.

16. Vidich and Bensman, *Small Town in Mass Society*, p. xviii.

17. *Ibid.*, pp. 317–318.

past. They were so well preserved because of the attempt of the residents of the town to maintain a familiar way of life and a traditional ideology in the face of a society that devalues that way of life. . . . The living characteristics of Springdale were part of the characteristics of the late frontier, of nineteenth-century industrial and commercial culture and of a belief in agrarian democracy and independence.[18]

What happened to a community clinging to these values?:

> Governmental, business, religious, and educational super-bureaucracies far distant from the rural town formulate policies to which the rural world can respond only with resentment. The urban proletariat has replaced the rural majority only in turn to be replaced in numerical primacy by the new middle classes and by service workers who are not primary producers. The "family farm," though it still exists, is now a big business industrialized in its operations and administratively organized; but for the most part, farming is now corporately organized. While decreasing in number, the units of production have greatly increased in size. Throughout the country the rural countryside and old farm houses have been invaded by the commuting industrial, white-collar, and professional classes.[19]

II

In the meantime, the nationalization of American life continues, though since the 1960s there has been increasing criticism of the "bigness" that is so obvious a feature of organizations and institutions of all kinds. Those critical of the direction that modern American society is taking have re-emphasized the traditionally "federative" character of

18. *Ibid.*, p. 322.
19. *Ibid.*, p. 323. In a similar study, *Small Town and the Nation: The Conflict of Local and Translocal Forces* (Westport, Conn.: Greenwood Publishing Co., 1969), Don Martindale and R. Galen Hanson probe the tension and stress created by the simultaneous existence of local and cosmopolitan ideals and patterns of activity. The town they studied—Benson, Minnesota—contained both "old style" inhabitants—those who sought to maintain the earlier, local style of life—and "new style" inhabitants—those who welcomed the newer, cosmopolitan style.

American life and have urged that local initiative, action in the communities where people actually live, become a central feature of the society once again. What such critics are asking for goes against the organizational grain of the last century, but implies that what people want is more important, and eventually more powerful, than what organization itself dictates in a setting of human inertia.

And, it must be added, the national government has responded, to some extent. In the 1960s, new programs in the area of health, education, and welfare featured direct aid to local or community "centers." Indeed, to this date, there is still no *uniform*, national financial program for health insurance, the school systems, and welfare recipients—activities, it should be recalled, that have had a strong tradition of local action. But even in areas where nationalization is obvious, federal bureaucracy has not necessarily followed suit: there is no cabinet-level department of consumer affairs and no federal law for the incorporation and licensing of national corporations. Recent efforts to return federal revenues to states and localities have become more strenuous, with conservatives arguing that the states would disperse the money more widely to rural as well as to urban elements in the population, and liberals arguing that, since the cities are where most of the people live, cities ought to be aided directly, without the inequitable syphoning off of funds that state legislatures would probably favor.

Even the social order seems to have resisted the centralization of power of the kind that was wielded by a small group of industrial and financial entrepreneurs at the turn of the last century, though sociologists and political scientists who have written about power and wealth in post-World War II American society are divided into what G. William Domhoff calls pluralists and power elitists. The pluralists, like Arnold Rose and Robert Dahl, argue that power is diffused among various groups to the point that each decision or action has to be examined on its own terms if we are to understand who exercised power to do what. The power elitists—particularly C. Wright Mills and Domhoff himself—argue that the pluralists ignore what has been a real concentration of power and wealth in the United States, what Mills calls, in effect, "power clusters" within the political, corporate, and military spheres. This elite has sufficient cohesion to affect profoundly the whole pattern of life for what Mills calls the mass society.[20]

20. C. Wright Mills, *The Power Elite* (New York: Oxford University Press, 1956), pp. 269–297; G. William Domhoff, *The Higher Circles: The Governing Class in America* (New York: Random House, 1970), pp. 309–355.

Still, whether or not one agrees that there has been a governing class since the 1920s in the United States, what seems indisputable is the enormous concentration of wealth and power in this century, a direct consequence of the nationalization of American economic and political life. The richest one percent of our people own about forty percent of our wealth. The bottom one fifth of American families have six percent of our income, while the top one fifth have forty percent. The two hundred biggest manufacturing corporations hold two thirds of the wealth of all such corporations. The biggest one percent of these corporations control eighty-six percent of the net profits of all manufacturing. The ten biggest commercial banks have one quarter of all deposits in such banks, whereas the ten biggest insurance companies have more than half of the assets of all life insurance companies in the country.[21]

A small group of families is worth millions, sometimes hundreds of millions of dollars apiece and has far-flung and varied financial, industrial, charitable, cultural, political, and foreign interests.[22] Even so, today's "super-rich" probably do not have the "visible" influence their turn-of-the-century predecessors had, and the chief instrumentality for the expression of private as opposed to public power—the corporation—is also probably less susceptible to the influence and direction of a dominant personality than it was in 1900.

Indeed, John Kenneth Galbraith, in his "final" assessment of the American economy—*Economics and the Public Purpose*—argues that economic power in contemporary America mainly flows, not from actions of the "super-rich" in their capacity as major stockholders and directors, but from the collective decisions taken by the management of mature, oligopolistic, national corporations; not, in other words, from what the nominal "owners" do, but from what the collective technical expertise of their managers suggests is most likely to protect or enlarge the activities of the firm. As oligarchy after oligarchy has emerged in different parts of industry, power has thus become far more impersonal; the real rulers of economic society are the legions of technocrats whose corporate giants have quietly removed huge areas of American economic life from the operations of a "market" system through the successful manipulation of costs, prices, wages, government policy,

21. Jack Newfield and Jeff Greenfield, *A Populist Manifesto: The Making of a New Majority*, paperback edition, (New York: Praeger Publishers, Inc., 1972), pp. 18, 45, 49, 61.

22. Ferdinand Lundberg, *The Rich and the Super-rich* (New York: Lyle Stuart, Inc., 1968).

and consumers' values. Modern bureaucratic organization in the form of the large industrial corporation has thus made power collective while harnessing corporate operations to the goal of never-ending growth and increasingly illusory "newness."

If Galbraith is right, then what is concentrated and powerful in contemporary society is the big, rich corporation, rather than a coterie of rich families. In any case, as the American economy became nationalized, popular sentiment in favor of open and fair competition was written into federal law in the form of antitrust laws. But the growing power of the federal government has not been used to stop the growth of national corporations, even though the popular ideal remains that of an openly competitive economic order. The oligarchies that dominate industry after industry are in many ways not competitive, however. In other words, the national government has not, since the 1930s, acted in response to a widely held ideal and has allowed the process of nationalization and concentration to go on apace. Antitrust proceedings are minimal. Organizational growth and the security of the rich take precedence over the less tangible existence of a common belief.

It should also be pointed out that farmers and laborers were organized in huge national organizations during the same period that industries were. Should they too be broken up and made competitive? Is popular sentiment inconsistent here? Should labor unions be national and monopolistic if industries are not also? The federal government has in fact acted to protect the concentrated labor union, through the establishment of the minimum wage and the guaranteeing of collective bargaining. Actually, those who favor reform do not generally want to do away with bigness in industry either. They want such things as a federal law to incorporate and license corporations; strict limits on concentration enforced by regulatory agencies truly looking out for the public interest; thoroughgoing tax reform; representation for minority or nondominant groups of all kinds on the governing bodies of every type of corporation and institution, from political parties to factories, from banks to foundations; and the nationalization of ·natural monopolies such as utility corporations. Galbraith goes even further and favors making public the mature, oligopolistic, national corporations—especially the weapons industry—as well as such activities as mass housing construction, health services, and rail transportation.[23]

23. Galbraith, *Economics and the Public Purpose* (Boston: Houghton-Mifflin Co., 1973), pp. 272-273, 277-285; Newfield and Greenfield, *A Populist Manifesto;* Morton Mintz and

If the federal government has not created an openly competitive society in the economic sphere, it has taken action on behalf of another American ideal, that of legal equality. With recent scientific opinion favoring racial equality, with blacks increasingly demanding that they be treated equally under the law, and with growing numbers of middle-class whites arguing that the time has come to live up to the principle of human equality, the federal government—Court, Congress, President—worked actively toward the goal of complete legal equality. The government thereby tried to open the national community to "outsiders" in a way that towns would never have done if left to their own local initiative, much as they had always tried to keep out the "stranger."

This progressive implementation of our revolutionary ideals can be said to give our national community some sense of purpose. But the crisis that surfaced in the mid-1960s has shattered the faith of many Americans. Persistent racial antagonism, festering ecological problems, growing uncertainty over what the proper role of the United States in the world of nation-states should be, the fear and high incidence of violent crime—all call into question the sunny optimism that many Americans often bestowed upon their beloved Union. Even celebrations and festivities are losing their nationalistic or religious character. Where are those great "national festivals of purpose" that Boorstin found such a commonplace part of nineteenth-century American life? Christmas can be viewed as the major consumer's holiday of the year; Thanksgiving is an exercise in gluttony; Independence Day is a summer's holiday weekend; and Washington's Birthday is a midwinter break, a "birthday" scheduled so that it always falls on a Monday. As Harvey Cox has shown, we have lost our capacity to be festive,[24] which means we no longer look outside the materialistic dimension of our own lives to celebrate the meaning of whatever larger historical and transcendent religious purposes there may be for out existence as a people.

Jerry S. Cohen, *America, Inc.: Who Owns and Operates the United States?* (New York: Dial Press, 1971). For a distinctive emphasis—that government regulation lead to the actual return of a genuinely open, competitive system—see Mark J. Green. *The Closed Enterprise System: Ralph Nader's Study Group Report on Anti-Trust Enforcement* (New York: Grossman Publishers, 1972).

24. Harvey Cox, *A Feast of Fools: A Theological Essay on Festivity and Fantasy* (Cambridge, Mass.: Harvard University Press, 1969); Boorstin, *The Americans: The Democratic Experience*, pp. 158–162.

III

In the midst of the pain and anguish of the present-day crisis, some writers have groped their way toward new definitions of community that will fit a population that seems itself to be searching for new forms of community. Thus, some observers detect a shift in definition from a geographic or physical emphasis to a social one. In this view, the urban dwellers' "community" becomes an association of relationships scattered about the metropolis, divorced from neighborhood and street. If so, this shift would appear to apply only to middle-class urbanites. The poor and the immigrants still have the old-fashioned type of community—whether in the form of the ghetto or the neighborhood. Perhaps the middle classes' success in developing a new definition of community in an urban setting, while the poor have not, at least contributes to the continuous tension among groups in our metropolises. Ironically, by having *retained* the older, presumably more workable form of community, the urban poor and ethnic groups are the least-satisifed elements in American society today. Whereas the villagers of the seventeenth, eighteenth, and nineteenth centuries *sought* to maintain a cohesive, homogeneous community, those in our ghettos are *forced* by circumstances to do so. The whole thing has flipped. What was the norm has become the exception, what was once desirable is now avoided.

Boorstin noted in his *The Americans: The National Experience* that migrants in caravans moving across the plains created transient communities as long ago as the middle decades of the nineteenth century, replete with mini-"Constitutions," laws, rules, and punishments for their infraction, even a hierarchy of officials. So, too, did farmers in the plains to the west of the Mississippi River; and miners, wherever a strike drew a crowd like a magnet, established "Claims Clubs," another form of transient community in which they too set up rules—for staking out claims—and the machinery for enforcing those rules: officials, courts, trials, juries, quick punishment. Indeed, from colonial times until the closing of the frontier in the 1890s, from the Atlantic to the Pacific, there was a consistent tradition of "vigilantism" in frontier communities, in settlements out ahead of the firm establishment of territorial or state law enforcement agencies. The inhabitants of such communities took the law into their own hands and, through posses and their own judicial and penal procedures, caught, tried, and punished those who broke their rules.[25] Thus, in the nineteenth cen-

25. Boorstin, *The Americans: The National Experience*, pp. 49–112; Graham and Gurr, editors, *The History of Violence in America*, pp. 154–226.

tury, the transient community was the deliberate creation of a restless, extremely mobile population.

Boorstin, in his latest writings, believes the entire nature of community in twentieth-century America has profoundly changed, right along with the nationalization of American life, by becoming far more transient and varied. The new communities are *like* the old ones in that they have "shared hopes," a "vividly shared present," and "shared expectation." But they are different in that

> they are fragmented, and they are everywhere. What holds members of these new communities together is not a shared religious or civic dogma, not a shared booster-enthusiasm, not even a shared economic interest, but something much vaguer and more attenuated. It is a shared consciousness, a shared awareness. People now think of themselves as members of groups and classes which were unimagined only a century ago.[26]

In other words:

> A new civilization found new ways of holding men together —less and less by creed or belief, by tradition or by place, more and more by common effort and common experience, by the apparatus of daily life, by their ways of thinking about themselves. Americans were now held together less by their hopes than by their wants, by what they made and what they bought, and by how they learned about everything. . . . These Everywhere communities floated over time and space, they could include anyone without his effort, and sometimes without his knowing. Men were divided not by their regions or their roots, but by objects and notions that might be anywhere and could be everywhere. Americans lived now not merely in a half-explored continent of mountains and rivers and mines, but in a new continent of categories.[27]

As America became nationalized, as life became more and more standardized, the places where people actually lived became one kind of "everywhere" communities. Appropriately, individuals who were

---

26. Daniel J. Boorstin, *The Decline of Radicalism: Reflections on America Today*, paperback edition (New York: Random House, 1970), p. 4.
27. Boorstin, *The Americans: The Democratic Experience*, p. 1.

remarkably inventive—Boorstin calls them "Go-Getters"—those who developed the technology that was the prerequisite for this increasingly evident uniformity were not tied to particular communities the way booster-businessmen of the mid-nineteenth century had been. Even transportation ceased to be "fixed" and confined:

> The national network of numbered highways was a symbol of the diffused destinations of the dominant American vehicle. A highway, no longer the "highroad" to a place of importance, or to any place in particular, was now part of a network that took the driver anywhere and everywhere. This was the beginning of the end of the single city center to which people came in public transportation from all over. . . . The airplane, when it became, second to the automobile, the principal means of intercity passenger transport, diffused the city still farther. In older times the point of arrival . . . had been a center of city life. But now the airport was on the outskirts, only ambiguously related to the city it served.[28]

The typical "everywhere" community of a specific, geographic character, the suburb, can be regarded as a twentieth-century version of the "Upstart Town," a new frontier "for the recurrent need to build new institutions for community purposes," with fresh opportunities for political participation in the shaping of new communities. But the suburb should also be viewed as a new version of a "Transient Community": "Instead of the wagon train, where people leaned on one another as they moved across the continent, Americans in suburbs leaned on one another as they moved rapidly about the country and up the ladder of consumption. A small town was a place where a man settled. A suburb was a place from which a person moved."[29] Indeed, the suburb was, above all else, an "Everywhere Community." The "boomers" who built it, unlike the boosters of the previous century,

> seldom intended to live in the community he was building. For him community was a commodity, a product to be sold at a profit. And the suburban home owner often moved into a whole town which had been shaped in advance by a shrewd developer's sense of the market. . . . In the late twentieth cen-

28. *Ibid.*, p. 271.
29. *Ibid.*, pp. 289, 290.

tury, to move from almost any suburb to almost any other of comparable class anywhere else in the United States was like moving from one part of a neighborhood to another. With few exceptions, the products and services available and the residence itself were only slightly different.[30]

For Boorstin, the amorphousness of "place" communities, especially metropolitan areas, is dramatic proof of the basic decline in the distinctiveness of towns and cities everywhere in the United States. As the physical shape of human habitation came to be more and more similar, less and less "legible," the very definitions of community altered:

> While the Census Bureau and the federal government used ["Standard Metropolitan Statistical Area"] . . . social scientists and citizens were also using new terms to describe the elusive, vaguely defined areas reaching out from what used to be called simply "towns" and "cities." A host of terms came into use: "metropolitan regions," "polynucleated population groups," "conurbations," "metropolitan clusters," "megalopolis," etc., etc. A century earlier, American city boosters had used the language of hope and hyperbole, dignifying villages as towns, towns as cities, and cities as metropolises: mid-twentieth-century Americans stretched their language with another purpose—to communicate uncertainty and penumbra.[31]

For Boorstin, the most important communities of modern America are not based on specific "places" at all, but are of a statistical nature. With the rise of a science of statistics since the late nineteenth century as an intellectual underpinning, Americans have learned to group themselves in communities based upon myriads of numerical categories, rather than on geography or class. Beginning with the 1850 census, a growing array of facts about the economic and social life of everyone were collected. After the turn of the nineteenth century, a federal Bureau of Standards flourished and became a "world leader in techniques of testing, measuring, and standardizing."[32] Americans learned to ask: How many? How much? How big?

---

30. *Ibid.*, pp. 290, 291. For a more detailed comparison, see same source, p. 274.
31. *Ibid.*, p. 268.
32. *Ibid.*, pp. 168–170, 170–173, 192.

The cash register and calculating machines brought precision to economic transactions and forced people to think quantitatively about the material aspect of their lives. Life itself became insured by an industry based squarely upon statistics. With the introduction of the income tax, Americans increasingly thought of themselves in income "brackets." Even poverty was defined statistically. Morality itself, especially sexual morality, came to be, to a considerable extent, a matter of adhering to "norms" of behavior defined through statistical inquiry. Even intelligence became associated with measurement by means of various "mental" tests. Market research and public opinion polls regularly checked the range or concentration of opinion among various groups or the population as a whole.[33]

By the mid-twentieth century, Americans thought of themselves as members of many groups defined statistically. To Boorstin, the most significant of these are what he calls "Consumption Communities." The consumption community is quick ("immigrants have found it easy to become Americans"), nonideological ("people of all races, beliefs, and religious and political creeds can join"), democratic ("the great American democracy of cash"), and "tends to become the model of all other communities" ("all experience tends to be treated more and more like the experience of consuming").[34] The consumption communities are

> far more numerous and far less intense than those of earlier ages, [indeed] are communities of men and women not in one another's presences . . . are diffused and dispersed over the country. . . . The modern American is tied—by the thinnest of threads and by the most volatile, switchable loyalties—to thousands of other Americans by nearly everything he eats, or drinks, or wears, or reads, or uses. Old-fashioned political communities and religious communities, themselves now become only two among many new, but once unimagined, fellowships. We are held to other men, not only by a few iron bonds, but by countless gossamer webs tying together the trivia of our lives everyday.

* * * * *

33. *Ibid.*, pp. 167–193; 200–244.
34. Boorstin, *The Decline of Radicalism*, pp. 31–32.

No American transformation was more remarkable than these
new American ways of changing things from objects of possession and envy into vehicles of community. Nearly all objects
from hats and suits and shoes men wore to the food they ate
became symbols and instruments of novel communities
[typically called into being and maintained by advertizers].
Now men were affiliated less by what they believed than by
what they consumed. In the older world almost everything a
man owned was one-of-a-kind. In the newer world the unique
object [generally] was an oddity and came to be suspect. If an
object of the same design and brand was widely used by many
others, this seemed an assurance of its value. . . . And there
were created many communities of consumers. Men who never
saw or knew one another were held together by their common
use of objects so similar that they could not be distinguished
even by their owners.[35]

In the "Everywhere Communities" of modern America, the vagueness and blurred lines Boorstin found in the geographically "unfinished" nation of the nineteenth century continue in other forms in
the mass society of the twentieth. Law and law-breaking or crime, what
was legal or illegal, became fuzzy and ill-defined. In the trans-
Mississippi West in the decades after the Civil War, the same individual
was often, by turns, law-enforcer and criminal. There were "Good Bad
Men" and "Bad Good Men," "Lawless Sheriffs" and "Honest De-
speradoes." In frontier areas, who really knew what the "law" was?
Similarly, those who devised means of enlarging the scope of corporate
enterprise frequently plunged into murky areas of ill-defined legal
practices. In the twentieth century, organized crime became, like government itself, a kind of "service institution," "selling to Americans
something that Americans wanted to prohibit by law"—like gambling
and prohibition.[36]

As for other examples, corporations, franchised-dealerships, and
installment credit all blurred the concept of "ownership." "Progressive" education tried to make the lines between the "schools" and "society" as indistinct as possible.[37] In fact, ambiguity and uncertainty
clouded vast ranges of American cultural and social life:

35. *Ibid.*, pp. 38–39, 89–90. A slightly altered version appears in Boorstin, *The Americans: The Democratic Experience*, pp. 147–148.
36. *Ibid.*, pp. 34–41, 53–64, 80, 77–87.
37. *Ibid.*, pp. 413–434, 496–501.

Was your language "right" or "wrong?" Were you speaking eloquently or crudely? Were you acquiring knowledge or false-hood, were you being educated, propagandized, entertained, or actually deceived? What were the roles of teacher or of pupil? What was knowledge and what was ignorance? What knowledge was "useless" and what was "useful?" Did art have to be "beautiful?" And if not, what was art anyway?[38]

Technological developments created further confusion. Pullman's sleeping and dining railroad cars blurred the distinction between home and travel. The use of glass as a common building material broke down the sharp dividing line between "inside" and "outside." The packaging of goods changed the nature of a product in that the selling or display of a thing became a real element of the thing itself. The growth of supermarkets, their distribution of all manner of goods for sale during many hours of the day and night, blurred kinds of stores and the dis-tinction between shopping and nonshopping time.[39]

Television went beyond everything else in altering the character of everyday experience:

The common-sense hallmarks of authentic firsthand experi-ence (those ordinary facts which a jury expected from a witness to prove that he had actually experienced what he said) now began to be absent, or only ambiguously present, in television experience. For his TV experience, the American did not need to go out to see anything in particular: he just turned the knob, and then wondered while he watched. Was this program live or was it taped? Was it merely an animation or a simulation? Was it a rerun? When, if ever, did it really occur? Was it happening to actors or to real people? Was that a commercial?—a spoof of a commercial?—a documentary?—or pure fiction?[40]

Boorstin finds that other technological innovations have produced change of an even greater significance:

The regularities of nature, by which men knew that they were alive and were only human—the boundaries of season, of in-

38. *Ibid.*, pp. 449–450.
39. *Ibid.*, pp. 332–336, 336–346, 434–447.
40. *Ibid.*, p. 395.

doors and outdoors, of space and time, and the uniqueness of each passing moment—all these were being confused. . . . The first charm and virgin promise of America were that it was so different a place. But the fulfillment of modern America would be its power to level times and places, to erase differences between here and there, between now and then. And finally the uniquness of America would prove to be its ability to erase uniqueness. . . . The American Democracy of Times and Places meant making one place and one thing more like another, by bringing them under the control of man.[41]

Condensed, regrigerated, canned, and frozen foods severed the link between eating and the seasons. Household running water and waste-disposal fixtures, along with central-heating and air-conditioning systems, cut off indoor living from the shifting conditions imposed by the seasons and geographic variations.[42] The skyscraper, the high-rise apartment building, and the shopping center greatly expanded the boundaries of such "controlled" settings:

> Americans could cease to be earthbound because they were no longer bound to the earth for their drinking water and washing water, for disposing of human wastes, for their means of keeping warm and cool, for their ways to communicate with neighbors. The skyscraper was the climactic symbol of man's ability to rise above the particular time and places to satisfy his needs, to keep comfortable and at work, making experience for all Americans, wherever they lived, more alike.[43]

Of even *greater* significance are the technological innovations that have. made experience "repeatable":

> The unrepeatability of the moment was the very meaning of life—and of death. It was another name for man's mortality. For only God was omnipresent. He could be everywhere and anywhere at once, He was not confined by space or by times, nor was He restrained by weather of the seasons. Only God could see all events as if they still happened, or happened all at

41. *Ibid.*, pp. 305, 307.
42. *Ibid.*, pp. 309–332, 346–358.
43. *Ibid.*, p. 346.

one time. Only God could see the moving forms and hear the voices of the dead. Now man could do all these things.[44]

Clocks and watches gave horological time a new precision. Work itself became "packaged," precisely measured and standardized: repeatable.

> The work ethic was based on the notion that each working moment was unique and irrevocable. There were morning hours and evening hours, and there was something different about the labor of each man. . . . Life was a series of unrelivable, unrepeatable episodes. Time was a procession of unique moments—each was now and never again. The past was what had gone beyond recall. . . . In twentieth-century America even this old truism would cease to be true. For time became "fungible," a series of closely measured, interchangeable units. Time was no longer a stream and had become a production line.[45]

The camera and photography, the phonograph and the tape recorder made possible the recreation of countless everyday occurrences. "Instant replay" on television and radio provided a public dimension to the repeatable experience, while copying machines extended such activity to written and printed language as well. The popularity of sports, criminal adventures, even weather reports, can be explained in part, Boorstin thinks, by their relatively unformed, unpredictable character. They are the most vivid examples of Americans "in search of the spontaneous."[46]

The technological revolution that has largely created the "everywhere communities" of modern America has also, Boorstin insists, extensively democratized American life. Like some later-day Tocqueville, Boorstin ransacks American civilization to produce evidence that this is in fact the case. Statistical communities are notably democratic, providing

> ways of clustering people into groups that made sense, without necessarily making invidious distinctions. Numbers are neutral. No person was "better" than another. The numbering of peo-

44. *Ibid.*, p. 359.
45. *Ibid.*, p. 361.
46. *Ibid.*, pp. 361–370, 386–389, 397–402, 402–408.

ple (one person, one vote) itself seemed to symbolize the equality at which a democratic society aimed. From their very nature, numbers offered a *continuous* series, a refuge from those sharp leaps between "classes" found in other societies."[47]

Corporations became "democratizers of property": "The United States was becoming a nation of citizen-stockholders." The franchise helped to democratize ownership. Television "democratized experience," "[just] as the printing press five centuries before had begun to democratize learning." As public speaking evolved from formal oratory to just plain talk, modern public discourse further democratized American politics.[48]

Marketing research and opinion polls increasingly turned production and politics into exercises in providing people with what they wanted. The revolution in marketing that department stores, five-and-ten-cent stores, chain-stores, supermarkets, and mail-order firms fashioned was certainly democratic in the sense that it made all goods available either for sale to or for the inspection of all. Ready-made clothing democratized the appearance of people. The advertizing of goods and services and the insurance of health, safety, and life were notably democratic enterprises in their reach and scope.[49]

Morality became for many little more than what was the "norm." Psychology, "the science of uniting the 'is' and the 'ought,' was the supremely democratic science. For it referred all questions of human behavior not to any Higher Authority, nor to some traditional scripture, but to the normal behavior of men." Philosophy, in the hands of its most popular twentieth-century practitioner, John Dewey, "idealized activity" and "erased many of the old distinctions in philosophy. Philosophers had ranked entities by putting the concrete individual fact or experience at the bottom, and giving the place of honor to the abstract, generalizing absolute. In Dewey's world there was no place for such hierarchies."[50]

Language, even in dictionaries, became increasingly that which was spoken and written by most people, and not by a linguistic elite. Education became the new religion, with the universities as its cathedrals, even though they were built before the parish churches, that is, the

47. *Ibid.*, p. 165.
48. *Ibid.*, pp. 413, 420, 428–434, 393, 462–478.
49. *Ibid.*, pp. 148–157, 91–130, 173–188, 137–145.
50. *Ibid.*, pp. 238–244, 230, 498.

public high schools. But, though the emergent educational system thus had the curious shape of an inverted pyramid, the more recent secondary schools were thoroughly democratic in character,[51] and the universities that capped the system were "Hotels of the Mind,"

> providing for each American community's mental and cultural activities many of the democratic conveniences which its hotel provided for their social and commercial activities. American universities tended to be public, popular, and democratic. But the common faith, far from producing any uniformity of standards, produced a fantastic, disorderly diversity, in the frenetic effort to find something uniquely suited for everybody.[52]

Even travel to foreign places was democratized through the introduction of the "packaged" tour.[53]

By steadily focussing on evidences of democracy such as these, Boorstin largely igornes other evidence—also statistical in nature—that reveals nondemocratic aspects to American life. Corporations may be the "democratizers of property," but they are also the vehicle for enormous concentrations of power and wealth. Poverty may have become "statistical" in definition, but it still embraces a significant portion of the population and shows no signs of becoming a thing of the past. The racial tension that divides our cities is a fundamental problem, and certainly worthy of more than the few pages Boorstin devotes to it. Even such "negative" but critically important consequences of technology as pollution and energy—or resource—scarcity are ignored. The discovery of the "Everywhere Community" is a great insight; but instead of viewing its emergence as a political and social problem of the first magnitude, Boorstin excitedly focusses on it as dramatic evidence of the shifting nature of "community" in modern America.

Boorstin is concerned about certain implications of both technology and democracy, however. "Democratizing everything enlarged the daily experience of millions; but spreading also meant thinning. . . . Attenuation summed up the new quality of experience. Attenuated experience was thinner, more diluted, its sensations were weaker and less poignant. It was life punctuated by commas and semicolons rather than by periods and exclamation points." In the "Everywhere Com-

51. Ibid., pp. 454–462, 478, 590–501.
52. Ibid., p. 480.
53. Ibid., pp. 514–520.

munity," as often as not, the old-fashioned live "crowd" was replaced by the "public," vast numbers of physically separate individuals "held together simply because they were all responding to the same distant stimuli."[54] What *standards* could the individual American refer to as he stood alone at the receiving end of the one-way communication of radio and television or in the aisles of mass-produced goods at the supermarket? And there were some wider questions:

> Did the very perfection of techniques for widening experience, and especially those for creating and diffusing the repeatable experience—did all this, somehow, impoverish experience in the very process of democratizing it? Was it inevitable that a democratized experience, however rich and technologically sophisticated, should be impoverished? Was there an inherent contradiction between the aim of democracy—to enrich the citizen's everyday life—and its modern means? Did the very instruments of life enrichment, once available to all, somehow make life blander and less poignant? Could it be possibly true that while *democratizing* (the process) enriched, *democracy* (the product) diluted?[55]

Like Henry Adams at the turn of the nineteenth century, Boorstin is also disturbed by the spectre of uncontrollable growth unleashed by technology in a democracy. Even "decision-makers," such as presidents, do not seem to be capable of deflecting the over-all momentum, something increasingly divorced from human will and purpose. For example, recent progress along the frontiers of technology "the exploration of the inconceivably miniscule inside the atom and the exploration of the inconceivably vast universe of outer space . . . both had the effect of deepening man's sense of momentum and accentuating his feeling of the new unfreedom of omnipotence."[56] Boorstin is led to the following conclusion:

> Momentum kept things going the way they were already going. . . . In a society, too, the force of momentum depended upon *size* and *speed*. And these, of course, were precisely the dimensions which had distinguished American history. . . .

54. *Ibid.*, pp. 306, 477.
55. *Ibid.*, p. 389.
56. *Ibid.*, p. 580.

Growth, ever more and faster, seemed to have become the nation's whole purpose. . . . Perhaps, then, the mission and doom of American technology were the continual discovery of new techniques. Perhaps the best things in democracy came not from having but from seeking, not from being well off but from becoming better off. Would a high standard of living, no matter how high, always open vistas that would become flat and stale? And was it necessary to keep the standard of living ever rising if the vistas were to remain wide and open and fresh?[57]

In short: "Man's problem of self-determination was more baffling than ever. For the very power of the most democratized nation on earth had led its citizens to feel inconsequential before the forces they had unleashed."[58]

Even if Boorstin's "Everywhere Community" be accepted as an adequate definition for community in contemporary America, his examples are not exhaustive. Page Smith, by contrast, sees new "pseudo-communities," such as Alcoholics Anonymous and Synanon (for drug addicts), and concludes that they are a by-product of the alienation and anomie characteristic of an urban society that he's convinced has failed to produce an organic community:

It may be that in a mass society, the creation of pseudo-communities of various kinds is the best hope of protecting the individual against the demoralizing effects of alienation. Yet it is difficult to see how enough such communities can be formed to seriously affect the sense of anomie that characterizes our culture. Pseudo-communities need a bond of common suffering to tie them together. The well-fed acedia of our society is poor material out of which to fashion communities of any kind. . . . It is certainly clear the pseudo-communities are more problematical and unstable than the type of community experience represented by the American small town.[59]

Neither Smith nor Boorstin refers to the hippie commune. Whether located in a countryside farmhouse or an urban home, these communal arrangements constitute a kind of rejection of liberal-

57. *Ibid.*, pp. 558, 390.
58. *Ibid.*, p. 558.
59. Smith, *As a City Upon a Hill*, p. 306.

capitalist society and are thus in the tradition of the utopian or Christian communitarian movements of the early and mid-nineteenth century. Though far less ideological, in a secular sense, than their predecessors and largely confined to youth, some of the more religiously oriented hippie communes show the same kind of genius for innovation that the Shakers and the Mormons displayed in the development of their faith. Now, as before, communes exist at the sufferance of the authorities and within the laws of the larger society. The movement of alienated youth into communes seems to have slowed down, but is not dying out, either.

If the recent emphasis on the fragmented, attenuated, transitory nature of community in contemporary America is properly placed, then Americans are indeed in a mess. What about the "old" political-territorial communities such as Boston, Hoboken, and Peoria, and all the other places that the U.S. Census Bureau lists as "real" communities. If one's clubs, shopping places, therapy-groups, and so on, are all to be regarded as communities on a par with Youngstown, Ohio, and Eureka, California, the American may well wonder what sense can be made out of such a patch-quilt of communal associations. Which one is to have priority? Which, if any, is *basic*, stable, deserving of his long-term loyalty?

If the proper image to have now is one of a nationalized mass society containing endless crisscross patterns of community life, then nationalism has indeed triumphed. But at what price? There are *still* all those disturbing "urban problems." And people *still* live in Boston, Deerfield, and Cooperstown—communities with real and lasting governments and laws and authority, however inadequately defined and displayed.

Americans have come a long way from the work of their earliest, large-scale "community'builders," the Puritans of Massachusetts Bay. They have lost the cohesion of an intolerant, spiritually oriented community and replaced it with the confusion of a tolerant, materialistically-oriented, varied, mass society whose people live in increasing numbers in crowded metropolitan areas. What have we lost? What have we gained?

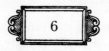

Americans: In the Aggregate, As Individuals, and In Families

The organizational scheme for American history suggested by the term *levels of communities* leaves out of account two facets of American life that are both broader and narrower than the concept of community. One is the American people themselves, either in the aggregate or as individuals. The other is the family.

I

One way to generalize about Americans as a people is to examine their character. Some able writers have done so, though with a considerable amount of confusion and contradiction. The subject is difficult to grasp and forever imprecise. Surely we all say, on occasion, "That is *so* American," realizing that whatever provoked our comment is typical, but not universal. There are those who say that the investigation of a people's character is *too* imprecise to be worth the bother of studying it.[1] Even if scholars did not, however, others would still talk about it —and write about it.

1. Thus, Boyd Shafer: "[There isn't] any such thing as national character. National characters if any exist are certainly of recent origin and the nations themselves have not been constant. Attempts to describe the national characters of the various peoples . . . are impressive in their bulk . . . But all generalizations, even the intelligent ones, are no more than tentative hypotheses. If they have any validity it is only for a particular moment and then with so many exceptions that they are inaccurate; if they contain any truth for the whole national group, they more than likely do not apply to any individual within the group; and if they have any meaning, this is not because of anything inherent in man and nature but only because different groups have different historically

The best sources on the subject are foreign travelers who have left dozens of accounts of Americans. Only in this century have Americans themselves studied their own character. Among the most noticeable researchers are social scientists, who have been both old-fashioned observers as well as takers of surveys. More recently, a few historians —most notably David Potter—have ventured into the field. What has emerged matches the presumed nature of the subject itself. Some have written about traits of character (such as practicality and inquisitiveness), while others are concerned about values (progress, freedom). Some think character is stable and is itself a determinant of political-economic-social life (Lipset), while others see a shift in character resulting from a shift in the nature of the society (Riesman).[2] Some present evidence for contradictory elements in the American character (Potter's idealism and materialism, individualism and conformity),[3] while others claim to find a basic source for that character (Potter, again: equality or abundance; Pierson: mobility; McLoughlin: pietism; Hsu: self-reliance; Turner: the frontier; and Schlesinger: the city).[4]

In spite of a number of suggestive propositions on the subject, writings on the American character are divergent, far from consensus on anything. One rightly wonders whether the subject or its newness as an area for historical inquiry causes such diversity. Basic questions remain unanswered: Why and how did Americans develop a national character? Does it go through the same process of nationalization that other facets of American life have undergone? Do regional and local

evolved cultures" (Shafer, *Nationalism: Myth and Reality*, paperback edition [New York: Harcourt, Brace, & World, Inc., 1955], pp. 228–229). It should be added, however, that Shafer's "different historically evolved cultures" gives back a lot that he had taken away.

2. David Riesman, *The Lonely Crowd* (New Haven, Conn.: Yale University Press, 1950); Seymour Martin Lipset, *The First New Nation*, paperback edition (New York: Basic Books, Inc., 1967) pp. 115–158.

3. John Higham, editor, *The Reconstruction of American History*, paperback edition (New York: Harper & Row, Publishers, 1962), pp. 197–220.

4. Michael McGiffert, editor, *The Character of Americans: A Book of Readings* (Homewood, Ill.: Dorsey Press, 1970), pp. 96–130, 146–156, 231–249; William G. McLoughlin, "Pietism and the American Character," *American Quarterly*, XVII (Summer 1965), 163–186. For statistical evidence of urban mobility, see Stephan Thernstrom, *Poverty and Progress* (Cambridge, Mass.: Harvard University Press, 1964); Peter Knights, *The Plain People of Boston, 1830–1860* (New York: Oxford University Press, 1971). For a general treatment of mobility, see George W. Pierson, *The Moving American* (New York: Alfred A. Knopf, Inc., 1973). For contradictory elements in the character of colonial Americans, see Michael Kammen, *People of Paradox: An Inquiry Concerning the Origins of American Civilization* (New York: Alfred A. Knopf, 1972).

variations make generalizing hazardous?[5] Do we associate characteristics with men only, without being conscious that we do? Are women[6] and children included? Are "outsiders," such as Negroes, Indians, immigrants, included? In short, to whom do we refer when we say something is "American" about a person's behavior, and has the reference substantially altered through the decades of American history? Has the nationalization of American life been accompanied by the development of a truly national character profile? To what extent does character determine the pattern of collective political, economic, and social life, and to what extent is character just a reflection of that life?

The evidence seems to be against Riesman's assertion that Americans changed from a typically inner-directed personality to a typically outer-directed one, a change prompted basically by industrialization and its consequences. Lipset, and indeed the early travelers' accounts themselves, show much evidence of the outer-directed personality type from the beginning, something that fits into the new emphasis on community dealt with in this book. But single-factor sources for character are easily disposed of because of their lack of universality. Thus, not everyone was regarded as equal, or shared in abundance, or moved about, or was influenced by the frontier or the city. These sources are more pertinent, however, if one gives a very tight definition of those who were *in* the American community and excludes Negroes, Indians, immigrants, women, and children.

It is impossible to list with assurance a composite character portrait of the American, though some general traits often mentioned in-

---

5. C. Vann Woodward cautions against applying the presumed determinants of national character indiscriminately to all sections of the country. Even the Puritan ethic, which Edmund Morgan found much in evidence in the colonial period, Woodward argues had far less influence in Southern life than elsewhere. See Edmund S. Morgan, "The Puritan Ethic and the American Revolution," *William and Mary Quarterly*, XXIV, no. 3 (January 1967), 3–34; C. Van Woodward, *American Counterpoint: Slavery and Racism in the North-South Dialogue* (Boston: Little, Brown & Co., 1971), pp. 13–46.

6. Certainly David Potter would argue that they are not. To avoid the trap of assuming that "the characteristics of American men are the characteristics of the American people . . . when one meets with a social generalization it is frequently worthwhile to ask concretely, does it apply to women, or only to the masculine component in the population? . . . The question seems worth asking, for it appears more than possible that many of our social generalizations which are stated sweepingly to cover the entire society are in fact based upon the masculine population, and that if we took the feminine population into account, the generalization might have to be qualified, or might even run into an entirely different direction" (David M. Potter, "American Women and the American Character," as quoted in McGiffert, p. 319).

clude individualism, conformity, idealism, materialism, practicality, inventiveness, inquisitiveness, experimentation, restlessness, exuberance, hopefulness, "good-naturedness," busy-ness, and changefulness.[7]

Arthur Schlesinger, Sr., remains the only scholar who has explored, however briefly and tentatively, the relationship between American character and the city. His exploration is suggestive of what has to be done if we are ever going to understand how the communities that most American now live in shaped their citizens' collective personality. Schlesinger found that "the national character . . . is . . . a mixture of long-persisting traits tempered by some newly acquired ones. . . . The rise of the city confirmed or strengthened many of the earlier characteristics, while reshaping others." Schlesinger suggests that urbanization has led us to consider cultural achievement important, has lessened aversion to specialization of talent, and fostered an increase in "voluntary associative activity" and the "discrediting of individualism as the automatic cure of social and economic ills."[8]

Unfortunately, the same sort of inquiry has not been undertaken with respect to the town. Smith asserts that the Protestant ethic as a source of values was given a "communal" emphasis in the town, but an "individualistic" emphasis in the city. The continued existence of the town's distinctive set of values led to the emergence of what Smith calls a "remarkable character type," a group of able, energetic youth who "constituted a self-conscious, articulate, aggressive company of 'inner-directed' men and women prominent in all areas of national life."[9] These gifted "small-town boys who made good" are what Smith thinks of as the finest product of the best facets of the American character. Atherton stresses the emphasis in the Midwestern town on the practical and useful, implying that cultural, intellectual endeavors usually were located in an urban setting. But this is all we have on the town and American character. It is not enough.

The only study to examine "regional" character is William R. Taylor's *Cavalier and Yankee: The Old South and American National Character*. Taylor attempts to show how stylized, stereotyped, indeed, mythological "character-types" found expression in literature and came generally to characterize "Northerners" and "Southerners" and

---

7. *Ibid.*, pp. 21–36, 41–82, 212–249.

8. Arthur M. Schlesinger, Jr., "What Then Is the American, This New Man?" as quoted in *Ibid.*, pp. 117, 115–116.

9. Smith, *As a City Upon a Hill*, p. 236.

even "Westerners." As he puts it, before the Civil War, "[in] parables and cautionary tales, Americans were instructed in the traits which would weaken them as individuals and as a nation, and in those which would make them strong. No region escaped this. Scrutiny of social virtues and vices, and a certain ambiguity played over the identifying characteristics of each section of the country."[10]

Thus, Westerners were enterprising and independent, but also wild and unruly. The New Englander was thrifty, industrious, and ascetic, but also mercenary, hypocritical, and excessively prosaic. The Southerner was indifferent to material acquisitions, polite, and genteel, but also weak, vacillating, self-indulgent, wild, vindictive, and self-destructive. What emerged by the time of the Civil War were two dominant character types who were direct descencents of those who fought in the English Civil War: the Northern Yankee, based upon the Puritan Roundhead, and the Southern Cavilier, based upon the English Cavalier. Taylor goes on at length to investigate the Cavailier, but his concern is "primarily with the dynamics of the legends rather than with the degree of their historical authenticity."[11] His study, the only sustained inquiry into the regional dimensions of character, is limited to manifestations of ideal-types in fictional writings—an important manifestation, to be sure, but not the only one.

* * * * *

At the other extreme in studies on Americans as a people is the "aggregate analysis" of demographers: the vital statistics of a whole population. Demographers concentrate on the growth or decline of a population, on birth, marriage, and death rates, on the age of citizens at marriage, the size of families, life expectancy, and information on the health of the population and on its rate of geographic mobility.[12] Sources are church, town, county, state, and national census records—or should be. Such study has largely been restricted, however, to colonial New England. Also, the federal census has not yet been adequately utilized. Only when it has been will we have a statistical pro-

10. Taylor, *Cavalier and Yankee*, paperback edition (Garden City, N.Y.: Doubleday & Co., 1963), p. xxi.

11. *Ibid.*, pp. x, xv, xxi.

12. E. A. Wrigley, editor, *An Introduction to English Demography from the Sixteenth Century to the Nineteenth Century* (New York: Basic Books, Inc., 1966).

file of our whole population through its historical experience. This profile could supplement studies done on national character; together, they could constitute a portrait of Americans in the aggregate, *outside of the perspective of their various communities.*

Such demographic studies must be restricted to those aspects of life just listed, or the statistics produced will provide information that deals with various facets of *community* activity, however. Listings of economic activity, occupations, church membership, social organizations, and so on, should also be used in studies of economic, social, and cultural history at various levels of community life. In sum, "vital statistics" have to be precisely defined if demographers are going to provide us with the proper statistical profile to accompany the character profile, which, though fuzzy, is definitely emerging.

II

To shift our focus from *Americans in the aggregate* to *the American as an individual* is to move from one end of the historical spectrum to the other. There is one connecting link, however: both involve "persons," whether in the abstract or in the particular.

Biography is one of the oldest forms of historical writing, and its future is assured. Having long ago replaced the filiopietistic memoir offered during the nineteenth century by descendants of notable figures, the life-and-times format of modern historical biographical writings shows no signs of being superseded and will not be, as long as historians are primarily concerned with the *interaction* between important individuals and their society. A proper balance is difficult to attain, however. Some biographers—Charles Wiltse's *John C. Calhoun*[13] is a good example—are so concerned with the public life of their subject that his personality and private life are overwhelmed. Such studies become more valuable as accounts of that aspect of life in which the historical figure was prominent than as sources for an understanding of the figure himself. Other biographers—Martin Duberman is perhaps the most notable—have insisted that historians who write about individuals make full use of psychologican concepts and methods to the extent that sources permit.[14] The most balanced definition for historical

13. Three vols. (New York and Indianapolis: Bobbs-Merrill Co., 1994–1951).
14. Martin Duberman, "The Abolitionists and Psychology," *The Journal of Negro History*, XLVII (July 1962), 183–192.

biography has come from Oscar Handlin: "The proper problem of the biographer is to assess the role of men in history. His subject is not the complete man or the complete society, but the point at which the two interact. At these points the situation can throw light on the character of the individual and the individual's reaction can illuminate the situation."[15] A recent series entitled "The Library of American Biography," of which Handlin is editor, alters the formula somewhat and focusses on outstanding individuals who contributed significantly to some whole aspect of American life. Generally, attention is now being given to important figures in many different areas of activity, not just political or economic. This new range is welcome.

But what must now be considered is the relationship between individuals and communities. Figures of national prominence in whatever aspect of life pose no difficulty as justifiable historical subjects. But what about those of lesser consequence, the so-called second- or even third-ranking figures? Given the national perspective of our historical writing up to this point, individuals of less than national prominence have appeared to be of peripheral importance. Even figures associated with a region or a state have been offered as good historical subjects because their contribution was wider, or national, in its impact.

But if American history is viewed about-face, and our perspective is town, city, state, and so on, then an individual whose prominence did not extend beyond his community could be investigated on his own terms. The justification would then be simply that he was of consequence in *a* community. Obviously, such individuals would have to be placed in the context of all those whose position was the same in the thousands of towns, hundreds of cities, or dozens of states at the same period of time—just as the history of a town, or city, gains meaning to the extent that it fits into the general category of local history; there is no difference. In this way, a growing awareness of the existence of simultaneous levels of community in American history may alter the character of biographical writing.

* * * * *

A relatively new, but related, type of historical writing, one that has yet to flourish in the American field, is group biography or "prosopog-

---

15. J. Joseph Hutchmacher, *Senator Robert F. Wagner and the Rise of Urban Liberalism* (New York: Atheneum, 1968), p. viii.

raphy," what Lawrence Stone calls "the investigation of the common background characteristics of a group of actors in history by means of a collective study of their lives."[16] The "elitist" approach—"the interaction, in terms of family, marriage, and economic ties, of a restricted number of individuals . . . usually . . . power elites"[17]—was pioneered by Charles Beard in his study of the Founding Fathers, published in 1913. Other scholars have written similar, interpretive works on such obviously important groups as the Anti-Federalists, the Radical Republicans, the Robber Barons, the Anti-Imperialists, the Old Republicans, the Abolitionists, the Redeemers, the Muckrakers, the Progressives, and the New Dealers.[18] Stone's prescription is

> to make a meticulously detailed investigation into the genealogy, business interests, and political activities of the group, the relationships being displayed by means of detailed case studies. . . . [in order to] demonstrate the cohesive strength of the group in question, bound together by common blood, background, education, and economic interests, to say nothing of prejudices, ideals, and ideology.[19]

This prescription has seldom been followed in all its details, but the elitist approach to group biography is unquestionably well established, particularly in the *political* sphere. Again, however, this is true largely on the *national* level. Prosopography, like biography, needs to be both broadened and deepened. There should be, for example, a thorough study of Boorstin's antebellum booster-businessmen or the founders of New England towns.

16. *Daedalus: Journal of the American Academy of Arts and Sciences*, C, no. 1 (Winter 1971), 46.

17. *Ibid.*, p. 47.

18. Jackson Turner Main, *The Antifederalists: Critics of the Constitution*, 1781–1788 (Chapel Hill: University of North Carolina Press, 1961); Norman K. Risjord, *The Old Republicans: Southern Conservatism in the Age of Jefferson* (New York: Columbia University Press, 1965); Richard O. Curry, editor, *The Abolitionists: Reformers or Fanatics* (New York: Holt, Rinehart, & Winston, 1965); Hans L. Trefousee, *The Radical Republicans: Lincoln's Vanguard for Racial Justice* (New York: Alfred A. Knopf, Inc., 1969); C. Vann Woodward, *Origins of the New South* (Baton Rouge, La.: Louisiana State University Press, 1951); Louis Filler, *Crusaders for American Liberalism*, second edition (Yellow Springs, Ohio: The Antioch Press, 1961); George Mowry, *Theodore Roosevelt and the Progressive Movement* (Madison, Wisc.: University of Wisconsin Press, 1946); Morton Keller, editor, *The New Deal: What Was It?* (New York: Holt, Rinehart, & Winston, 1963).

19. *Daedalus: Journal of the American Academy of Arts & Sciences*, C, No. 1, (Winter, 1971), p. 47.

Another kind of prosopography, by contrast, has dealt more broadly with various categories of individuals in American life, and that is the short, encyclopedic, neutral, largely noninterpretive collections of group biographies, such as the government-sponsored *Biographical Directory of Congress* and *The Dictionary of American Biography*, concerning prominent Americans in all aspects of life. Similar collections for states and cities have been published since at least the nineteenth century. Thus, information on thousands of Americans of various kinds in various communities is available. But this information has not been adequately *interpreted*. The only way we are going to extend our understanding of recognizable and definable groups beyond the most obvious ones of national prominence is for scholars to subject the many entries of the *DAB* and the *EDC* and other, similar, collections to statistical analysis at *the same time* that they delve into and interpret the lives of representative individuals within these groups.

III

The most influential recent scholarly treatment of the origins of the modern family in the broad context of Western civilization is that of French historian Philip Ariés: *Centuries of Childhood: A Social History of Family Life*. William O'Neill neatly summarizes Ariés's thesis:

> At the risk of mutilating his subtle and richly illustrated argument, what Ariés discovered was that the family as we understand it did not come into being until about the sixteenth century. Before then, the family performed a function by guaranteeing the transmission of life, property, and names, but "it did not penetrate very far into human sensibility." Life was polymorphous, promiscuous, and collective to a high degree. Family, relatives, servants, and friends lived together, not only in the same house but usually in the same rooms. Children were unimportant as long as there were enough of them, and were apprenticed out or sent to other families for training as pages at an early age. The upper-class family, at least, was essentially a public institution that made few demands upon its members, who lived primarily not in the family but in society.
>
> In the sixteenth and seventeenth centuries, the modern conjugal family began to emerge in consequence of the discovery of the child. Once it was established that the primary obligation

of the family was to train and nurture children, the apprentice-ship system was gradually replaced by formal education. As family life became progressively more oriented around the child, privacy and domesticity increased, and the family commenced to lose its old public character. Until the end of the seventeenth century, real privacy was rare, but in the eighteenth century, the family began to push society back. The modern house with its several rooms opening on corridors made it possible to separate servants from the family, while collateral relatives were banished altogether. Among the middle classes, the conjugal family became the normal type, formal visiting was introduced in place of the old casual social relations, and the home came to be marked by the modern characteristics of comfort, privacy, isolation, and domesticity.

Relations between husband and wife grew more intimate, and both became preoccupied with the health and education of their children. The child-centered society was born and the retreat from sociability completed. This movement, which began with the bourgeoisie, spread finally to the other classes and widened the gulf between them. Ariés believes that the old polymorphous social body in which everyone lived in proximity to each other was broken up into big groups called classes and small groups called families.[20]

In brief, the "private" family as the universal, basic unit in society is a phenomenon of comparatively recent origin in modern Western history.

* * * * *

In the specifically American context, family history, long the private preserve of "old-stock" Americans with an interest in genealogy, has only in recent years been considered by professional historians as a subject worthy of serious historical investigation.[21] As in the case of

20. William O'Neill, *Divorce in the Progressive Era* (New Haven, Conn.: Yale University Press, 1967), pp. 4-6.

21. Edward Saveth, "The Problem of Family History," *American Quarterly*, XXI (Summer, 1969), 311–329. The pioneer in the history of the American family was Arthur C. Calhoun in his study, first published 1917 to 1919, reprinted in paperback as *A Social History of the American Family*, 3 vols. (New York: Barnes and Noble, Inc., 1960). Calhoun's

local or town history, scholars working on colonial New England history have provided our only solid foundation for an over-all understanding of the role the family has played in our historical experience. Edmund Morgan was the pioneer: his *The Puritan Family: Religion and Domestic Relations in Seventeenth Century New England* presented a full portrait, based largely on sermons, of the better-off colonial New England family. In 1970, John Demos presented *A Little Commonwealth: Family Life in Plymouth Colony*, in which he examined a broader range of sources, including public records, and offered a view of *all* families within that early period.

What emerges from these studies is an interpretation of the family that Bernard Bailyn, in an essay entitled *Education in the Forming of American Society*, places in the broader context of American history. Simply put, our history begins with the family, in many ways like our own in *structure*, playing many different *roles* relating to the whole transmission of culture from one generation to the next that separate, distinct institutions have since taken over. Easily the most important unit in colonial society, the family was, as Demos put it (at least in Plymouth Colony), a business, school, vocational institute, church, house of correction, welfare institution, hospital, orphanage, old people's home, and poor house.[22]

And Morgan indicates that the more prominent Puritan family, at least, was clearly authoritarian and father-centered. Fathers provided instruction for their children so that they could understand the word of God and His world and find a suitable "calling." There were formal procedures for courting and marriage that required parental consent.[23]

study, heavily descriptive, based upon literary sources, has a broad definition: "The three volumes . . . attempt to develop an understanding of the forces . . . operative in the evolution of family institutions in the United States. They set forth the nature of the influences that have shaped marriage, controlled fecundity, determined the respective status of father, mother, child, attached relative, and servant, influenced sexual morality, and governed the function of the family as an educational, economic, moral, and spiritual institution as also its relation to state, industry, and society in general in the matter of social control" (pp. 9-11). Modern scholars have not expanded the subjects Calhoun takes into account—indeed, much of his terminology has a modern tone, in so much as they have asked new questions and brought into play new kinds of evidence, mainly of a statistical character.

22. John Demos, *A Little Commonwealth: Family Life in Plymouth Colony*, paperback edition (New York: Oxford University Press, 1971), pp. 183–184.

23. Edmund S. Morgan, *The Puritan Family: Religious and Domestic Relations in Seventeenth Century New England*, paperback edition (New York: Harper & Row, Publishers, 1966), pp. 29–108.

However, Page Smith gives a quite different emphasis. He argues that "while law required that a suitor obtain the permission of his intended's father, the law was seldom invoked. . . . What is striking about Puritan marriage is the degree of mutuality that characterized it. . . . Marriages were not contracted. . . . For perhaps the first time in history, young men chose their brides and brides their husbands." With the institution of "pre-contract," "a kind of semi- or trial marriage . . . [it] is clear most Puritan marriages originated in physical attraction." This community of saints thus allowed a "new kind of human encounter" among its members, as "[the] preservation of the Puritan community superseded the more traditional concern with male succession; it was God's word which must be perpetuated, not a male succession." For a time, "[piety] was more important than property."[24]

Demos and Greven add further details to the picture. The family—at least in colonial Andover—was not "extended," as scholars once thought, but "nuclear," though "extended kinship groupings" (children living with their own families nearby) were common. Fathers maintained their influence by delaying the time when their sons took over full ownership of the land that their fathers had granted them. Families were typically larger than they now are, and the prominent ones had servants and apprentices (that is, children from poorer families who were to be broadly trained in exchange for their services). Marriages typically occurred at a somewhat later age than at present. Those who lived until twenty-one had a life expectancy quite similar to our own. But, in contrast to contemporary society, the child grew up in a world in which family life merged naturally with religious and community life.[25]

The question that obtrudes at this point is: Did the family, after the colonial period, decline in importance (as suggested by the Bailyn thesis) in the process of shedding its various social roles, or did it increase in importance (as suggested by the Ariés thesis) as it became more "private" and conjugal everywhere in the modern Western world?

24. Smith, *Daughters of the Promised Land: Women in American History* (Boston: Little, Brown & Co., 1970), pp. 41, 42.

25. Philip J. Greven, Jr., *Four Generations: Population, Land, and Family in Colonial Andover, Massachusetts* (Ithaca, New York: Cornell University Press, 1970), pp. 21–99; Demos, *A Little Commonwealth*, pp. 60–125. See also Robert W. Wells, "Demographic Change and the Life Cycle of American Families," in *The Family in History: Interdisciplinary Essays*, edited by Theodore K. Rabb and Robert I. Rothberg, paperback edition (New York: Harper & Row, Publishers, 1973), pp. 85–94.

David Rothman, reviewing the Bailyn thesis, sides with Ariés, and concludes that the family's stability and continued importance in the lives of individuals were not directly linked to such developments as the shrinking size of the household, the emancipation of women and children, or even to the decline of the father's authority.[26]

Two scholars who have written broadly on the changing character of the American family in the nineteenth century also stress the continued centrality of the family in American society. William Bridges asserts that, as the family became less authoritarian and hierarchical and more democratic, it also became a "refuge." Bridges, who assumes that family life and the value patterns of a society reflect one another, argues that, since American society was increasingly atomistic, impersonal, and competitive, child-rearing practices revealed a stress on the impersonal—that is, on emotional nondependence and detachment. The child was generally thought to be indpendent, in order that he might take advantage of different kinds of opportunities and different sorts of occupations in a fast-growing society, something that resulted in a relatively active, manipulative approach to people and things. Such training was difficult and often led to at least partial failure. In this setting, the home became a retreat from the world, a shelter from the impersonality and competitiveness of society: the home became *both* a training ground and a retreat. The home and the economy thus became the foci of opposite sets of values, each more extreme because of the presence of the other, each acting as a restraint on the other. What was the result? "A tense amalgam of advance-with-safety, progress-with-restraint, exploit-with-control."[27]

Frank Furtenberg also finds strains and stresses in the evolving patterns of family life for this period, basing his conclusions on forty-five accounts of foreign travelers who commented extensively on this subject. As to "courtship and mate-selection," the free choice of mates based upon love was the prevailing pattern, though greater freedom of movement and earlier courtship was generally in accordance with strict moral standards. The resulting strain led to earlier marriages, bad choices, and inadequate preparation. As for the "conjugal relation," there was a great loss of freedom for women when they married because of demanding domestic obligations and a lack of employment opportunities as an alternative. American women made dutiful and af-

---

26. David J. Rothman, "A Note on the Study of the Colonial Family," *William and Mary Quarterly*, XXIII, no. 3 (1966), 627–634.

27. William Bridges, "Family Patterns and Social Values in America, 1825–1875," *American Quarterly*, XVII (1965), 3–11.

fectionate wives and had power in the home over domestic matters, though they deferred to their husbands in case of disagreement.

As for parent-child relations, large families were common and the children were well taken care of, with permissive child-rearing patterns much in evidence. Children typically appeared self-confident, independent, poised, mature, left home as soon as they could, and married early. As for the position of American women, beauty was generally a feature confined to youth; it was premarital. The domesticated married woman was treated with reverence and respect. Barbara Welter adds that her cardinal virtues were piety, purity, submissiveness, and above all, domesticity. Furtenberg believes that the deferential treatment was superficial and deceptive, however—that women actually occupied an ambiguous position in a presumably democratic society. Domesticity made woman inferior, something that also produced strain. The deference paid her was basically compensation.[28]

Furtenberg concludes that mate-selection, the marital relationship, and parent-child relations all assumed their modern form in the United States *before* Americans became industrialized, and all owe more to a democratic family ideology than to modes of production. Even the stresses and strains antedate the creation of our present society: the voluntary choice of a mate, the loss of freedom for women at marriage, women's discontent arising from total domesticity, the lack of discipline in American children, and the inferior position of women—all provided strains in family life long before the presence of a mass society. Indeed, these tensions may have in a sense made it easier for Americans to adapt to an industrialized society when it developed. A lack of parental restrictions on children and the desire of women to improve their position in society provided an appropriate familial setting for industry. Finally, Furtenberg adds, the lack of attention paid to adolescence, divorce, and old age may have indicated that these aspects of family life weren't sources of strain then, as they are now.[29]

William O'Neill, in his study of the changing character of family life at the turn of the century, from 1890 to 1920, documents the way in which one aspect of family life not on Furtenberg's list also became a source of strain: divorce. To O'Neill, the emergence of divorce as a

28. Frank Furtenberg, Jr., "Industrialization and the American Family: A Look Backward," *American Sociological Review*, XXXI (June 1966), 325–338; Barbara Welter, "The Cult of True Womanhood, 1820–1860," *American Quarterly*, XVIII (1966), 150–174.

29. Furtenberg, p. 337.

family problem was perfectly natural, given the evolution of modern
family life:

> If we regard the Victorian patriarchal family as an essentially
> new institution, rather than as the last gasp of a dying one, we
> can see why divorce became a necessary part of the family sys-
> tem. When families become the center of social organization,
> their intimacy can become suffocating, their demands unbear-
> able, and their expectations too high to be easily realizable. Di-
> vorce them becomes the safety valve that makes the system
> workable. Those who are frustrated or oppressed can escape
> their families, and those who fail at what is regarded as the
> most important human activity can gain a second chance. Di-
> vorce is, therefore, not an anomaly or a flaw in the system, but
> an essential feature of it. When the modern family came to
> dominate society in the nineteenth century, divorce became
> common.[30]

The debate over divorce at the turn of the century was, O'Neill argues, over values, over the proper nature of the family in society. In a
manner very much in keeping with the emphasis in the writings of
Bridges and Furtenberg, O'Neill makes the bald assertion: "The
emergence of the modern family has had very little to do with the industrial revolution, which it predated, but instead has been substantially influenced by ideology."[31]

What has the family become in the twentieth century, in our own
time? There has been much writing on the subject by sociologists, but
their investigations are marred by a lack of historical perspective. In
1953, John Sirjamaki tried to summarize such literature. He concluded
that

> [the American family] is a small nuclear family centered largely
> upon its immediate members, settled in independent residence,
> dissociated from all but closely connected relatives, and lasting
> only through the adult years of its spouses and often not even
> so long. While it is quite as indispensable to its members as the
> institution of the family has ever been in any society, its useful-
> ness for Americans has been slanted to an emphasis upon it as

30. O'Neill, pp. 6–7.
31. *Ibid.*, p. 17.

the primary group which provides its members with affection and security in each other and less as a kin group essential to their survival and common welfare. . . . As a consequence of such characteristics, marriage now tends to be regarded very much as a private affair of the spouses. Once couples have wed, they are expected to manage their family and household by their own devices, without much further regulation by public authorities or assistance from others. . . . Within the home, moreover, the concern for the family as an institution is currently small, while that for individualization of family members . . . is large. The members are likely to view the family as existing for them and not they for it. From it, they covet principally satisfaction of their basic needs for love and companionship but more and more, also, as an increasing part of their lives is expended in the other social institutions of society, they expect it to enable them to participate in these with some degree of effectiveness. Thus, while they have a great dependence upon the family, at the same time they can engage in enterprises outside their home. . . . The family has . . . not been comparably strengthened as a social institution by legislation or other means, nor are its members ordinarily trained to consider it as having an existence apart from themselves. It is not a property-holding entity nor are taxes or other legal liabilities assessed against it, nor is it any longer to any extent even a producer group. Instead, its rights and duties are generally assigned to its individuals as citizens of the society rather than as members of their families.[32]

Sirjamaki found that this type of family reflects the character of American society. The small, mobile family is appropriate to an economic system that "tends to employ workers as individuals and to train, transfer, or dismiss them according to its own necessities without much more than casual recognition that they live in families"; to a political system that "espouses a respect for human personality and equality of opportunity as fundamental values of the people";[33] to an educational system that affirms "learning is an individual matter [with] each student . . . treated . . . as a person temporarily without a family so that

32. John Sirjamaki, *The American Family in the Twentieth Century* (Cambridge, Mass.: Harvard University Press, 1953), pp. 193, 194.
33. *Ibid.*, pp. 196, 197.

his training may proceed according to his abilities";[34] to a religious order that emphasizes "the salvation of each human being" and sustains "the individualization of family members and the development of democratic relations among them"; to a social system "comprised of open competitive classes in which the people strive for preferment as individuals rather than as members of family groups."[35]

The difference between Sirjamaki's twentieth-century family and Morgan's and Demos's colonial family appears to be immense. But why didn't capitalism, representative government, Christianity, and open educational and social systems—all in evidence from colonial times onward—lead to the family we know far *earlier* in our historical experience? The patriarchal, authoritarian, family-centered character of colonial society is a fact, as much as any historical generalization is. Why and how and when the role of the family changed into what it now is are still questions without satisfactory answers, in spite of the efforts of Bridges, Furtenberg, and O'Neill. Their studies do reveal, however, that in the critical transitional period of the nineteenth and early twentieth centuries, changing values or ideology were of crucial importance to the democratization of family life, more important than industrialization. In view of all this, do historians dare generalize at all about the family through American history?

Page Smith argues that a profound change in the nature of marriage has had vast consequences for Americans in their capacity as husbands and wives, fathers and mothers:

> Freedom in the choice of a mate and in courtship [in colonial New England] was only allowable because the ultimate aims were universally agreed upon and the necessary social disciplines thoroughly internalized and vigorously enforced by the community. The consequence was that, when marriage became an essentially private matter, of concern only to the parties involved, the institution was stripped of all social supports and constraints which both enhanced and stabilized it. When a young man and a young woman entered into matrimony. in the seventeenth century, they did so with the sense [that] they were serving a vital social, and, indeed religious purpose. They were enlisting in the service of Christ with the responsibility of producing more faithful Christians to carry on His work and with

34. *Ibid.*, 197.
35. *Ibid.*, p. 198.

an almost equally important if mundane function in the community. The choice of a mate was personal, but the marriage was notably public.[36]

In time, marriage became personal,

> and . . . what was, at best, a complex and precarious union was deprived of the forms, orders, and social imperatives that had formerly helped to sustain it. For the first time in history, the full weight of this inherently difficult relationship fell on the over-burdened egos of husbands and wives.[37]

But in other areas of family life, historians have not found such clear-cut change. Indeed, Phillip Greven rather persuasively argues that family structure, at least, has not neatly evolved in any general, linear manner through time. Studies of contemporary life "have demonstrated the persistence of widespread kinship groups and extended family structures."[38] Immigrant groups in particular have exhibited these characteristics.

> Indeed, it is now apparent that there has been an astonishing degree of continuity in the forms of families in communities and societies, whether traditional or modern, rural or urban, agricultural or industrial. . . . Under many different circumstances, from the mid-sixteenth through the mid-twentieth centuries, one can find nuclear households and extended households, nuclear families and extended families, mobility and rootedness, autonomy and dependence. Many basic characteristics of family thus have remained remarkably unchanged during the past four centuries. . . . The process of change, though, is far more complex than we have generally assumed; it is not simply a long-term change from extended family to the nuclear family, coinciding with industrialization and urbanization. Changes in family structure usually occur *within* definite periods, within particular places, whether urban or rural, and within particular societies, whether agrarian or industrial. The shapes and the natures of families depend upon the circums-

36. Smith, *Daughters of the Promised Land*, p. 62.
37. *Ibid.*
38. Greven, *Four Generations*, p. 285.

tances in which they are functioning and upon the wishes, assumptions, and actions of the people involved. In a sense, families often experience a fluctuating process of expansion and contraction, with the structures of families usually being built upon nuclear households, but with the degree of extension varying according to particular demographic, economic, and social circumstances.[39]

But what of the undeniable diminution of the family's duties in society? When and under what circumstances did it relinquish its role as the major transmitter of culture, when did it stop being a business, school, church, vocational institute, house of correction, welfare institution, hospital, orphanage, old people's home, and poor house?[40] David Rothman, in a significant study entitled *The Discovery of the Asylum: Social Order and Disorder in the New Republic*, points to the Jacksonian Era—the 1820s and the 1830s—as the period during which institutions for at least the "deviant and dependent" members of society were established in many communities around the United States. The "asylum" thus is a cover term for "penitentiaries for the criminal, asylums for the insane, almshouses for the poor, orphan asylums for the insane, almshouses for the poor, orphan asylums for homeless children, and reformitories for delinquents."[41]

Americans in the colonial period, Rothman argues, believed that man was a sinful creature with significant flaws and weaknesses. Therefore, criminals, poor people, orphans, delinquents, and the insane were a natural part of society:[42]

> [The colonists] relieved the poor at home or with relatives or neighbors; they did not remove them to almshouses. They fined or whipped criminals or put them in stocks or, if the crime was serious enough, hung them; they did not conceive of imprisoning them for specific periods of time. The colonists left the insane in the care of their families, supporting them, in case of need, as one of the poor. They did not erect special buildings for incarcerating the mentally ill. Similarly, homeless

39. *Ibid.*, pp. 287–288.
40. Demos, *A Little Commonwealth*, pp. 183–184.
41. Rothman, *The Discovery of the Asylum: Social Order and Disorder in the New Republic* (Boston: Little, Brown & Co., 1971), p. xiii.
42. *Ibid.*, pp. 3–56.

children lived with neighbors, not in orphan asylums. To be sure, there were some exceptions to these general practices. Large colonial towns did build almshouses, but only to meet unusual conditions, to confine persons so sick and disabled that no household could function as caretaker, and, in addition, to cope with strangers to the community. The few institutions that existed in the eighteenth century were clearly places of last resort.[43]

By contrast, the middle-class officials who established the asylums of the early nineteenth century, anxious about the disorder of a fast-growing and changing society, responded to the deviant and the dependent with a

vigorous attempt to promote the stability of the society at a moment when traditional ideas and practices appeared outmoded, constricted, and ineffective. The almshouse and the orphan asylum, the penitentiary, the reformatory, and the insane asylum all represented an effort to insure the cohesion of the community in new and changing circumstances. Legislators, philanthropists, and local officials, as well as students of poverty, crime, and insanity were convinced that the nation faced unprecedented opportunities. The asylum, they believed, could restore a necessary social balance to the new republic, and at the same time eliminate long-standing problems. At once nervous and enthusiastic, distressed and optimistic, they set about constructing and arranging the institutions. . . . The nation had a new sense of its society. Americans now wrote voluminously about the origins of deviant and dependent behavior, insisting that the causes of crime, poverty, and insanity lay in the faulty organization of the community. From this perspective they issued harsh and bleak judgments on the functioning of society and the perils that citizens faced. Yet at the same time they shared a keen sense of the promise of social action, for the diagnosis seemed to contain the cure. This viewpoint led directly to the discovery of the asylum. . . . The asylum was to fulfill a dual purpose for its innovators. It would rehabilitate inmates and then, by virtue of its success, set an example of right action for the larger society. There was a uto-

43. *Ibid.*, p. xiii.

pian flavor to this first venture, one that looked to reform the deviant and the dependent and to serve as a model for others. The well-ordered asylum would exemplify the proper principles of social organization and thus insure the safety of the republic and promote its glory.[44]

What resulted were institutions that emphasized regimentation, uniformity, and order, similar to that of the military or the emergent factory.

Rothman suggests that reform, or the desire for institutional innovations, at least, was based upon a fear of social disorder—rather a new emphasis for the reform crusades of the antebellum period. He also links the objectives of officials to those of the communitarian reformers who, like Owen, also sought to establish model communities that the society at large could emulate.

By the 1850s, the new institutions were clearly failing to achieve their founders' goals. With the asylums a relatively cheap means of maintaining social order, especially with the arrival of large numbers of alien immigrants swelling the rank of deviants and dependents, Americans allowed a second generation of officials to turn the discipline that was to lead to reform into a mere custodial operation—dreary, monotonous, and long-term, if not terminal, in duration. Thus, the asylum remained the physical means by which Americans kept their deviant and dependent out of sight, long after they no longer believed such action would lead to the restoration of normality.[45]

But by the turn of the century,

> [as] America became increasingly industrialized, new methods replaced the asylum for dealing with social problems. When American industrial output surpassed that of every other nation, when the city population outnumbered the rural, and when immigrants flocked to the new world and its factories, then citizens began to substitute foster homes and adoption procedures for the orphan asylum, to experiment with probation and parole systems that would avoid or curtail imprisonment, to organize pension and social security plans that would replace the alsmhouse, and to begin to operate out-patient centers in order to avoid hospitalizing the insane.[46]

44. *Ibid.*, p. xviii, xix.
45. *Ibid.*, pp. 237–295.
46. *Ibid.*, pp. xvi–xvii.

Even if Rothman overstresses fear of social disorder as the most significant reason for the actions of asylum officials, even if he overdraws the relationship between what they built and the model communities of the communitarian reformers (Did asylum officials really want *all* Americans eventually to live in an asylumlike setting?), there is no question that his study is an important initial inquiry into the ways in which institutions took over the tasks largely fulfilled by the colonial family.[47]

Similarly, Michael Katz, in his *The Irony of Early School Reform: Educational Innovation in Mid-Nineteenth-Century Massachusetts*, argues that reformers who became education officials in that state and set the pace for change tried to impose a rationally conceived and outlined system upon urban and industrial communities with growing numbers of working class immigrants:

[The] people of most wealth and prestige in communities, often joined by those of more middle-level social position, supported educational innovations, especially the establishment of high schools. These people shared an ambivalent perception of the growing urbanism and industrialism that marked the commonwealth. Cities and factories were necessary, good, and should be promoted; cities and factories brought social and familial disintegration and chaos. Related to their ambivalent perception of society were their contentions concerning the virtues of educational reform in general and the high school in particular. The high school would foster urbanism and industrialism by creating communal wealth, by training skilled workmen, by assuming the functions of outmoded apprenticeships, by providing necessary channels for mobility. The high school would curb the evils of urbanism and industrialism by unifying and civilizing the community and the family, by overcoming the hostility and apathy of parents to education that would help build modern industrial cities permeated by the values and features of an idealized rural life. The relation between expenditures on education, high school establishment, and the nature of communities reveals the depths of commitment to this ideology, for it was in the more urban and indus-

47. On juvenile delinquency in particular, see Joseph M. Hawes, *Children in Urban Society: Juvenile Delinquency in Nineteenth-Century America* (New York: Oxford University Press, 1971).

trial communities, those in need of educational innovation according to the ideology, that educational change was most apparent. Educational change, however, was not a gentle process: educational promoters, convinced of the value of their wares, harangued and badgered the mass of reluctant citizens; the style of reform was imposition. . . . [But] the high school was not usually attended by the working class whom it was allegedly intended to benefit; it was not welcomed by the people for whom it was supposedly established.[48]

The organization of the new system paralleled developments in industry:

Women made up an increasing proportion of the industrial as well as the educational labor force. In industry the growth of larger units of production was part of a process of rationalization: the subdivision of processes in the manufacture of goods and the gathering of all workers engaged in making a product under one roof. Workers, moreover, were given training to increase their efficiency. Educational reorganization reflected the same trends. The teaching process was to be subdivided; each teacher, ideally would be responsible for but a part of a student's education, and the teachers would be trained in the new normal schools. Overlap between schools, where possible, was to be eliminated and larger, more efficient units created through regrouping. Rationalization, the division of labor, training, and feminization all marked both industry and education.[49]

Finally, on the nature of the educational process and the ultimate purpose of schooling, there was basic agreement:

The sordid materialism of society bred personalities that took as their standards for action, their cues for behavior, the vain and often dangerously immoral code of those around them. The duty of the school was to supply that inner set of restraints upon passion, that bloodless adherence to a personal sense of

48. Katz, *The Irony of Early School Reform: Educational Innovation in Mid-Nineteenth-Century Massachusetts* (Cambridge, Mass.: Harvard University Press, 1968), pp. 49–50.
49. *Ibid.*, pp. 59–60.

right, which would counteract and so reform the dominant tone of society. This goal was to be attained through nicely balancing intellectual, moral, and physical education; and the forms of that education were to stress hard work and the provision of the models that, more than lecturing, would form the personality of the child.[50]

There was, then, much about the development of educational institutions that paralleled what Rothman found in the asylums for the deviant and the dependent: in both, reformers were concerned about social order and the imposition of values and behavior patterns through institutions designed uniformly and specifically for those purposes by the reformers themselves in a society experiencing the dislocations that everywhere attended modern urbanization and industrialization.

* * * * *

Historians have not sufficiently studied the members of the family unit—mother-wife, father-husband, and children—either. Curiously, though the vast bulk of historical writing focusses on adult male activity, the man as husband and father has been the subject of very little of that writing. For instance, we do not even know very much about what Americans have thought the "good" or "successful" father and husband *ought* to be, or what his image has been throughout our history. And though Morgan's colonial Puritan father is clearly what we call an authoritarian figure, as well as a patriarchal one, we know little about the timing and manner in which his role within the family evolved into what it is now: still nominal head, but sharing his authority with spouse and various institutions.

Similarly, there is much that we do not understand about the changing role of women within the family. Unlike men, women have been the subject of only a small number of historical studies. Indeed, their very existence poses a problem for a profession whose categories have evolved with the presumption that it was men who were the historical actors. How are women to be categorized? They are most definitely not a minority group, as they comprise approximately half the adult popu-

50. *Ibid.*, p. 131. For the relationship between reform and social control, with reference to another "crusade," see David J. Pivar, *Purity Crusade: Sexual Morality and Social Control* (Westport, Conn.: Greenwood Press, 1973).

lation. But women, until recently, have obviously been dealt with un-
equally in legal, political, economic, social, and cultural-intellectual
terms. Because of this, they have been presented in the guise of either
an oppressed minority or a militant reform group. The story of the
American woman and the development of female equality in our society is a complicated one, but it can be far more effectively told when
women are presented as half the adult population and thus an integral
part of any explanation of political, economic, social, or cultural-
intellectual development in the national, regional, state, urban, town,
or rural level.

Page Smith's *Daughters of the Promised Land: Women in American
History*, the first general treatment of the subject, is disappointing,
largely because of its failure to define the subject in the manner just
suggested. His inquiry is restricted in the colonial period almost entirely to New England, in later periods to the North, and throughout to
the urban middle class. This makes even tentative generalization extremely difficult and forces Smith to restrict the applicability of his
conclusions, even in the act of making them. For instance: "The reader
hardly needs to be reminded that the women about whom I have been
talking are primarily urban middle-class women of the North. I have
had little to say about Southern women or about fronteir women, the
women of the great westward migration." Or: "Thus, if the argument
offered here can be accepted, American women, more particularly
middle-class city dwellers (who were, to be sure, a small minority of the
population)." Even more restrictive is the large amount of space devoted to women reformers, something Smith explains, but does not
justify: "As a historian I started out to treat them as 'history,' interesting
and touching curiosities from an earlier age, but they broke through
my scholarly defenses and became what I had not at all anticipated or
intended, the heroines of this book."[51]

Smith obviously wants to stimulate further study on the subject;
and, in fact, does not "care whether [others] find me right or wrong so
long as in so doing they help to illuminate the role of women in American history." The problem is that his book is presented as a *general*
treatment, when in fact it exhibits many of the same limitations as his
earlier study on towns. In both there is a preoccupation with one region
(at first New England, and later, the North more generally) and with
one type (in one, the covenanted town; and in the other, first the
better-off Puritan and later the urban reformer). Men may well have

51. Smith, *Daughters of the Promised Land*, pp. 215, 66, 345.

"deprived women of their history, and, in consequence, of an important part of their identity, by the simple expedient of not telling
it"[52]—as Smith claims. But his own presentation could have had far
greater impact if he had dealt with all areas, all classes, and all aspects of
life with equal emphasis.

Even so, the level of generalization based upon illustration goes well
beyond anything that has yet appeared in print. Smith correctly makes
the over-all role of women in American life the most significant aspect
of their history, even if reform activity receives much more of his attention. In ancient Greece and Rome, women were classified and divided
into several distinctive functions: mother/wife, mistress, concubine,
courtesan, slave girl, religious woman, and so on. It was thought that
"[feminine] sexuality could be reconciled with an orderly and creative
society only if the functions of women were separated and sharply defined, if, indeed, they were represented in different categories of
women . . . each category limited to its sphere." Christianity, by contrast, "offered the fragmented, divided women of specialized
function . . . a new wholeness," as women were accepted on a basis of
equality with men as the children of one God. Men and women who
married were to love and obey God and to have sexual intercourse for
procreation.[53]

In colonial America, Smith concludes, the Puritans carried the
Christian concept of the wholeness and spiritual equality of women to a
new high point.[54] But as American society became less primitive, more
settled, more complicated, women were again defined, as in Greece
and Rome, in terms of specific functions. The long-term aim of female
reformers was to gain secular equality, something the Christian
churches had long argued existed in the spiritual realm. However, the
women's rights movement developed at the same time that increasing
specialization and secularization overwhelmed the simple colonial society that had permitted a fuller development of the Christian concept
of woman. The emergence of secular equality and a renewed insistence
that women no longer be reduced to distinctive sexual roles has therefore occurred in a society that has placed a great emphasis on
specialized role-playing. In a sense, women's reform movements represent a triumph over practical, social imperatives, just as the primitive
Christian ideal in big, specialized, imperial Rome had. But equality as

52. *Ibid.*, pp. ix-x, 340.
53. *Ibid.*, pp. 15, 22, 24–25.
54. *Ibid.*, pp. 40–43, 54, 56.

an ideal has been central to the American experience; it has been used by all groups who have felt oppressed as their justification for demanding legal equality in a society whose very structure became, with the growth of industrialization, increasingly complicated.

The usual aspects of life receive far less attention in Smith's study. He is fitfully concerned with the various roles women came to play from the mid-eighteenth century onward, but he is only marginally concerned with economic, cultural, intellectual, social, or political life as such. Only religious experience is probed extensively, and even in this case the reason is that religion and reform were linked in the feminist movements as in all others.

Still, Smith's point about woman's changing role in our society is well worth further interpretation. What he says, in effect, is that, after the mid-eighteenth century, at the same time that women came to play a variety of *sexual* roles—wife/mother, mistress, promiscuous sexual partner, whore, slave girl—their *economic* role became increasingly restrictive. As Smith explains:

> It was not until the end of the colonial era that the idea of a "suitable" or "proper" sphere of feminine activites began to emerge. Women were thought of primarily as wives or mothers and their functions defined positively in terms of these basic roles. There were, in the early years, very few negative definitions—that this or that activity was unsuitable or inappropriate for a woman to engage in. In consequence, colonial women moved freely into most occupations in response to particular needs and opportunities rather than abstract theories of what was proper. Most frequently they took over a dead husband's or father's business, and we find them acting as shopkeepers (in very considerable numbers), teachers, blacksmiths, hunters, lawyers, inn-keepers, silversmiths, tinworkers, shoemakers, shipwrights, tanners, gunsmiths, barbers, and butchers.[55]

David Potter, in his article "American Women and the National Character," tried to account in general terms for the evolving role of women in our society and, in doing so, investigated some of the categories that Smith tends to ignore. Industrialization created the need for female office personnel and assembly-line workers. Once the male monopoly on jobs outside the home was broken, the historical basis for female subordination was swept away. Legal equality, first in

55. *Ibid.*, p. 54.

the political sphere and more recently in the economic sphere, followed. But even though more than a third of American women now have occupations outside the home, the majority are still only keepers of the house and all continue to bear primary responsibility for rearing the children. Potter, unlike Smith, stresses the fact that woman's role in our society is still *primarily* that of mother and wife.

In colonial times, Morgan and Demos portray her as having a distinctly subservient, though important, role in family life.[56] Potter adds that the man was typically the producer of food, fuel, dwelling, and raw materials for clothing, whereas the woman not only cooked, kept house, and cared for the children, but also processed the things her husband produced, thus making the home largely a closed economic unit.

Industrialization and its attendant mechanization has "largely eliminated the need for brute strength and great physical stamina in most forms of work," thus providing a kind of equality of economic opportunity between men and women. Occupations are apart from homes, and women have increasingly mechanized homes. In the process, the mother figure has replaced the father as the central authority, as the father is absent most of the time while the children are being reared. Potter also emphasizes the special occupational character of the woman as child-rearer/housekeeper/consumer. Her work is still general and broad-ranging in an age of specialization; she is, in fact, virtually the last of Boorstin's "versatile amateurs." And, as such, her work pattern is without the neat compartmentalization of work-time and leisure-time and alters far less dramatically through her married life than that of her husband's. Amazingly, even though she is charged with responsibilities of enormous importance—rearing the children and supplying the family—"the housewife is the only worker who does not get paid" and, indeed, as the major consumer, "is an object of condescension . . . someone who need not be treated as a mature person." The modern American woman, Potter concludes, retains a social inequality that stems from the biological fact of child-bearing and the social-economic fact that the child-bearing, consumer-housewife is not even paid for her fundamentally important activities; both circumstances produce an ambivalence in the position of woman in our society. "The inescapable fact that males can have offspring without either bearing them or rearing them means that the values of family life and of personal achievement can be complementary for men, where they

56. Morgan, *The Puritan Family*, pp. 29–64; Demos, *A Little Commonwealth*, pp. 82–99.

are conflicting values for women. . . . This one immutable and timeless fact, more than anything else, seems to stand forever in the way of the complete and absolute equality of men and women."[57]

Potter's contribution on the subject of women in American history is certainly not exhaustive. Indeed, it is not in the form of a well-documented inquiry, but rather is a generalized account based upon observations that seemed self-evident to the author; but he has left us with a general framework that should be utilized in further study.

Unlike men, women in American society have always had an image or ideal—at least in the minds of men. The good and virtuous woman has always been depicted in our literature, art, and folklore. The extreme expression of the cult of womanhood was a Southern regional one and pertained to the aristocratic white female in a hierarchical, caste system. But this cult was in evidence everywhere, from frontier to eastern seaboard. In an article based upon women's magazines, gift books, and religious tracts, Barbara Welter concludes that there was a fixed, static cult of true womanhood (at least in the 1820–1860 period) in a volatile, changing society. A true woman's cardinal virtues were piety, purity, submissiveness, and, above all, domesticity.[58]

The only study to link women to community is Anne F. Scott's *The Southern Lady: From Pedestal to Politics, 1830–1930*. Focussing on the peculiar caste character of Southern society before the Civil War and the distinctively, persistently rural setting of the region throughout the century studied, she concludes that the image of the Southern woman—essentially that which Welter found—was considerably different from the reality of a restricted, hard-working domestic life, on all levels of society, even on the plantation. After the Civil War, industrialization, the growth of towns, and increasing economic opportunity outside the home led to a more complex setting and, thus, to greater diversity in female roles than was the case before the war. But such changes had important restrictions: "Even prosperous country women were still exceedingly busy with related chores of house and farm, and the far greater number of poor farmers' wives were so burdened as to be quite out of the mainstream of modern life. The town, by contrast, provided servants, leisure, the stimulation of group activity—in short, the essential milieu in which the new woman could develop."[59] From

57. Potter, "American Women and the American Character," in *The Character of Americans*, edited by Michael McGiffert, pp. 318–334.

58. Welter, "The Cult of True Womanhood, 1820–1860," pp. 150–174.

59. Anne F. Scott, *The Southern Lady: From Pedestal to Politics, 1830–1930* (Chicago: University of Chicago Press, 1970), p. 228.

such women came the reform movements of the late nineteenth and early twentieth centuries.

* * * * *

According to Morgan and Demos, children in colonial times were regarded as miniature adults after about the age of six and thus never had what we call adolescence. Children were to love, respect, honor, and revere their parents, while parents were to love, provide for, instruct, and train their children. Reading, writing, ciphering, vocational skills, and religious instruction were all family-centered educative activities. The child's world was the patriarchal family, which merged imperceptibly with the wider life of the community. Preaching in church and instruction in private schools supplemented what was, under law, a family responsibility in the first instance.[60]

By the middle of the nineteenth century, according to Richard Rapson, outsiders thought children in the United States were "precocious"—"saucy, self-reliant, wild, spontaneous, immodest, independent, demanding, irreverent."[61] Observers noticed a blurring of the lines between parent and child. The family itself appeared to have become democratized: parents were open and friendly and permissive with their children, in fact, were *like* their children. Likewise, homes were "loose," the opposite of warm and cozy and orderly. American society had come to worship the very youthful qualities that its children had been allowed to develop. In America, even adults were childlike and admired what was youthful. By contrast, the emergent public school system was becoming the major source of discipline, presumably taking over the role that the family had played.

David Potter[62] has given further emphasis to the permissiveness of the modern American way of raising children by pointing to material abundance as a factor of great consequence. Bottle-feeding replaced breast-feeding and thus emphasized early the "separateness of the infant as an individual," while at the same time producing better initial

60. Morgan, *The Puritan Family*, pp. 65–108; Demos, *A Little Commonwealth*, pp. 62–106.

61. Richard L. Rapson, "The American Child as Seen by British Travelers, 1845–1935." *American Quarterly*, XVII (Fall 1965), 520–534, 532. The beginning of a distinct "adolescence" during the nineteenth century is explored in Joseph F. Kett, "Adolescence and Youth in Nineteenth-Century America," in *The Family in History: Interdisciplinary Studies*, edited by Theodore K. Rabb and Robert I. Rotberg, pp. 95–110.

62. Potter, *People of Plenty*, pp. 189–208.

nourishment. Household space has added to the sense of apartness of the American child. Heated homes have given him physical freedom from heavy, restrictive clothing, by giving him warmth in cold weather. The disposable diaper and washing machine have allowed a permissive system of toilet training.

Likewise, abundance has profoundly affected the family as a whole. For instance, it has made possible earlier marriages and thus younger parents, along with conditions for prolonging life and producing parents who will live to rear their own children. Abundance has, to be sure, also broken up the old economy of scarcity based upon a family's working at home. But though a father works away from home, he has more leisure time to spend with his children, as does a mother with young children because of labor-saving devices and outside services. Although modern parents have more leisure time to spend with their children, however, those same parents have lost control of their children's peer group, which has moved beyond family siblings with the development of the public school system. Abundance has permitted marriage on the basis of emotional attachment, bringing to the union all the instability inherent in this kind of relationship. Abundance has also fostered a capacity for independent decision-makiing and self-reliant conduct in dealing with economic diversity and opportunity, and fathers instill these traits into their children. Abundance also allows for an increasing delay in economic responsibility for youth. Thus, the years of schooling are protracted, with laws "setting minimum ages for leaving school, for going to work, for consenting to sexual intercourse, or for marrying. . . . Delays in reaching economic maturity are not matched by comparable delays in other phases of growing up. . . There is a kind of imbalance between the postponement of responsibility and the quickening of social maturity,"[63] which makes American adolescence a difficult age.

Potter's study, like his article on women, is a wide-ranging commentary on familiar features of American life which, in this case, he believed could be explained by reference to relative economic abundance. Unlike his article on women, however, this broader inquiry is difficult to place in time. Nowhere does Potter indicate what period of time he is referring to. The whole process of child-bearing in a society of abundance thus has an annoyingly timeless and static quality. Potter also ignores certain aspects of the subject, most notably child labor during industrialization. Though Rapson's and Potter's writings do not by

63. *Ibid.*, p. 207.

any means exhaust the need for study on children and the family, we can at least begin to understand from them the breakdown of a family-centered transmission of culture from generation to generation, even though neither explained how, why, or when family life evolved into something quite different from what it was in the colonial period.

What the family did in colonial times was not totally *replaced* by social, cultural, and religious institutions during the nineteenth century, but those institutions certainly challenged the parents for control of educative functions that were once largely the family's own. Occupational training, religious and ethical instruction, academic study—all came to be formally imposed from outside. Governments passed laws establishing compulsory education, regulating child labor, forming a selective-service system, and defining at what chronological age adulthood is attained, just as in colonial America—at least, in New England—provincial assemblies made such matters the responsibility of parents. Also, juvenile courts have been created to adjudicate infractions of the laws committed by minors. The result has been the development of adolescence, a distinctive stage between childhood and adulthood. This stage has lengthened in recent years, as social and economic maturity have been further separated from biological maturity, resulting in the boredom and alienation of a mass youth culture. In the meantime, the family has come to play a much greater psychological role at the same time that outside institutions have assumed a much greater educative role.

The period during which children become adults is probed in a general way by Oscar and Mary Handlin in their *Facing Life: Youth and the Family in American History.* With a well-developed capacity to convey the essence of a broad development in succint but convincing prose, the Handlins reveal (1) that the apprenticeship system was the way in which most young Americans came to an occupation until well into the nineteenth century; (2) that schools, from the students' perspective, have mainly been a place for those whose parents have wanted them to learn basic skills, to be inculcated with moral and religious values, or, more recently, to attain status or important positions; and (3) that schools, under the direction of educators, have taken on a bewildering variety of functions in this century, but reflect society by turning learning and knowledge into a kind of industry at the same times as they provide the setting for prolonged adolescence for an ever-increasing percentage of the population.

In colonial times:

Schools appeared in response to felt needs that arose either out of the shortcomings of existing arrangements for education in the family or out of the situation of dependent groups in the population. . . . It was wasteful of time and effort for each laboriously to tutor his own charges, when any competent adult could instruct a whole group at once. The service was worth a moderate price. A wide variety of types of instruction arose as a response to the demand. . . . Apprenticeship remained the most common form of getting a boy out of the home. Attendance at college became a varient for people with aspirations toward a higher social rank than that of the artisan. When the conditions of life in the colonies eased, some families could afford to provide their sons with an interval of study between childhood and adulthood . . . Apart from those destined for the ministry, the students had no clear idea of why they were in college . . . To survive, [such institutions] sought to provide a gentlemanly liberal education to young men in the awkward age between childhood and independence. Yet for the time being most Americans found alternative means of leaving home more attractive, so that the college, whatever its future importance, remained peripheral to colonial life.[64]

From 1770 to 1870:

The forms of apprenticeship by which boys acquired training and left home were not quite as varied after 1770 as before. In those occupations in which the level of skill was relatively low, employers used wage labor, especially after immigration increased the supply of hands and the factory provided the techniques for managing large numbers. A succession of mechanical inventions made it cheaper to take on help by the hour, day, or week rather than to get ensnared in the cumbersome apprenticeship arrangement. . . . Furthermore, in many callings, the family aspects of the apprenticeship relationship faded away. Informal arrangements replaced the written contract or indenture, terms were rarely fixed or precise, and the youth often lived with his own parents or in a boardinghouse rather than with the master. In many cases, the labor and wages in-

64. Oscar and Mary Handlin, *Facing Life: Youth and the Family in American History* (Boston: Atlantic-Little, Brown & Co., 1971), pp. 45, 59, 61.

volved became more important to both parties than the discipline and instruction. . . . Occasional efforts to restrict access to the professions of law, medicine, and the ministry had little effect. Popular hostility to monopolies, privileges and licenses of every sort put the right to practice within the reach of many who had only perfunctory training.[65]

As for formal education,

The school . . . offered parents custodial service for children, to whom it imparted a broad education in behavior, ideas and skills; and it also tried to give instruction that would aid young people to locate themselves in advantageous callings. . . . No central authority between 1770 and 1870 imposed order upon the designs which expressed the variety of American educational intentions; each state made its own laws and each locality implemented them in its own fashion and, in addition, any individual or group could put its own schemes into practice. . . . Confusing as the outcome was, it set a wide array of choices before parents and children. . . . The nineteenth-century colleges bore many resemblances to the other schools through which young people left home; and to a considerable degree all these institutions competed for students among the same pool of parents with children between the ages of twelve and twenty. . . . Most students interested in getting on with careers did not find the university necessary or helpful. In the scrabble for customers the colleges competed not only with one another but also with better, or at least more direct avenues into vocations—apprenticeship, the academies, the professional schools and the institutes. . . . The dominant influence upon the college was the function it served in providing certain boys with an exit from the family. . . . Such youths were aimless and haphazard in the choice of a career; college was an interlude for indecision, sometimes entered to relieve parents of anxiety, sometimes to escape the need for making up one's own mind. In this refuge, young men who could afford it separated themselves from their fathers with communal approbation and began to chart independent courses through life. . . . The college in effect assumed the task of disciplining young men with

65. *Ibid.*, pp. 84–85, 90.

whom the family could not cope at home. . . . Americans did
not admit to themselves, but concealed, with inflated rhetoric,
the purpose the college served—to control their sons. . . .
Whatever else the college aspired to be, its first responsibility
was to supply some youths with the training for life in society
that parents were unable or unwilling to impart directly. Its
duty was to inculcate traditional morality in a fortunate minority too old to be any longer subject to father's discipline and not
yet within reach of the controls of society. This way of leaving
home protected the outside world against disruption by reck-
less young people whom it thereby absolved from the necessity
of as yet assuming full responsibility for their actions.[66]

From 1870 to 1930:

In the decades that followed, the belief that adolescence was
the time for all to study hardened into absolute certainty. A
properly organized system of schools would prepare all youth
for life, compensate for the deficiencies of the family and fill
up the interval before independence. . . . [In high school]
youths who lived at home could attend to the age of eighteen,
gain additional skills or prepare for college or professional institutions. If nothing more, the high schools provided an interval in which career decisions could be postponed. It was true
that those who followed this course also postponed the age of
leaving home and thereby created profound new emotional
tensions within it. . . . The function of that institution was,
however, unclear, for it attempted to provide something to do
for a heterogeneous student body. . . . The majority [of young
people] felt the pressure of . . . preparing for a job that would
earn them a livelihood as soon as possible; the detour through
a college without a clear vocational purpose was beyond the
means of boys and girls who had to scramble for a place and an
income early in life. . . . The function of the college as custodian of culture . . . affected its receptivity to science. The day of
the learned amateur was all but over; mastery of a subject now
called for highly technical skills, for access to extensive libraries
and laboratories, and for close communication with peers
throughout the world. Science developed an organization by

66. *Ibid.*, pp. 97, 98, 114–115, 120, 123–124, 134–135.

disciplines, set up internal standards for the accreditation of practitioners and for the validation of results, and claimed recognition of its competence by society at large. . . . Scholarship did not, however, become an activity of autonomous academies, museums, technical schools, institutes or state agencies, as had been the earlier American expectation. . . . [Instead] state institutions grew . . . through the agglomeration of functions. . . . The University—private as well as public—became a holding company incorporating a variety of institutes and faculties, some of which had formerly been separate, some of which still received students directly from high school, and some of which had only remote links to other units in the conglomerate. But the central element with which the whole was identified was the undergraduate college. . . . The outcome . . . represented the triumph of the concept of the university-college as custodian of culture.[67]

Finally, after 1930:

That education was an appropriate means for furthering equality and for preparing youth for life was by now so thoroughly taken for granted as hardly to merit discussion. Teachers and administration expressed a heady confidence in the ability of their institutions to reform the whole society. . . . The schools were critical because they commanded the knowledge vital to all and because they transmitted the skills essential to the operations of modern technology. In addition, they modeled their products for appropriate places in life.[68]

* * * * *

But what of the relationship between the family and the community that surrounded it? Since the family interacted with its setting, any attempt to understand our society's fundamental unit must involve the various levels of community that the family has lived in.

Not surprisingly, the fullest treatment of the family and the town focusses on a colonial community: Andover, Massachusetts. Phillip

67. *Ibid.*, pp. 154, 157, 166, 190, 190–191.
68. *Ibid.*, p. 217.

Greven has utilized both the "family reconstitution" and "aggregative analysis" methods suggested by demographers to show the relationship between family and economic activity—agriculture—within a pioneer town along the Atlantic coast. In the first three generations of family life in this early American town, patriarchal families were established. The process involved late marriages for the sons, delays in the transference of land from fathers to sons, prolonged paternal controls of various kinds over lands already conveyed to sons, "extended kinship groups," or sons and daughters with their own families in nearby households—all together creating large, healthy, patriarchal families and a stable community. This situation altered by the mid-eighteenth century, when siblings became geographically and economically mobile, because of complex, interrelated factors involving declining birth rates, higher death rates, earlier marriages, diminished land holdings, and rising land prices.[69]

In its concentration on both family and town, Greven's work stands somewhere between, say, Lockridge's and Demos's. But the only connection examined is that provided by economic activity. What about the relationship between family and church or school or town government? In what ways did families interact with these local institutions to effect changes? Greven demonstrates how economic life altered an initially patriarchal family life and *vice versa*. He should—indeed, he promises—to go further.

Edmund Morgan, in his study of the Puritan family, points to the laws of colonial New England as having been a reflection of the whole pattern of family life in colonial New England. He sees the family as the prime determinant of life in that society. The Puritans, he argues, believed that, if man could only be good, there would be no need for civil and ecclesiastical institutions. The family could then stand alone as the only necessary unit in human society. With this view of life, Puritans created communities, governments, and churches only because man was a sinner and needed social order that went beyond the family.[70] This social order was hierarchical, as everything else was hierarchical, both in an individual sense and in the social sense: first, family; second, church; third, commonwealth. "[Old] men were superior to young, educated to uneducated, rich to poor, craftsmen to common laborers, high born to low born, clever to stupid." Morgan continues: "The es-

69. Greven, *Four Generations*, pp. 21–99, 222–223, 272–273.
70. Morgan, *The Puritan Family*, p. 133.

sence of the social order lay in the superiority of husband over wife, parents over children, and master over servants in the family, ministers and elders over congregation in the church, rulers over subjects in the states."[71]

Richard Bushman's *From Puritan to Yankee: Character and Social Order in Connecticut, 1690–1765* extends Morgan's thesis in an attempt to link family life with community and character. Bushman gives the three equal billing, and so his study does not fit neatly into family or town history or even into the study of character. Also, the setting shifts from town (or "community life") to state (the unit chosen for investigation) to region (this is a Puritan society).

The hallmarks of Bushman's Puritan community of 1690 are law, authority, order, and co-ordination in a hierarchical or patriarchal society whose aims were clearly defined. Such a society

> molded the character of its members, establishing for each
> their rudiments of an identity . . . and [producing] personalities
> marked by rigorous moral standards, but even more by a pre-
> possession of authority. . . . The key to the Puritan character
> can be found in the responses of individuals to the series of
> stern fathers who stood over them in the homes of their child-
> hood, in the church, in society, and in the state. . . . [But] the
> firm hand of authority, structuring all of life, framed steady
> and resolute personalities, sure of the world in which they lived
> and as stern in exercising authority as their fathers. Puritans
> quickly moved from the role of child to that of father, playing
> both with equal conviction.[72]

This occurred in a society whose rules—political philosophy—stressed both the laws of rulers and the rights of the ruled. At the center of this social order was the family, "for the Puritans knew that the pattern of submission set in the home fixed the attitude throughout life and that strong family government prevented disorder in the state. The father was the model for all authority—magistrates were called fathers of the people—and the Biblical command to honor parents was expanded to include all rulers."[73]

71. *Ibid.*, pp. 18–19.
72. Richard Bushman, *From Puritan to Yankee: Character and Social Order in Connecticut, 1690–1765* (Cambridge, Mass.: Harvard University Press, 1967), pp. 18, 19–20.
73. *Ibid.*, p. 14.

Puritans became Yankees for a lot of reasons, but of most significance was a shift in religious dogma combined with an increasing emphasis on material wealth and growth in the population, which resulted in "outlivers" living apart from the original community. The revivalists of the eighteenth century argued that salvation comes from an inner experience—conversion—and not from obedience to the law and authority of God's magistrates. Guilt felt about ungodly, wordly pursuits could be dissipated with the knowledge that faith in a loving God could replace oppressive authority figures. Greven adds that, as mid-eighteenth-century families (at least in Andover) became more mobile and independent than their seventeenth-century predecessors, they became uprooted, possibly anxious and dislocated, and moved to communities where they often took part in such religious revivals. And Clark argues that revivalism most naturally flourished in relatively unsettled, quasi-frontier areas in New England—the kind of places toward which Greven's "uprooted" would have gravitated.[74] Thus, the sheer growth of a tight, hierarchical society, produced—through changes in beliefs and values—a loose and open one, whose people were characterized by independence, avarice, and shrewdness, who were more free, but "also learned the sorrows of rootlessness, fear, [new kinds of] guilt, and loneliness"—in short, the Yankee, who, in his New England habitat in the century after the revolution "produced a flowering of individualism, a magnificent display of economic and artistic virtuosity."[75]

The relationship between family life and community life as Puritans became Yankees also receives attention in sociologist Bernard Farber's *Guardians of Virtue: Salem Families in 1800*. Testing the validity of Ariés's and Weber's theses on family history, but restricted, like Greven, to an examination of one town, Farber utilizes both statistical and literary evidence to show that the structures and functions of families in all three of Salem's "classes"—the merchant, the artisan, and the new laboring—contributed to the growth of a commercial spirit. The authoritarian, hierarchical Puritan family of colonial times provided both the patriarch-entrepreneur and the patriarch-artisan. In a context of intense competition, the patriarch-entrepreneur pooled family resources and created family alliances in a search for security; and the patriarch-artisan, in a setting of social mobility, emphasized the Puritan work-ethic in the training of apprentice-relatives or of the young

74. *Ibid.*, pp. 183–232; Greven, *Four Generations*, pp. 276–279; Clark, p. 87.
75. Bushman, p. 288.

from the laboring class, whose loose, non-Puritan pattern of family life also left them open to communal forms of control from above, whether under the guardianship of town overseers or incarceration in charity houses.

Page Smith is the only writer to present a generalized picture of the relationship between the family and the town. His words have both the eloquence and the vagueness that come with sweeping generalization:

> The word *hometown* has deep meaning in America. The town was home. It was an extended family. . . . The town was made up, like the family, of a number of individuals who lived, for the most part, in a face-to-face relationship, a community in which were acted out the great human dramas of birth, marriage, death, sin, and redemption. . . . The town, like the home, became the symbol of a world of intimacy, warmth, acceptance, and security. . . . In the center of the family group and of the town as the extended family was the mother. . . . If the mother was the central, loving, inspiring, life-giving figure in the home, mother and town merged in the depths of the psyche. . . . In the founding of most towns, the "father-authority" figure was of great importance—the leader, the oracle, the wise judge, the model of excellence. . . . The man, the perpetually optimistic architect of new enterprises, was better suited for establishing communities than for making them thrive. . . . As the town matured, it pressed in upon the man and defeated him or drove him out. . . . The woman became, by the end of the nineteenth century, the dominant figure in the community. From having been strangely patriarchal in its early years, the town became matriarchal. The mother rather than the father became the central image, the strong, compelling individual. . . . The town, built by the man, and so often the tomb of his ambitions, was the perfect setting for the woman. The female presence pervaded the town's life; the female as mother—cooking, baking, admonishing, loyally supporting the beaten husband, sponsoring culture, maintaining the church, upholding the old values, pushing her children, plotting, planning, saving, and finally subduing the town, making it into a larger mother, the place where trust and love and understanding could always be found, making the town one of

America's most persistent and critical symbols—the town as mother, comforter, source of love.[76]

Thus did the patriarchal man of the early and mature town give way to the matriarchal woman who took charge of the town's imitative cultural, artistic, educational, and reform activities by the late nineteenth century. "The ecstasies, the hysteria, and the violence" of the Woman's Christian Temperance Union, its image of "the sodden and defeated male,"[77] were thus the expression of female resentment against the inadequacies, the loss of status and self-confidence of the man in the town.

The "small-town boy," by contrast, lived in a world that brought confidence, because he could encompass it physically and try to understand it. The boy felt he belonged to the whole community and developed a deep sense of security. He joined in adult activities at an early age and was naturally educated into adult society. Boys had a great deal of physical freedom within their security. Within the town, churches and schools educated the child in a certain life-style based upon the town's version of the Protestant ethic.[78]

Smith also characterizes the town as a way-station for rural families who moved into villages before later moving on to cities;[79] and so it must have been, for *some* families. Others, of course, stayed in towns for a number of generations, even towns that grew into cities. The migratory patterns of families are surely complex, and one can easily think of other patterns: from town *out* to countryside, from countryside *directly* into city, from town to city, of course, and more recently, from city to town.

The only study of the American family in an urban context is sociologist Richard Sennett's *Families Against the City: Middle-Class Homes of Industrial Chicago, 1872–1890*. Sennett's study is a sometimes difficult-to-grasp combination of his discipline's grand theories, occasional references to historians' theses, bits of literary evidence, many charts, and a lot of sociological terminology. He subjected the 1,200 people of the Union Park section of Chicago to a statistical analysis, to explore certain dimensions of middle-class family life in a burgeoning city of the late nineteenth century for which literary evidence is inade-

76. Smith, *As a City Upon a Hill*, pp. 215–216, 216–217, 171–172.
77. *Ibid.*, p. 173.
78. *Ibid.*, pp. 213–234.
79. *Ibid.*, p. 257.

quate, particularly the relationship of such families to their work. Sennett's hypothesis is that "the family was used as the immediately available tool by which men such as those in Union Park tried to shield themselves from the disorder and diversity of the city."[80] Sennett found that

> [The] young did not leave the parental home, for the most part, until they themselves were ready to marry. . . . Few of the young men were alone . . . or living as wanderers without occupation; the end of the discipline of school marked the beginning of the discipline of work. Indeed, [it would appear that] . . . young men waited to move to homes of their own until they had established themselves in work, so that success in the economic order of the city came to be joined to the "adequacy" of a young man for marriage. . . . A host of sexual taboos and prohbition of child labor in this middle-class community made abstinence not only possible but a compelling necessity.[81]

The result was the development of a kind of "intensive" family whose posture toward its community was determined by *fear*:

> A guiding force was fear: fear of marrying too soon or having too many children, fear of not being stable. . . . [The] family was enshrined out of a sense of its peril in the city. . . . A confused passage from one's home to a home of one's own should have created fear about what was happening; there was no clear communal pattern to refer to, and unlike the older farm or village, the options for choice and for error in this immense city must have been so great as to be overwhelming. For a person in transit between the family of his parents and a family of his own, the lack of a common means of transition could only have produced anxiety about how one was to work the matter out. . . . The satisfaction of being married as soon as one was an adult thus became counterbalanced by the evident will to make the family stable, to sustain it by steadily working away at the job. In the midst of a city growing at a rapid rate, where businesses failed as often as they succeeded, where bureaucratic rules for advancement were not standardized, where, in

80. Richard Sennett, *Families Against the City: Middle-Class Homes of Industrial Chicago, 1872–1890* (Cambridge, Mass.: Harvard University Press, 1970), pp. 141–142.
81. *Ibid.*, p. 118.

short, entrepreneurial dynamism was characteristic of the city's
life as a whole, a very young, married worker was not free to
explore, the way other people were. . . . Would it not be
reasonable, with such tangible signs of fear about work, that
the place of the family would be that of a defensive refuge
from the work world? A well-articulated secondary literature
now exists about the fear, in general, that people of the time
had of cities; surely the family played a specific role in the expression of this fear. The upbringing of children in such a society would not focus on their participation in the city. Nor
would the husband and wife turn to the community for social
activity. Rather, the family would become the instrument of defense against the increasing complexity and uncertainty of the
city environs. The family would thus become a retreat from
perceived disorder.[82]

Out of this came a more democratic family, to be sure, but one with
problems stemming directly from the decline in the authority of the
father:

[The] privacy and seclusion, whether a willful imposition of
order against the disorder of industrial Chicago or an involun-
tary recoil, ended in cutting off fathers from those they had
brought to maturity, so that fathers appeared weak, the
mothers strong and the quality of the upbringing, in a modern
phrase, "counterfeit" . . . . These good family men, a first generation of the industrial city's middle class, did not take the
plurality of urban society into their own lives, but rather sought
to maintain the singleness and purity of their emotional lives in
the sanctity of the home. This defense against emotional plurality in themselves, this unwillingness to give themselves up to

---

82. Ibid., pp. 119, 146–147. Warner places the kind of middle-class family that Sennett writes about in the physical setting of the new suburbs of the late nineteenth century:
"To middle-class families the suburbs gave a safe, sanitary environment, new houses in
styles somewhat in keeping with their conception of family life, and temporary neighbors
who would reinforce an individual family's efforts to pass on its values to its children. The
surrounding evenness of wealth also gave adults a sense of community of shared experience, and thereby gave some measure of relief from the uncertainties inherent in a world
of highly competitive capitalism . . . In 1900 the new metropolis lacked local communities that could deal with the problems of contemporary society at the level of the
family and its immediate surroundings" (Warner, *Streetcar Suburbs*, pp. 157, 160).

the disunity of the city, but a desire rather to preserve a region of intimate life which, in its privacy, was sheltering and intense, led the fathers to disaster in the family itself. The father in the eyes of his offspring became a weakling who did not count, who failed to prepare the sons for their own tasks in the world. This failure in turn led the young people to re-establish, out of their anomie, a refuge for themselves in families of their own and so perhaps perpetuate the cycle of "counterfeit-nurtuance" of the young for social life. . . . Out of this failure in pluralism, the family lost its inner balance and condition of intergenerational respect.[83]

Thus, whether in the context of the town or of the cities, writers like Smith and Sennett find a marked shift away from a father-centered toward a mother-centered family life in the late nineteenth century. As man-created towns declined, fathers lost their vitality and mothers became the focal point of community life for the small-town family. As cities burgeoned and the character of economic life became uncertain, middle-class urbanites grew fearful, turned away from the community, and at the same time that fathers of such families lost the authority and confidence they once enjoyed. This interplay of family and community thus had a significant impact on the development of the modern American family.

* * * * *

Future studies in family history will most likely assume three different forms. One is "family biography," or the study of important or representative families *through the generations*, with particular attention to the shifting economic, social, and political position of such families in their communities and to the persistence of certain characteristics, values, and objectives.[84] Another form is the investigation of certain types of "elitist" families, such as Morgan's better-off Puritans or Virginians, or the Boston Brahmins, or prominent Southern planters,[85] whether

83. Sennett, pp. 214, 216.

84. Bernard Bailyn, "The Beekmans of New York: Trade, Politics, and Families," *William and Mary Quarterly*, XIV, no. 3 (1957), 598–608.

85. Edmund S. Morgan, *Virginians at Home* (Williamsburg, Va.: Colonial Williamsburg, Inc., 1952); Frederic C. Jaher, "Businessmen and Gentlemen: Nathan and Thomas Gold Appleton—An Exploration in Intergenerational History," *Exploration in*

in a state, region, or the nation. Beyond this, *all* families in a given area, such as Greven's Andover families or Demos's Plymouth or Bristol, Rhode Island, families,[86] can be subject to analysis based upon statistical and public records, that is, what demographers call "family reconstitution," the amassing of demographic information about all members of all the families through a significant period of time. Out of such study should come a picture not only of the changing role of the family in our society, but statistical information about its structure and size, the average age of its members at marriage, average life-span, and so on.

The most intractable problem confronting family historians is, in exaggerated form, the same problem that has plagued those who have written about local history: how to generalize significantly.[87] Statistical evidence garnered from public records can tell us much about such vital statistics as size, birth, marriage, and death, but other important aspects of family life, such as its functions and the way in which it transmitted culture or values from one generation to the next, can not *by their nature* be quantified by demographers. Thus, significant areas of family life await the slow process of accumulation—family by family, type by type—that in local history has led to the credible attempts at synthesis provided by Zuckerman, Lockridge, Clark, Dykstra, Atherton, Smith, Bridenbaugh, and Wade.

While there are hundreds of cities and thousands of towns, however, there are countless numbers of families. And though it is a safe assumption that families *share* characteristics in the way that towns do—as Morgan and Demos have already demonstrated—the immense number of units involved and the insurmountable difficulties in the way of significant measurement make convincing generalization even more difficult when applied to Americans as members of families. Similarly, the interaction between any historical activity and others that relate to it creates further difficulties. To what extent do political, economic, social, cultural, and intellectual developments shape family life as to class, occupation, political loyalty, and so on, and to what extent does family life influence these aspects of American society?

Entrepreneurial History, IV, no 2 (1966-1967), 17-39; Paul Connor, "Patriarchy; Old World and New," *American Quarterly*, XVII (Spring 1965), 48-62.

86. John Demos, "Families in Colonial Bristol, Rhode Island: An Exercise in Historical Demography," *William and Mary Quarterly*, XXV, no. 3 (1968), 40–57.

87. Edward Saveth abundantly illustrates the dimensions of this problem in his article "The Problem of Family History," *American Quarterly*, XXI (Summer 1966), 311–329.

Community life complicates the matter even further: To what extent has family life been shaped by the type of town, city, or region it has existed in? And, to be fair, to what extent does family life itself influence the pattern of community life? These kinds of question, always present in any historical inquiry, are particularly nagging to the family historian because of the distinctively large number of interacting factors he should take into account. Even the biographer, with his built-in anxiety over the proper emphasis between "life" and "times," does not fully share his colleagues' difficulty. At least the biographer has a distinctive reference point in the shape of the individual he is writing about.

* * * * *

The patriarchal colonial family as sketched by Bailyn and refined by Morgan, Demos, Greven, and Bushman fits neatly into a larger view of early American society. If Bailyn's thesis can fairly be *added* to, at all, it can be postulated that the patriarchal family pattern was present in *other* significant areas of colonial and early national life. In politics, factions—indeed, even the first party system—were characterized by family alliances and dominant figures. In economic life, the family business was common. In social, cultural, and intellectual life, there was a small group of individuals from prominent families who dabbled as talented amateurs with wide-ranging interests. Small clusters of eminent families thus constituted a kind of governing class.

After 1830, the whole pattern of life in America became institutionalized, specialized, and, at least in *form*, increasingly democratized. Factional politics became, under the Jacksonians, a largely standardized, nationwide, federal organization with a life not at all dependent on who its congressional and presidential adherents were. And yet, Jackson and his assistants controlled that party as surely as heads of factions had controlled theirs. The family enterprise increasingly gave way to corporate enterprise. And yet, control was often centralized in the hands of entrepreneurs or managers, much as fathers and sons had directed every phase of their operations. The creation of schools, penitentiaries, insane asylums, almshouses, orphanages, reformatories, hospitals, universities, museums, laboratories, public lecture and concert halls and theatres, as well as the specialization and professionalization of law, medicine, science, theology, academic scholarship, and corporate-financial management—all evolving at different rates and times—led to the progressive fragmentation of many other facets of life and resulted in the breakdown of a social order *dominated* by handfuls of families.

American life thus ceased to be patriarchal in nature—at least, in the old sense of the term. And though there continued to be an upper class based mainly on wealth and not on family, character, or virtue, the role of that class was reduced to that of a social model for other Americans in the sense of a materialistic style of living. But *power* itself has been retained by "power elites," small groups of individuals whose office, wealth, or persuasive character results in significant decision-making by a few within large bureaucratized, theoretically democratic institutions.

Thus, what began as a patriarchal, hierarchical, family-centered society became, under the impact of industrialization, a hierarchical, institutionalized society whose "patriarchs" became, not fathers in families, but, for example, industrialists in huge corporations or even middle-class reformers who sought to maintain social control through the operation of institutions that would properly mold the deviant, dependent, and immigrant elements of the population. In this century, the "patriarchs" of old have become "power elites" at the apex of such nationwide interest groups.

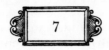

The Comparative Approach
To American History

The comparative approach to historical study is indispensable, for many reasons. The American historical experience, like everything else, can be better understood if we know how it compares with the experience of other nations and societies. What is truly significant and distinctive will stand out only if we can place our past in a worldwide perspective. This work must be in addition to our attempting to place each aspect of our history in proper relationship to the whole of our history.

But other kinds of comparisons are important, too. What became, first, a nation and, more gradually, a society, began as part of the British Empire, as colonies of imperial Britain. Therefore, to measure properly the distinctiveness of Americans, one has to compare their colonial society directly with seventeenth- and eighteenth-century England, the land that the colonists left behind. And similar comparisons should also be made with other European nations, as immigrants from other countries entered North America through the eighteenth, nineteenth and early twentieth centuries. Only in this way can the impact of a new environment on the waves of migrants who made up the American population be assessed. This is the approach that Oscar Handlin used in his famous *The Uprooted: The Epic Story of the Great Migrations that Made the American People*. And this must be in addition to study on the relationship between native-born Americans and *their* natural environment.

Also, because Americans were on the frontier of western civilization, because their society was an outpost of that civilization, all developments in their society continued to show the influence of corresponding developments in Britain and Europe, at least until the end of the nineteenth century. From the beginning, the revolutionary ideals expressed in the Declaration of Independence and the developmemt of republican government in an expanding nation influenced others around the world, and Americans of all descriptions believe in the special mission of their Union. But, as R. R. Palmer has pointed out, the American Revolution was not really exportable, in that the American colonies, populated by transplanted white Europeans, were modeled largely after British society, while, by contrast, Asian, African, and Latin American revolutionary movements consisted of native, nonwhite people in undeveloped lands who forcibly severed their connection with a small colonial clique. The relevance of the American example to these later upheavals is restricted to the revolutionary ideology that the American rebels had, in turn, imported from Europe and applied to their own situation.[1]

In the twentieth century, however, the United States has become the dominant nation in the West, meaning that influence flows largely in the other direction. Indeed, American life has influenced not only Europeans, but also neighboring Canadians and Latin Americans, as well as Asians and Africans to some extent. Therefore, any facet of American life should be studied comparatively, in terms of *outside influence*, whether of Europe on the United States or of the Americans on the rest of the world.

The relationship between the world that the colonists left behind and colonial America is described in several different ways by those who have recently written on town and family. Lockridge, criticizing Powell's earlier study of the origins of New England towns,[2] stresses the continuity between the old and new world towns by calling both "closed corporate peasant communities," whereas Zuckerman is concerned to show what was distinctive about the colonial New England town. For Lockridge, the frame of reference is outward; for Zuckerman, it is inward. Bridenbaugh shows how the largest colonial towns · rather quickly outgrew their essentially medieval character and emerged as commercial and cultural trading centers between England and a rural-village population, but he does not refer to developments in the

---

1. C. Vann Woodward, editor, *The Comparative Approach to American History* (New York: Basic Books, Inc., 1968), pp. 47–61.

2. Chilton Sumner Powell, *Puritan Village: The Formation of a New England Town*, paperback edition (New York: Doubleday & Co., Inc., 1965).

larger English towns at the same time, and so does not offer direct comparisons of the kind that allow an assessment of how distinctive these nascent cities were. Greven concludes that studies of English families in the seventeenth century show *more* flux and mobility than his own study of Andover families showed, which means that new world families were *more* settled, stable, patriarchal, and had more typical "extended-kinship groupings" than their counterparts in England at the same time.[3]

As for the world that *later* immigrants left behind, Oscar Handlin's *The Uprooted* soundly established the importance of examining the whole process of migration from the "old" world to the "new." The contrast between rural Europe and urban (even rural) America had a profound impact on the lives of the sporadic waves of migrants who constituted new elements in the population. John Higham, comparing American immigration to that of other nations, finds that it has been not so numerous in proportion to the total native population as some, but has been much more diverse in origins. The first migration (1680s–1770s) made the "chartered group" in the American nation a diversified one. The second migration made the United States a Catholic as well as a Protestant country and made possible the fast creation of an industrial labor force that built the cities and a transportation network and heavy industry.[4]

The continued influence of European nations on developments in the young American nation has been documented for literature and the fine arts, industrial processes, reform movements (particularly abolition), and would be shown in a host of other areas as well, if historians regularly considered the European in addition to the American story. A pioneering effort is David F. Bowers, editor, *Foreign Influences in American Life*, a group of essays published during World War II under the auspices of the Program of Study in American Civilization at Princeton University. Included are bibliographic listings on immigration and assimilation as well as on the economic, political, artistic and literary, religious and philosophic impact. The model scholarly study in this area is Frank Thistlewaite's *America and the Atlantic Community: Anglo-American Aspects, 1790–1850*, in which the British influence on such areas of life as economic development, political radicalism, humanitarian activity, the antislavery and feminist movements, educa-

3. Greven, *Four Generations*, pp. 261–270; Bridenbaugh, *Cities in the Wilderness*, pp. 467–481.

4. Woodward, editor, *The Comparative Approach*, pp. 91–105.

tional reform (where influence moved in both directions) are discussed.

As for outright comparisons between the "American way" and the way of others, there is beginning to be a respectable literature. Page Smith compares American towns with Rampura and Rani Khera in India, Tedoztlan in Mexico, "Peyrane" in France, "new towns" in Britain, and towns in general in Australia.[5] By so doing, Smith is able to show more strikingly what was distinctive about the American experience. Ruth Sutter, in *The Next Place You Come To: A Historical Introduction to Communities in North America*, makes a more extensive inquiry and describes the changing character of local communities in the areas that became the United States, Canada, and Mexico.

In 1966, the "Voice of America" asked C. Vann Woodward to prepare a series of lectures and interviews on American history for its audiences abroad. Woodward chose the comparative approach, to enable people in other societies to find out how the American experience compared with their own, with respect to such common historical experiences as the colonial phase, the Enlightenment, revolution, frontiers, immigration, mobility, slavery, civil war, reconstruction, the Negro since freedom, industrialization, political parties, the coming of big business, socialism and labor, imperialism, social democracy (1910–1918), World War I, the great depression, World War II, and the Cold War.

We learn, among other things, that American and European cities differ in their social profile, with the rich in the center and the poor at the outskirts in centers across the Atlantic; that the frontier experience in Russia, Canada, Brazil, Australia, and the United States differed widely because of geographic, institutional, and cultural factors; that American economic enterprise became corporate but competitive long after European countries retained family-controlled firms and sometimes allowed cartels; that the two-party system is a rarity in the world and is restricted largely to the political offspring of the British; that the United States is distinctive as the only major industrial power not to have had an effective socialist party; that Progressive and New Deal reforms both reflected and influenced similar movements abroad; and that the American experiment in imperialism (involving actual colonies) was shorter than that of the British of French, the by-product of other events, but distinctive in the insistence of the United States that

5. Smith, *As a City Upon a Hill*, pp. 284–295.

colonies be thoroughly Americanized.[6] The contributors to this volume are all well-known historians in their respective fields. Though Woodward thought this collection of brief but concentrated essays "will inspire further interest in the comparative approach among professional historians,"[7] such has not generally been the case. In fact, studies on national developments still very rarely include direct comparisons as an *integral* part of their subject. Elkins's *Slavery* stands out as a refreshing exception, with its sections on the Latin American and North American slavery systems.

Woodward's hope will not become a reality until scholars automatically think of comparative analysis as a necessary and proper adjunct of their methodology. There are, of course, difficulties. One is the misleading oversimplification that comes from forcing out of context a subject that is examined in isolation. A related problem is that whoever is writing knows more about his own subject than he does about the subject he is comparing it to.

These difficulties are outweighed by the pressing need for American historians to overcome a parochialism that has always pervaded historical writings on the United States, something related to the widely-held assumption that American life *is* unique and superior. This belief has led to a lot of tall claims for American distinctiveness that do not stand the test of open, direct comparison. From Bancroft to Boorstin, those who have most successfully generalized about our historical experience have emphasized our distinctiveness, and not necessarily out of ignorance of Europe. Bancroft, Boorstin, and Beard, if not Turner, are quite discerning about European life. What is needed are studies of all types with a built-in comparative framework. Boorstin's work stands as a kind of model. His *The Americans: The Colonial Experience* is filled with contrasts between European and American life, a technique that all but vanishes in *The Americans: The National Experience*, but reappears with a fair degree of regularity in *The Americans: The Democratic Experience*.

Of course, foreign observers who have written about American life have a built-in comparative approach. The problem with their accounts is that they tend to overstress and overgeneralize upon those facets of life that seemed most unlike their own. To take two examples: Tocqueville stressed equality as the basic fact of American life in the

6. Woodward, editor, *The Comparative Approach*, pp. 187–205, 75–90, 220–237, 206–219, 238–252, 271–284, 296–314, 253–270.

7. *Ibid.*, p. ix.

1830s, whereas, from our perspective, we find a caste society. But, in contrast to Tocqueville's Europe, the Americans *were* characterized by their egalitarianism. So too, can a modern scholar of Chinese origin, Francis Hsu, argue that the basic characteristic of the Americans is their self-reliance, because, in contrast to the Chinese, this trait *does* indeed characterize American life. But the weight of recent scholarly opinion is very much to the contrary.[8]

It seems clear that the soundest comparative history centering on the United States as the subject of primary concern will be written by American historians who have learned enough about other societies to make comparisons that are dependable. As Page Smith makes the point: "What is involved, essentially, is a new frame of mind in which the historian's study of a single period or event in a single nation is broadened to include the whole spectrum of similar events in other nations."[9]

II

Some historians who have reflected on the rise of the nation-state in the modern world have argued that the establishment of national fields of scholarship and study has obscured as much as it has revealed about the recent history of mankind. Page Smith argues that modern Western professional scholarship has, since the nineteenth century, served, not God, or one's ancestors, but the developed nations of Europe and North America. True,

> [the] Western nations, confident and poised, are able to affect considerable sophistication about their respective histories. They have shown commendable rigor in reducing overblown histories to their proper proportion, in separating myth from fact, in criticizing their own excesses of nationalistic zeal. With all this, their histories are still cast in an essentially nationalistic and parochial mold.[10]

8. Alexis de Tocqueville, *Democracy in America* (New York: Alfred A. Knopf, Inc., 1945), p. 3; Francis L. K. Hsu, "American Core Value and National Character," in *Psychological Anthropology*, edited by Francis Hsu (Homewood, Ill.: Dorsey Press, 1961).

9. Page Smith, *The Historian and History* (New York: Alfred A. Knopf, Inc., 1964), p. 224.

10. *Ibid.*, p. 219.

Western historians can forestall the misguided efforts of scholars from newly emerging nations from producing "particularistic histories in which truth is submerged in legend,"[11] that is, to repeat the myth-laden, spurious early histories of the Western nation-states.

For Smith, the "overriding theme for the century ahead . . . is the unity of mankind." In his opinion, history should be used "as a means of creating the true unity of mankind." Calling national histories "obsolete, Smith nevertheless thinks that the prospect of historians in the United States, Britain, France, and Germany "abandoning their primarily nationalistic orientation . . . wildly Utopian. It runs counter to all the tendencies and prejudices of our day. Specialization and compartmentalization are everywhere in the ascendancy."[12]

Boyd Shafer elaborates on the nationalistic focus of modern scholars:

> The customary method of historians in our times, and for the last two centuries, has been to write national histories, to study national institutions, to attempt solution of national problems. It is easier and more convenient, the material can be more readily collected and synthesized, they themselves are nationalists, it is politic, and it has become a tradition. They also do it because the nation has become the most important social unit and the most obvious one to study. People in our time live in nation-states and possess national consciousness; most of their vital activities are carried on within the framework of the nation-state. . . . [Nationality] is the most significant contemporary group distinction. . . . [Scholarship is usually the] study of national thought and action, study of but fragments of men particularly as they differ from other fragments. The whole scholarly orientation is thus toward the elaboration of differences rather than concentration upon commonness or similarity. . . . [To] study men as if they existed only in segments, to ignore what they have in common and how they are alike is not to approximate the whole truth. It is partial, incomplete, and in a sense false. . . . [Historians], diplomats, social scientists, journalists, and novelists have all been trained by their education and conditioned by their societies to seek the different, to bring out the peculiarities, and to build

11. *Ibid.*
12. *Ibid.*, pp. 219, 221.

their policies, their theses, and their stories upon these, not upon the likenesses among men. . . . [They] have nearly all overlooked the simple fact that men as individuals and men in groups are in many ways more alike than different.[13]

Shafer goes on to make the case for a return to the study of humanity:

[Whatever] "progress" men have achieved is the result of the common efforts of many men, nationalities, and races. Genius knows no national, racial, or any other boundary. Like imbecility it is uncommon in all groups, and at the same time common to all. . . . All inventions and discoveries are built upon previous ones and these in turn . . . came from men of many nationalities and races located everywhere on the earth and living at least as long ago as the classic Greeks. . . . A group, be it a nation- or city-state, cannot be described . . . as if it were a single man, an individual with very special qualities. Reasoning by analogy is often helpful; it is never accurate . . . As with physical traits the mental and spiritual characteristics of the individuals in any one nation overlap those of individuals of other nations. . . . As men have set about to solve their similar problems, they have naturally evolved similar institutions. . . . Government . . . A class system . . . A church . . . Since man in the plural is men and since men inhabit a common earth, they have met common problems and erected common institutional answers.[14]

He concludes:

Of the individual differences among men, of their national and racial dissimilarities, the studies are many and some profound. They err chiefly in that they are based upon partial observation. They are incomplete because they are so exclusively histories of nations and national heroes, analyses of national problems, and descriptions of national institutions. All that is argued here is that the whole truth be sought, and not just the

---

13. Boyd C. Shafer, *Nationalism: Myth and Reality*, paperback edition (New York: Harcourt, Brace, & World, Inc., 1955), pp. 215, 216, 217.
14. *Ibid.*, pp. 219, 232–233, 236.

national truth. . . . Scholars who stress the differences to the
exclusion of the known similarities do so at the expense of
truth and to their own and mankind's great peril. . . . [There] is
no basis, historical, biological, psychological, for believing this
nationalism must be or will be permanent. Below the surface of
their national pecularities, men remain, so far as we know,
more alike than different.[15]

The built-in comparative approach to the study of any historical
subject referred to earlier would project outward the line of inquiry of
nation-bound historians and is the only practical way of attaining the
objectives outlined by Smith and Shafer. In terms of research, the mul-
tiarchival approach of diplomatic historians would have to be extended
to other aspects of human life.

Such an approach, if rigorously pursued, would undoubtedly
greatly enhance our understanding of humanity's past. Surely we will
know more about individual, family, community life if we learn what is
common to all humanity and not merely what is distinctive to particular
portions of it. But there is a problem here. In *recent* Western history, as
both Smith and Shafer readily agree, the nation-state *has* dominated
the life of mankind. To repeat Shafer's words: "People in our time live
in nation-states and possess national consciousness; most of their vital
activities are carried on within the framework of the nation-state."[16] It
may well be, as both of these historians assert, that this will not be the
case in the future, as it was not in the more distant past. But will international studies distort what was *common* among people around the world
in the last two centuries in the same way that early national histories
inflated national distinctions?

In the political sphere, efforts to achieve an international system
have taken the form of a Woodrow Wildon-inspired worldwide organization, but one consisting solely of sovereign nations—in other
words, an organization that has kept in place the nation-state system
and even actively encouraged its growth elsewhere in areas colonized
by Western powers. The universalization of the nation-state system in
our time and the recognition that that system has received by the
world's only international political institution, the United Nations, has
meant that people everywhere are divided into citizens residing in
political entities, all of which have equal weight in the world's "legisla-

15. *Ibid.*, pp. 236–237.
16. *Ibid.*, p. 215.

ture," the United Nations General Assembly.[17] Such a system equates the mature nations, such as Britain and France, where common language, culture, traditions, history, and institutions have fitted snug, territorially defined political units, with such new nations as Gambia or Guyana. In political terms, the world is like some giant metropolitan region: a patchwork of political jurisdictions, often bearing little resemblance to cohesive societies, or communities, given a social, economic, or cultural definition.

If the world be viewed in economic terms, many factors suggest that economic activity is not *naturally* linked to political units such as nation-states. These factors include the expansion of trade, the acquisition of colonies (of such countries as Britain, France, the United States, Japan, Germany, and Russia), the recent development of supranational, regional economic units like the Common Market, and the spread of largely American-controlled multinational corporations and trade unions. In much the same way, expansionist metropolitan centers and regional economic development in the United States transcended political boundaries within that nation-state.

Similarly, the dissemination of popular and sophisticated culture and thought—whether of American or of some other origin—through large areas of the world and the greatly facilitated movements of ideas, goods, and people that have accompanied revolutionary developments in transportation and communication illustrate the sievelike character of national boundaries in the twentieth century. Once again, American urban centers fulfilled a similar function as their cultural "mix" spilled out into their growing hinterlands.

Finally, large numbers of people in the modern Western world have shared certain forms in common, such as the development of Christianity, representative government, and capitalism. These were facets of Western life that transcended national boundaries, whether during the village-dominated societies of the seventeenth, eighteenth and nineteenth centuries or of the mass societies of the twentieth. Varied though they have been across the Western world, they have given definition to the civilization that has become imperialistic and exported its ways around the world.

It is possible, especially if increasing uniformity in the pattern of life on this planet becomes more evident, that an international level of

---

17. George Kennan made this point in his Charles R. Walgreen Foundation Lectures at the University of Chicago, published as *American Diplomacy*, 1900–1950 (Chicago: University of Chicago Press, 1951), pp. 50–79.

community—the community of mankind—should be added to the proposal outlined in this essay. If historians move in this direction, they will be confronted with an enormously awkward and complex subject, but one that, as Smith and Shafer suggest, will constitute a much-needed corrective to the excessive emphasis on national history.

Some argue that, if there is growing uniformity in the world, it is the product of the Americanization of the West—or of Russian influence over other countries with communist governments. Or, as Crane Brinton put it: the radical wings of Western civilization, the United States and Russia, have overwhelmed the center, Europe. If this is the case, then the study of American influence abroad becomes an important part of "international history" in the twentieth century. With the passing of the age of two super-powers, however, we should expect that influence to diminish during the years to come.[18]

III

Internationalism of another kind is evidenced in the way historians have labored to put together the scheme this book outlines. The authors of key studies referred to in earlier chapters acknowledge their indebtedness to other scholars, particularly in France and Britain. The whole concept that there is a world we have lost, a pre-industrial village society, comes from the work of Peter Lazlett,[19] as Lockridge is quick to point out.[20] David Rothman refers to Aries's *Centuries of Childhood* as a reference point for further study on the family and concludes that it offers an alternative view of the over-all role of the family to Bailyn's—a concept worth exploring.[21] Both Lockridge and Greven pay tribute to the work of first French and then English historians on towns.[22] *An Introduction to English Historical Demography*,[23] published by the Cambridge Group for the History of Population and Social Structure in 1966, contains articles with actual procedures for research and

18. Crane Brinton, *A History of Western Morals* (New York: Harcourt, Brace, & World, Inc., 1959), pp. 402–412.

19. Peter Lazlett, *The World We Have Lost* (London: Methven & Co., Ltd., 1965).

20. Lockridge, p. xii.

21. Rothman, "A Note on the Study of the Colonial Family."

22. Especially true of Lockridge, *A New England Town*, pp. 186–190, which is a bibliographic essay.

23. Edited by E. A. Wrigley and others and published in London.

is also cited with approval by Greven and Lockridge as a guide for future demographic study as applied to family and town. Perhaps the greatest work to examine an area through levels of community, however, showing the interrelationship between geographic setting, social ideas, beliefs, and the development of community life from village to empire is Ferdnand Braudel's *The Mediterranean and the Mediterranean World in the Age of Philip II*. Braudel's unit of study is more than a nation and less than the world: it is a geographic region, the lands around the Meditteranean. His masterpiece brought together for one part of Europe for one period of time much of what this author is asking American scholars to do in general accounts of American history. Of great influence in Europe since 1949, Braudel's massive study has only recently been translated into English.

Historians of other countries ought to investigate the usefulness of a scheme for historical study that embraces individual, family, countryside, village, city, state or province, region, nation, and people in the aggregate, especially those whose nation is of comparatively recent origin. Italy, Germany, Russia, and Canada are obvious examples. The scheme being presented here is, *in theory*, applicable wherever people have built towns and cities and forged states and nations.

IV

It is appropriate to refer here to the obvious interdisciplinary influences on our historical writing, a kind of comparative methodological approach to historical inquiry itself. Much of what is "new" about the way we write history has come from other disciplines, from the social sciences especially, but also from philosophy, theology, literature, and the arts. In this century, especially, shifts in methods, areas of study, questions asked, and sources used have either been borrowed from these other disciplines or have been developed by historians inspired by work already done in other disciplines.[24]

In the American field, political historians such as Lee Benson have developed the field of mass political behavior through the statistical measurement of voting. Economic historians such as Douglas North and Stuart Bruchey have statistically analyzed economic growth. Social

24. See for example, Fritz Stern, editor, *Varieties of History: From Voltaire to the Present* (New York: Meridian Press, Inc., 1956); Hans Meyerhoff, editor, *The Philosophy of History in Our Time* (New York: Doubleday & Co., 1959).

historians such as Elkins have used sociological studies of recent phenomena to add to our understanding of the psychological and social aspects of institutions.[25] These are three well-known examples from a fast-growing list. Quantification is a new methodological device that cuts across old historical categories—political, economic, or social—and allows for statistical measurement of a great range of human activity recorded in town, city, county, state, and national administrative and judicial records, as well as the records of basic institutions such as churches and corporations.

Of course, the best historians fit methods borrowed from other disciplines to questions and evidence appropriate to historical inquiry. There are many questions that quantification will never adequately answer and for which literary evidence is clearly more dependable: those pertaining to motivation and purpose, for example. Also, there are many gaps in statistical evidence and that which is available is frequently not what scholars would like to be available. Even when the statistics are what we want, they are susceptible to varying interpretations, just as old-fashioned literary evidence is.

All this is obvious, but bears repeating now because, whatever its limitations, the quantification of historical evidence is here to stay. And it is as popular with those who have made significant contributions to family and community history as it is with any other group of American historians.

The measurement of statistical evidence by itself does not generally create controversy. After all, literary, or written or oral evidence is also usually quite restricted and fragmentary. Historians should know how to use *both* kinds of evidence, in mixtures determined by their subject and the material available.

Where controversy obtrudes is over the question: To what end? As articles and monographs and textbooks proliferate, as more and more areas of human life are subjected to historical analysis, historians such as J. H. Plumb and Page Smith rightly ask: Of what purpose is such work? Of the textbook and the survey course, Smith says:

25. Lee Benson, *The Concept of Jacksonian Democracy;* Douglas North, *The Economic Growth of the United States, 1790–1860*; Stuart Bruchey, *The Roots of American Economic Growth, 1607–1861: An Essay in Social Causation* (New York: Harper & Row, Publishers, 1965); Stanley Elkins, *Slavery*. In the field of family history, see *The Family in History: Interdisciplinary Studies,* edited by Theodore K. Rabb and Robert L. Rotberg, paperback edition (New York: Harper & Row, Publishers, 1973). In the field of urban history, see *Nineteenth Century Cities: Essays in the New Urban History,* edited by Stephen Thernstrom and Richard Sennett (New Haven, Conn.: Yale University Press, 1969).

All facts are more or less equal. Once we submitted to the compartmentalizing and fragmenting of historical knowledge, it was difficult, if not impossible, to find a principle of selection. We thus yielded without a struggle to the autocracy of the fact. We are obliged to "cover" a certain body of material; we must avoid "gaps." But, as we know very well, the essence of teaching (and of scholarship) is selection.[26]

And, of the monograph:

What is demanded . . . is that the historian do what by the nature of his craft he has been most reluctant to do, that is, distinguish between that which is important and that which is unimportant. The monograph, which includes everything of any conceivable relevance to its subject, is the model of indiscriminate history and involves the abdication of the process of selection and arrangement that is the essence of good history.[27]

Similarly, Plumb charges the so-called *Annales* school of French historians, whose mentors were Marc Bloch, Georges Lefebvre, and Ferdnand Braudel of studying trivia, of losing sight of the important developments in their past.[28]

To Smith, the proper goal of the historian is of vital importance to the health of his society:

[It] is [the historian's] concern for the future which induces him to turn his attention to the past. The future can only take place when that portion of the past which must be preserved has been distinguished from that portion which must be abandoned, and this can only be done by reference to a future which commands the deepest faith and the highest aspirations of the present. For this reason, history is important; for this reason, we pay heed to it. . . . Historians are the custodians of the common memories of mankind. In a very real sense it is upon their wisdom and resolution that the destiny of man depends. The Hebrews discovered history; the Christians made it the heritage of all men. . . . The responsibility of the modern

26. Smith, *The Historians and History*, p. 163.
27. *Ibid.*, p. 225.
28. *New York Times Book Review*, December 31, 1972, pp. 8, 14.

historian, like that of the prophets of Israel, is to speak of those things which must continue to claim our loyalties and engage our faith . . . the future given a shape by our faith, or condemned to drift and disaster by our indifference. . . . History is our greatest reservoir of self-images, ideas, and "life-styles"; it is of vast importance therefore that we preserve a clear vision of our past. If we create and promote as the truth an account of the past which reinforces our modern sense of powerlessness and anomie, we encourage this trend. If we see history more truly as the creation of man's effective will and action—and this is what historical investigation shows it to be—we can find the heart, as other generations have done, to act as men; to assert boldly, if not our complete dominance over process, at least the dignity and validity of human action. . . . If the more responsible and enlightened members of a society do not dare to say what must be done, what must be kept and what must be discarded, what is good and what is evil, the least responsible elements will insist on elevating an individual or a class to perform this function, however badly.[29]

What *should* history be, then?:

Great history, the history that has commanded men's minds and hearts, has always been narrative history, history with a story to tell that illuminates the truth of the human situation, that lifts spirits and projects new potentialities. The detailed, analytical history that is the standard produce of our academies has little to say to the ordinary man. Indeed, it often seems to have only contempt and scorn for him. . . . The textbook . . . by its deceptively bland offering up of the "facts" or of equally limp generalizations, deprives us of the most essential reality of history—that it is unfinished and imperfect, always being challenged to yield up answers to new dilemmas as well as to the recurrent questions posed by every age. . . . Out of the vast legions of the past, the few souls who have won earthly immortality—whether in history or in literature—have done so because of their power to universalize the particular, to involve themselves so deeply and percipiently in their own time or in an earlier time that they transcend time by the power of their love.

29. Smith, *The Historians and History*, pp. 226, 228, 213, 164.

Their passion speaks with such accuracy and insight of the men and events that moved them that others are equally moved and stand in spirit with them.[30]

Similarly, though more broadly, J. H. Plumb has said that "history without events is no history at all—and by events I do not mean the pitter-patter of everyday life—but the wars, the catastrophes, the conflicts of institutions and religions, class struggles and ideologies, political decisions at the center, avd also the inventions, the ideas, the books that have molded human history. These things have made us what we are and what we may be."[31]

What Plumb and Smith call for is a return to history as narrative, as drama, as a story on the scale of the great romantic historians of the mid- and late-nineteenth century, such as Bancroft and Parkman. The analytical approach is leading, they claim, to a greatly injurious trivialization of the past. Modern scholarship, reaching out methodologically and taking in ever-increasing varieties of sources and subjects, has produced a huge volume of published writing that has not brought us an appreciably greater understanding about what is *important* in humanity's historical experience.

By aping social scientists—who are as personal and biased in their assumptions as anybody else, but pose as objective purveyors of scientific analysis[32]—historians prostrate a great discipline, whose very nature precludes final consensus:

[The historian] should recognize that the truth is less in his sources than in himself. The sources will reveal no more to him than he has the wisdom to elicit from them. . . . [The good historian's] insight is the consequence not of a lack of involvement but of the deepest commitment to the people, the period, and the events about which he is writing. Such devotion does not, of course, preclude honesty, fairness, and balance. It rather makes these qualities essential if the work is not to degenerate into a simply panegyric. Honesty in the treatment of sources and judiciousness in the assessment of individuals, parties, and partisans must of course be exercised—and these may be achieved through patience and determination to subdue

30. *Ibid.*, pp. 142, 164, 228–229.
31. *New York Times Book Review*, December 31, 1972, p. 14.
32. Smith, *As a City Upon a Hill*, pp. 298–300.

one's prejudices. . . . To say that a historian is subjective is simply to state that he is a living human being who grasps the past through a kind of extension of his sensory apparatus, with the help of his critical faculties—which is the only way in which the past can be properly grasped. To say that he is objective suggests that he exists somehow outside of time, outside of the flux of human events, and thus views mankind with cold, Olympian detachment. . . . [The] expectation of making the discipline of history into a science implies, however its champions might deny it, a determinism, a complete conditioning. Unless by scientific history they mean calculable patterns of individual and social response based on man's behavior under similar conditions in the past, they do not mean *science* at all and had better abandon the term once and for all. If they simply mean methods of research and investigation that are as painstaking, as thorough, and as accurate as possible, they have no more claim to the word *science* than any honest and careful intellectual craftsman.[33]

Smith goes on to divide historical phenomena into "existential" history—"the most dramatic and sharply defined episodes of the past"—and "symbolic" history—"the creation of the historian. It has no existence, no reality, other than that given it by the researches of the professional historian. . . . Events in this category are not given names by those involved in them; they are named, and thus called into life, by the historian."[34] Existential history consists of definable events that participants are aware of living through: "At the epoch-making moments in history, the critical and analytical faculties of the participants are sharpened and intensified. The issues, heightened and dramatized, are presented in vivid form; the degree of self-consciousness of those involved in the crisis is raised to a higher level."[35] Such history is best written close to the event by participant-historians who have time to view the larger significance of what has just happened. Later history of such events has serious shortcomings:

[Such] formulations . . . cannot be more true than the statements of the men who lived, believed, acted, and . . . died in

33. Smith, *The Historian and History*, pp. 147, 155–156, 211–212.
34. *Ibid.*, pp. 202–203.
35. *Ibid.*, p. 204.

the name of certain principles and ideals. Individuals in history achieve authenticity through their actions, and historians cannot arbitrarily deprive these lives of their meaning by judgments imposed long after the event. . . . We cannot truly transcend the explanations of participants as to why they were involved in these momentous episodes; the unity of the actors and their actions has a kind of inviolability that makes it difficult and precarious to separate the two and intrude between them the conclusions of a historian writing many years or cultures after the event.[36]

Symbolic history, by contrast, "brought with it, as part of its critical and comparative method, a universal skepticism which it applied indiscriminately to the past. Symbolic history rested, quite clearly, on generalization and interpretation. Dazzled by the success of this approach, historians undertook to apply it to all history, existential and symbolic alike, with a heavy-handed uniformity."[37]

Smith admits that "topics in the area of symbolic history are concerned, in general, with the more conditioned aspects of man's behavior in history . . . [while] the dramatic and crisis events of existential history correspond most directly to man's experience of free will."[38] He also admits that "symbolic" developments in the form of

day-to-day trends move through a series of crises, [and] are generally beyond the comprehension of contemporaries; they move too slowly, lie too deeply buried, involve too wide a range of phenomena to be fully grasped by the individuals who are borne along on their slow tide. They involve ideas, inchoate mass movements, social change, modifications in economic systems, new conceptions of the role of the individual or institutions."[39]

But why restrict the study of history to those portions of the past that show off human will or that contemporaries themselves were aware of? This essay is full of references to good but thoroughly *analytical* studies that ask important, fresh, historical questions, that probe neglected but significant aspects of human experience. Is such

36. *Ibid.*, pp. 206–207.
37. *Ibid.*, p. 208.
38. *Ibid.*, p. 212.
39. *Ibid.*, p. 214.

writing of no consequence because it does not necessarily focus on people making their own world out of dramatic efforts of the will, or because it is concerned with something that contemporaries were unaware of? It may be intellectually arrogant to pursue historical study with the blanket assertion that we understand more than the people we are studying knew about themselves, but surely it distorts the nature of human beings to argue that what they comprehend about their existence is automatically more insightful than any later effort. Perspective does matter. The long-term developments Smith relegates to symbolic history can be better understood in the fullness of time.

The linkage of narrative history with measurable dramatic events is also disturbing. Smith comes close to saying that whatever makes a good story, whatever engages the attention of a group of a people and gives their lives excitement, is the only stuff out of which history can be made. But, are these the only threds in our past that are of *importance* to the development of our contemporary world? Narrative historical writing, that which is characterized by its closeness to fictive accounts of life, is full of long, detailed stories of political debates, diplomatic maneuverings, and military campaigns. Have these studies contributed any *more* to our understanding of the shaping of the modern world than have some of the more analytical ones focussed on the trivia that Plumb and Smith rightly chastise? It is doubtful.

The fact is that great narrative history can treat the subjects of "symbolic" history to great effect. Oscar Handlin's *The Uprooted* is probably the most poetic evocation of the essential character of the experience of immigration ever written; yet, it contains much of an "analytical" character. Is immigration simply "existential" or "symbolic" history? In either case, who can deny that an understanding of it is essential to anyone who would comprehend our past? In books such as *Facing Life*, the Handlins combine analytical synthesis with a chronological frame and buttress all with an abundance of detail about individuals, to produce a study for which the terms *narrative* and *analytical* are relatively meaningless. Indeed, is life in the small town, a subject about which Smith has written so eloquently, simply "existential" in character? It can now be seen that Smith's great emphasis on the covenanted community was natural, in that here were communities with a spiritual purpose. Here, too, was natural drama: Would the inhabitants live up to their ideals, or not? Because all small towns were not covenanted ones, however, Smith was forced to analyze their changing character, something he did with balance and judgment unequalled by any other writer. Similarly, Boorstin's *The Americans* time and again shows the significance of facets of our past that we thought were of little consequence—the trivia of symbolic history—and weaves together fresh observation and dramatically alive detail to produce a compelling blend of narration and analysis. In sum, all kinds of human experience, if widely perceived, contain elements of tragedy, comedy, joy, sorrow, folly, stupidity, wisdom, courage, and cowardice. Why limit our study to what contemporaries saw as definite events?

The point is this: Smith's categories of existential and symbolic history won't hold. Are people always ignorant of long-term trends? What about our own society? Are we not aware of such developments? Do not our social scientists, indeed, our historians who write about symbolic history, repeatedly call our attention to this dimension of our lives? People may be more alive when participating in dramatic events that give their lives excitement, but are they any less aware of the fact that they live in families, in levels of communities, in a society with certain values and patterns of life? If a person's life does not concern family and community, what on earth does give it structure and meaning?

The best analytical studies of recent years—often written by students of Handlin's, incidentally—have greatly extended our understanding of the character of our historical experience. They have not focussed on trivial matters; what has animated these inquiries and given them real vitality is the conviction that all those glorious narrative histories of the nineteenth century failed to provide the kind of understanding that we can at least attempt to achieve of our world as it is today. The work of writers like Demos, Lockridge, Zuckerman, and Rothman should have a broad impact on students and scholars of American history.

But will they have any influence on the thinking of that vast audience for which national and local historians such as Bancroft and Sheldon wrote during the later half of the nineteenth century—the kind of people who today are members of local genealogical and historical societies—who buy the kind of books featured by the History Book Club? The social scientists' mode of conceptualized, analytical inquiry into human behavior that flourished in Germany during the nineteenth century and was best exemplifed by the writings of Max Weber has generally failed to interest people with an interest in the past—other than students and professors at universities. The same people who at least tolerate charts, graphs, statistics, and analysis couched in a specialized, conceptualized language for social scientific studies of contemporary society insist on an essentially literary form for historical writing and have continued to equate history with the story, whether of their own ancestors, or of their community. Why? There is not a readily apparent explanation, unless it be that history—unlike the largely one-dimensional study of the present—involves time, change, and completed lives, and thus has the elements associated in the popular mind with myth, parable, anecdote, novels, short stories, and poems.

And it must be said in Plumb's and Smith's defense that much of academic scholarship *is* divorced from the question of value or purpose, theory or philosophy, *is* written without reference to the perennial questions with which all people grapple, and *is* sometimes focussed on matters whose importance is not established. Of what worth is an article or a monograph, even to other scholars and students, if it fails these tests? The justification that a piling up of such writing will lead to an ever-increasing shared understanding or consensus is—can only be—a false one. Instead, there is the morass of endless revision.

In any case, there is no reason why the new scheme being outlined in this essay can not be presented in an essentially narrative, chronological framework. Such an effort would be far broader than, say, Bancroft's, or, more recently, Morison's; but it would share with these earlier efforts their essentially story-book character. There is no inherent contradiction between the narrative approach and a well-organized, wide-ranging line of inquiry, as the best work by Smith, Handlin, Boorstin, and others show. A chronological treatment can carry a large freight of subjects. It is imperative, however, that whoever is bold enough to write such an account be able to distinguish—as Plumb warns—the important from the trivial. Attention must be steadily focussed on those agencies of change that created the world we now have out of the world we have lost. But, in order to do this, the historian should pay attention to family and village life, to what was going on in states and regions, as well as to what was gripping the nation. The great narrative historians of the nineteenth century did not do this, though local antiquarians and chroniclers such as George Sheldon did; and Sheldon had a wide *local* audience, just as Bancroft was immensely popular nationally.

It is to be hoped, then, that a well-written narrative history, weaving together statistical and literary evidence and dealing with the story of families and communities and how they changed over three centuries, will reclaim the audience that historians have lost and make the best historical writing of interest to a broad segment of the population—as it was before there was a historical profession, when *amateurs* like Sheldon and Bancroft were Keepers of Our Past.

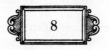

8

The New Scheme: Problems

The preceding chapters contain an account of the more successful efforts to generalize in a significant way about the historical dimensions of the American family, town, city, state, regions, nation, and character as a people. The total impact of this work, and subsequent efforts, should change the way we regard our past—a change so great that it could amount ultimately to a popular as well as to an elitist revolution in historical understanding.

There are, of course, enormous gaps in our understanding—particularly with respect to the family and the town, the kind of gaps that allow Lockridge to generalize on the basis of one town on the grounds that "the forces which most shaped the history of this town . . . were general forces which must have affected other towns."[1] Perhaps. But Lockridge, whose study is in many ways contradictory to Zuckerman's, ironically relies on Zuckerman's investigation of fifteen Massachusetts towns for some evidence that what happened in his town was, in fact, typical. Zuckerman's conclusions about New England towns in the eighteenth century turn out to be based upon far fewer than his title suggests. Greven's general comments on family follow an investigation of four generations of families in one town. Though he admits that "any attempt to determine whether or not Andover was 'typical' of other towns or to generalize extensively about other families and communities in early America must remain largely in the realm of intuition and speculation,"[2] this admission does not stop him from intuiting or

1. Lockridge, *A New England Town*, p. 165.
2. Philip J. Greven, Jr., *Four Generations: Population, Land, and Family in Colonial Andover, Massachusetts* (Ithaca, N.Y.: Cornell University Press, 1970), p. 275.

speculating, basing his comments on a smattering of other writings on family.

The problem with this kind of generalizing, even though it is cautiously framed and tentatively offered, is its narrow basis in specific historical studies. Generalizations in such circumstances are likely to fluctuate rather wildly. As in archeology, each important new find will suggest a grand new thesis. Part of the difficulty is the large number of towns and even greater number of families. Few of either have been studied in any depth. But beyond this, there is an obstacle that arises from the uneven geographical focus of the recent literature. Much of what we know about families and towns is based upon colonial New England—on Massachusetts, particularly. How valid are generalizations that refer repeatedly to inquiry focussed on one section, one state, one community? The Puritan society of colonial New England may well have had a cohesiveness and distinctiveness quite lacking in the mid-Atlantic or Southern colonies. Smith is so captivated by the covenanted town that he missed an opportunity to investigate towns in all areas and periods. Much of what he says about the small town is based on either the New England colonial town or its later Midwestern derivative. And much of what is said in general terms about the family relates to the conclusions of Morgan, Demos, and Greven in their specialized studies on New England.

All of this amounts to a kind of "regional imperialism" in our historical writing that has led to many new insights at the same time that it may be leading to distortions. Perhaps the most pressing need in American historical writing is for family and community studies dealing with areas and periods *other* than colonial New England. It is, therefore, foolish and incorrect to argue that American history is an "overworked" field. In contrast to other fields, it may appear to be; but the hierarchical, federated scheme that family and community studies postulate means that there is a need for innumerable future studies to substantiate or to alter the views sketched out by the pioneers whose work has already been assessed. New studies of those thousands of families, hundreds of towns, dozens of cities, and of the many aspects of life in the regions and the nation, should exhibit the same combination of detail and observation, of illustration and generalization as, say, Lockridge's or Greven's. And those generalizations ought to be framed with reference to the earlier efforts. Only in this inept, clumsy way will historical writings within a family-community framework grow into a body of literature that compels the attention of everyone seriously interested in the study of our past.

* * * * *

Even with the gaps and possible distortions, what these studies already suggest as a whole outline for American history is far more convincing than what appears in our textbooks, which unquestionably distort our past in several basic ways. By focussing primarily on government and politics, they have created periods of American history that make no sense at all when applied to many other aspects of life. And by concentrating on big and dramatic events, they largely ignore the normal functioning of groups and institutions in American society. By doing these things, our textbook writers hide from us both "the world we have lost" and many of the answers as to how and why we have gained the world we now have. How did our originally patriarchal, hierarchical society become a liberal democratic one, but one that is also bureaucratic and institutionalized—an impersonal, mass society? How and why did we lose our only historically viable small community and gain what we now call liberalism and freedom in a wider community that seems to be falling apart? These are questions that cannot be answered so long as our general accounts focus more on the activities of the national government than they do on such things as urbanization and industrialization.

In spite of a great profusion of monographic and periodical literature, the over-all outline of our textbooks on American history has not changed since the 1930s. The table of contents can be guessed before a new text is opened. This is a remarkable state of affairs for one of the largest groups of scholars in any discipline anywhere. It is not only unnecessary; it is harmful. As long as school children and university students see their past from a national and political perspective, there isn't much they will ever understand about that past.

All historical categorization is schematic and distorts reality. Such is the nature of human inquiry. The chief test of any categorization should be the extent to which it makes comprehensible the whole range of evidence that the historian has access to. A general scheme that focusses on the individual, the family, and the levels of communities they have lived in, with the emphasis gradually shifting from the town to the city to states to regions and finally to nation—such a scheme reveals more about our past than does the one we now find in our textbooks.

* * * * *

There are, of course, many difficulties in fleshing out the bones of this proposal. One is how to create the proper balance between important events and the normal functioning of individuals, groups, and institutions in American society. By focussing on dramatic political events—political controversy over big issues, crises and wars with other nations, or civil strife within the United States itself—our textbook writers have equated that which is most worthy of attention from our past with the exceptional, the unusual, or the memorable occurrence, just as modern journalism came to define news in the mid-nineteenth century. But much of our best historical writing since the 1940s has focussed on the role and function of groups, institutions, and activities, and the way they work or grow and decline and relate to others. Textbook authors have taken such writings into account by including occasional chapters on economic, social, cultural, and intellectual developments—that is, information whose significance doesn't depend on its relationship to important events. But there has been no attempt to strike a balance between event and function, between the dramatic and the humdrum, between the political-economic and the social-cultural aspects of American life. Surely, we can now agree that it is wrong to leave the impression that historical developments can normally be explained by reference to exciting, cataclysmic change involving human actors who are powerful and have fascinating personalities. Historical development is far more complicated; it involves the measurement and evaluation of a complex web of individuals, groups, and institutions whose activity—on occasion—resulted in something dramatic but more typically did not, and whose motivation and purpose involved more than what a few leaders thought, said, and did.

It is difficult to *blend* an accounting of the flow of events *with* an analysis of the essentially static functioning of institutions or communities, though the historian is aided in this endeavor by the fact that there is seldom a clear line of demarcation between an "event" and a long-term "development." In any case, historians typically view political events as somehow more natural, important, and worthy of attention than other kinds. But are they? Should scholars continue to assume, as they have in the past, that events of an economic, social, cultural, or intellectual character merit less space in general accounts than political ones? The assumption of power by a new group in a town, the establishment of a branch plant in a small community, the annexation of a suburb to a fast-growing city—these and countless other events must be given the same chance to "mean" something as, say, the tariff act of 1828. Events on the local, state, and regional levels—*in the aggregate*—may have had far more impact than the national political events we have all at least heard of.

* * * * *

Another difficulty is how to show the ways in which all aspects of human activity interact and relate to one another, with particular concern for the *direction* of influence from one to another. The problem with the *Marxist* or *economic* or *Christian* or any other *single factor* approach to the study of human behavior in the past is that one element is assigned a general primacy and is automatically referred to as the basic causal factor in any change. But if the determinants of human behavior are regarded as a mixture of elements, then the historian's task is immeasurably more difficult. He should not conclude that there can never be a primary factor, but he must be very suspicious if it ever appears that there is only one operative factor. In a sense, the historian has a special duty to sustain a comprehensive view of human behavior. He must never regard people as "political," or "economic," or "social," or "cultural," or "intellectual" beings, as those in other humanistic and social science disciplines to some extent do. He alone has the responsibility to view humanity in its wholeness. This perspective should give to historical studies a dimension lacking in all other disciplines that have human societies and individuals as their subjects.

Historians who probe particular subjects now *do* typically find a variety of factors that they assess before making final judgments. Those who write textbooks fail on two counts, however: They almost always have a national perspective and concern themselves with the "lower levels" of American society only when they need to look elsewhere for an explanation of national events; and they present almost everything from the perspective of government, so that other facets of life take on importance only when they are mixed up with government. These perspectives have the attractiveness of all schemes based upon a single reference point. But they are based upon false premises, namely, that Americans should be viewed through their history from a national perspective, and that something becomes important only as it becomes involved with government. The first false premise has already been discussed. The second requires a little discussion.

Human societies are made up of many activities and institutions. And though government is of great importance because it has power that is exercised with reference to the whole population under its jurisdiction, neither the existence nor the character of development of other activities and institutions is dependent solely on government. Both the range and the limitation of governmental authority has waxed and waned and is in constant flux in human societies. The family, the church, values, economic activities—all have important roles to play in the history of any society. Government is not the only active agency of human change, development, or decline.

Those who would now make a new account of the American past have to be extraordinarily sensitive to the complex interplay of political, economic, social, cultural, and intellectual aspects of life; they must be very perceptive about the directions of influence and about what caused change and what reflected it. Identifying the strands of human activity and assessing developments in each, they also have to avoid presenting these strands in isolation from everything else. And they have to do even more: They have to decide what is appropriate to their discussion of family and community life. Once again: it is a mistake for those—such as Zuckerman and Greven—who have written on the family and towns and cities to lump their subjects under the rubric of social history. This is wrong because their subject is really of a different character, of a different order of things. They are confusing categories of human *behavior* with categories of human *communities* or *groups*. Political, economic, social, cultural, and intellectual life is carried on within the nation, to be sure, but also in the region, state, city, town, and family.

There is no easy way to decide which aspects of life should be discussed in the context of family or the various kinds of communities. The only seemingly valid generalization is that whatever activity occurs *primarily* in the context of either the family or a particular kind of community should be linked with it. Also, what is basically regional and national in scope will of course continue to take place in local communities, but the level of *organization* will be beyond the countryside, the town, and the city. For example, nationwide corporations, labor unions, associations of all kinds, communications such as television and radio, transportation by air and rail are all nationwide and can not be studied from any other perspective than the national one. But they are located in particular communities, even though they go outside those communities. By contrast, to study such things as churches and—at least until recently—schools, outside the context of town or city or even, in a general way, the states, would not make any sense, either. Of course, some things, like political parties, are important on all levels and would have to be part of any inquiry directed at each of those levels.

Therefore, though future general accounts of American history should be chronological in format, the prospect that our past will be viewed through the shifting perspectives of *different levels* of family and community life means that the unilinear, continuous sequence of earlier "national" accounts such as Bancrofts' or Morison's or that of any number of textbooks will have to give way to a repetitive probing of a given period, seen first from the vantage point of the family, then of the town, the city, the state, the region, and finally the nation.

* * * * *

A third difficulty in the creation of a new general scheme for our history texts is how to establish a proper balance between elitist history and mass history, a balance that, to date, our textbook writers have certainly not achieved. What happens is typically attributed to small elites, usually politicians, who have power or influence—this, in spite of the impressive writings that have focussed on masses of people and large institutions. It bears repeating here that the papers of elite groups are not our only source. The availability of records held by the administrative and judicial organs of local, state, and national government, along with those preserved by churches, the most common and widespread institution outside government until recently, have allowed for the statistical measurement and evaluation of the behavior of the mass of people in our history. What is needed now is an estimation of the *relative* importance of the mass and the elite or leadership groups. Surely it is too simplistic to study our past as if influence moved in only one direction. Even the most totalitarian of societies have rulers who must reflect as well as shape popular sentiments, opinion, and values. To argue that the masses have always been duped by power elites is as wrongheaded as it is to assert that every society has the rulers it deserves. Every society *does* have leaders, those who have power, wealth, and influence; every society also has its masses. But it would be as much a distortion to study a society from the bottom up as it has been to study it from the top down. Either perspective by itself is incomplete. We need judicious appraisals of the relative influence of elites and masses.

Politicans, business leaders, religious spokesmen, educators, scientists and technocrats, reformers, inventors, artists, even occasional theorists—all have acted singly and in groups, in ways that have had important consequences for their society. But they also reflected popular sentiments and movements, and what they did can not be fully understood apart from what the masses were doing in their political, economic, cultural, intellectual, or social capacity. Indeed, history ought to be written in such a way that terms such as *elitist history* or *history of the masses* lose their meaning, for the proper perspective is outside and beyond both. That these terms have had some meaning, however, is because of the unnecessarily restricted focus of those who write history. This is not to say that the over-all direction of influence can never be either from the top down or from the bottom up. Sometimes such a pattern will be found. But neither "elites" nor "masses" must ever be studied *in isolation* from the other.

* * * * *

A fourth problem involves periodization. Our textbooks now contain the quite unsatisfactory arrangement of periods defined by government and politics, coupled with more loosely structured chapters on other aspects of life that are somehow supposed to fit into the political periods, but don't. Developments in art, architecture, recreation and leisure, economic activity, thought, education, religion, and so on, do not ordinarily evolve through time in lockstep with politics. And it distorts our past unnecessarily to pretend that they do. What appears to be a well-marked area in one is meaningless in another. Dramatic events or changes may affect one or several categories, but generally leave many others unscathed.

Only four times in our history have Americans been in crises of such dimension that it can at least be argued that the whole society felt the impact: the Revolution, the Civil War, the Depression, and the crisis that began in the mid-1960s. The depth and breadth of these crises can be debated. Many say that the Revolution resulted in political independence but nothing else of consequence that would not have happened anyway.[3] Others say that the Civil War ended the possibility that whites, if not blacks, in any geographic region would try to secede from the Union, but settled nothing beyond that.[4] The depression, it is sometimes argued, led to reform whose major purpose was to preserve our system, not to alter it in any fundamental way.[5] It is too soon to say anything about the most recent crisis.

3. Edmund S. Morgan, *The Birth of the Republic, 1763–1789* (Chicago: University of Chicago Press, 1956).

4. Carl Degler, *Out of Our Past: The Forces that Shaped Modern America*, paperback edition (New York: Harper & Row Publishers, 1962), pp. 228–237.

5. Bernstein, editor, *Towards a New Past*, pp. 263–288.

But however restricted the long-term impact of these crises is judged to have been, no one can doubt their immediate impact. The Revolution became an internal colonial civil war, in addition to being a rebellion against the imperial British government. The Civil War divided the nation when a secession movement led to the creation of a new government over a large portion of the territory of the old union and to a war that was the bloodiest internal conflict of any modern nation-state. The depression seriously affected the material-economic security and stability of a large portion of the population and created uncertainty in the rest. The present crisis involves deep fissures in the American community at various levels, deep conflict over the proper role of the United States in the world, and great concern over the impact of American life on the environment within and around the territory of the United States.

Each crisis appears, at least, to have been deeper and broader than the last. Many were neutral and not involved in the fighting of the Revolution. Many fought, but many did not, in the Civil War. A large portion of the population was economically insecure in the depression, though some were not. But who is wholly unaffected by the present crisis?

Whatever their dimensions, all of these crises offer convenient dividing lines for general accounts of American history. To some extent they have already served as such. The colonial period is typically regarded as a distinctive unit in our history, and so is the period between the Revolution and the Civil War. What is less certain is what goes after. The present scheme would break the remaining period into two: from the Civil War through the Great Depression and World War II; and from World War II to the present. These four periods would be the *only* periods. No longer would there be the shorter "political periods." These divisions are, in some sense, as arbitrary as the older, shorter political ones, in that not everything was dramatically affected by each of the crises. Even so, they did disrupt the whole society for a time. And the new periods are longer than the old and allow significant change in all fields of human activity a much better chance of being noticed and placed in proper perspective in relationship to each other.

* * * * *

A final problem that will have to be confronted if a new over-all scheme for our past is to be constructed is how to discuss both change and stability within each of the four periods in a clear, organized manner. Surely the factors making for change and for stability are the essence of any worthwhile interpretation of the past. Just as surely, any account that has pretensions of being comprehensive has to probe *both*. Any society with a relatively long life can not be understood if the only focus is on what produced changes in it. For a society to endure, it must also have stability.

Americans, in the long view of things, have had stability to an extraordinary extent. The population consists of white migrants from all of Europe, black forced-migrants from much of Africa, "yellow" migrants from Asia, and "red" natives. The white element formed a nation that quickly expanded across the whole continent, an economy that quickly became the greatest industrial machine on earth, a society that became progressively more egalitarian, and a political system that quickly became democratic. The *pace* of all these developments is dizzying when placed in proper perspective. And yet, the American governmental system is the oldest continuously functioning system in the modern Western world. Economic life has not produced sustained, violent clashes among workers and managers. Social life has exhibited sufficient flux and mobility to block the development of well-defined, antagonistic classes. Americans were not deeply divided over the kind of society they wanted. There has been wide agreement on the fundamentals of life. The United States became a giant among nations quickly—and with surprising stability. Any interpretation that fails to deal with this is seriously defective.

Of course, change was just as basic. But what needs more emphasis is the wide range in the *character* of change in our past. Some things have developed and become fixed or static at a certain point, remaining stable thereafter: the rise of a legitimate opposition, the creation of uniform electoral machinery for elections (such as the date and frequency of kinds of offices to be filled, types of electoral districts, and so on), and the loss of a cohesive governing class. Others have been cyclical—that is, they have waxed and waned over and over: party loyalty in Congress, government regulation of business corporations, free trade and protection, economic growth and recession, nativism, educational and other kinds of reform. Still other things have changed progressively through time at a somewhat regular pace: the extension of the franchise, industrialization, urbanization, specialization.

To complicate the matter further, some, but by no means all change has involved—obviously—the replacement of something old with something new. But another kind has been the attempted return *to* something old, something that *used* to be. For example, the rebels of 1776 wanted the British government to stop what it was doing and act the way it had before 1763. The Jacksonians wanted to undo what government had done, to dismantle legislative programs with a long history, to turn government away from a path that, in their judgment, had led to the misuse of governmental power. During those same years, school and asylum officials and theorists sought to construct institutions for the dependent and the deviant that would recreate the social order that they believed had existed in earlier times. The Progressives stressed the importance of government to act in such a way that the open, democratic society of the early nineteenth century would replace the increasingly oligarchical social order of their own time. These reformers were at first divided over what government should do, but *in practice*, they largely favored Populist-like regulation, rather than Jacksonianlike dismantling of governmental programs. There are many other examples of groups who wanted to change things into what they used to be or were imagined to be in a purer, simpler past. The innovator and the reactionary both seek change. Visions of the good life refer both to the future and to the past.

Those who spend their lives consciously seeking to change society in order to improve or perfect it are properly called reformers, and what gives them their name is their willful intention to do so. Reformers in American history have almost always been middle- or upperclass in their background. They have shared both a sense of personal anger over the discrepancy between the ideals and practices of their community and society and the conviction that they *knew* how to improve or perfect that society if only their solutions were adopted. Some have been concerned about the imposition of order upon an awkward, mobile, rapidly developing society through the establishment of certain kinds of institutions and practices or through the abolition of others deemed evil or harmful. Most have sought to preserve the basic character of their society and have tried to persuade others to work for ameliorative change.

Americans have always had communities in which various forms of utopian thought have been of great consequence. The reformist impulse has flourished in Puritan and communitarian towns—Massachusetts, Rhode Island, and Pennsylvania colonies, and much of the New England region, to name some obvious examples. Indeed, the national community from its inception in 1776 and 1789 has always had a utopian mystique about it. The Declaration and Constitution proclaim the creation of a special, unique human society in which mankind will perfect itself. But the character of the population that came together in the United States during the eighteenth, nineteenth, and twentieth centuries was so varied that early *local* efforts to create pure, homogeneous, utopian communities were overwhelmed. Utopian objectives were shifted to the national level during the nineteenth century. But since the "national covenant" tolerated diversity within a federated society, the main effort of reformers has been to perfect the behavior and institutions of a varied people whose basic pattern of life was fixed by the time that covenant was drawn: liberal, politically; capitalistic, economically; broadly Christian, religiously; open, socially. National reformers, like the local and regional ones before them, thus operated within a given framework.

It is true that labor and farmer reform leaders in the 1820s and 1830s and again in the 1870s and 1880s favored broad, deep social reform, at times bordering on the utopian or socialist, as Edward Pessen and Gerald Grob indicate. For example, Pessen analyzes the thought of the middle-class leaders of the Workingman's Parties and the craft unions of the earlier period. Appalled by both the existence of poverty and the greed of the rich, lashing out at the concentration of private property, the excesses of the factory system, and the constant threat of monopoly, the leaders demanded basic change through political action that would result in the creation of the co-operative principle in the distribution and consumption of goods and lead to the development of universal and public education. Anticipating the broad reform movements that farmers and laborers supported later in the century through the Knights of Labor, the Grange, the Farmers' Alliances, and the Populist Party, these reformers gave a wide definition to labor, who, they believed, "suffered more than did any other group in American society . . . [In their minds] the greatest crime in society was the denial to the actual producers of wealth of the good things they had created."[6] But labor leaders were not united on an alternative: some, like Owen, favored the development of model communities within the existing society; others favored basic change for the whole society. The implications of Pessen's study are rather far-reaching, for it would appear that the reform-minded leaders of major groups in nineteenth-century America wavered between piecemeal and wholesale reform

6. Pessen, *Most Uncommon Jacksonians*, p. 202. For the same view with reference to the radical abolitionists, see Aileen Kraditor, *Means and Ends in American Abolitionism: Garrison and His Critics on Strategy and Tactics, 1834–1850* (New York: Pantheon Books, 1969).

and cannot be as sharply distinguished from the "communitarian" utopians or socialists, such as Owen, as was once thought.

Even so, those who have, from time to time, clearly offered a basically different kind of community have been outlawed or banished or ignored or absorbed; consider Roger Williams in seventeenth-century Massachusetts, the Loyalists during the Revolution, the communitarians of the early nineteenth century, the socialists and the communists of the late nineteenth and twentieth centuries and the hippies of the late twentieth century. The Liberal-Capitalist-Christian-Open Society has undergone various crises, but the Loyalists in the Revolution, the Southerners in the Civil War, the communists and socialists in the depression, and the young radicals and hippies in the most recent crisis have not provided alternatives that the dominant portion of American society has agreed to.

Reformers who accepted the national covenant and the society that it provided a framework for have typically organized on a federal basis, with national, state, and local chapters, have sustained propaganda campaigns or crusades to persuade the public of the importance of their cause, or have sometimes exerted pressures on government to enact appropriate legislation. This was true of antislavery and the temperance and later W.C.T.U. and Prohibition crusades, the later Negro rights campaigns, the woman's rights and later feminist movements, as well as the peace and pacifist organizations. Reform did not come easily or quickly. Indeed, the impulse often waxed and waned several times before government action was taken, which means that reform groups acted as a kind of goad, a reminder that the nation's ideals were not being practiced. Reformers have created a climate of opinion that has galvanized sympathetic politicians to act. But the swiftest action has occurred when some of the politicians themselves have been reformers, such as Jefferson and other rebel leaders in the new state legislatures of the 1780s, the abolitionists in Congress during the Civil War, Radical Republicans during Reconstruction, Progressives during Theodore Roosevelt's, Taft's, and Wilson's administrations, and the New Dealers during Franklin Roosevelt's administration.

In general, change of a positive character with an ameliorative effect has been the result of many intertwining factors, of which the efforts of self-proclaimed reformers is one—sometimes an important one, sometimes not. But important changes have also resulted from the activity of groups who did not picture themselves as reformers. Boorstin's pioneer businessmen, the boosters, brought much that is distinctively American to our cities. Industrial or financial entrepreneurs such as Rockefeller, Carnegie, Morgan, and Ford integrated economic processes in an efficient and profitable manner, creating the national corporations characteristic of the twentieth century. Inventors such as Eli Whitney and Thomas Edision profoundly influenced the development of economic and social life. But none of these groups thought of themselves as reformers, as, say, the Abolitionists or the New Dealers did—innovators, yes, but not crusaders for a more moral or just society. And yet, both the innovators and the crusaders were active, willful human agents of change. What they did had either an indirect or a direct impact, sometimes of great consequence, on their society.

Change in the context of community life has had a typically ambivalent character. The Puritan covenanted town in New England certainly exhibited a utopian-reformist impulse, but, as Smith points out, those who were colonizers, those who founded new towns in the Midwest, were typically those who backed off from the parent community because it wasn't pure and holy enough, which makes the colonizers the conservative ones. Even family life in colonial New England, Greven finds, was more stable, more authoritarian in the colonial frontier than it was in old, settled England, which again makes change in the new world conservative in nature. And, as Zuckerman adds, the strenuous efforts of the Puritan towns to be "peaceable kingdoms" or homogeneous, harmonious communities meant that orthodox beliefs and common ways of doing things kept out the diversity that is central to modern liberalism.

And yet, ironically, this was the same region that, in the nineteenth century, produced much of the innovative and reformist impulses that affected American life as a whole. The South assumed at the regional level some of the same characteristics of the New England town in the colonial period. Its insistence upon orthodoxy; a homogeneous community suspicious of outsiders; a concern for the peculiar character of the community; the lack of understanding and appreciation of it by outsiders; a belief in the superiority of the community's whole pattern of life; even the presence of colonizers who carried that way of life ever westward—in all these ways, Southern regionalism in the nineteenth century was a copy of New England localism in the colonial period.

At the same time, the booster spirit of communities in the Midwest assured *rapid* copying of the old ways as Americans settled the vast interior river valleys of the continent. Boorstin documents the way in which this competitive spirit among towns and would-be cities led to what he calls "innovative" practices and institutions. Upon closer examination, however, the "booster press" is much like the colonial press, back East; many of the innovations first displayed in the "palaces of the public," or early hotels, turn out to be the products of hotels in Boston and New York; "the booster college" was the western counterpart of a phenomenon that was eastern, as well; and even the "balloon-frame" house, though started in the fast-growing Midwestern cities, was publicized elsewhere and before long became standard everywhere.[7] If Midwestern communities *were* distinctive, it was in their intense competitiveness and fast growth, not in their innovative character. And even competition and expansion were not entirely unique to the Midwest and to the antebellum period.

In a general sense, towns were imitative in their forms and institutional patterns as they were founded on a succession of "frontiers" from ocean to ocean, and both territories and new states were formed under procedures largely fixed as early as the 1780s. Thus community life had a kind of continuity during the eighteenth and nineteenth centuries, long before the progressive nationalization of American life brought over-all uniformity. In the United States, the local community itself has thus provided an underlying continuity as the nation grew. It was against this steady background that the society changed. The context for that change has been the largest cities (in the cultural and economic spheres) and, since the turn of the nineteenth century, the nation.

The true safety-valve in the steady growth of the nation was not the frontier, at least not in the sense that Turner had in mind. The most common means of escape for those who have been dissatisfied with community life at any point has been the "secession" of the alienated portion from the community, of *whatever* kind. Lockridge documents the way in which those who concluded they could not sensibly join in life at the community center in colonial New England towns petitioned the legislature for permission to establish their own new town. Smith rather dramtically demonstrates the way in which others among the disaffected became Midwestern colonizers. Boorstin rightly portrays the Southern states that seceded in 1861 as being a regionwide example of an old impulse that began with the secession of the colonies from British Empire in 1776.[8] What he fails to mention, however, is that this

7. Boorstin, *The Americans: The National Experience*, pp. 113–168.

8. Lockridge, pp. 93–118; Smith, *As a City Upon a Hill*, pp. 37–54; Boorstin, *The Americans: The National Experience*, pp. 417–430.

tradition of secession extends all the way down to the "outlivers" of colonial New England towns. Those who have seceded have not generally succeeded in establishing the better community that they sought, but the impulse goes on.

* * * * *

A far-reaching study concerned with the twin themes of stability and change is Rowland Berthoff's *An Unsettled People: Social Order and Disorder in American History*. Writing with a medieval conception of the proper social order for a people, Berthoff asserts that

> all human concerns are properly linked according to a hierarchy of values. Some aspects of life exist, that is, for the sake of others, and these latter are more important. At the base of the hierarchy lie the economic values, necessary but subservient, of adequate production and equitable distribution of material goods. Upon that system rest the specifically social values of satisfactory relationship among men in a reasonably stable, secure institutional structure. . . . But a stable social structure is less important in itself than as the foundation, in turn, for other, loftier values of mind and spirit—aesthetic and intellectual achievement of some excellence and perhaps even what is variously called self-fulfillment, redemption from sin, or salvation of the soul.[9]

The great tragedy of American history is that Americans,

> especially in the nineteenth and early twentieth centures, when they virtually denied the existence of any hierarchy among values [, concluded] that economic values were [not] in any practical way inferior to social values [,indeed, that] economic relationships were . . . the most important social relationships as well. And except for increasingly perfunctory genuflections toward a rapidly receding God, the pragmatism and pluralism of popular attitudes and liberal thought abandoned the dominant position once held by cultural and spiritual values.[10]

9. Berthoff, *An Unsettled People: Social Order and Disorder in American History* (New York: Harper & Row, 1971), p. xiii.
10. *Ibid.*, pp. xiii–xiv.

The resulting experience demonstrated "the ethical imperative of a ruling hierarchy of values. Abandoning it resulted, at too many points, in an unsatisfactory social structure (and, for that matter, a defective economic system)."[11]

More recently, Berthoff finds a growing sense of a "need for an orderly, equitable social community—and for a more satisfying cultural and spiritual life." It is *possible*, therefore, that "American society may eventually complete the cycle of development which this book describes, from adequate order through excessive disorder and back again toward some satisfactory order." The social cycle, Berthoff believes, parallels, though it lags behind "the cycle of economic development—from mercantilist controls of the eighteenth century through the liberal individualism of the nineteenth and latterly once again to a kind of neomercantilist system."[12]

In colonial times, the earliest Americans created a society characterized by the essentially medieval ideal of an organic, status-bound, hierarchical social order, interlocking family, community, and church. The colonists, thus, were generally successful in their effort to continue the pattern of life that they had left behind. Economic change was gradual and allowed them to cling to their old ways. In the century following the Revolution, however, fast-paced commercial and industrial development shook apart the old social order, freed the individual from institutional contstraints to pursue his own material gain, and led to the equation of the ends of society with a human being's economic betterment. Since the late nineteenth century, Americans have acted to reassert the power of government over their economic activity, but have *not* acted to re-establish the old social, institutional restraints. In fact,

> [the] argument now ran that the good society . . . was that which set the individual free from institutional constraints, whether public or private. Even while in their economic affairs Americans were progressively repudiating the maxim that the best government governs least, they took to preaching permissiveness as the right principle for their social institutions. The progressives and liberals of the twentieth century, who were foremost in refastening public restrictions upon the individual's freedom of economic contract, at the same time

11. *Ibid.*, p. xiv.
12. *Ibid.*

abandoned, in theory at least, the little that remained of the old social sanctions against free choice in personal relations. . . . Whether the new personalism amounted to elevating the American concept of individual liberty from the material level to a higher social, cultural, and spiritual plane . . . was still not at all clear by 1945.[13]

Berthoff's reading of American history is refreshing and quite outside the mold of the liberal view of our past. Frankly conservative—indeed, "orthodox medieval"—his conception of the good society presumes a much greater *harmony* between public order and individual freedom than Americans have experienced since their Revolution. The whole drift of American history is thus viewed from a distinctive perspective, one that throws up in bold relief colonial American life as the best or most satisfactory that Americans have yet experienced. Berthoff goes on to trace our "descent" into a liberal society in which the ends of being become hardly distinguishable from material comfort or success. Though open to the charge of being over-schematic, he nevertheless fastens on to a theme from which liberally-oriented historians can not entirely escape: With the decline of the organic, medieval conception of the good society, what has replaced it, other than the "freed" individual, the rootless modern person, awash with *anomie* and alienation, without a direction or a purpose any larger than his own immediate material and personal desires? What price freedom?

Berthoff's study is thought-provoking; but his accounting of change in American society from a conservative to a liberal social order would have benefitted from an investigation of the various levels of family and community life. With such reference points, the explanations he offers for this great shift in the character of American life would have been clearer and fuller.

13. *Ibid.*, p. 360.

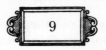

The New Scheme:
A Brief Sketch

And so, the new accounting of American history will have to assess a much greater array of factors than our textbook writers have done thus far. The basic outline of family to town to city to states to regions to nation in periods from 1600 to 1789, 1789 to 1865, 1865 to 1945, and 1945 to the present appears to be simple enough. But the actual presentation of American history with reference to such a scheme in an account that blends information with analysis, narrative with interpretation, is formidable.

The story becomes increasingly complicated as the nature of American life moved from the relatively simply toward the ever more sophisticated. Interrelationships between the seventeenth-century family and community are easier to study than later ones. Sheer growth of the population, development of more formally fashioned institutions with greater specialization, rapid advancement of processes (such as industrialization and inventions in transportation and communication) creating increasingly complicated, interrelated patterns of life, and the shift of influence gradually away from village to city, state, and nation—all make relationships and the direction of influence (if it can be detected at all) much more difficult to grasp. Still, the proposed scheme maintains a steady yet wide-embracing framework that allows for a more sophisticated analysis of these matters than the old, national governmental scheme has.

The reader will note that there is no mention made of the American character in the sketch that follows. This omission is deliberate. Until some measure of consensus is achieved as to what constitute the chief characteristics of the American people, whether or not those traits of character have changed and in what ways, and what relationship they have had to developments in the social, cultural, intellectual, economic, and political life of Americans—it is too soon to indicate how an analysis of character would fit in with the other segments in the scheme below. This is unfortunate and, of course, constitutes a serious omission. One thing seems evident, however: The place in the following sketch for discussions of character when they *do* become feasible is at the end of each section on the national community for each period.

* * * * *

Textbook accounts of the first period—the colonial—need less alteration than others. So much recent scholarship on family and community has been restricted to our prenational existence that it would be surprising if no attention were given to towns, rural areas, and family life, especially since there wasn't a nation to focus on!

Indeed, new accounts will have to begin, as the old have, from an international perspective. The "European background" is necessary. An analysis of the conditions leading to British colonization and a comparison with Spanish and other European nations is also indispensible, for the founding of America was entirely under the auspices of an imperial government that went about its business in a way quite different from other European powers. The founding of particular colonies should then be dealt with from the perspective of particular trading companies and proprietors. *Then*, however, the focus should shift to the colonists themselves—who they were and why they came. At this point, family life throughout the colonies should be analyzed with reference to communities, whether towns, countryside, or coastal cities. Activities and institutions of an essentially local character should be discussed. Only *then* should the emergent pattern of life in particular colonies be assessed. And only after *that* should the British colonial system and relationships between the colonies and the imperial government be outlined. Particular attention should be paid to what these colonies shared in common, *but also* to the ways in which they were distinctive. Throughout these discussions, factors making for both stability and continuity should be included.

In this way, it may be hoped, family and community life that existed simultaneously at various levels can be viewed and the interrelationships and influences among all components can be explained. According to Morgan, Demos, Greven, and Zuckerman, the direction of influence went from family and town upward, or outward.

The only ambiguous element in all this is "regionalism." Briden-baugh and Schlesinger divided colonial society into coastal cities, the rural backcountry, and the frontier, thus pushing towns out of the picture altogether and creating regions that were vertical, not horizontal, in geographic terms. Others have written on New England and the South. The best case for a distinctive region can be made for New England. The Puritan community spread through Massachusetts Bay and Connecticut and gave a unity to organized life in these colonies that was lacking elsewhere. And, as Charles Clark shows, Massachusetts tried, with partial success, to determine the character of community life in New Hampshire and Maine, as well. True, the Virginia rural-county pattern of settlement also spread through much of the South, but the pattern of life in Southern colonies lacked the homogeneity of the New England town. Certainly the British government often thought the New England colonies were peculiar and distinctive—economically, politically, socially, and in religious terms, as well. Friction between New England provincial governments and the imperial government was a regular feature of our colonial period, but because New England was so distinctive, it is important not to make developments, of whatever character, there, *synonymous* with colonial development generally—an unfortunate tendency of some of our best scholarship.

As for the causes of the Revolution, the focus should shift back to family and communities. Greven suggests:

> [It] is not inconceivable, for example, that the slow, and subtle, but nevertheless tremendously important, changes in the relationships between fathers and sons might have been connected closely with the movement for independence itself during the third quarter of the eighteenth century—that period in which the fourth generation in Andover was coming to maturity and establishing its own independence from fathers and families. . . . For Andover's fourth generation, Thomas Paine's call for independence in 1776 from the mother-country and from the father-king might have been just what Paine claimed it to be—common sense. In their own lives, this generation had come to take for granted that young men ought also to be independent men—freed of ties to their parental families, freed often of responsibilities of aging parents, economically independent and able to follow their own interests. Surprising though it may seem, political independence in 1776 might have

been rooted in the very character of many (but not all) American families.[1]

Zuckerman argues persuasively that, in Massachusetts, at least, the position of the towns is central to any understanding of the Revolution. At the heart of the matter was "the British edict against the town meeting in the Intolerable Acts of 1774, and it was [the towns'] defiance of that edict . . . that ignited the rebellion." Thus, "the Revolution was largely formed in the towns and sustained by the towns."[2]

Britain's "almost unprecedented intrusion on local autonomy" in 1774 thus struck at the vitals of this colonial society, and, not surprisingly, brought forth rebellion from communities who fought in order "to preserve their old patterns of peace and harmony." Since the towns were the center of political, economic, and community life in Massachusetts Bay, it is not surprising that they simply assumed full political authority with the collapse of the provincial government in 1774. Setting up Committees of Investigation to find and reform Loyalists to prevent disunity, the towns declared their independence with unanimity, created Committees of Correspondence to act as their political and constitutional voice in the outside world, paid and equipped soldiers, sent delegates to a constitutional convention in 1780 and later ratified what they wrote, were given the power to amend the new constitution, and continued to be the unit of representation for the state legislature until 1857. Thus, in what was essentially a political revolution, the towns of Massachusetts *naturally* established the sovereignty of the people and created a state "conceived in terms of a proto-federalism of communities."[3]

There have not been studies of families and towns comparable to those of Greven and Zuckerman for other colonies. But towns probably played as great a role in other New England colonies as they did in Massachusetts Bay. Bridenbaugh documents the relationship of the coastal cities to the prerevolutionary colonial resistance and finds those cultural-eonomic centers natural focal-points in that resistance. His study stops short of the war itself, however. At the state level, we already know a lot about the formation and activities of the new state governments during the revolution: they exercised essentially the

---

1. Greven, *Four Generations*, pp. 280–282.
2. Zuckerman, *Peaceable Kingdoms*, p. 223.
3. *Ibid.*, pp. 249, 223, 247–252, 212.

same powers as their colonial predecessors had.[4] At the regional level, once again, New England appears to have been the most distinctive. As William Nelson demonstrates, New Englanders provided, relative to other sections, the fewest Loyalists and most Rebels. Even communities founded by New Englanders around the periphery of the region were in favor of the rebellion, though adjoining towns were not.[5]

From the national and international perspectives, the course of British policy and the efforts at a united colonial response should be examined, as they have been in the past. Gordon Wood's *The Creation of the American Republic* analyzes the birth of a nation from the viewpoint of political thought, that is, the emergence of a republican creed embodied in a constitution whose legitimacy rested upon the sovereignty of the people. Wood is convincing in his explanation of how Americans (at least that small element of them who contributed to the written and oral debates) worked their way toward new views of government. He is not primarily concerned, however, about the complicated process whereby a *hierarchy if communities* created a political nation, each playing a role in that process. In short, his primary concern is not the kind of thing Zuckerman considers with the towns in Massachusetts and that Forrest MacDonald does for the states in connection with the framing and ratification of the Constitution.[6] An assessment of what those who were influential said about what should be created is not the same as an analysis of what people in towns, cities, countryside, and states thought should happen. The relationship between popular thought and elitist utterance needs further study.

On a related matter, Richard Merritt, in *Symbols of American Community 1735–1775*, shows that the colonists developed, especially under the spur of controversy, a sporadically increasing sense of "community awareness" in the years before the fighting started. By computing newspaper references to such phrases as "American" colonies and "American" colonists, he finds some evidence for prerevolutionary

4. Merrill Jenson, *Articles of Confederation: An Interpretation of the Social-Constitutional History of the American Revolution* (Madison, Wisc.: University of Wisconsin Press, 1948), and *The New Nation: A History of the United States During the Confederation, 1781–1739* (New York: Alfred A. Knopf, 1950). More recently, there is Jackson Turner Main, *The Sovereign States, 1775–1783* (New York: New Viewpoints, 1973) and *Political Parties Before the Constitution* (Chapel Hill, N.C.: University of North Carolina Press, 1973).

5. William Nelson, *The American Tory* (New York: Oxford University Press, 1961), pp. 94–104.

6. Forrest MacDonald, *We the People: The Economic Origins of the Constitution* (Chicago: University of Chicago Press, 1958).

"national" identification. The implication is that people living in colonies from New Hampshire to Georgia had to think about—have a mental image of—a continental political unit before they could try to create one.

In any case, at all levels of community, close attention should be paid to the impact, if any, of the Revolution on the character, patterns, and structure of American life. Was there a significant shift among those who held political, economic, and social power, or not? Did the society become more democratic and open, or not?[7] Also, the reasons for the division of the population into rebels, loyalists, and the uncommitted should be dealt with at all levels, from family to nation. Defining the Revolution as a kind of civil war, albeit an unequal one, forces attention on the problem of nationalism. To what extent was there an "American" society, when so many did not favor the creation of an American nation? Does the national perspective of these years offer anything more than a fledgling Congressional government comprised of people leading a rebellion the outcome of which was in doubt until the very end of the war?

Finally, the whole revolutionary experience of these years should be related to other revolutions of the same period, as well as to those that came later in different parts of the world. R.R. Palmer suggests that the American Revolution shared, with other revolutionary movements in Europe in the late eighteenth and early nineteenth centuries, a "liberal creed."[8]

Thus, though some shifts have to be made, there is a good deal already in the more recent accounts of our colonial period that could remain relatively undisturbed.

* * * * *

The segment of our textbook accounts most in need of revision is that dealing with the period from the Revolution to the Civil War. The typical account begins with a national perspective and retains it throughout, except for occasional forays into regional history, which are regarded as necessary to an explanation of the Civil War. Such a

---

7. The most recent inquiry into the nature of colonial society during the Revolution is Jackson Turner Main's *The Social Structure of Revolutionary America* (Princeton, N.J.: Princeton University Press, 1965).

8. Woodward, editor, *The Comparative Approach to American History*, p. 57.

perspective is improper. Instead of George Washington and the Congress, we should be told about families, then towns, then cities, then states, then regions, and only then about the nation—i.e., the same scheme as for the colonial period.

Unfortunately, there are no studies dealing with family life in general for this particular period.[9] But there are several short studies of families in a community context. Frederic Jaher has made several suggestions about the nature of a regional elite: the Boston Brahmins. He believes that the Brahmins achieved aristocratic status in a capitalist society that emphasized material acquisition and business success, by dominating the source of wealth in the area: first commerce, and then industry. They retained their position from the 1780s to the 1860s because of an industrious, aggressive, imaginative, entrepreneurial spirit, not only in economic life, but also in politics, education, religion, scholarship, and culture. When their economic pre-eminence declined after the Civil War, along with their region's relative economic position, their over-all leadership also declined.[10]

Paul Connor argues that the regional elite of the South, the planter aristocracy, quite literally retained the classical, patriarchal family structure whose virtue was defended by Southern apologists at a time when the family and institutions elsewhere were undergoing a kind of democratization.[11]

What is missing from the literature on family life between the Revolution and the Civil War is what gives balance to similar writings on the colonial period: the statistical evaluation of masses of families in a given community and even the nonstatistical evaluation of family life in a number of important aspects. Until studies such as Greven's, Morgan's, and Demos's are made, we will not have a secure foundation for the early national period of the kind already being constructed for the colonial years.

Boorstin's "booster" community is too ill-defined to be regarded as applicable to towns only, or even to communities outside the Midwest

9. Bridges, "Family Patterns and Social Values in America, 1825–1875," and Furtenberg's, "Industrialization and the American Family: A Glance Backward" are too broadguaged in their concerns to apply to this period in particular.

10. Frederic Jaher, "Businessmen and Gentlemen: Nathan and Thomas Gold Appleton—An Exploration in Intergenerational History," *Explorations in Entrepreneurial History*, IV, no. 2 (1966–1967), 17–39.

11. Paul Connor, "Patriarchy: Old World and New," *American Quarterly*, XVII (Spring 1965), 48–62.

during the period. There is nothing on the town to compare to Wade's *Urban Frontier* on the city—a study whose thesis and analysis of institutions and activities should form the basis for any discussion of the nature of urban life from the Revolution to the Civil War, though it would be helpful to know how America's urban frontier communities compared to others elsewhere in the world at the same time. Unknown, too, is the extent to which the replacement of towns and counties by population as the basis for representation in the lower house of state legislatures led to a shift in political power away from the towns and cities to the states. Neither the general character nor the pace of this shift has yet been studied. But we do know that the states remained the dominant level of government above the local community long after the adoption of the Constitution. And yet how little an impression this well-known fact appears to have made on our textbook writers!

State governments either abolished slavery or (later) enacted slave codes, ended primogeniture and entail, disestablished churches, fixed punishment for civil offenses and criminal acts, established public schools and asylums of all kinds. They incorporated and regulated towns and cities, as well as financial, economic, and private educational institutions. They used public money to subscribe to the stock of private corporations whose members were afraid to invest much capital in enterprises judged to be risky yet necessary for the public weal, such as banking, roads and canals. State governments sometimes gave tax concessions and land grants to foster the same sort of enterprise; they supported a bill of rights for both their own constitutions and the federal one in 1790, supported expansions of the franchise leading to white manhood suffrage by the 1830s, and legislated on other subjects that historians have not deemed worthy of attention.

To be fair, some historians have examined developments at the state level during this period: there is Katz's work on the public schools; Rothman's, on asylums; Cunningham's, McCormick's and Bensons's, on political parties; Sharps's, on an important political issue, banking; Handlin's, Hartz's, and Heath's, on the relationship between government and the economy—all studies considering developments from the perspective of the states.

But such efforts remain small in number when compared to the many studies that take account of regionalism, something that received the most concentrated attention that Frederic Jackson Turner ever gave any subject less specific than the frontier. To Turner we owe the easily imagined concepts of the "North," the "East," the "West," and the "South" for this period.[12] Textbooks still abound in such terminology, to the point that precision is lost altogether. The only question that should guide us is: Was whatever we are studying truly *organized* on a *regional* basis, or wasn't it? Some things were. Many things just as clearly were not.

The most basic difference between colonial regionalism and that of the antebellum period is that the earlier version was a by-product of local developments, whereas the later version was the result of the organization of certain facets of life on a regionwide basis. Thus, much of colonial New England was the sum total of largely homogeneous and autonomous Puritan villages. And to the extent that there was a colonial South, its area covered the territory in which there were largely isolated farms producing staple crops with slave labor, under the jurisdiction of counties.

In the postrevolutionary period, "Southern" regionalism gradually became sharp and distinctive and compelling in the minds of both those who considered themselves to be Southerners and those who did not. The reason for this development was not primarily economic, geographic, social, or cultural unity, but rather the belief that the South was peculiar, that it had a way of life within a caste society of the free and the enslaved that was distinctive to itself, and whose hierarchical and patriarchal character was more akin to colonial society than it was to that of the early national period. When this distinctiveness was threatened, "*the* South" became increasingly a closed society.

New England, by contrast, became an increasingly open society with the breakdown of the homogeneous Puritan village society. True, it retained enough of the singularity so evident in its colonial period to make possible some short-lived secession movements in the first decades after independence. But for the long term, New England's distinctiveness was shown in the ways it contributed to *national*, or at least much wider, developments. Boorstin analyzes its role in the application of economic processes and inventions, in the "Americanization" of the common law, and in the attempted "reformation" of American life. Beyond this, New Englanders spread out through the mid-Atlantic and Midwestern areas, bringing what remained of the distinctive patterns of their life with them.

But what of Turner's West? If it be defined as the "frontier," then, of course, it contained all the distinctiveness that the edge of settlement

---

12. Frederic Jackson Turner, *The United States, 1830–1850: The Nation and Its Sections* (New York: Henry Holt & Co., Inc., 1935).

had from colonial times onward. Regionalism so defined is transitory, geographically mobile, and never involved very many people relative to the whole population. Even so, it is at least a definable region in this period, as in others, through 1890. If the "West" be defined as the "old Northwest," however, its people were an amalgam of migrations from the South, the mid-Atlantic, and New England areas, and historians have failed to find a well-defined regional consciousness. If the "West" is the area covered by Boorstin's "booster" communities, then it extends to the Rockies, and it isn't known whether there was something about the geographic territory that made boosterism flourish, or whether the "West" is just a by-product of boosterism in the way that New England reflected the Puritan village in colonial times. If the "West" is the "Far West," it resembles nothing so much as a many-pronged effort at migration, each prong quite unlike the others. And if the "West" is the territory between the Appalachians and the Mississippi River Valley, then, of course, it cuts right through the "South."

The fact is that "East" and "West" have no meaning before the Civil War beyond being convenient names for vaguely defined areas. The efforts of Turner and those he influenced to turn the politics of this period into "regional bloc" patterns and alliances of "East," "West," and "South" is contrived and can't overcome the evidence that politicans did not *normally* act with "regional" interests in mind. After all, they were not elected by nor responsible to constituencies of a regional character, since the American governmental system formed in the 1770s and 1780s had not given political existence to regions.

Douglas North's attempt to explain economic growth with reference to interregional trade patterns[13] is also schematic to the point of irrelevance, simply because regions also had no economic existence. To compile economic statistics for the "South," the "Northeast," and the "Northwest," as North does, is almost meaningless, since such "regions" did not have economic independence, like some early "common market."

Since the whole character of life in Western areas was so consistently influenced by the East, it is clear that regionalism makes sense if it is applied only to "the South" and "the rest of the nation." The "North" is also a misleading term, because it implies an attachment to a region that no scholar has ever been able to show existed. People living in New Jersey, New York, Pennsylvania, Ohio, Indiana, and Illinois did not think of themselves as "Northerners," willing to act in defense of

13. North, *The Economic Growth of the United States, 1790–1860*, pp. 101–121.

important and distinctive "Northern" interests if they were threatened —which is what happened in the South.

Still, there were a number of developments in this period that were confined to the "rest of the nation," or, at least, did not noticeably influence the South. European white immigration, early labor movements, the spread of public education, and the development of social reform movements—all were generally kept out of the South. These were important aspects of life in the United States that were neither clearly national nor regional. Our understanding of all would be enhanced from the comparative investigation of the kind Thistlewaite suggested in his pioneering study of the European or British influence on American life during this period.

It makes sense to see the South as an island of regionalism in the sea of a loosely-knit nation-state. Such a view comes readily to mind when American regionalism is compared to the phenomenon elsewhere, particularly to Quebec in Canada. Both Quebecers and Southerners have been vitally concerned about the distribution of political power in a federated system. Both have had strong representation in the national government. Both have developed secession movements. Both have been more hierarchical and stratified in their social structure than the rest of the country. Both have contained most of those who have constituted a significant and distinctive minority in the population. Both contain a population that has had both a sense of identity with the region and a conviction that the region is indeed different and peculiar.

There are, of course, basic differences that also have to be mentioned if comparisons of this sort are to illuminate rather than distort. The South did secede; Quebec has not. The French Canadians are not negro slaves. English-speaking Canadians are an important "indigenous" element of the population in Quebec to an extent that Northern whites never were in the South. Here, as elsewhere, it would be helpful if American historians built the comparative approach right into their line of inquiry.

A comparison of another kind is suggested by Beard and especially by Boorstin and should be further developed: a comparison of the American Civil War to the American Revolution. In this comparison, the South plays the role of the rebelling colonists and the North plays the role of Britain. The "Whole" that was the empire becomes the nation. As Boorstin puts the question: What, in both conflicts, was the proper relationship of the part to the whole, and what could the part do if it felt oppressed by the whole? In short, in neither case was the prob-

lem of secession resolved short of armed conflict. Neither the "unwritten" constitution of the Empire nor the written constitution of the nation made any provision for withdrawal. In both cases, the part rebel-
led rather than submit further to the tyrannical use of power by the
central authority.[14] In both cases, the rebelling "part" set up its own
government modeled in many of its operational aspects after that of
the old central government. In both cases, the economic activity of the
"part" was largely financed, processed, and marketed by a succession
of middle-men in the "whole." In both cases, the rebels defended their
local autonomy and freedom from excessive interference by the central authorities. In both cases, the rebels were upset about efforts to
close off further settlement in territory to the West. In both cases,
communication broke down, and the central authority failed to assess
properly the actual situation in the seceding part, and *vice versa*.

Of course, there were differences. Southerners were directly—indeed, prominently—and not "virtually" represented in the central
government. The freedom that Southerners fought for was in the
name of human inequality, and not equality. The South was a closed
society, in many respects, and certainly in ways that the rebelling colonists were not. And it would be foolish to argue there was a "civil war"
in the Confederacy on the same level as there had been in the colonies
during the Revolution.

What of the national perspective? Textbook writers who present
accounts from this perspective obviously distort the reality of American life before the Civil War far more than they illuminate it. This
much is obvious. But what references *should* be made to the national
community for this period?

Stanley Elkins's suggestive, interpretive study of slavery provides a
proper frame. Though his chief concern was to find an explanation for
the distinctive character of the American slave system, his conclusions
involve national life generally. Simply put, the institutions of American
society were weak in comparison to those of European societies, especially Spanish and Spanish-dominated ones. There was no centralized
government or church or army or anything else that could provide the
power to integrate American life.[15] Boorstin, a year before Elkins,
reached a similar conclusion about colonial society in comparison with
British society: the whole structure of colonial life—in the professions,
in churches, in schools, in culture generally, even in the armies— was

14. Boorstin, *The Americans: The National Experience*, pp. 400–430.
15. Elkins, *Slavery*, pp. 27–52.

"looser," far less tightly-structured, much less professional and specialized than the British.[16] Unfortunately, Boorstin chose not to follow through on this comparison in his second volume. But he *is* concerned about the vagueness, or sense of incompleteness, that permeated American life, a vagueness manifested in territorial growth, geographic ignorance, exciting feelings about a wide-open future, and blurring of fact and fiction in "tall-talk" as well as in inflated declamatory rhetoric.[17]

That the very definition of nation was unsettled can clearly be seen in the lack of agreement on national symbols and in persistent regionalism in folklore and mythology. True, the Constitution—or, as Smith would have it, the "national covenant"—gave specific powers to a new central government similar in character to those the old imperial government exercised. But all attempts of "nationalist"-minded politicians to legislate comprehensive "national" programs conspicuously failed. Such attempts failed because of continued fear about the centralization of power in any general government, because of a strong tradition of state (or colony-wide) action in domestic or internal affairs, and because of the essentially local character of at least some of the matters that the new government dealt with.

In areas not closely related to the constitutionally "enumerated" Congressional powers, the failure to legislate for the nation was constant. Talk about an American university located in the nation's capital remained talk. Hopes for a truly national transportation system of roads and canals to supplement the national communications system of post offices and roads were never fulfilled, though there were many debates and proposals and even occasional appropriations for a "national" road.

Even matters that no one doubted were within Congressional jurisdiction, such as the regulation of foreign trade, were not dealt with comprehensively. Tariff rates were, by turns, raised, lowered, or neither consistently raised nor lowered, primarily because, though national jurisdiction was beyond debate, the impact of such legislation was unquestionably local, which was also true of internal improvements proposals and even banking systems with respect to the establishment of subsidiary offices. Tariff rates, roads and canals projects, and branch banks all affected in tangible ways the economic life of par-

16. Boorstin, *The Americans: The Colonial Experience*, pp. 145–265.
17. Boorstin, *The Americans: The National Experience*, pp. 221–324.

ticular communities throughout the nation. This meant that even *national* legislation was the result of primarily local pressures.

Only on issues that allowed congressmen to establish positions with reference to pressures other than local ones did congressional action approach the consistency and wholeness of a national program. Presidential leadership in foreign affairs and congressional authority over currency and the public lands were sufficiently general grants of power—grants that were general and not local in their affect—that politicians could allow such things as party loyalty, congressional debate, and presidential exhortation, rather than pressure from the constituency to determine their position. Thus, banking, public lands, and foreign policy issues were far more the product of party and of debate in national councils than were other issues. This is not to suggest that there were not deeply felt popular and political divisions on these issues; obviously, there were. What is suggested is that the major sources of such divisions transcended purely local considerations.

Even constitutional debate on the nature and extent of presidential and congressional authority turned on the question of whether an issue was primarily general or local in character. Foreign relations, foreign trade, the public lands were general matters, so debate turned on the proper *extent* of national power. If legislative action resulted in local or regional variations or antagonisms, was the national authority being properly used? If tariff duties created a kind of protection for domestic industry in certain localities and areas, but *not* in others, were such duties proper? If congressional control over public lands and territories led to a distinction between the free movement of human and material property, was not such control improper if one area (the South) was restricted in a way that others were not? And how could a national transportation system be created, even if Congress were given specific power through a Constitutional amendment to appropriate public funds for such a purpose, since roads and canals would benefit particular areas, particularly inland ones—far more than others, essentially coastal ones?

To be sure, such debate also occasionally turned on considerations of class. Protection would benefit an industrial class, some argued. A national banking system would benefit a capitalist class, others claimed. And some Southern spokesmen—particularly Calhoun—perceived the emergence of a distinctive class system as a natural byproduct of industrialization. But such themes were definitely secondary to those discussed above. Class consciousness was not the conspicuous feature of American life that it came to be in the late nineteenth century, nor what it *had* been in the colonies in the form of a social hierarchy. True, class as a frame of reference for national politics in the antebellum period was used in party rhetoric, but it was imprecisely used. One party was the "people's" party, the other was the "aristocratic" party—and the appeal of parties to the political nation was *never* such that those who could vote divided into neat class or occupational groupings. If voters had, there could never have been two major parties, as most Americans were farmers or craftsmen.

The most significant role of the major parties, as Boorstin points out, was to make a federated political system operative. The selection of rival candidates, the election of officials, and the integration of diverse political activity in towns, cities, counties, states, regions, and the nation through federated organizations—all this was the work of parties. Even so, the system did not work very well, and it never became sufficiently nationalized. Its looseness can easily be seen in the quiltwork of state-level political groupings whose activities had, even in times when the national parties were flourishing, only the most sporadic and indirect relationship to the activities of politicians in Washington.

Washington itself remained—significantly—a mere village until at least the middle of the century.[18] The division of power between the branches of the government and the mistrust of centralized power even among those elected to the new national government—both were mirrored in the physical layout of a capital that was rather sharply divided between a presidential area with the executive mansion, administrative offices, foreign embassies, and a congressional area containing temporary residences in the form of boardinghouses. Such an arrangement required a strong party leader to unite a majority of the Congress with a president in support of common objectives. Only Jefferson, and later Jackson, Van Buren, and Polk had that kind of talent to a conspicuous extent. And even these able politicians failed to attain the complete uniformity they obviously sought on matters that they considered to be of vital importance. In the no-party era between the first- and second-party systems, the highest degree of uniformity in voting occurred among those who lived in the same boardinghouses![19]

18. Constance M. Green, *Washington: Village and Capital, 1800–1878* (Princeton, N.J.: Princeton University Press, 1962).

19. James S. Young, *The Washington Community, 1800–1828* (New York: Columbia University Press, 1966).

Many who stood out in state politics were elected to Congress in this period. But the rate of turn-over among the members of the national legislature was high. Congressional careers were typically short. And a considerable number of those who "retired" returned to a *further* career in state politics, which suggests that state government was still regarded by many as the focal point of power in the American system, above the level of the local community, at least. The number of politicians who had long congressional careers and thus acted consistently from a national perspective was small until at least the time of the Civil War. A disproportionately large number of such individuals were from the South whose hierarchical social structure led to the continuation of a fairly cohesive governing class long after the rest of the country had changed. A disproportionately low number were from the mid-Atlantic states, where the sophisticated state of party politics was such that loyal party men appear to have served a brief term out of service to their organization.[20]

The American political system was, from whatever angle one chooses to view it, not at all like the centralized governments of many European nation-states, such as Britain, France, and Spain. It was, instead, something like Canada, Italy, and Germany as they moved toward confederation about the same time that the American Union fell apart. When an issue arose that forced Southerners to *think* of themselves as different and then to *act* as if they were different, the central political authority in the United States collapsed, and nearly half of the national politicians left the government and created one of their own.

Other central institutions in American life also divided. The national councils of Protestant churches—never very authoritarian or influential—divided in the late 1840s and early 1850s because of differences over slavery. With the outbreak of war, the national army—a skeleton force to begin with—split in two, the allegiance of officers and soldiers generally depending upon the region with which they most easily identified. Economic activity that involved more than small areas or even regions—that which connected Southern agriculture with Northern commerce and industry—was disrupted, of course; but since the economy had not become generally nationalized, the severance of such connections did not result in massive dislocations.

In short, by viewing the American nation as Elkins and Boorstin do, the weakness of national institutions in comparison with certain Euro-

20. *Biographical Directory of the American Congress* (Washington: U.S. Government Printing Office, 1961), *passim.*

pean nations makes the triumph of regionalism over nationalism more understandable than it is otherwise.

But why was slavery the issue that toppled those institutions? White Americans were generally racists, and most never favored legal equality for a race believed to be inherently inferior. There was nothing in the American value system that suggested such a course of action as long as the principle of human equality applied only to the white race. Even the emergence of a new social philosophy—that the hierarchical social order as defined in seventeenth-century towns was wrong; that all should have equality of opportunity in a mobile, open society—even this view was not inconsistent with human equality, so long as the mind made a place for caste, for slavery. But when abolitionists emphasized the human qualities of the black slave, Americans became upset and confused. The slavery issue could never have become so emotional in character without this agitation. And without the emotion, Americans could have continued to live with slavery, especially since they did not change their view on race until the 1930s and thereafter. With the agitation, many Northerners became convinced that slavery was unjust for any human being, even though they did not conclude that the black man was their equal. Only under the emotion-charged atmosphere of the immediate postwar era, harried by the widespread fear that white Southerners might reimpose slavery, could even so skillful a group of politicians as the Radical Republicans have persuaded Congress to legislate legal equality for the freedman—only to have the program dismantled in subsequent decades because of public indifference.

Thus, slavery became the central issue because of the way in which abolitionists probed the most glaring inconsistency between the ideal of human equality and practice of human enslavement. It is obvious that Northern opposition was materialistic as well as moralistic, but fear of competition from slave labor, by itself, could never have moved the slavery issue to its central position. It was when Southerners in significant numbers thought that the very *existence* of slavery was threatened that secession and war came. That which made Southerners *unite and act* was the threat that abolitionists posed to the whole pattern of Southern life. Once that propaganda was fixed in the minds of Americans, their subsequent action had to take account of it. Thus, Americans lived with the inconsistency of dividing over the justness of slavery while remaining largely united in their belief in racial inequality.[21] As

21. Allan Nevins was the first—at least for the antebellum period—to view the problem in its dual aspects: slavery and race relations (Allan Nevins, *The Emergence of Lincoln*, 2 vols. [New York: Charles Scribner's Sons, 1950], I, 532–544).

this was a phenomenon shared by western civilization as a whole in the nineteenth century, studies such as David Brian Davis's *The Problem of Slavery in Western Culture* bring a needed international perspective to study of the subject.

The Civil War itself would also benefit from such inquiry. Potter is the only one who has placed the event in the broader context of Europe in the mid-nineteenth century. Potter concludes that the Union government, unde Lincoln's leadership, successfully linked the cause of nationalism to the cause of liberalism, both having been under attack in Europe. By insisting upon the preservation of a nation whose purpose was liberal, Lincoln associated these two forces in a distinctively American way, in contrast, say, to Bismarck and, later, to Hitler, Mussolini, and Stalin.[22] The comparative approach should also involve direct comparisons between the American Civil War and other Civil Wars —for example, that of the English in the 1650s, of the Russians in 1917–1918, the Spanish in the 1930s, and the Chinese in the 1940s.

The war should also be investigated for its impact on American life, something begun by Allan Nevins.[23] In particular, to what extent did it, paradoxically, have a nationalizing affect, in the sense that people in towns and cities all over the divided nation were forced to view events from a "national" perspective. Was community life linked to Union or Confederate efforts with sufficient regularity that Americans became identified with the national community, even though reduced in size, to a significantly greater extent than before?[24] After all, the Civil War was the first great event involving the whole "national" community that occurred *within* the United States since its creation as a nation. Historians are in general agreement that the war did not create a "revolution" in the over-all pattern of political, economic, social, and cultural-intellectual life, however.

There is, of course, no historical writing of a general character to probe the role that families, towns, or cities played in the coming of the war. Our minds are blank on this matter. But if families and local communities continued to be central to American life, is it sensible to assume that they can be left out of account in any explanation of the war?

The Civil War, like the Revolution, had an aftermath that is most appropriately discussed along with the conflict, and, indeed, has been

22. Woodward, editor, *The Comparative Approach to American History*, pp. 135–145.

23. Allan Nevins, *The War for the Union*, 6 vols. (New York: Charles Scribner's Sons, 1959–1971).

24. For example, see George W. Smith and Charles Judah, editors, *Life in the North during the Civil War: A Source History* (Albuquerque, N.M.: University of New Mexico Press, 1966).

traditionally discussed at that place in textbook accounts. Reconstruction should continue to receive attention, but, as is the case with the Articles of Confederation and the Constitution, it should be analyzed from a national perspective, as the national government's effort to reconstruct the Union.

* * * * *

Textbook accounts of the period from the Civil War to the Great Depression also need considerable revision, though not the complete recasting of the previous period. There is usually a break in the smooth flow of the national and government-oriented narrative in the textbook version of the post-Civil War decades. Suddenly the reader has to adjust to a new focus: a "New West," a "New South," "The Ordeal of Industrialization," the "Urban Society," sometimes even "Intellectual and Cultural Trends." Though the shift represented by these typical chapter headings is beneficial, the change is not basic enough nor consistent enough. By the time of the "Progressive Era," the standard subject once more is national politics, which is never again lost sight of, except perhaps for a final chapter entitled "Modern American Society," or "The Face of the Future."

New accounts *should* begin again with the *family*. Unfortunately, however, there are no studies of a general kind on this subject for this period.[25] Until there are, comment will have to be of the most tentative character. Atherton's study of the small Midwestern town, by contrast, provides a ready-made frame of reference for the specific ways in which the small town in America lost its relative self-sufficiency and isolation as various facets of American life became nationalized. This single study thus has to bear an enormous responsibility in the absence of similar inquiries into towns in other areas. Its substance acts as a kind of pivot, revealing the ways in which the preindustrial village society is transformed into the mass industrial society of our time.

Unfortunately, in the absence of a general interpretive study of cities for the 1865–1945 period, the precise role that urban centers played in the nationalization of American life, especially in its economic and cultural aspects, is not clear. Warner's studies of Boston and Philadelphia for this period are sufficiently broad to indicate

25. Sennett's *Families Against the City*, focussed as it is on the interplay between middle-class families and city life, is not really a general study of family life for this period.

something of the nature of the urbanization process in particular cities across the country, even if the influence of the city on the rest of the population is left out of account. Urban study for the decades from about 1870 to 1920 is of particular importance because these were the years, as Handlin reminds us, of the making of the modern metropolis.

We also need to know more about the states, particularly about how and when they lost their power as the dominant government in domestic affairs in our federal system. Their continued vitality is evident in their pioneering effort to regulate large-scale industrial enterprise—rail transport to be precise—and in their being models or laboratories of Progressive reform before that movement had made much of an impact on national politics.[26] By the advent of the depression of the 1930s, however, most states could not cope with a situation that threatened the existence of the entire American system. At that point, if not before, the states could not deal effectively with a society whose organization and whose problems were national in scope.

Regionalism does have a role to play in the early part of this period. It is proper to focus on the last frontiers in the plains and Far West. They, like the earlier frontiers, contained a distinctive, though transitory society. But the frontiers of the trans-Mississippi West should not receive any *more* attention than the earlier ones, as they typically do in textbook accounts. Since the Far West frontiers, from the 1850s on, existed within a worldwide pattern of frontier expansion, the American version of this phenomenon ought to be compared to experience elsewhere.

With respect to the South, the theme should be the decline of distinctiveness as the area developed features of American life that its people pointedly avoided before the Civil War and as its former slaves—the main basis of its peculiarity—migrated to urban centers all over the Union.[27] The "South" is now basically a "historical" experience that still affects its inhabitants, in the way that those who lived in the original states must have shared the historical experience of their respective colonies for years after independence.

---

26. There ought, for instance, to be a synthesis of all those studies on the progressive reform movement in particular states.

27. Both the persistent distinctiveness and the movement toward assimilation are ably treated in the "History of the South" series: C. Vann Woodward, *Origins of the New South, 1877–1913* (Baton Rouge, La.: Louisiana State University Press, 1951) and George B. Tindall, *The Emergence of the New South, 1913–1945* (Baton Rouge, La.: Louisiana State University Press, 1967).

The proper focus for the nation in the post-Civil War period is, of course, the progressive nationalization of American life, not only in government, but in all other significant institutions and activities. Fortunately, there is already a masterful synthesis that probes the actual forms that the nationalizing process assumed: Robert Wiebe's *The Search for Order, 1877–1920*. Though ostensibly covering only a part of the period now being considered, Wiebe's thesis is in reality central to an understanding of American life from the Civil War to the depression. Wiebe begins with the proposition that the "island community" or isolated small town was still central to American society in the 1870s, but that such communities entered into a prolonged period of crisis during the headlong rush into industrialization, urbanization, and immigration that characterized the last decades of the nineteenth century. There was much confusion and disarray in this crucial transitional period; indeed, American society became distended. It was in this setting that a bureaucratic-minded, largely urban, "new" middle class developed a set of values, a point of view that stressed "continuity and regularity, functionality and rationality, administration and management."[28] This impulse, this passion for the imposition of order upon a disordered society is like the attitude that Rothman and Katz found in the middle-class officials who organized and managed the first institutions for the deviant and dependent members of society in the 1830s. Both groups feared chaos; both sought to impose order from above; both believed that they or their kind should be society's managers.

In the case of the Progressive at the turn of the century, the bureaucratic passion for order resulted in (a) the sudden organization of the professions, of industry, of labor, of occupations generally, on a national scale, rather than on the basis of particular communities; (b) the reduction of values, of thought, to a bureaucratic ideal that emphasized "frugality, promptness, foresight, efficiency," and so on; (c) the development of a government filled with "trained, professional servants . . . broadly and continuously involved in society's operations"; and (d) the development of major corporations whose businessman-leaders moved "to extend the range and continuity of their power through bureaucratic means."[29]

In place of the "personal, informal ways" of the island communities with their local autonomy and weak communications, a new pattern of life

28. Wiebe (New York: Hill & Wang, 1967), p. viii.
29. *Ibid.*, pp. 146, 160, 181.

derived from the regulative, hierarchical needs of urban-industrial life. Through rules with impersonal sanctions, it sought continuity and predictability in a world of endless change. It assigned far greater power to government—in particular to a variety of flexible administrative devices—and it encouraged the centralization of authority. Men were now separated more by skill and occupation than by community; they identified themselves more by their tasks in an urban-industrial society than by their reputations in a town or city neighborhood.[30]

Wiebe's synthesis is a powerful blend of narrative, a great deal of well-chosen specific references, and apt analysis. It is hard to imagine a more effective general account focussed on the nationalization of life that this essay makes so much of. *The Search for Order* will remain the reference point for future studies concentrated on the national level of American life during the years from the Civil War to the depression.

Our understanding of the depression itself would benefit from thorough, comparative study of the kind that William Leuchtenburg has asked for.[31] Not only should the international character of the depression be investigated but so should the extent to which Americans copied what Europeans were doing or had already done. The American solution—the New Deal's pragmatic kind of welfare capitalism, something between Socialism or Communism and Fascism—became a kind of model for other governments, but was itself partly the product of foreign examples. We also need to know why the depression was more severe in the United States than anywhere else, and why the relationship of the American government to the economy before the depression was as distinctive as it was. The impact of the depression on all aspects of American life has received some attention, but few have studied its affects on states, cities, towns, and family life.[32]

The depression, like previous crises, had an aftermath, but one of a peculiar character. Only World War II brought economic recovery, so an account of the war should be presented along with any analysis of the depression. Included in this account should be an investigation of

---

30. *Ibid.*, p. xiv.

31. Woodward, editor, *The Comparative Approach to American History*, pp. 296–314.

32. Barnard Sternsher, editor, *Hitting Home: The Great Depression in Town and Country* (Chicago: Quadrangle Press, 1970), is a beginning, in that it contains scholarly articles on the impact of various facets of the depression on particular towns and cities, such as Ann Arbor, Sioux City, Atlanta, Philadelphia, and New York; counties such as Cedar (in Iowa), Custer (in Nebraska), Harlan (in Kentucky), and Orange (in California); and states, such as Oklahoma and Arizona.

the impact of wartime mobilization, particularly with reference to its nationalizing effects on all aspects of American life presented from a national perspective. Once again, life in towns and cities must have focussed, as during the Civil War, on what the whole national community was experiencing.

* * * * *

Accounts of the most recent period of American history are much too government-centered, but at least their national perspective is warranted. With the nationalization of life the dominant feature of American society since World War II, such a perspective is the appropriate one *for the first time* in any general history of the Americans.

After surveying the national character of American society and analyzing the nature of the role of the United States in the world, the new account should then stress the altered substance of family life and of community life in regions, states, cities, and towns—indeed, what Boorstin thinks is a basic change in the definition of community itself to what he calls statistical social communities, rather than geographic ones. But what Boorstin fails to emphasize is that, at the same time that Americans nationalized their life, they produced three crises, one within their major "old-fashioned" community, the metropolis; another in their collective relationship to their environmental setting; and a third in their use of power in the community of nation-states. As more and more Americans move into urban areas, the problems of sustaining a human community of such a scale and variety increases, especially since nonwhite elements in the population pack into well-defined ghettos around the centers and become dissatisfied, alienated, and hateful Americans with legal equality but lacking economic well-being and social status. At the same time, the industrialization of the American economy has led to pollution of the air, water, and soil, as well as to the depletion of nonrenewable resources. Finally, American military, diplomatic, and economic power has led to involvement in the internal affairs of other nations to such an extent that Americans are bewildered and divided over their proper role in the world. At the heart of any analysis of the recent period in American history, therefore, should be an accounting of the *successful* nationalization of a mass, industrialized society, along with the concomitant *lack* of integration within the kind of local community that most Americans actually live in, as well as the absence of agreement on the proper relationship of Americans to their environment and of the United States to the outside community of nations. In this contradiction lies much of what ails American society today.

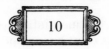

Conclusion

American intellectuals have often pondered the nature of community as they assessed or criticized their society. By and large, they have dwelled upon local communities, where people actually live. Morton and Lucia White, in their *The Intellectual vs. the City: From Thomas Jefferson to Frank Lloyd Wright*, find a persistent tradition of anti-urbanism, or a definite bias in favor of the town and countryside:

> [The] negative attitude of the intellectual toward the American city is of interest in its own right, especially because it is voiced in unison by figures who represent major tendencies in American thought. . . . Because these figures dominate or sum up certain phases of American intellectual development, they form a body of intellectual lore and tradition which continues to affect thought and action about the city today. There is a contemporaneity about some of their views which is not obscured by the fact that they speak from the past; they continue to be read by those who are interested in the general history of the United States and also by those who are curious about our literary and philosophical tradition. They virtually constitute our intellectual tradition as it is known today. They make up the core of our intellectual history and one must go to them if one wishes to know what the articulate American conception of urban life has been.[1]

1. Morton and White (Cambridge, Mass.: Harvard University Press, 1962), p. 3. The figures included are Jefferson, Emerson, Thoreau, Hawthorne, Poe, Melville, Henry Adams, Henry James, William Dean Howells, Theodore Dreiser, William Norris, John Dewey, Jane Addams, Louis Sullivan, Frank Lloyd Wright, and Robert Park.

Thus, until our own time, our most influential intellectuals have criticized the community most of us have come to live in.

Similarly, Jean Quandt, in *From Small Town to the Great Community:
The Social Thought of Progressive Intellectuals*, indicates that a number of
the leading Progressives[2]—members of the very group that Wiebe
finds played a central role in the nationalization of American life
—adhered tenaciously to the small-town view of life that they grew up
with, even in the act of prescribing for a society whose nature had
changed drastically from what it had been in their youth. These
latter-day "communitarians" faced the "problem of community" in the
following manner:

> What the communitarians claimed to see when they looked
> about them was the breakdown of the small, close-knit group
> under the impact of urbanization and industrialization. A social
> organization based upon family, neighborhood, and small-town
> solidarity was being replaced by one based upon the more im-
> personal and tenuous ties of the market place. The division of
> labor, together with modern methods of communication and
> transportation, had created a physical unity based upon the in-
> terdependence of parts, but a moral unity corresponding to
> this economic web had not yet emerged. . . . A greater psychic
> and moral integration to match the increasing physical integra-
> tion of society was essential to the realization of their notion of
> community. As they saw it, the growing unity of the social or-
> ganism only laid the groundwork for that interpenetration with
> the whole which characterized a sense of community. With all
> interests now intertwined, modern communication could create
> greater mutual understanding and common purpose. Thus the
> Great Society provided the material basis for its moral equival-
> ent, the Great Community. . . . In this vision, the small com-
> munity became the scale model for the larger one. Its values of
> intimacy, mutual identification, and face-to-face communica-
> tion appeared in the blueprint for the city, the province, and
> the nation. At the same time, the small local community be-
> came the training ground for a larger loyalty, a link in the
> chain that would lead from neighborhood to nation. But the

2. The nine figures included are William Allen White, Frederic Howe, Jane Addams,
Mary Parker Follett, John Dewey, Josiah Royce, Franklin Giddings, Charles Horton
Cooley, and Robert Park.

optimism of the circle was tempered by the suspicion, if not the clear recognition, that the forces of modern society were working against as well as for them. In their view, the growing complexity of social organization was obstructing the re-creation of mutual sympathy and full communication on a large scale. Furthermore, the trend toward economic integration was weakening local loyalties.[3]

In short, the effort of some intellectuals to make the new, nationalized and urbanized community over into the small town's image failed—was, in fact, doomed to failure. But note: they still tried. The small town still provided their standard.

Of course, the Whites and Quandt are quite selective. The fact is that not all intellectuals favored rural life over urban. Indeed, since the 1920s and the 1930s, increasing numbers of them have chosen city life and, until recently, at least, have praised its diversity, its freedom, its intellectual and cultural attainments, and heaped scorn on the bigotry, provinciality, and over-all narrowness of the town and the countryside.

The American intellectual has thus been ambiguous in his attitude toward community life in America, an ambiguity that has found expression in the writings of our historians as well. Local antiquarian-chroniclers such as George Sheldon were too much a part of the town they wrote about to feel estranged or at all critical. And modern writers such as Page Smith still think that the small town—especially one with a spiritual purpose—is the most successful community that Americans have yet devised. Daniel Boorstin seems caught up in the sheer excitement of community-building, if his prose in any way reflects his feelings. Other writers, like Zuckerman, are concerned about the antiliberal side of rural or village life. But until recently, historians who wrote about cities reflected the antiurban bias of other intellectuals by reducing the study of urban life to a series of problems, something the present-day urban crisis may foster once again.

What sets apart the work of our most influential and popular historical synthesizers is their search after a meaning for *American* history, and not just that of particular types of local communities. Bancroft, Turner, Beard, and Boorstin thus placed their gifts in the service of the nation-state. As Americans gained a sense of nationhood, they did so,

3. Quandt, *From the Small Town to the Great Community (New Brunswick, N.J.: Rutgers University Press, 1970)*, pp. 17, 20.

in part, because these writers gave them a shared feeling for a common past.

It is clear that Bancroft *imposed* a national purpose and meaning on a society whose life was in fact dominated by local communities. He did so by referring to a larger theme of human progress and the growth of liberty illustrated with distinctive clarity in the British colonies that became the United States of America as the result of a Revolution that pitted those concerned about the advancement of liberty against a tyrannical imperial government.

At the end of the nineteenth century, with the end of American territorial expansion and the closing of the frontier within that added territory, Frederick Jackson Turner concluded that what gave American life its distinctiveness was something peculiar to America, or, at least, not shared with Europe: the continued existence of a frontier. From this conviction came Turner's preoccupation with the regional aspects of national life. For Turner, the most important facet of American life after 1789 was its persistent regionalism—whether on the frontier or in settled areas. This focus influenced the character of much historical writing in the United States for four decades after 1900.

Yet another view, shared by the so-called Progressives and most effectively articulated by Charles Beard in his textbook, *The Rise of American Civilization* (1927), also influenced the character of historical writings on the United States during the same period. Beard wrote from a national perspective, and like Bancroft, he argued with reference to a theme that transcended the American historical experience—namely, that the economic factor is basic in human life and largely determined the character of that life. In the American context, economic and class antagonism and conflict took the form of an agrarian-commercial division that permeated all aspects of American life. When such divisions coincided with the regionalism that Turner stressed, the cataclysm that was the Civil War resulted. Beard and the Progressives wrote in a period when their society—which they wished to reform—appeared to have the same divisions that they found in the historical experience of Americans. The depression of the thirties simply underscored the primacy of the economic factor.

The national perspective is also central to the works of the best-known liberal-consensus historians, such as Hofstadter and Hartz. Writing during the "cold war," in a world seemingly dividing into free and totalitarian Communist nations, those who had a liberal-consensus point of view tried to explain what united Americans internally and made them distinctive with reference to the world outside. These historians found agreement on fundamentals from the beginning of the historical experience of those who became Americans.

The crisis of the 1960s and its sudden focus on who is "in" and who is "outside" of the American community has prompted the development of a radical point of view that once again gives primacy to division, antagonism, strife, and conflict. But instead of concentrating on what divided "liberal" society, as Beard had done, the "Young Radicals" are more concerned about views and elements in the population that lay *outside* of the liberal consensus. To them, American society is not split down the middle in a great agrarian-commercial division. American society is split across, horizontally, between those who are "in" and those who are "out." They want to study the "outs."

All this is a quick and familiar summation of those viewpoints that have dominated the historical consciousness of educated Americans. What hasn't been sufficiently recognized, however, is the extent to which Bancroft, Turner, Beard, and Hofstatder all imposed upon American history an unhistorical perspective. What Bancroft *hoped* was a nation, what Turner and Beard saw *emerge* as a nation, and what Hofstatder *knew* was a nation, was not *always* a nation. And to impose a national perspective on American history from 1607 onward has created a distortion as great as anything to be gained from these writers' conception of what is basic to the character of America's past.[4]

This is why Boorstin's work is so refreshing. And this is why it is probably the greatest of all the influential attempts at historical synthesis. Though he blurs his definition of community to the point that distinctions between rural areas, towns, and cities are obliterated, Boorstin is our first important synthesizer to convey the sense of nationhood *coming out of* community-building at the local level.

We now have the bare outline of a new organizational scheme through which to view our past. No organizational scheme—by its nature—can be perfectly satisfying. What has been presented in outline form in this essay, however, is more revealing than what we have had from the time when general textbooks first appeared.

How did the preindustrial village society become transformed into the mass industrial society that threatens the very balance of nature itself? How did Americans lose the small, viable, homogeneous, sometimes intensely spiritual community that stifled liberty and gain a large, heterogeneous, libertarian, mostly secular community that threatens

---

4. For a general survey of the historical profession, see John Higham, *History: Professional Scholarship in America* (Englewood Cliffs, N.J.: Prentice-Hall, Inc., 1965).

to fall apart? How have Americans lost a patriarchal, hierarchical, stratified, but personal society and gained a more democratic but also more impersonal, bureaucratic, institutionalized, but still stratified society? Out of these transformations has come the world's mightiest liberal society, the full flowering of many old European notions and ideals. What have the liberals wrought?

There exists now a magnificent opportunity for historians with the narrative flair of a Bancroft or a Morison, the analytical sweep of a Handlin or a Hofstadter, the gift for finding the memorable illustration of a Boorstin, and Turner's capacity to probe to the essence of something. The story of Americans goes beyond the worship of God or of one's ancestors, beyond the praise of one's nation. It involves more than the curiosity of old American families, the good citizenship of school children, and the patriotism of their parents. It takes in more than wars, political debates, and exciting leaders. It is the story of how a portion of humanity organized itself into families and communities and created the most powerful nation on earth. The motives and purposes, successes and failures, the joy and the sorrow of these people is certainly a story worth telling, and worth telling in a way that will reclaim the attention of those in historical and genealogical societies, or the History Book Club—in short, those whose predecessors read the history of a Sheldon or of a Bancroft in the days when we understood and cared about a lot less than we dare to today.

Bibliography

Note:
This is a selective bibliography,
restricted to writings referred
to in the text.

I: Historical Writing

Bass, Herbert J., editor. *The State of American History*. Chicago: Quadrangle Books, 1970.

Gay, Peter. *A Loss of Mastery: Puritan Historians in Colonial America*. Berkeley, California: University of California Press, 1966.

Higham, John. *History: Professional Scholarship in America*. Englewood Cliffs, N.J.: Prentice-Hall, Inc., 1965.

Hofstadter, Richard. *The Progressive Historians: Turner, Beard, Parrington*. New York: Alfred A. Knopf, Inc., 1968.

Meyerhoff, Hans, editor. *The Philosophy of History in Our Time*. New York: Doubleday & Co., 1959.

Plumb, J. H. *The Uses of the Past*. London: Macmillan & Co., Ltd., 1969.

Smith, Page. *The Historian and History*. New York: Alfred A. Knopf, Inc., 1964.

Stern, Fritz, editor. *Varieties of History: From Voltaire to the Present*. New York: Meridian Press, Inc., 1956.

Van Tassel, David. *Recording America's Past: An Interpretation of the Development of Historical Studies in America, 1607–1884*. Chicago: University of Chicago Press, 1960.

II: Community

Braudel, Ferdnand. *The Mediterranean and the Mediterranean World in the Age of Philip II*, 2 vols. Translation. New York: Harper & Row, Publishers, 1972–1973.

Buber, Martin. *Paths to Utopia*. Paperback edition. Boston: Beacon Press, 1958.

Boorstin, Daniel J. *The Americans: The Colonial Experience*. New York: Random House, 1958.

——— . *The Americans: The National Experience*. New York: Random House, 1965.

——— . *The Americans: The Democratic Experience*. New York: Random House, 1973.

König, Rene. *The Community*. London: Routledge — Kegan Paul, Ltd., 1968.

Laslett, Peter. *The World We Have Lost*. London: Methuen & Co., Ltd., 1965.

Quandt, Jean. *From Small Town to the Great Community: The Social Thought of Progressive Intellectuals*. New Brunswick, N.J.: Rutgers University Press, 1970.

Redfield, Robert. *The Little Community*. Chicago: University of Chicago Press, 1956.

Stein, Maurice. *The Eclipse of Community: Toward a Theory of American Communities*. Princeton, N.J.: Princeton University Press, 1960.

White, Morton, and Lucia White. *The Intellectual vs. the City: From Thomas Jefferson to Frank Lloyd Wright*. Cambridge, Mass.: Harvard University Press, 1962.

III: Towns

Allen, James B. *The Company Town in the American West*. Norman, Okla.: University of Oklahoma Press, 1966.

Atherton, Lewis. *Main Street on the Middle Border*. Bloomington, Ind.: Indiana University Press, 1954.

Clark, Charles E. *The Eastern Frontier: The Settlement of Northern New England: 1610–1763*. New York: Alfred A. Knopf, Inc., 1970.

Curti, Merle. *The Making of an American Community: A Case Study of Democracy in a Frontier County*. Stanford, Calif.: Stanford University Press, 1959.

Dykstra, Robert R. *The Cattle Towns*. New York: Alfred A. Knopf, Inc., 1968.

Grant, Charles. *Democracy in the Connecticut Frontier Town of Kent*. New York: Columbia University Press, 1961.

Green, Constance M. *Washington: Village and Capital, 1800–1878*. Princeton, N.J.: Princeton University Press, 1962.

Lockridge, Kenneth. *A New England Town–The First Hundred Years: Dedham, Massachusetts, 1636–1736*. New York: Wm. Norton & Co., Inc., 1970.

Martindale, Don, and R. Galen Hanson. *Small Town and the Nation: The Conflict of Local and Translocal Forces*. Westport, Con.: Greenwood Publishing Co., 1969.

Powell, Chilton Sumner, *Puritan Village: The Formation of a New England Town*. Middleton, Conn.: Wesleyan University Press, 1963.

Reps, John. *Town Planning in Frontier America*. Princeton, N.J.: Princeton University Press, 1969.

Rutman, Darret B. *Winthrop's Boston: A Portrait of a Puritan Town*. Chapel Hill: University of North Carolina Press, 1965.

Sheldon, George. *History of Deerfield, Massachusetts*. 2 vols. Deerfield, Mass.: Pocumtuck Valley Memorial Association, 1895–1896.

Sternsher, Barnard, editor. *Hitting Home: The Great Depression in Town and Country*. Chicago: Quadrangle Books, 1970.

Smith, Page. *As a City Upon a Hill: The Town in American History*. New York: Alfred A. Knopf, Inc., 1966.

Vidich, Arthur J., and Joseph Bensman. *Small Town in Mass Society: Class, Power and Religion in a Rural Community*. Princeton, N.J.: Princeton University Press, 1958, 1968.

Young, James S. *The Washington Community, 1800–1828*. New York: Columbia University Press, 1966.

Zuckerman, Michael. *Peaceable Kingdoms: New England Towns in the Eighteenth Century*. New York: Alfred A. Knopf, Inc., 1970.

IV: Cities

Bridenbaugh, Carl. *Cities in the Wilderness*. New York: The Ronald Press Co., 1938.

———. *Cities in Revolt*. New York: Alfred A. Knopf, Inc., 1955.

Callow, Alexander B., editor. *American Urban History: An Interpretive Reader with Commentaries*. New York: Oxford University Press, 1969.

Frisch, Michael. *Town Into City: Springfield, Massachusetts, and the Meaning of Community, 1840–1880*. Cambridge, Mass.: Harvard University Press, 1972.

Green, Constance M. *American Cities in the Growth of the Nation*. Tackahoe, N.Y.: John de Graff, Inc., 1957.

Handlin, Oscar, and John Burchard, editors. *The Historian and the City*. Cambridge, Mass.: The M.I.T. Press, 1963.

Jackson, Kenneth T., and Stanley K. Schultz, editors. *Cities in American History*. New York: Alfred A. Knopf, Inc., 1972.

Knights, Peter. *Plain People of Boston: A Study in City Growth*. New York: Oxford University Press, 1971.

Lynch, Kevin. *The Image of the City*. Cambridge, Mass.: The M.I.T. Press, 1960.

Mumford, Lewis. *The City in History: Its Origins, Its Transformations, and Its Prospects*. New York: Harcourt, Brace & World, Inc., 1961.

Schlesinger, Arthur, Sr. *The Rise of the City*. New York: The Macmillan Co., 1933.

Thernstrom, Stephan. *Poverty and Progress: Social Mobility in a Nineteenth Century City*. Cambridge, Mass.: Harvard University Press, 1964.

———. *The Other Bostonians: Poverty and Progress in the American Metropolis, 1880–1970* Cambridge, Mass.: Harvard University Press, 1973.

——— and Richard Sennett, editors *Nineteenth Century Cities: Essays in the New Urban History*. New Haven, Conn.: Yale University Press, 1969.

Wade, Richard. *The Urban Fronter: The Rise of Western Cities*. Cambridge, Mass.: Harvard University Press, 1962.

Warner, Sam B., Jr. *Streetcar Suburbs: The Process of Growth in Boston, 1870–1900* Cambridge, Mass.: Harvard University Press, 1962.

———. *The Private City: Philadelphia in Three Periods of Its Growth*. Philadelphia: University of Pennsylvania Press, 1968.

———. *The Urban Wilderness: A History of the American City*. New York: Harper & Row, Publishers, 1972.

Weber, Adna. *The Growth of the City in the Nineteenth Century: A Study in Statistics*. New York: The MacMillan Co., 1899. Reprint. Ithaca, N.Y.: Cornell University Press, 1963.

Weber, Max. *The City*, edited by Don Martindale and Gertrud Neuwirth. Glencoe, Ill.: Free Press, 1958.

V: States

Benson, Lee. *The Concept of Jacksonian Democracy: New York as a Test Case*. New York: Princeton University Press, 1961.

Cunningham, Noble, Jr. *The Jeffersonian Republicans: The Formation of Party Organization, 1789–1801*. Chapel Hill, N.C.: University of North Carolina Press, 1957.

————. *The Jeffersonian Republicans in Power: Party Operations, 1801–1809*. Chapel Hill, N.C.: University of North Carolina Press, 1963.

Elazar, Daniel J. *The American Partnership: Intergovernmental Co-operation in the Nineteenth-Century United States*. Chicago: University of Chicago Press, 1962.

Handlin, Oscar, and Mary Handlin. *Commonwealth: A Study of the Role of Government in the American Economy: Massachusetts, 1774–1861*. Cambridge, Mass.: Harvard University Press, 1947.

Hartz, Louis. *Economic Policy and Democratic Thought: Pennsylvania, 1776–1860*. Cambridge, Mass.: Harvard University Press, 1948.

Heath, Milton. *Constructive Liberalism: The Role of the State in the Economic Development in Georgia to 1860*. Cambridge, Mass.: Harvard University Press, 1954.

Key, V. O. Jr. *American State Politics: An Introduction*. New York: Alfred A. Knopf, Inc., 1956.

McCormick, Richard. *The Second American Party System: Party Formation in the Jacksonian Era*. Chapel Hill: University of North Carolina Press, 1966.

MacDonald, Forrest. *We the People: The Economic Origins of the Constitution*. Chicago: University of Chicago Press, 1958.

Main, Jackson Turner. *Political Parties Before the Constitution*. Chapel Hill, N.C.: University of North Carolina Press, 1973.

————. *The Sovereign States, 1775–1783*. New York: New Viewpoints, 1973.

Nevins, Allan. *The American States During and After the American Revolution*. New York: The Macmillan Co., 1924. Reprint. New York: A. M. Kelley, 1969.

Patterson, James T. *The New Deal and the States: Federalism in Transition*. Princeton: Princeton University Press, 1969.

Sharp, James P. *The Jacksonians versus the Banks: Politics in the States aftr the Panic of 1837*. New York: Columbia University Press, 1970.

VI: Regions

Billington, Ray A. *The Far Western Frontier, 1830–1860*. New York: Harper & Row, Publishers, 1956.

Jensen, Merrill, editor. *Regionalism in America*. Madison, Wisc.: University of Wisconsin Press, 1952.

North, Douglas. *The Economic Growth of the United States, 1790–1860*. Englewood Cliffs, N.J.: Prentice-Hall, Inc., 1961.

Odum, Howard and Harry E. Moore. *American Regionalism: A Cultural-Historical Approach to National Integration*. New York: Henry Holt & Company, Inc., 1938.

Philbrick, Francis S. *The Rise of the West, 1754–1830*. New York: Harper & Row, Publishers, 1965.

Potter, David M. *The South and the Sectional Conflict*. Baton Rouge, La.: Louisiana State University Press, 1968.

Tindall, George B. *The Emergence of the New South, 1913–1945*. Baton Rouge, La.: Louisiana State University Press, 1967.

Turner, Frederick Jackson. *The Significance of Sections in American History*. New York: Henry Holt & Co., 1932.

——— . *The United States, 1830–1850: The Nation and Its Sections*. New York: Henry Holt & Company, Inc., 1935.

Woodward, C. Vann. *American Counterpoint: Slavery and Racism in the North-South Dialogue*. Boston: Little, Brown & Company, 1971.

——— . *Origins of the New South, 1877–1913*. Baton Rouge, La.: Louisiana State University Press, 1951.

——— . *The Burden of Southern History*. Baton Rouge, La.: Louisiana State University Press, 1960, 1968.

VII: The Nation

Ahlstrom, Sydney. *A Religious History of the American People*. New Haven, Conn.: Yale University Press, 1972.

Arieli, Yehoshua. *Individualism and Nationalism in American Ideology*. Cambridge, Mass.: Harvard University Press, 1964.

Baltzell, E. Digby. *Philadelphia Gentlemen: The Making of a National Upper Class*. Glencoe, Ill.: Free Press, 1958.

Bancroft, George. *The History of the United States of America from the Discovery of the American Continent*. 10 vols. Boston: Little, Brown & Co., 1834–1874.

Barnouw, Eric. *The Image Empire: A History of Broadcasting in the United States*. 3 vols. New York: Oxford University Press, 1966–1970.

Bernstein, Barton J., editor. *Towards a New Past: Dissenting Essays in American History*. New York: Pantheon Books, 1968.

Berthoff, Roland. *An Unsettled People: Social Order and Disorder in American History.* New York: Harper & Row, Publishers, 1971.

Blum, John M. *The Republican Roosevelt.* Cambridge, Mass.: Harvard University Press, 1954.

Boorstin, Daniel J. *The Decline of Radicalism: Reflections on America Today.* New York: Random House, 1969.

Bremner, Robert H. *From the Depths: The Discovery of Poverty in the United States.* New York: New York University Press, 1956.

Cox, Harvey. *A Feast of Fools: A Theological Essay on Festivity and Fantasy.* Cambridge, Mass.: Harvard University Press, 1969.

Cremin, Lawrence. *American Education: The Colonial Experience.* New York: Harper & Row, Publishers, 1970.

Degler, Carl. *Out of Our Past: The Forces that Shaped Modern America.* New York: Harper & Row, Publishers, 1959.

Danhoff, Clarence H. *Change in Agriculture: The Northern United States, 1820–1870.* Cambridge, Mass.: Harvard University Press, 1969.

Domhoff, G. William. *The Higher Circles: The Governing Class in America.* New York: Random House, 1970.

Donald, David. *Lincoln Reconsidered: Essays on the Civil War Era.* New York: Alfred A. Knopf, Inc., 1956.

Elkins, Stanley. *Slavery: A Problem in American Intellectual and Institutional Life.* Chicago: University of Chicago Press, 1959.

Gabriel, Ralph. *The Course on American Democratic Thought.* Second edition. New York: The Ronald Press Co., 1956.

Galbraith, John Kenneth. *Economics and the Public Purpose.* Boston: Houghton-Mifflin Co., 1973.

Genovese, Eugene. *The Political Economy of Slavery: Studies in the Economy and Society of the Slave South.* New York: Pantheon Books, 1965.

Graham, Hugh D., and Ted R. Gurr, editors. *The History of Violence in America: Historical and Comparative Perspectives.* Paperback edition. New York: Bantam Books, Inc., 1969.

Grob, Gerald N. *Workers and Utopia: A Study of Ideological Conflict in the American Labor Movement, 1865–1900.* Evanston, Ill.: Northwestern University Press, 1961.

Hays, Samuel P. *Conservatism and the Gospel of Efficiency: The Progressive Conservation Movement, 1890–1920.* Cambridge, Mass.: Harvard University Press, 1959.

Hayter, Earl W. *The Troubled Farmer, 1850–1900: Rural Adjustment to Industrialism.* De Kalb, Ill.: Northern Illinois University Press, 1968.

Hofstadter, Richard. *Anti-Intellectualism in American Life.* New York: Alfred A. Knopf, Inc., 1962.

Hugins, Walter. *Jacksonian Democracy and the Working Class: A Study of the New York Workingman's Movement, 1829–1837.* Stanford, Calif.: Stanford University Press, 1960.

Jensen, Merrill. *The Articles of Confederation: An Interpretation of the Social-Constitutional History of the American Revolution.* Madison, Wisc.: University of Wisconsin Press, 1948.

––––––. *The New Nation: A History of the United States During the Confederation, 1781–1789.* New York: Alfred A. Knopf, Inc., 1950.

Kennan, George. *American Diplomacy, 1900–1950.* Chicago: University of Chicago Press, 1951.

Kohn, Hans. *American Nationalism: An Interpretive Essay.* New York: The Macmillan Co., 1957.

Kolko, Gabriel. *The Triumph of Conservatism: A Reinterpretation of American History, 1900–1916.* Glencoe, Ill.: Free Press, 1963.

Link, Arthur S. *Woodrow Wilson and the Progressive Movement, 1910–1917.* New York: Harper Brothers, Publishers, 1954.

Litwak, Leon F. *North of Slavery: The Negro in the Free States, 1790–1860.* Chicago: University of Chicago Press, 1961.

Lundberg, Ferdinand. *The Rich and the Super-Rich.* New York: Lyle Stuart, Inc., 1968.

Main, Jackson Turner. *The Social Structure of Revolutionary America.* Princeton, N.J.: Princeton University Press, 1965.

Meade, Sidney. "The 'Nation with the Soul of a Church'." *Church History,* XXXVI (September 1967), 262–283.

Mencher, Samuel. *Poor Law to Poverty Program.* Pittsburgh: University of Pittsburgh Press, 1967.

Merritt, Richard. *Symbols of American Community, 1735–1775.* New Haven, Conn.: Yale University Press, 1966.

Miller, Douglas T. *Jacksonian Aristocracy: Class and Democracy in New York, 1830–1860*. New York: Oxford University Press, 1967.

Miller, Perry. *The Life of the Mind from the Revolution to the Civil War*. New York: Harcourt, Brace, & World, Inc., 1965.

Mills, C. Wright. *The Power Elite*. New York: Oxford University Press, 1956.

Mintz, Morton, and Jerry S. Cohen. *America, Inc.: Who Owns and Operates the United States*. New York: The Dial Press, 1971.

Nagel, Paul. *One Nation Indivisible: The Place of the Union in American Thought, 1776–1861*. New York: Oxford University Press, 1964.

———. *This Sacred Trust: American Nationality, 1798–1898*. New York: Oxford University Press, 1971.

Nelson, William. *The American Tory*. New York: Oxford University Press, 1961.

Nevins, Allan. *The Emergence of Lincoln*. 2 vols. New York: Charles Scribner's Sons, 1950.

———. *The War for the Union*. 6 vols. New York: Charles Scribner's Sons, 1959–1971.

Newfield, Jack, and Jeff Greenfield. *A Populist Manifesto: The Making of a New Majority*. New York: Praeger Publishers, Inc., 1972.

Pessen, Edward. *Most Uncommon Jacksonians: The Radical Leaders of the Early Labor Movement*. Albany, N.Y.: State University of New York Press, 1967.

———. *Riches, Class, and Power Before the Civil War*. Lexington, Mass.: D. C. Heath & Co., 1973.

Rae, John. *The American Automobile*. Chicago: University of Chicago Press, 1965.

Rudolph, Frederic. *The American College and University: A History*. New York: Random House, 1962.

Saloutos, Theodore. *Farmer Movements in the South, 1865–1933*. Berkeley and Los Angeles: University of California Press, 1960.

Schlesinger, Arthur, Jr. *The Age of Roosevelt*. 3 vols. Boston: Houghton-Mifflin Co., 1957–1960.

Smillie, Wilson G. *Public Health, Its Promise for the Future: A Chronicle of the Development of Public Health in the United States, 1607–1914*. New York: The Macmillan Co., 1955.

Smith, George W., and Charles Judah, editors. *Life in the North During the Civil War: A Source History*. Albuquerque, N.M.: University of New Mexico Press, 1966.

Stover, John. *American Railroads*. Chicago: University of Chicago Press, 1961.

Toffler, Alvin. *Future Shock*. New York: Random House, Inc., 1970.

Trattner, Walter I. *From Poor Law to Welfare State: A History of Social Welfare in America*. Riverside, N.J.: The Free Press, 1974.

Wiebe, Robert H. *Businessmen and Reform: A Study of the Progressive Movement*. Cambridge, Mass.: Harvard University Press, 1962.

———. *The Search for Order, 1877–1920*. New York: Hill & Wang, 1967.

Wood, Gordon S. *The Creation of the Amrican Republic, 1776–1787*. Chapel Hill, N.C.: University of North Carolina Press, 1969.

VIII: Americans: In the Aggregate, as Individuals, and in Families

Ariés. Philip. *Centuries of Childhood: A Social History of Family Life*. New York: Random House, 1962.

Bailyn, Bernard. *Education in the Forming of American Society*. Chapel Hill, N.C.: University of North Carolina Press, 1959.

———. "The Beekmans of New York: Trade, Politics, and Families." *William and Mary Quarterly*, XIV, no. 3 (1957), 598–608.

Biographical Directory of the American Congress. Washington: United States Government Printing Office, 1961.

Bridges, William. "Family Patterns and Social Values in America, 1825–1875." *American Quarterly*, XVII (1965), 3–11.

Bushman, Richard. *From Puritan to Yankee: Character and Social Order in Connecticut, 1690–1765*. Cambridge, Mass.: Harvard University Press, 1967.

Calhoun, Arthur C. *A Social History of the American Family*. Paperback edition. 3 vols. New York: Barnes & Noble, Inc., 1960.

Connor, Paul. "Patriarchy: Old World and New," *American Quarterly*, XVII (Spring 1965), 48–62.

Daedalus: Journal of the American Academy of Arts and Sciences, C, no. 1 ["Historical Studies Today"] (Winter 1971).

Demos, John. *A Little Commonwealth: Family Life in Plymouth Colony*. New York: Oxford University Press, 1970.

————. "Families in Colonial Bristol, Rhode Island: An Exercise in Historical Demography." *William and Mary Quarterly*, XXV, no. 3 (1960), 40–57.

Farber, Bernard, *Guardians of Virtue: Salem Families in 1800*. New York: Basic Books, Inc., 1972.

Furtenburg, Frank, Jr. "Industrialization and the American Family: A Look Backward." *American Sociological Review*, XXXI (June 1966), 325–338.

Greven, Philip J., Jr. *Four Generations: Population, Land, and Family in Colonial Andover, Massachusetts*. Ithaca, N.Y.: Cornell University Press, 1970.

Handlin, Oscar, and Mary Handlin. *Facing Life: Youth and the Family in American History*. Boston: Atlantic-Little, Brown & Co., 1971.

Hawes, Joseph M. *Children in Urban Society: Juvenile Delinquency in Nineteenth-Century America*. New York: Oxford Universtiy Press, 1971.

Jaher, Frederic C. "Businessmen and Gentlemen: Nathan and Thomas Gold Appleton—An Exploration in Intergenerational History." *Explorations in Entrepreneurial History*, IV, no. 2 (1966–1967), 17–39.

Kammen, Michael. *People of Paradox: An Inquiry Concerning the Origins of American Civilization*. New York: Alfred A. Knopf, Inc., 1972.

Katz, Michael. *The Irony of Early School Reform: Educational Innovation in Mid-Nineteenth-Century Massachusetts*. Cambridge, Mass.: Harvard University Press, 1968.

McGiffert, Michael, editor. *The Character of Americans: A Book of Readings*. Homewood, Ill.: The Dorsey Press, 1970.

Morgan, Edmund S. *The Puritan Family: Religious and Domestic Relations in Seventeenth-Century New England*. Paperback edition. New York: Harper & Row, Publishers, 1966.

————. *Virginians at Home*. Williamsburg, Va.: Colonial Williamsburg, Inc., 1952.

O'Neill, William. *Divorce in the Progressive Era*. New Haven, Conn.: Yale University Press, 1967.

Pierson, George W. *The Moving Americans*. New York: Alfred A. Knopf, Inc., 1973.

Potter, David M. *People of Plenty: Economic Abundance and the American Character*. Chicago: University of Chicago Press, 1954.

Rapson, Richard L. "The American Child as Seen by British Travellers, 1845–1935." *American Quarterly*, XVII (Fall 1965), 520–534.

Rothman, David J. "A Note on the Study of the Colonial Family." *William and Mary Quarterly*, XXIII, no. 3 (1966), 627–634.

——— . *The Discovery of the Asylum: Social Order and Disorder in the New Republic*. Boston: Little, Brown & Co., 1971.

Rabb, Theordore K. and Robert I. Rotberg, editors, *The Family in History: Interdisciplinary Essays*, Paperback edition. New York: Harper & Row, Publishers, 1973.

Riesman, David. *The Lonely Crowd*. New Haven, Conn.: Yale University Press, 1950.

Saveth, Edward. "The Problem of Family History." *American Quarterly*, XXI (Summer 1966), 311–329.

Scott, Anne F. *The Southern Lady: From Pedestal to Politics, 1830–1930*. Chicago: University of Chicago Press, 1970.

Sennett, Richard. *Families Against the City: Middle Class Homes of Industrial Chicago, 1872–1890*. Cambridge, Mass.: Harvard University Press, 1970.

Sirjamaki, John. *The American Family in the Twentieth Century*. Cambridge, Mass.: Harvard University Press, 1953.

Smith, Page. *Daughters of the Promised Land: Women in American History*. Boston: Little, Brown & Co., 1970.

Taylor, William R. *Cavalier and Yankee: The Old South and American National Character*. New York: George Braziller, Inc., 1961.

The Dictionary of American Biography. New York: Charles Scribner's Sons, 1932–1958.

Welter, Barbara. "The Cult of True Womanhood, 1820–1860." *American Quarterly*, XVIII (1966), 150–174.

Wiltse, Charles. *John C. Calhoun*. 3 vols. Indianapolis, Ind.: Bobbs-Merrill Co., 1944–1951.

IX: The Comparative Approach

Bowers, David F., editor. *Foreign Influences in American Life*. Princeton, N.J.: Princeton University Press, 1944.

Davis, David Brian. *The Problem of Slavery in Western Culture*. Ithaca, N.Y.: Cornell University Press, 1966.

Hayes, Carlton. *Nationalism: A Religion*. New York: The Macmillan Co., 1960.

Handlin, Oscar. *The Uprooted: The Epic Story of the Great Migration that Made the American People*. Boston: Atlantic-Little, Brown & Co., 1951.

Lipset, Seymour Martin. *The First New Nation*. New York: Basic Books, Inc., 1963.

Shafer, Boyd. *Faces of Nationalism*. New York: Harcourt, Brace, Jovanovich, Inc., 1972.

Sutter, Ruth E. *The Next Place You Come To: A Historical Introduction to Communities in North America*. Englewood Cliffs, N.J.: Prentice-Hall, Inc., 1973.

Thistlewaite, Frank. *America and the Atlantic Community: Anglo-American Aspects, 1790–1850*. Paperback edition. New York: Harper & Row, Publishers, 1963.

Woodward, C. Vann, editor. *The Comparative Approach to American History*. New York: Basic Books, Inc., 1968.

Wrigley, E. A., editor. *An Introduction to English Demography from the Sixteenth Century to the Nineteenth Century*. New York: Basic Books, Inc., 1966.

Index of Proper Names

Subject Index

317